THE CAMBRIDGE COMPANION TO
NEW RELIGIOUS MOVEMENTS

New religions emerge as distinct entities in the religious landscape when innovations are introduced by a charismatic leader, or a schismatic group leaves its parent organization. New religious movements (NRMs) often present novel doctrines and advocate unfamiliar modes of behavior, and have therefore often been perceived as controversial. NRMs have, however, in recent years come to be treated in the same way as established religions – that is, as complex cultural phenomena involving myths, rituals, and canonical texts. This *Companion* discusses key features of NRMs from a systematic, comparative perspective, summarizing results of forty years of research. The volume addresses NRMs that have caught media attention, including movements such as Scientology, New Age, the Neo-pagans, the Sai Baba movement, and Jihadist movements active in a post-9/11 context. An essential resource for students of religious studies, history of religion, sociology, anthropology, and psychology of religion.

Olav Hammer is Professor of the History of Religions at the University of Southern Denmark. He is author of *Claiming Knowledge: Strategies of Epistemology from Theosophy to the New Age* (2001), and co-editor of *Polemical Encounters: Esoteric Discourse and Its Others* (with Kocku von Stuckrad, 2007), *The Invention of Sacred Tradition* (with James R. Lewis, 2007), and the *Handbook of the Theosophical Current* (with Mikael Rothstein, 2012).

Mikael Rothstein is Associate Professor of the History of Religions at the University of Copenhagen, and Visiting Professor at the Vytautas Magnus University, Kaunas. He is author of *Belief Transformations* (1996), editor of *New Age and Globalization* (2001), and co-editor of *Secular Theories in the Study of Religion* (with Tim Jensen, 2000).

CAMBRIDGE COMPANIONS TO RELIGION
A series of companions to major topics and key figures in theology and
religious studies. Each volume contains specially commissioned chapters
by international scholars which provide an accessible and stimulating
introduction to the subject for new readers and non-specialists.

Other titles in the series

THE CAMBRIDGE COMPANION TO CHRISTIAN DOCTRINE
edited by Colin Gunton (1997)
9780521471183 hardback   9780521476959 paperback

THE CAMBRIDGE COMPANION TO BIBLICAL INTERPRETATION
edited by John Barton (1998)
9780521481441 hardback   9780521485937 paperback

THE CAMBRIDGE COMPANION TO DIETRICH BONHOEFFER
edited by John de Gruchy (1999)
9780521582582 hardback   9780521587815 paperback

THE CAMBRIDGE COMPANION TO KARL BARTH
edited by John Webster (2000)
9780521584760 hardback   9780521585606 paperback

THE CAMBRIDGE COMPANION TO JESUS
edited by Markus Bockmuehl (2001)
9780521792615 hardback   9780521796781 paperback

THE CAMBRIDGE COMPANION TO FEMINIST THEOLOGY
edited by Susan Frank Parsons (2002)
9780521663274 hardback   9780521663809 paperback

THE CAMBRIDGE COMPANION TO MARTIN LUTHER
edited by Donald K. McKim (2003)
9780521816489 hardback   9780521016735 paperback

THE CAMBRIDGE COMPANION TO ST PAUL
edited by James D. G. Dunn (2003)
9780521781558 hardback   9780521786942 paperback

THE CAMBRIDGE COMPANION TO POSTMODERN THEOLOGY
edited by Kevin J. Vanhoozer (2003)
9780521790628 hardback   9780521793957 paperback

THE CAMBRIDGE COMPANION TO JOHN CALVIN
edited by Donald K. McKim (2004)
9780521816472 hardback   9780521016728 paperback

THE CAMBRIDGE COMPANION TO HANS URS VON BALTHASAR
edited by Edward T. Oakes, SJ and David Moss (2004)
9780521814676 hardback   9780521891479 paperback

THE CAMBRIDGE COMPANION TO REFORMATION THEOLOGY
edited by David Bagchi and David Steinmetz (2004)
9780521772242 hardback   9780521776622 paperback

Continued at the back of the book

NEW RELIGIOUS MOVEMENTS

Edited by Olav Hammer

and

Mikael Rothstein

CAMBRIDGE
UNIVERSITY PRESS

209
CAM

CAMBRIDGE UNIVERSITY PRESS
Cambridge, New York, Melbourne, Madrid, Cape Town,
Singapore, São Paulo, Delhi, Mexico City

Cambridge University Press
The Edinburgh Building, Cambridge CB2 8RU, UK

Published in the United States of America by Cambridge University Press, New York

www.cambridge.org
Information on this title: www.cambridge.org/9780521196505

© Cambridge University Press 2012

First published 2012

Printed and bound in the United Kingdom by the MPG Books Group

A catalogue record for this publication is available from the British Library

Library of Congress Cataloguing in Publication data
The Cambridge companion to new religious movements / edited by Olav Hammer,
Mikael Rothstein.
   p.   cm. – (Cambridge companions to religion)
Includes bibliographical references and index.
ISBN 978-0-521-19650-5 (hardback) – ISBN 978-0-521-14565-7 (paperback)
1. Cults. I. Hammer, Olav. II. Rothstein, Mikael.
BP603.C35 2012
209–dc23
2012015440

ISBN 978-0-521-19650-5 Hardback
ISBN 978-0-521-14565-7 Paperback

Contents

Contributors

David G. Bromley is Professor of Religious Studies and Sociology in the School of World Studies at Virginia Commonwealth University. He has authored or edited over a dozen books on the subject as well as many book chapters and journal articles. Recent books include *Cults and Religious Movements: A Brief History* (with Douglas Cowan, 2008) and *Teaching New Religious Movements* (2007). He is founder of the series Religion and the Social Order, sponsored by the Association for the Sociology of Religion, past editor of the *Journal for the Scientific Study of Religion*, and past president of the Association for the Sociology of Religion.

George D. Chryssides studied philosophy and theology at the University of Glasgow, and gained his doctorate from the University of Oxford. He has taught philosophy and religious studies at various British universities, becoming Head of Religious Studies at the University of Wolverhampton, England, in 2001, a post which he held until 2008. He is currently Honorary Research Fellow in Contemporary Religion at the University of Birmingham. He has published extensively in the field of new religious movements, and recent publications include *A to Z of New Religious Movements* (2006), *A Reader in New Religious Movements* (2006, co-edited with Margaret Z. Wilkins), *The Study of Religion* (2007, with Ron A. Geaves), *Historical Dictionary of Jehovah's Witnesses* (2008), *Christianity Today* (2010), *Heaven's Gate* (2011, edited), and *Christians in the Twenty-first Century* (2011).

Peter B. Clarke (1940–2011) was Professor Emeritus of the History and Sociology of Religion at King's College London (University of London) and professorial member of the Faculty of Theology at the University of Oxford, where he lectured in anthropology of religion. He also taught at universities in Africa, Brazil, and Japan. He joined King's College London in 1978, and was the founder there of the Centre for New Religions. His research included the study of new religious movements from a global perspective with special reference to modern Japanese religions outside Japan and African-Brazilian religions. He carried out research on contemporary Islam in different parts of the world including Africa and in Europe. He was the founder and co-editor with Dr Elisabeth Arweck of the *Journal of Contemporary Religion*.

Douglas E. Cowan is Professor of Religious Studies at Renison University College, University of Waterloo, in Ontario, Canada. He is the author of numerous books, the most recent of which are *Sacred Terror: Religion and Horror* *on the Silver Screen* (2008) and *Sacred Space: The Quest for Transcendence in Science Fiction Film and Television* (2010).

Asbjørn Dyrendal is Professor at the Department of Archaeology and Religious Studies, NTNU (Norwegian University of Science and Technology). He has published extensively on modern Satanism, conspiracy theory, and contemporary religion. His most recent publications include *Fundamentalism in the Modern World* (2 vols., ed. with Ulrika Mårtensson, Jennifer Bailey, and Priscilla Ringrose, 2011).

Reuven Firestone is Professor of Judaism and Islam at Hebrew Union College in Los Angeles. Among several other volumes he is the author of *Jihad: The Origin of Holy War in Islam* (1999); *Who Is the Real 'Chosen People'? The Meaning of Chosenness in Judaism, Christianity and Islam* (2008); and *Kibbush: The Revival of Holy War in Judaism* (in press).

Olav Hammer is Professor of the History of Religions, University of Southern Denmark. He has published extensively on religious innovation in Europe, New Age religiosity, and new religious movements in the theosophical tradition. His publications include *Claiming Knowledge: Strategies of Epistemology from Theosophy to the New Age* (2001); *Polemical Encounters: Esoteric Discourse and Its Others* (ed. with Kocku von Stuckrad, 2007); *The Invention of Sacred Tradition* (ed. with James R. Lewis, 2007); *Alternative Christs* (ed. 2009); and the *Handbook of the Theosophical Current* (ed. with Mikael Rothstein, 2012). He is executive editor of the journal *Numen*.

Graham Harvey is Reader in Religious Studies, the Open University, UK. He is author of *Listening People, Speaking Earth: Contemporary Paganism* (1997) and the editor of *Religions in Focus: New Approaches to Tradition and Contemporary Practices* (2010) and of *Rituals and Religious Belief* (2005). He is President Elect of the British Association for the Study of Religions. He is working on a book entitled *Food, Sex and Strangers: Redefining Religion*.

James R. Lewis is Associate Professor of Religious Studies at the University of Tromsø, Norway, and Honorary Senior Research Fellow at the University of Wales, Trinity Saint David. He edits Brill's Handbooks on Contemporary Religion series, and co-edits Ashgate's Controversial New Religions series. Recent publications include *The Children of Jesus and Mary* (with Nicolas Levine, 2010); *Violence and New Religious Movements* (2011); and *Religion and the Authority of Science* (ed. with Olav Hammer, 2011).

Sabina Magliocco is Professor of Anthropology at California State University, Northridge. She grew up in Italy and the United States. A recipient of Guggenheim, National Endowment for the Humanities, Fulbright, and Hewlett fellowships, and an honorary Fellow of the American Folklore Society, she has published on religion, folklore, foodways, festival, and witchcraft in Europe and the United States. Her books include *The Two Madonnas: The Politics of Festival in a Sardinian Community* (1993 and 2005); *Neo-Pagan Sacred Art and Altars: Making Things Whole* (2001); and *Witching Culture: Folklore and Neo-Paganism in America* (2004). Along with documentary film maker John M. Bishop, she produced and directed a set of documentary films entitled *Oss Tales* (2007), on a May Day custom in Cornwall and in California.

Susan J. Palmer is a tenured teacher in Religious Studies at Dawson College, and a Research Associate and Lecturer at Concordia University in Montreal, Quebec. She specializes in the sociological study of new religious movements, and has authored four books including *Moon Sisters, Krishna Mothers, Rajneesh Lovers: Women's Roles in New Religions* (1994); *AIDS as an Apocalyptic Metaphor* (1997);. and *Aliens Adored: Raël's UFO Religion* (2004). She has co-edited three volumes: *The Rajneesh Papers* (1993); *Millennium, Messiahs and Mayhem* (1998); and *Children in New Religions* (1999).

Jesper Aagaard Petersen is Associate Professor, NTNU (Norwegian University of Science and Technology). He has published extensively on modern Satanism and related currents. He is the editor of *Contemporary Religious Satanism: A Critical Anthology* (2009) and the co-editor, with James R. Lewis, of *Controversial New Religions* (2005) and *The Encyclopedic Sourcebook of Satanism* (2008). He is co-editor with Per Faxneld of *The Devil's Party: Satanism in Modernity* (2012).

James T. Richardson is Professor of Sociology and Judicial Studies, University of Nevada, Reno. He is an expert in the area of minority religious movements, and has published a dozen books and over 250 journal articles in refereed journals and chapters in books. His most recent books include *Regulating Religion: Case Studies from Around the Globe* (2004) and *Saints under Siege: The Texas State Raid on the Fundamentalist Latter Day Saints Community* (with Stuart Wright, 2011).

Mikael Rothstein is Associate Professor of the History of Religions, University of Copenhagen, Denmark. He is also tenured Visiting Professor at the Department of Sociology, Vytautas Magnus University, Lithuania. He is author and editor of several volumes on new religions and comparative religion in general. Among his English-language publications are *Belief Transformations* (1996); *Secular Theories in the Study of Religion* (ed. with Tim Jensen, 2000); *New Age and Globalization* (ed. 2001); and *Handbook of the Theosophical Current* (ed. with Olav Hammer, 2012). Presently Rothstein is engaged in the study of various new religions and indigenous peoples' religions, especially in Borneo and Hawai'i.

James A. Santucci is Chair and Professor of Comparative Religion at California State University, Fullerton. He became a member of both the Religious Studies (now the Comparative Religion Department) and Linguistics Departments at California State University, Fullerton in 1970. In 1993, he became a full-time member of the Comparative Religion Department. James Santucci has authored five books, including *An Outline of Vedic Literature* (1976); *La società teosofica* (1999); and (co-authored) *An Educator's Classroom Guide to America's Religious Beliefs and Practices* (2007), and has authored over forty-five articles. He was also a contributor to *Agni: The Vedic Ritual of the Fire Altar* (vol. II, ed. Frits Staal, 1983). He is the editor of *Theosophical History* and *Theosophical History Occasional Papers*.

Mark Sedgwick is Professor at Aarhus University, Denmark. His research and teaching cover both the Islamic world and the West, with an emphasis on recent centuries and on religious and intellectual history. He has published widely on Sufism, and in particular on neo-Sufi movements and their influence in the West. Among his publications on the topic of Sufism are *Saints and Sons* (2005) and *Sufism: The Essentials* (2000, 2nd edn. 2003).

Bryan Sentes is Professor of English at Dawson College, Montreal, Canada. He holds a BA (Philosophy) and MA (English Literature). He is the author of three books of poetry and of scholarly works on NRMs and the UFO mythology, most recently in *UFOs and Popular Culture* (ed. James R. Lewis, 2000) and *Alien Worlds* (ed. Diana G. Tumminia, 2007).

Marat Shterin is Lecturer in the Sociology of Religion at King's College London. His academic interests include minority religions, in particular new religious movements across religious traditions, church–state relations, with special reference to religion and law, and religion and conflict. He has published a number of academic articles and edited volumes on these issues and is currently completing his monograph *Religion in the Remaking of Russia.*

Tulasi Srinivas is Assistant Professor of Cultural Anthropology at Emerson College, Boston. Her interdisciplinary and innovative research centers around the processes of cultural translation and cultural renewal through a study of religious experience, knowledge, and subjectivity set against the political-economic backdrop of globalization. Srinivas' specific focus is on understanding the analytics of faith through Indian religious traditions, particularly Hinduism. She is the author of *Winged Faith: Rethinking Globalization and Religious Pluralism through the Sathya Sai Movement* (2010), on the culture of the global Sathya Sai Movement, and is currently working on a second monograph on Hindu priests and devotees in Bangalore city, tentatively titled *Abiding Faith: Innovative Ritual, New Knowledge, and Ambivalent Globalization in Hindu Temples in Bangalore.*

Garry W. Trompf is Emeritus Professor in the History of Ideas at the University of Sydney. He has been Professor of History at the University of Papua New Guinea and held Visiting Professorships to the universities of California (Santa Cruz), Utrecht, and Edinburgh. His major works include *The Idea of Historical Recurrence in Western Thought* (1979); *Cargo Cults and Millenarian Movements* (ed., 1990); *In Search of Origins* (1990, 2nd edn. 2005); *Payback* (1990); and *Melanesian Religion* (Cambridge, 1991); He is editor of the monograph series Studies in World Religions; Gnostica; and Sydney Studies in Religion.

Catherine Wessinger is the Rev. H. James Yamauchi, SJ Professor of the History of Religions at Loyola University, New Orleans. Her books include: *Women's Leadership in Marginal Religions: New Roles Outside the Mainstream* (ed. 1993); *How the Millennium Comes Violently: From Jonestown to Heaven's Gate* (2000); *Millennialism, Persecution, and Violence: Historical Cases* (ed. 2000); *Memories of the Branch Davidians: Autobiography of David Koresh's Mother* by Bonnie Haldeman (ed. 2007); and *The Oxford Handbook of Millennialism* (ed. 2011). She is co-general editor of *Nova Religio: The Journal of Alternative and Emergent Religions.*

Introduction to new religious movements

OLAV HAMMER AND MIKAEL ROTHSTEIN

NEW RELIGIONS AND RELIGIOUS INNOVATION

Religions resemble living organisms. They emerge as distinct entities in the religious landscape when, for example, innovations are introduced by a charismatic leader or a schismatic group leaves its parent organization. They gain momentum if they manage to attract adherents, often shifting shape in the process: the leadership of the charismatic individual is replaced by a more bureaucratic institution, or the initial emotional effervescence of the schismatic group subsides. Some religions disappear in the earliest, formative stages, while others manage to survive the turbulent first years. As time passes, they may enter into a phase of relative stability. Changes still take place, but often at a pace that is so slow that established doctrines and rituals seem to be seamlessly transmitted from generation to generation. Only when a new charismatic authority figure takes center stage, a schismatic group breaks out of the organization, or when external forces undermine the stability of the tradition, do changes once again become visible as equilibrium becomes threatened. Finally, even traditions that have subsisted for centuries or millennia can pass into insignificance or oblivion. Gods that were venerated in the distant past – Marduk of the Babylonians, the Egyptian goddess Isis, Zeus of classical antiquity, and countless others – are reduced to names in the annals of research, as rituals in their honor are no longer performed and stories about them cease to be told.

One of the most important aspects of this life cycle is that the rate of religious change is greatest when a movement is young, and in times of social change or crisis. The rapidity with which innovations are introduced makes religious novelty obvious for all to see: charismatic figures can impose radically unfamiliar doctrines and patterns of behavior on their followers, guidelines for belief and action that were adhered to in the early days of a religious movement may be superseded by new doctrines only a few years later, and modes of behavior declared essential for salvation while the founder was alive can be replaced by a radically different ethos under his or her successors. Established traditions also change, but do so at a pace that is so slow that their adherents manage very gradually to adapt, or even fail to notice any changes. An optical illusion thus sets time-honored religions in opposition to younger movements that can seem radically alien.

The 1960s and 1970s saw the emergence of a number of highly visible new religious movements. The Children of God (later to be known as The Family), the Unification Church, the Church of Scientology, the Rajneesh movement, the Divine Light Mission, ISKCON (the "Hare Krishnas"), and many other young religions caused alarmed reactions from concerned outsiders. These and other new movements seemed so outlandish that many people saw them as evil cults, fraudulent organizations or scams that recruited unaware people by means of nefarious mind-control techniques. Real or serious religions, it was felt, should appear in recognizable institutionalized forms, be suitably ancient, and – above all – advocate relatively familiar theological notions and modes of conduct. Most new religions failed to comply with such standards. The scholarly study of new religious movements, or NRMs (as the young religions of that period came to be called), originated around this time in an attempt to come to grips with the most pressing questions that these developments raised. Who converted to these movements, and how did the process of conversion take place? How did these movements organize? What made them spring into existence, and what did the typical life cycle of such movements look like? Why did so many of these movements exist in a state of seemingly perpetual conflict with surrounding society? And not least: did these movements pose a danger to society?

STUDYING NEW RELIGIOUS MOVEMENTS AS SOCIAL PHENOMENA

Over the years, a sizeable body of literature emerged that addressed such issues. Much of this literature has been written by social scientists, and is based on methods such as participant observation, surveys, and interviews. The picture revealed by this research (summarized in a chapter by David G. Bromley in this volume) was that many of the most alarmist claims about new religions were misguided. For instance, their recruitment strategies often failed abysmally. Only a tiny proportion of those who were approached by missionaries of the new religious movements converted, and of those who did, most left the movement again after a shorter or longer period of engagement. The "brain-washing" techniques that some critics believed were used by these movements to coerce outsiders simply did not exist.

It also became apparent that the differences between the new religions and their older counterparts had been greatly exaggerated in the media and in popular perception. Literature on the new religions noted that their modes of organizing, their doctrines, and their rituals were, under an often exotic veneer, quite familiar from older religions. In a perhaps more innocent age, established religions seemed to come with an automatic stamp of approval. However, classifying NRMs as "ordinary" or "normal" religions was not intended as an endorsement of their essential goodness. It just meant that they were not inherently different, and that even the traits that critics identified as problematic were in fact well known from older traditions. The secret teachings of Scientology, for instance, resembled the mystery cults of antiquity. The strong emotional bonds between some members of NRMs and their charismatic leaders were quite similar to the affective ties found between disciples and leaders in older religions. The fact that members of some movements surrendered their finances and autonomy to such leaders did not seem in any way qualitatively different from, say, the desire of some Christians to abandon their previous lifestyles and yield to monastic discipline. The flamboyant display of wealth of some leaders of NRMs could easily be matched by the demonstration of affluence in established religions. The purported absurdity of the doctrines of some new religions lies entirely in the eyes of the beholder – after all, established theological traditions risk seeming just as absurd to critical outsiders. Even the new religions that had descended into a spiral of violence, such as the Peoples Temple in Guyana, whose members either committed mass suicide or were murdered, or the Aum Shinrikyo movement, which perpetrated gas attacks in the Tokyo subway, demonstrated that violence in ways matched by older religions. Besides, it was also clear from the sociological literature that such cases were exceedingly rare.

Years of sociological and anthropological research on unconventional religions thus confirmed the impression with which we started this chapter: new religions are just young religions, and tend to resemble all other young religions. And equally: old traditions such as Christianity, Islam, and Buddhism were once young religions, and as far as the interpretive difficulties allow us to judge from the sources, faced the same challenges and issues as all other young religions, and experienced the same degree of conflict with surrounding society. As Paul puts it in 1 Corinthians 1:23, emergent Christianity was a scandal to the Jews and folly to the Greeks.

Most young religions are thus received with a mixture of distance and mistrust by outsiders, and conversely adherents of most young religions view majority society as misguided or corrupt. This was certainly the case in the formative age of now well-established traditions (as the turbulent history of early Christianity amply attests) and this remains the case to this day. Many new religions are characterized by an elitist self-perception. Many promote doctrines that seem truly odd to outsiders, and some reserve access to their core doctrines to initiated members. Quite a few new religions encourage a lifestyle that differs markedly from that of the social majority: members may wear distinctive clothes, choose new names, adopt a mode of communal living that sets them physically apart from others, or adopt dietary restrictions or other modes of behavior that make them stand out as a distinct group. Controversies and conflicts tend to arise with such groups, an issue that is surveyed in James Richardson's chapter. Since tensions with surrounding society are so common, several of the chapters that describe specific movements also deal with this question. Examples include the Church of Scientology, known not least for its policy of entering into litigation with critics (see the chapter by James R. Lewis). As seen in the chapter on Satanism (by Asbjørn Dyrendal and Jesper Aagaard Petersen), conflict can be a constitutive part of the religious movement's identity to such a degree that the most potent symbol of cultural subversion, Satan, is used as a self-designation.

Nevertheless, not all religious innovation entails tension. A chapter on the New Age (by George Chryssides), documents a form of religiosity that tends to reject parts of the mainstream Christian heritage, embraces concepts such as reincarnation, accepts alternative views of history, crafts new rituals and so forth, but is nevertheless rarely seen as a social menace, and has become part of popular culture in much of the West. The main reason for this low level of tension, we suspect, is the fact that New Age interests do not impel people to switch lifestyle to any significant degree, and allow them to pick and choose religious elements without necessarily deferring to the authority of a charismatic leader.

Other topics that have received much attention in the social science-based literature concern the use of modern communications, and the global presence of NRMs. Until quite recently, contacts between members of religious movement were largely face-to-face. Earlier global new religions were spread through the personal efforts of the leaders, who at great cost and with considerable personal hardship set out on worldwide missionary tours. Present-day NRMs benefit from the ease and low cost of global communications. A chapter by Douglas Cowan discusses the consequences of the Internet for creating and maintaining religious communities.

Globalization affects NRMs across the board. Movements that have originated in the West have gained an international membership. On the other hand, NRMs that emerge in contexts outside of North America and Western Europe are cognizant also of developments in the West, and the creation of new religions takes place on a global scale. Chapters by Marat Shterin and Peter B. Clarke discuss NRMs in Russia and Africa, respectively. Indeed, the conditions for religious innovation are global to the extent that Jihadist movements in the contemporary period, arguably some of the most "alien" of all new religions from a Western perspective, display all the characteristics of new religious movements described in the sociological literature (see the chapter by Reuven Firestone).

STUDYING NEW RELIGIOUS MOVEMENTS AS RELIGIONS

The study of new religious movements was thus concerned with a fairly narrow range of (often sociological) questions, but the field has gradually gone beyond this initial focus and has begun to apply the same theories and methods to new religions as to more familiar traditions. The repertoire of basic elements of religions, as found anywhere in the world and throughout recorded history – myths, rituals, sacred texts, conceptions of history, visions of the future – can also be found in young religions, and the theories and methods applied to studying these elements in established traditions can also be profitably applied to NRMs. The mechanisms that promote innovation in religions are also similar in established and in new religions: appeals to charisma or to tradition, the creative reinterpretation of the religion's heritage of concepts and practices, and so forth. Many chapters in the present volume are concerned with such fundamental elements as these are manifested in new religions, and the basics can be briefly summarized here.

Charismatic leadership

Many new religions are the creations of specific individuals. The founding figure will be vested with the right to direct the everyday activities of the group and define its doctrinal positions. The authority to do so derives from the unique status attributed to these leaders, who already in life, and to an even greater extent after their death, are presented in mythological narratives that transform them into exalted beings. An illustrative example is the founder of Scientology, L. Ron Hubbard (1911–1986), who to his followers is not only "every human's best friend," but also the most brilliant individual who has ever lived. It is believed that Hubbard gained ultimate insight into virtually all important areas of life, and that the discoveries that he was able to impart to his fellow humans is the only hope for our species. During the first years of his movement, Hubbard played a very visible role, but as his organization grew, he largely withdrew from public life and became inaccessible to his disciples. In particular after his death, a vast hagiographic tradition has been constructed by his organization, and in a sense Hubbard has become freely available again as the center of Scientological devotion, albeit now through texts, videos, and recordings (a phenomenon known in the sociology of religion as the routinization of charisma). Historians of religions and others have documented a less flattering reality regarding Hubbard, but this is a matter of little or no concern for Scientologists, who continue to view Hubbard as an unparalleled genius.

Mythological historiography

A mythologically based historiography that places the movement, its leader, and everything the movement stands for at a crucial point in time and space is another characteristic element of many new religions. Many religions present themselves as the culmination of all previous history: the spiritual insights found in existing scriptures and the revelations imparted to the prophets of bygone times are merely precursors to the absolute truths available through the new religion. Millenarian or apocalyptic theories of what the future will entail are other typical features of the mythological perspective of many young religions. For instance, according to the theologians of the Unificationist movement (also known as Unification Church or informally as "the Moonies," after the movement's founder and leader, Sun Myung Moon, b.1920), the very existence of the movement is the result of a divine plan. All problems, whether individual or global, are said to be the result of sinful behavior, and it is claimed that the original sin – the disregard of divine command – originated with Adam and Eve, who failed to form a perfect, divine family. The movement teaches that Jesus was sent to earth to establish the first ideal, "God-centered" family from which a new humanity should rise, but that he also failed. Now, however, "the Third Adam" has appeared in the guise of Moon. The redeemer or savior has finally arrived, and according to unificationist theology we are therefore living in an age of transformation. As expressed by Moon: "I have encountered the living God through a lifetime of prayer and meditation, and have been given this absolute truth. Its remarkable contents clarify all the secrets hidden behind the entire universe, behind human life and behind human history."[1] The history of sinful humanity has come to an end, and with the presence of Moon and his wife, the foundation has been laid for a coming golden age.

Reusing existing religious elements

Religions throughout history have incorporated and reused existing religious and cultural elements, and have recombined and reinterpreted myths, doctrines, and rituals that were already available. The foundational canon of Christianity not only refers to numerous events in the Hebrew Bible, but has appropriated the entirety of its predecessor's scriptures as the Old Testament. The emergence of Buddhism is predicated on the critical use and appropriation of pan-Indian concepts such as karma and reincarnation. Similarly, modern religions have roots in already existing religions, and can be classified in a small number of types or "families," depending on whether the main source of inspiration is, for example, Christian, Hindu, or Buddhist. In some cases, the links are easy to detect. The Sathya Sai Baba movement, for instance, is clearly an offshoot of the vast family of Hindu traditions (see the chapter by Tulasi Srinivas). In others, the reuse of tradition is freer, and "tradition" can in some cases be a modern invention. The various neopagan movements, documented in a chapter by Sabina Magliocco, may bear some vague relationship to the pre-Christian nature religions that they wish to recreate, but are essentially new religions. The neo-Sufi movements described by Mark Sedgwick in his chapter draw partly on Islamic sources, but can be very free in their interpretation of what these sources say.

Very rarely, a recombination and re-use of earlier elements becomes the fertile point of departure of a family of its own. One of the most successful of all new religions of the late nineteenth and early twentieth century is the Theosophical Society. The mother organization lost much of its momentum after the 1930s, although it still has thousands of members worldwide. The main reason for including a chapter on Theosophy (by James Santucci) in the present volume is, however, not its status as a somewhat older NRM, but rather because Theosophy as a set of concepts and doctrines has influenced contemporary popular religion to an unprecedented degree. Theosophical understandings of reincarnation, the human aura, and the chakras (focal points of "energy" in occult human physiology), for instance, have become known to millions of people.

Finally, NRMs do not only reuse materials from older religions, but have a much vaster pool of resources at their disposal. By incorporating elements from contemporary culture, such quintessentially modern phenomena arise as religions with a psychotherapeutic aim and religions based on an appeal to science (see the chapter on Scientology by James R. Lewis).

Two chapters in the present volume are specifically devoted to the creative crafting of religious texts and rituals (by Olav Hammer and Mikael Rothstein, and Graham Harvey, respectively). The selective adaption and creative reuse of existing elements is, however, apparent in all the case studies of specific religions presented in this volume. A particularly apt example of a movement that has used existing elements to create something that at first glance may appear radically innovative is the Raëlian religion (as documented in a chapter by Susan Palmer and Bryan Sentes). On the one hand, it presents itself as a scientistic UFO-based religion: its mythology focuses on the deeds of hyper-technological extraterrestrials, whose scientific insights are to be emulated by the human race. On the other hand, its beliefs can also be seen as a radical reinterpretation of Jewish and Christian mythology. The prophet Raël rooted his teachings in biblical narratives, but with the crucial qualification that the Bible had hitherto been thoroughly misunderstood. The creator, Elohim or God, is not really a deity, but actually refers to a group of highly evolved space beings who created life on earth by means of advanced genetics, and the Temple mentioned in the Old Testament is in reality a veiled reference to their laboratories. The "immaculate conception" of mainstream Christianity refers to medically facilitated extra-uterine conception, and "eternal life" to repeated cloning of the same individual.

In most cases, however, new religions recycle old beliefs and rituals in less radical ways. Usually a balance is sought between the innovative and the traditional, so that innovative elements remain rooted in existing traditions. In fact, one of the most frequent ways of justifying the introduction of novel elements is to insist that they represent a return to forgotten truths and ancient revelations. Hence, the adherents of many new religions vehemently deny that there is anything new about the doctrines and practices that they follow.

Notes

1   See www.reverendsunmyungmoon.org/teach_read_unification_theology.html.

Further readings and other resources

A significant number of academic publications on new religions have appeared during the last decades. Some books offer a general discussion, others are devoted to specific religions, yet others are thematic; some are strictly sociological, others multi-disciplinary. References to books and articles on specific new religions or on particular themes can be found after each chapter, but here are a few general titles that can serve as introductory guides for relative newcomers to the field. We limit ourselves to literature in English.

Books

Arweck, Elisabeth, *Researching New Religious Movements: Responses and Redefinitions* (London, 2006).

Chryssides, George D., *Exploring New Religions* (London and New York, 1999).

Chryssides, George D. and Margaret Z. Wilkins (eds.), *A Reader in New Religious Movements* (London and New York, 2006).

Clarke, Peter B., *New Religions in Global Perspective: A Study of Religious Change in the Modern World* (London, 2006).

Clarke, Peter B. (ed.), *Encyclopedia of New Religious Movements* (London, 2008).

Cowan, Douglas and David G. Bromley, *Cults and New Religions: A Brief History* (Malden, MA and Oxford, 2008).

Lewis, James R. (ed.), *The Oxford Handbook of New Religious Movements* (Oxford, 2004).

Partridge, Christopher (ed.), *Encyclopedia of New Religions: New Religious Movements, Sects and Alternative Spiritualities* (Oxford, 2004).

Journals

International Journal for the Study of New Religions
www.equinoxpub.com/IJSNR
Journal of Alternative Spiritualities and New Age Studies
www.asanas.org.uk
Journal of Contemporary Religion
www.tandf.co.uk/journals/cjcr
Nova Religio: The Journal of Alternative and Emergent Religions
www.novareligio.org

Academic websites

http://networkingreligiousmovements.org/
www.cesnur.org

Part I

Social science perspectives

1 The sociology of new religious movements

DAVID G. BROMLEY

New Religions Studies (NRS), an emerging area of specialization in the academic study of religion, has as its primary mission the study of new religious movements (NRMs). While NRS has its roots in a variety of disciplines – anthropology, history, psychology, religious studies, and sociology – the discipline of sociology has played a particularly prominent role in its emergence and development. NRS arose in the context of the proliferation of countercultural movements during the 1960s and 1970s, and the initial orientation of area of study was heavily influenced by the cult controversy of that era. NRS has subsequently transcended this initial narrow focus and become an important area of theory and research on religious movements. The development of NRS benefited from a historic first, the existence of a group of scholars with sophisticated theoretical and methodological tools for studying the movements and a cohort of developing movements to study, a combination that had not existed for prior cohorts of NRMs.

The area of study that has become NRS has now been taking shape for nearly half a century, and a substantial corpus of scholarship on NRMs has been amassed. The emergence of NRS has made it possible to produce a steadily growing body of knowledge about how religious organizations form and grow. Scholars have been able to observe the basic components of religion – myth, ritual, conversion, leadership, and organization – while they are being constructed. As NRS has evolved, key issues for sociologists have included defining the area of study (NRMs) as well as distinguishing different types of NRMs; analyzing the patterning of conversion to new religious traditions; describing distinctive features of NRM myth and ritual, organization, and leadership; and exploring potential trends in NRM development. This chapter reviews the theory and research on these issues with the objective of identifying how this work has advanced our understanding of religious movements and, more generally, of religion.

IDENTIFYING ESSENTIAL SIMILARITIES AND
DIFFERENCES IN NRM ORGANIZATION

One of the first issues confronting NRS scholars has been defining, delimiting, and organizing the area of study. While NRS originated with research on a small number of the most high-profile and controversial NRMs, scholars quickly became aware of the plethora of groups that appeared during the last half of the twentieth century. NRS scholars initially were able to treat these new movements as a set simply because they were either all new religious organizations or were new to their host societies. It soon became apparent, however, that it was necessary to formulate both a more systematic conceptualization of "new religion" and some means of distinguishing groups that varied significantly in terms of originating faith tradition, guiding myth and ritual, style of leadership and organization, and degree of societal acceptance or rejection. The long-established church–sect typology, even incorporating the subsequently developed concepts of denomination and cult, simply did not adequately describe either the characteristics that NRMs shared in common or their social and cultural diversity. NRS scholars have therefore developed several approaches to distinguishing key similarities of NRMs as movement organizations as well as identifying important differences among them that draw on but reconstruct the basic logics of church–sect typologies.[1] Three basic questions have been paramount in orienting theory and research on NRMs: what are the identifying markers of NRMs that distinguish them from other types of religious groups?; what are the different types of NRMs and how do these different types relate to the established institutional order of the host society?; and what are the most important ways that NRMs respond to the sociocultural dislocation that leads to their formation?

One foundational issue for NRS is what constitutes a new religion. Eileen Barker argues that one of the most critical features of NRMs is that they are first-generation movements.[2] Viewed in this way, characteristics of NRMs include:

- Converts – NRMs are made up entirely of converts who have experienced some measure of identity transformation, which typically yields high commitment levels, a dichotomous worldview, expectations of dramatic change, and distancing from conventional society.
- Atypical membership – NRMs tend to be formed from specific, limited segments of the population, which reflect social class,

education, age, degree of social encumbrance, creating both limitations and potentialities for new movements.

- Charismatic authority – NRMs are led by charismatic figures who rely on novel revelations or insights that constitute the basis of their authority and who are not constrained by institutionalized tradition and authority.
- External antagonism – NRMs are likely to be met with hostility as a product of factors such as belief systems that are regarded as implausible, deviant practices and lifestyles, social and geographic isolation, and what is deemed excessive submission to the movement leader.
- Movement transformation – NRM organizational transformations are likely to be more radical and rapid as a result of a variety of factors: movement growth, movement accommodation, and issues resulting from integrating a second generation of members.

Building on Barker's formulation, NRMs may also be viewed as new organizations with specific developmental requisites. For example, Rodney Stark has stipulated several organizational characteristics that are exhibited by religious groups that have achieved a prominent presence in the religious landscape.[3] These characteristics include an adequate level of leadership authority to ensure organizational effectiveness, high levels of member commitment, sufficient fertility levels to maintain movement size, effective socialization mechanisms, and a combination of internal solidarity and openness to ties outside the group. Describing NRMs as new organizations consisting entirely of converts brings into sharp relief the developmental challenges NRMs face as organizations and organizational characteristics that are associated with successful movement development.

Another equally important issue for NRS is how to distinguish different types of newness since NRMs are extraordinarily diverse in terms of originating tradition, mythic and ritual structure, and leadership and organization. One approach to describing the diversity of NRMs, that is, different forms of newness, involves grouping NRMs in terms of their relationship to the institutional order of the society. David Bromley and J. Gordon Melton have developed this approach, categorizing NRMs in terms of the type and degree of their alignment with the established institutional order.[4] Alignment involves both cultural and social components and is always a matter of degree. At any specific historical moment, the alignment of a group is the product of its claims to a religious status and the response to those claims by the established institutional order. What emerges from this approach are four broad types of religious groups:

- Dominant tradition groups are those that are most highly aligned both socially and culturally with the established institutional order.
- Sectarian tradition groups are those that are culturally aligned with the dominant social order but establish independent, oppositional organizations.
- Alternative tradition groups are those that are socially but not culturally aligned with the dominant institutional order.
- Emergent tradition groups are those that are neither socially nor culturally aligned with the dominant institutional order.

The composition of dominant tradition groups has been quite stable historically and is best exemplified by liberal Protestant churches (e.g., Episcopalianism). With respect to NRMs, three types of movements can be identified. Sectarian tradition groups roughly correspond to the traditional category of sect (Calvary Chapel or Marian apparition groups). Alternative tradition groups consist, for example, of Buddhist, Hindu, Western Esoteric groups. Emergent tradition groups include both those that claim no connection to an existing tradition (e.g., Scientology) and those that have had their claims to existing traditions rejected (Unificationism, Hare Krishna, The Family International, Mormon polygamous groups). The assumptions of this approach are that the three types of NRMs have different developmental trajectories and that movement organizational characteristics grow out of the movement–societal relationship. The emergent group category was a particular focus of early NRS scholarship. It is a particularly interesting set of groups as the movements are new and confront a unique set of developmental problems by virtue of being denied status as representing a legitimate expression of either the dominant or an alternative religious tradition. While acknowledging the importance of emergent movements, Bromley and Melton argue that NRS can be broadened by incorporating the entire array of NRMs.

Another issue in the development of NRS has been how to connect current NRMs to the sociocultural dislocation that led to their formation. A widely used approach to this issue focuses on how new movements represent alternative responses to the same structural conditions. Some of these movements extend the dominant societal logic in a more radical, prophetic form while others embody an alternative logic that resists the dominant social order. Roy Wallis describes the former as "world-affirming" and the latter as "world-rejecting" movements; Bromley refers to them as "adaptive" and "transformative" movements, respectively.[5] Wallis and Bromley are in substantial agreement that both types of movements represent alternative reactions to characteristics of the dominant social order. Wallis identifies these characteristics as rationalization, materialism, secularism, and loss of community. Bromley argues that tension is created by a growing ascendancy of contractual forms of organization over traditional covenantal forms. The important point here is that both of these analyses concur that, confronted with the same structural conditions, some movements (Scientology, quasi-religious therapy groups, New Age groups) are creating radical forms of individualism, achievement, self-actualization, and material success while others (Unificationism, The Family, Hare Krishna) are seeking to build tight-knit spiritual communities rooted in family and religion. The logics of the two sets of groups move in opposite directions. World-affirming/ adaptive movements seek to empower and transform individuals who then become the agents of social change; world-rejecting/transformative movements sacralize the group and embed members in the group, which becomes the vehicle for promoting social change.

NRM ORGANIZATION AND DEVELOPMENT

The world-affirming/adaptive and world-rejecting/transformative distinction has been particularly useful in analyzing NRMs because the two orientations are clearly reflected in their styles of organization. The characteristics of the two sets of NRMs therefore reflect both the oppositional posture that they share and the direction of their response to the structural dislocation of the period. I consider here the central components of contemporary NRMs as religious movements: myth and ritual, organization and leadership.

Religious myths are narratives that contain the foundational assumptions from which members of a religious tradition reason and act. They address issues such as humankind's origins, separation from its original or natural state, and requisite pathways back to original meaning and purpose. NRMs construct alternative mythic narratives, offer novel interpretations of the human condition, and challenge established logic. Correspondingly, NRM rituals confirm and demonstrate the reality and power of their mythic narratives.

World-affirming/adaptive movements construct individualistically oriented origination myths in which humans possess god-like qualities or potential. The ultimate reality is "I-ness." For example, in

Scientology individuals are understood to actually be immortal Thetans who once were gods of their own universes. Rajneesh taught followers that they were innately divine. J. Z. Knight, who channels Ramtha, revealed that each individual is a representation of the mind of God. In each of these origination myths the god-like qualities that individuals possessed were obscured when individuals lost touch with their true essence and potential. The primary mission of each of these movements is restoring individuals to their original, natural state of empowerment. Rituals in world-affirming/adaptive movements empower members by connecting them with their infinite potential and immortality. For example, a central ritual of the Raëlians is baptism during which Raël (or his representative) holds the initiate's head and establishes a telepathic link with the Elohim (the advanced race that created humans). The Elohim then register the member's DNA, setting the stage for later cloning, and hence immortality. In Scientology, trained auditors locate debilitating "engrams" (stored records of traumatic experiences through one's lifetimes); as engrams are "cleared," the practitioners move up the "Bridge to Total Freedom" and toward restoring their qualities as Thetans. Enhanced feelings such as aliveness, creativity, spontaneity, autonomy, and control are demonstrated during the rituals and are taken as evidence of progress toward experiencing one's true selfhood.

The origination myths of world-rejecting/transformative movements, by contrast, take a more collectivist bent by stressing love, trust, family, and community. The ultimate reality is "We-ness" rather than "I-ness." These movements envision the natural state of humans as being embedded in a deity-centred family, one that is centred on love of and love from deity. The discontinuity individuals experience in their lives results from their separation from a deity-centred lineage that transcends their individuality. Unificationism, The Family International, and the Branch Davidians conceive of themselves as faithful remnant movements that are rebuilding deity-centred families and lineages through their prophetic leaders. Each of these movements thus assigns itself a pivotal role in the process of restoration of humanity to its original state, and each member's identity derives from membership in the deity-centred family and lineage. The rituals in these movements are organized to bring outsiders into the NRM family and to bring members into the proper relationship with divine purpose. In The Family International, for example, members alternated between "witnessing" (joining outsiders in prayer that would assure the outsiders' salvation), "litnessing (distributing the true message of divine purpose) to attract converts, and "flirty fishing" (engaging in sacrificial

displays of God's love by meeting the physical needs of potential converts). Unificationists similarly engaged in proselytization to bring non-
members out of Satan's domain and into God's domain. The central
group ritual, the blessing, involves the formation of God-centered marriages under the authority of Reverend Moon, the Lord of the Second
Advent, who uses his messianic authority to move couples into a God-
centered lineage.

World-affirming/adaptive movements are typically organized as
classes, clinics, training sessions, workshops, and other limited involvement forms that dispense skills requisite for individual empowerment. Group embeddedness is regarded as a primary impediment to
full expression of individuality, and so a primary focus of group activity is heightening rational control by rooting out unruly emotions that
might compromise voluntaristic, self-interested behavior. Therefore,
training in est and auditing in Scientology are organized as services
that individuals may choose for their own personal growth. Since
these movements have an announced purpose of empowering autonomous individuals, participants are expected to graduate and become
autonomous individuals who embody and display enhanced abilities.
Leaders are often described as guides, trainers, counselors who, formally at least, typically have more limited authority than counterparts in world-rejecting/transformative movements. Channels, such
as J. Z. Knight, become ordinary individuals outside of the channeling
events, and auditors in Scientology and trainers in est possess authority only within the group rituals.

World-rejecting/transformative movements are organized as collec-
tives, families, and communes. Group embeddedness is not confining
but liberating as it is through collective commitment to a transcendent purpose that individuals achieve their true nature and identity. The
primacy of collective purpose means that members create organizations designed to eliminate egoism and self-reliance in favor of those
that emphasize commitment, love, and emotional expressiveness.
These goals are reached by organizing as spiritual communities and
families. The symbolism is exemplified in group names such as The
Family International or the Unified Family (one of the early names
for Unificationism) and the designation of members as "children" or
"brothers and sisters." Since these movements are collectivist in organization, maintain strong separation from conventional society, and
diminish individuality, movement leaders are more likely to exhibit
strong charisma claims, whether through a guru system (Hare Krishna)
or messianic status (Unificationism).

CONVERSION TO NRMS

By far the most thoroughly researched issue in the study of NRMs by sociologists, and other scholars as well, has been conversion. Conversion has traditionally been understood as involving a radical transformation of identity and a paradigmatic shift in worldview, a transformation involving an encounter with the numinous. NRS has begun to explore conversion more directly as simply an individual–group relationship. As the study of conversion to NRMs has progressed, a more complex perspective on conversion has emerged that indicates it involves several dimensions: the macro-social conditions under which individual transformations occur, the nature of the change that is involved, and the process of a conversion career. Although a single theory incorporating all of these dimensions has yet to be formulated, theoretical statements on the separate dimensions provide a more sophisticated understanding of conversion.

Of the three dimensions of conversion considered here, the macro-social conditions have received the least attention, but it seems clear that a variety of societal conditions shape the potential for individual transformations. The availability of specific pools of potential converts, such as age and gender groups, is one such factor. During earlier eras, for example, a surplus of women was associated with polygamous marriage in Mormonism and the membership base in Shaker communities. For contemporary NRMs, age has played a significant role in movement building. The existence of a large cohort of young adults who experienced a period of sociocultural dislocation, were not encumbered by institutional commitments, and were concentrated on college campuses and in countercultural centres proved to be a critical resource in NRM recruitment campaigns. The sheer size of the pool of unattached young adults open to lifestyle experimentation was a major factor in allowing a large number of movements to grow simultaneously. The availability of groups with which potential converts could affiliate was equally important. All other things being equal, the greater the number and diversity of groups the more likely it is that there will be competitive recruiting by new groups and more choices for potential converts. The 1960s and 1970s were decades during which there was a proliferation of social movements and new religions of various kinds. There were New Age movements (e.g., channeling, personal growth, and firewalking groups), quasi-religious therapies and corporations (Erhard Seminar Training, Lifespring, Amway), a diverse array of intentional communities, and a host of political movements. In addition, the revision of US laws during the 1960s that had precluded Asian immigration created a wave of Asian religions and religious teachers arriving on American shores. Potential converts therefore had many choices and could move among the variety of available groups.

The process of individual affiliation with NRMs has been much more fully developed. Theories of identity reconstruction and shift in social network commitments illuminate the dual dimensions of recruit–movement attachments while group influence–individual agency theories offer different models of the relationship between individual initiative and group socialization in effecting conversion. Further, conversion is now understood as a potentially symmetrical process in which individuals often affiliate with and then disaffiliate from NRMs as part of a conversion career.

Based on their study of Nicheren Shoshu Buddhism, Snow and Machalek emphasize the reconstruction of individual identity through a process that includes recreation of one's biography; adoption of a single, all-encompassing source of explanation ("master attributional scheme"); the replacement of analogical with more literal reasoning that treats group ideology as ultimate truth; and embracing a convert identity so that individual and movement interests coincide.[6] Through these processes converts symbolically align themselves with the movement. By contrast, John Lofland and Rodney Stark, based on their study of early US Unificationism, conceptualize conversion in terms of change in social network commitments, which they posit occurs through problem-solving activity on the part of the convert.[7] They identify a set of "predisposing conditions" and "situational contingencies" that together produce a conversion. The former includes dissatisfaction with current life circumstances that produces motivation tension, defining that tension as having religious meaning, and being dissatisfied with one's present religious affiliation. The latter involves reaching a turning point in life where a change of direction seems necessary, establishing affective bonds with the new group while weakening those bonds with outsiders, and increasing behavioral involvement in the new group. Both Snow and Machalek and Lofland and Stark implicitly treat conversion as the product of individual initiative while acknowledging group influence.

Some scholars have taken on the issue of individual agency–group influence more directly since it is evident that conversion is best understood as an interactive process. The relationship between individual agency and group influence in the conversion process has been subject to considerable debate. A number of scholars have emphasized individual agency in the movement affiliation process. Based on findings from

Scientology, for example, Straus has emphasized conversion as an "individual accomplishment." Drawing on interviews with 800 members of a variety of groups, Levine concluded that affiliations with NRMs constituted "temporary detours" by youth seeking to assert independence from parental control during adolescence. Bromley and Shupe, drawing on interviews with Unificationists, found that extreme conformity by recent converts could be better understood as role playing rather than group commitment.[8]

Other scholars have given greater attention to the role of groups in structuring participant behavior. One of the most sophisticated analyses is Kanter's study of communal groups in which she identifies three types of commitment mechanisms that these groups use to shape both individual identity and regulate individual conduct: instrumental, affective, and moral. Each of these has a corresponding set of practices (sacrifice and investment; renunciation and communion; and mortification and transcendence) that promote collective over individual interests.[9] What is particularly striking about Kanter's findings is that the groups she studied appear to have independently rediscovered an array of commitment-building mechanisms that generate high levels of individual allegiance, and the more successful groups institutionalized some mixture of those mechanisms. A typology that anticipates varying combinations of individual agency and group influence has been developed by John Lofland and Norman Skonovd. They identify six types of individual–movement connection (intellectual, mystical, experimental, affective, revivalist, and coercive).[10] Each type reflects a different combination of factors that structure the conversion process (social pressure, temporal duration, affective arousal, affective content, and ordering of belief and group involvement). With respect to individual–group influence, the first four types suggest greater individual agency, and the latter two greater group control. It is therefore likely both that different movements will employ different kinds of influence mechanisms and that movements will confront the problem of integrating individuals who present varying kinds and levels of motivations. This kind of perspective is particularly helpful in analyzing NRMs because it theoretically connects the conversion process to the organizational challenges facing developing religious movements.[11] What has slowly emerged from these various strands of work is the recognition that conversion is a complex process involving both social and symbolic dimensions in which individual agency and group socialization mechanisms each play a role.

Finally, NRS has contributed to an understanding of conversion generally by developing the concept of "conversion careers."[12] Since

conversion historically was regarded as a transformative spiritual experience and a "change of heart," it did not easily incorporate the notion of
an exiting process. Indeed, the primary corresponding concepts, such as
"falling from the faith" and "apostasy," have a negative connotation.
What NRM research has demonstrated is that conversion theory needs
to conceptualize a larger process that potentially involves an affiliation–
disaffiliation sequence.[13] In fact, research indicates that contemporary
NRMs have extremely high rates of membership turnover.[14] Analogous
to the affiliation process, the disaffiliation process can involve several modes of disconnection. The severing of bonds with a movement
may involve cognitive disillusionment with the group's beliefs, practices, leadership, or potential for success; erosion of emotional energy,
attachment, belongingness, and solidarity; or organizational isolation
or separation. Severing group ties cognitively, emotionally, morally, or
physically increases the attractiveness of alternative personal, domestic, and occupational opportunities.[15] The concept of conversion careers
is also expansive and flexible enough to incorporate post-movement
careers, most notably apostasy. For both historical and contemporary
NRMs, apostates (movement leavetakers who ally themselves with
oppositional movements in an adversarial role) have played a key role
in the developmental trajectories of their former movements.[16]

The study of conversions to NRMs has essentially both problematized the concept of conversion and offered a variety of theoretical
approaches that yield a more sophisticated understanding of the conversion process. What emerges from the study of conversion in NRMs
is that sociocultural factors shape the availability of both movements
and potential converts; it is a multidimensional process in which both
individual and group have some degree of influence; individuals and
groups connect in diverse ways; personal transformation may be symbolic and/or social; and involvements may be short-term or long-term.
This multidimensional conception of conversion moves theorizing
away from traditional religious/spiritual interpretations and toward a
sociopolitical process of shifting individual alliances and social network
identification. The study of conversion to NRMs is also revealing about
the process of movement development. For example, research suggests
that many individuals deemed converts may in fact be initially connecting on either an individual identity or a social involvement dimension, but not both, and that the relationship between individual agency
and group control mechanisms may vary among groups.[17] Given a mixture of types and levels of involvement, it becomes clear that movement organizations are much less stable or monolithic than they might

appear. A major problem for developing movements is finding a means of channeling diverse types of involvement. Particularly if movement attractiveness is related to sociocultural crisis, movements may founder if they rely simply on a temporary supply of potential recruits and a heightened level of motivation. Sustained development requires cultivating an institutionalized context for continued membership, a solution that has eluded many NRMs.

MOVEMENT TRENDS AND DEVELOPMENTS

It has now been a half century since the contemporary cohort of NRMs began to form. Movement organization is now well developed; the founding leaders have either died or are reaching the ends of their lives; first-generation members who have remained in the movements have raised children who have reached ages at which they can determine whether to follow in their parents' footsteps. The maturation of these movements has created an opportunity for NRS scholars to assess trends in these NRMs since their inception and to identify issues that have receded over time and those that continue to pose challenges.

Some of the changes that are occurring support traditional sociological theory. Most of the movements have experienced a loss of membership in several ways. The overwhelming majority of individuals who affiliated with these movements have since disaffiliated. The most productive recruiting years for these movements were those in which the youth counterculture was at its zenith and experimentation with lifestyle alternatives was widespread and attractive. Since that time recruitment rates, particularly in Western nations, have declined while defections have continued to erode the membership base. Movements such as Unificationism, Hare Krishna, and The Family that grew so rapidly in the late 1960s and early 1970s declined with equal rapidity as recruitment rates plummeted and now are relatively small and quiescent. Added to the defection among early converts has been the loss of second-generation members who have reached adulthood, although some movements have fared better than others. For example, losses have been severe for Hare Krishna, both because parents and children were separated so that adults could continue serving movement goals and because the schools (gurukulas) proved to be abusive environments for the children. The Family fared somewhat better, its period of sexual experimentation notwithstanding, as it sought to integrate teenagers into movement leadership. The loss of membership has had an organizational ripple effect through NRMs as it has eroded the economic base of even the wealthiest movements, such as Scientology and Unificationism.

NRMs generally have become not only smaller in size and wealth, they have also become more settled organizationally. One major factor in the tempering of these movements has been the death of the charismatic founder/leaders. Rajneesh/Osho, Prabhupad (Hare Krishna), L. Ron Hubbard (Scientology), and Moses David Berg (The Family) have all died and been replaced by leaders who function primarily as administrative leaders. Gone is the more radical experimentation of the early days. Unificationists gave up their experimentation with Moon personally picking marriage partners, The Family has foresworn its controversial practice of using sexual allure ("flirty fishing") to recruit new members; Hare Krishna members no longer roam airports selling copies of the Bhagavadgītā, having become largely a diasporic Hindu church. Historically, few communal groups have survived more than a few decades, and the communal lifestyles that characterized a number of the more radical movements have given way to more conventional lifestyles even more rapidly. The shift to single-family households has been accompanied by more conventional career patterns, further weakening movement cohesiveness. Many of the movements that initially boasted a millennial or apocalyptic ideology, with members expecting imminent world-transforming events, have revised such expectations and now are discussing longer-term futures and express less certainty about the end of human history. One early development that has continued is the transnational organization of these movements. Arising in the wake of World War II, the emergence of global-level capitalist organization and movements for gender and racial equality, NRMs developed as transnational entities. From the outset, Unificationism was underwritten by a multinational network of corporate entities; The Family created an international network of homes that eschewed national identities; Amway and Scientology blended international corporate organization and religion. Hare Krishna, Unificationism, and The Family also built their respective movements around multi-racial, multinational families and communities. None of these patterns has changed; indeed the pattern of transnational organization has been accentuated.

There has been significant change in the issues surrounding the more controversial movements in Western societies. NRM recruitment campaigns, public fundraising, and high-demand lifestyles have been abandoned by the most visible and controversial groups, dramatically reducing some of the most intense conflicts. Most prominently, as NRM recruitment success declined, the brainwashing debate that consumed the study of NRMs as well as media coverage of NRMs has largely sub-sided. Organized anti-cultism has diminished in most nations, and the accompanying strategy of entrepreneurial, coercive deprogramming has largely been eliminated. Likewise, fears of a succession of homi-cide/suicide events in the manner of Peoples Temple, Heaven's Gate, Aum Shinrikyo, Solar Temple, and the Branch Davidians have not been realized.

The maturation and settling of most of the NRMs around which NRS was established present scholars with promising issues for fur-ther development of the area of research. One is the matter of when a new religion is no longer new. No systematic answer to this question has yet been offered, but an answer is necessary to delimit the field of study. It is likely that the process of movement settling does not occur evenly or in a linear fashion, and so it will offer new opportunities for theory construction. A second issue is what movements will supple-ment the current cohort of NRMs as focal points of NRS. Perhaps the most logical alternative is to broaden the range of movements of inter-est. There have been some modest efforts to incorporate earlier NRM cohorts into NRS, but there remains a wealth of untapped information on historical movements that could be used to advance NRS theory. Of even greater potential is the inclusion of contemporary movements outside of the West. There is an enormous pool of largely unexplored NRMs in Japan and China, Africa, and South America that offers the opportunity to broaden and deepen an understanding of NRM forma-tion and development. Moving in this direction would also broaden the range of scholars who could contribute to NRS. An expansion of NRS that does incorporate greater historical and cross-cultural perspective would be an important step toward insuring that NRS will fulfill its considerable promise.

Notes

1   Traditional church–sect logic has moved in two directions. The first is to identify internal organizational characteristics, such as mem-bership base, style of worship, inclusivity/exclusivity, group size, and leadership style. The second is to focus on group–societal relation-ship, generally expressed in terms of degree of tension or acceptance/rejection. It is important to emphasize that the existence of multiple ways of categorizing NRMs is highly useful because typologies are heuristic devices that allow us to illuminate pivotal dimensions of NRMs.
2   Eileen Barker, "What Are We Studying? A Sociological Case for Keeping the 'Nova'," *Nova Religio* 8 (2004), pp. 88–102.

3 Rodney Stark, "Why Religious Movements Succeed or Fail: A Revised General Model," *Journal of Contemporary Religion* 11 (1996), pp. 133–46.

4 David Bromley and J. Gordon Melton, "On Reconceptualizing Types of Religious Organization: Dominant, Sectarian, Alternative, and Emergent Tradition Groups," *Nova Religio* 15:3 (2012), pp. 4–28.

5 Roy Wallis, *The Elementary Forms of the New Religious Life* (London, 1984); David G. Bromley, "A Sociological Narrative of Crisis Episodes, Collective Action, Culture Workers, and Countermovements," *Sociology of Religion* 58 (1997), pp. 105–40.

6 David Snow and Richard Machalek, "The Sociology of Conversion," *Annual Review of Sociology* 10 (1984), pp. 167–90.

7 John Lofland and Rodney Stark, "Becoming a World-Saver: A Theory of Conversion to a Deviant Perspective," *American Sociological Review* 30 (1965), pp. 863–74.

8 Roger Straus, "Religious Conversion as a Personal and Collective Accomplishment," *Sociological Analysis* 40 (1979), pp. 158–65; Saul Levine *Radical Departures: Desperate Detours to Growing Up* (New York, 1984); David Bromley and Anson Shupe, "Just a Few Years Seem Like a Lifetime: A Role Theory Perspective on Conversion to a Marginal Religious Group," in Louis Kriesberg (ed.), *Research in Social Movements, Conflict and Change* (Greenwich, 1979), pp. 169–96.

9 Rosabeth Kanter, *Commitment and Community* (Cambridge, 1972).

10 John Lofland and Norman Skonovd, "Conversion Motifs," *Journal for the Scientific Study of Religion* 20 (1981), pp. 373–85.

11 More extreme theories of "brainwashing" have also been debated. While most scholars have rejected a brainwashing approach to conversion, there is general acknowledgement of the importance of examining the group structure within which individual commitments develop. See, for example, Benjamin Zablocki and Thomas Robbins (eds.), *Misunderstanding Cults* (Toronto, 2001); David G. Bromley and James T. Richardson (eds.), *The Brainwashing/Deprogramming Controversy* (New York, 1983).

12 James Richardson, *Conversion Careers: In and Out of the New Religions* (Beverly Hills, CA, 1978).

13 David G. Bromley, "Affiliation and Disaffiliation Processes in New Religious Movements," in Eugene V. Gallagher and W. Michael Ashcraft (eds.), *New and Alternative Religious Movements in America* (Westport, CT, 2006), vol. 1, pp. 42–54.

14 Eileen Barker, "Defection from the Unification Church: Some Statistics and Distinctions," in David G. Bromley (ed.), *Falling from the Faith: Causes and Consequences of Religious Apostasy* (Newbury Park, 1988), pp. 166–84; Marc Galanter, *Cults: Faith, Healing, and Coercion* (New York, 1989); Stuart Wright, *Leaving Cults: The Dynamics of Defection* (Washington, DC, 1987).

15 Janet Jacobs, *Divine Disenchantment: Deconverting from New Religions* (Bloomington, 1989); Stuart Wright, "Leaving New Religious

Movements: Issues, Theory, and Research," in Bromley (ed.), *Falling from the Faith*, pp. 143–65.

16   David G. Bromley, *The Politics of Religious Apostasy* (Westport, CT, 1998).

17   Theodore Long and Jeffrey Hadden, "Religious Conversion and the Concept of Socialization: Integrating the Brainwashing and Drift Models," *Journal for the Scientific Study of Religion* 22 (1983), pp. 1–14.

Further reading

Bainbridge, William S., "New Religious Movements: A Bibliographic Essay," in David G. Bromley (ed.), *Teaching New Religious Movements* (Cambridge, 2007), pp. 331–55.

Bromley, David G. and Jeffrey K. Hadden (eds.), *Handbook on Cults and Sects in America*, 2 vols. (Greenwich, CT, 1993).

Dawson, Lorne, *Comprehending Cults: The Sociology of New Religious Movements* (Toronto, 2006).

Lewis, James R. (ed.), *The Oxford Handbook of New Religious Movements* (New York, 2004).

2 New religious movements and the evolving Internet

DOUGLAS E. COWAN

Beijing is used to days like this. April 25, 1999. Mild temperature, medium humidity, and almost no wind combined with the ever-present smog to lower visibility in one of the world's most populous and polluted cities. Patchy drizzle washed over the Zhongnanhai, the leadership complex of the Chinese government, glistening on the pavement and darkening the brick-red background of the large slogan mounted next to the south entrance: "Long live the indomitable thought of Mao Zedong." Government functionaries passed through the gates, while tourists, student groups, the generally curious, and, as always, the police strolled the square. Another grey day outside China's new "forbidden city."

Less familiar, however, were the large groups of people gathered along the streets of the Zhongnanhai, standing silently, politely, and, as it seemed, immovably. By the end of the day, around 10,000 Falun Gong practitioners stood there in mute protest against the government that had included them in a sweeping campaign against popular superstition and unauthorized spirituality in the People's Republic of China (PRC).[1] The *New York Times* described the 1999 Zhongnanhai protest as "the biggest illegal rally in Beijing since the 1989 Tiananmen democracy movement," something all the more impressive because the group seemed to manage it without alerting the authorities.[2]

A form of self-cultivation rooted in *qigong* traditions, Falun Gong (also known as Falun Dafa) began in 1992 and grew rapidly, finding fertile ground among the millions who joined by late April 1999. Within a few months of their protest, though, the group was officially banned in China, and since then the Zhongnanhai has mounted a relentless campaign of propaganda and repression against it. Indeed, at a 2007 conference on new religions held in Shenzhen, just across the PRC border from Hong Kong, many Chinese academics (and others) uncritically repeated government claims that Falun Gong is *xiejao*, an "evil cult."

According to scholars Mark Bell and Taylor Boas, when he was asked how the group was able to organize such a large protest in 1999,

29

particularly when they were already under suspicion (and, arguably, surveillance), Falun Gong founder Li Hongzhi replied on the movement's main website that "they learned [about] it from the Internet."[3] Famously reclusive, Li now communicates with his followers mainly through the Web and all the group's texts are available for free download.[4] More important, though, is the impression that the Internet, then a relatively new technology with very shallow social penetration in mainland China, and the worldwide potential of which very few understood, was crucial to the organization of the Zhongnanhai protest.

Demonstrating one of the principal frustrations with Internet research, however, the web page cited by the authors is no longer active and a Google search for the reference returns only the Bell and Boas article. Although they point out quite correctly that "many such assertions of Falun Gong's Internet use are anecdotal or overstate the case," in the wake of the protest commentary from academics to pundits proclaimed the significance of the Internet as a means of resistance organization. "Falun Gong's Internet savvy," writes media scholar Stephen O'Leary, "was a crucial factor in its ability to organize the unauthorized demonstration under the noses of Chinese intelligence."[5] In a rather breathless article written after the official ban on Falun Gong, Barbara Crossette wrote in the *New York Times* that the government's reaction in the wake of the protest "demonstrates in a flash of instant history" – whatever that means – "that totalitarians, already flummoxed by the fax machine and the cellular phone, may be facing the biggest high-tech challenge of all in the Internet."[6]

The question, though, which is at least implicit in the comments of both O'Leary and Crossette, is: was it? That is, was the Internet as important to the Zhongnanhai protest as Western observers would like it to be? Actually, it seems rather unlikely. Consider: according to Internet World Stats, in 1999 just over 4 percent of the world's population had access to the Internet and most of that was through dial-up service. Broadband access did not begin to make serious progress until well after the Zhongnanhai protest. Indeed, according to the China Internet Network Information Center, by mid 1999, two months after the protest, China counted only 4 million people with Internet access, a miniscule fraction of its population, which stood then at 1.26 billion.[7] That some of the Zhongnanhai protestors may have heard about the event through electronic bulletin boards seems plausible; that the Internet was the crucial organizational factor somewhat less so.

What this demonstrates, however, is how quickly the Internet – and its potential – captured the late modern imagination. Online communication and social networking; the World Wide Web as a weapon in the battle for social capital and control; the inextricable relationship between online and offline behavior; the tendency to hyperbolize both the reality and the effects of the Internet – all of these shaped (and continue to shape) the emerging contours of the online world and the place of new religious movements within it.

E-SPACE AND CULTURAL CHALLENGE

Few communications technologies have so quickly or profoundly influenced the way large numbers of human beings interact as the Internet – or changed the manner in which they think about interacting. Indeed, for hundreds of millions of users worldwide, the thought of a personal or business life without constant, immediate access to the World Wide Web, to email, to the expanding and contracting aggregations of the "daily me" is, in a word, unthinkable. No technology has so quickly achieved the depth of social penetration – and the height of commercial hyperbole – as that which allows us to "Go Online and Get Connected!" In 1982, *Time* magazine named "The Computer" its "Man of the Year," and as I write this chapter nearly a generation later, a CNN headline reveals that, in addition to some of its creators, the Internet itself has been nominated for the 2010 Nobel Peace Prize – not a little ironic given that the US State Department's 2009 human rights report indicates that many governments committed more resources in that year to curtailing Internet access than in any other. This paradox notwithstanding, and even though only 25 percent of humankind has Internet access at this point, few announcements could better illustrate how pervasive at least the idea of online influence has become.

First introduced to consumers in the mid 1990s, and despite a number of persistent and significant digital divides (e.g., age, gender, race and ethnicity, nationality, economic status), since its inception the World Wide Web has become all but ubiquitous in developed and lately some developing countries. Once the domain of the desktop computer, the Internet is now the constant companion of hundreds of millions through laptops, netbooks, cell phones, and an expanding variety of handheld devices. Social networking through MySpace, Facebook, and Twitter; the aggregation of "McNews" and "infobytes" through RSS feeds and "intuitive" browsers; and the sociotechnological moves from Web 1.0 to Web 2.0 and, according to some, Web 3.0, have provoked both utopian and dystopian visions of the virtual future.

Although some significant work has been done on religion and the Internet, relatively little has considered new religious movements in the context of Internet use and online controversy. Using examples drawn principally from modern Paganism and the Church of Scientology, the rest of this chapter addresses three basic issues: (a) the Internet as a vehicle for religious experimentation and identity formation; (b) the Internet as a contested information space in which new religious movements and anti-NRM countermovements seek to control an expanding (though, paradoxically, also self-limiting) pool of symbolic and actual resources; and (c) the Internet as medium for the "daily me" phenomenon – the personal trend to aggregate information according to individual taste and prejudice that is aided and abetted by advances in Internet technology and what some commentators have called the mobile digital lifestyle – and its potential impact on the cultural perception and social reception of new religions.

E-SPACE PARTICIPATION AND SUBCULTURAL IDENTITY: MODERN PAGANISM

"On the Internet, nobody knows you're a dog" – the caption to Peter Steiner's now famous 1993 *New Yorker* cartoon, depicting one dog logged on the family computer while talking to another dog sitting on the floor – illustrates one of the principal interests among those who study online behavior and interaction. Who are we when we are online? Who can we be? And how do we maintain these identities? For some, online identity is as simple as changing one's name: Bob becomes Bill as a quick and easy means of anonymity. Gender-bending was (and remains) a popular means of identity experimentation, though it was not long before researchers discovered that our offline identities almost inevitably leak through into our online personas, revealing us, if not for who we are, then at least for who we are not. Hundreds of thousands of people worldwide are devoted to online role-playing games such as *World of Warcraft* and to interactive environments such as Second Life, and their online avatars provide important venues for identity manipulation and exploration.

Although Internet technology affords certain advantages in identity play, the reality is that little takes place online that does not happen offline. Massive multiplayer online role-playing games may look radical and new, and they may involve players on a much larger scale, but how different are they from the extensive *Dungeons and Dragons* games on which many of us were weaned pre-Internet? In many religious communities, the assumption of a different name – and by implication a new identity – is commonplace. In the modern Pagan context, for example, Miriam Simos (b.1951) becomes Starhawk, author of the enormously popular modern Pagan text *The Spiral Dance*, and Tim Zell (b.1942), one of the founders of the Church of All Worlds, becomes Otter Zell, then Otter G'Zell, later Oberon Zell, and now Oberon Zell-Ravenheart, as his sense of personal Pagan identity evolves. Thus, as I point out at length in *Cyberhenge*, while there is the initial appearance of enormous online creativity and innovation, what happens on the Web is more often than not a reflection or a refraction of offline activity. All that said, the Internet presents three distinct advantages for identity exploration in a new religious context: subcultural contact; identity performance; and authority entrepreneurship.

Hunched over a laptop in her bedroom, a dog-eared copy of *new-Witch* open on the desk beside her, a young girl – call her Louise – types out a message on her friend's Facebook wall. "Did my first spell tonite," she writes. "Waaaay cool." Enchanted, as it were, by the concept of Wicca portrayed in pop cultural products such as *Charmed*, *Buffy the Vampire Slayer*, *Practical Magic*, and *The Craft*, Louise first did what many teenagers do these days when they want to learn about anything: she googled "Wicca." Millions of sites are returned in the search results, a bewildering assortment, with some offering magical supplies for sale, others advertising online schools of wizardry and witchcraft, still others promoting membership in this or that discussion site or Facebook group. What she learns from this welter of input (which, it should be noted, is not the same as information) is that she is not alone in her interest. Above all, she knows now that there are others out there who care about the same things. And this may come as a shock to a young girl raised in a small town in the southern United States, perhaps brought up in a politically and religiously conservative environment, sent to a parochial school where witchcraft is talked about in dread whispers if at all, and where the local bookstore is prey to the overprotective instincts of would-be censors. As she begins to interact online, though, she realizes that others are asking similar questions – and questioning the same social and cultural orthodoxies – as she. What's so bad about being a witch? How do I learn more? Are there others close to where I live?

In a manner only palely approximated by such things as pen pals, the Internet provides the communicative space for like-minded individuals to connect in ways unheard of only three decades ago. Suddenly, Louise is videochatting in real time with a girl her own age in another state who has just created a Facebook group for young women interested in modern Paganism. She is downloading modern Pagan music and podcasts to her iPod. She has begun to see the world around her through the lens of her burgeoning interest in Wicca. And, most importantly, she has begun to share that interest with others. She may not, strictly speaking, have discovered a community, but she has at least made a few friends. In this case, the Internet is not the relationship – this, too, is important to remember – but access to the World Wide Web facilitates the relationship between these two young women. Subcultural contact has been made.

As her interest in Wicca develops and her circle of online contacts both expands and deepens, Louise begins to experiment with a Wiccan identity of her own. Online, she now goes by the Craft name Willowsilk – a combination of her favorite character from *Buffy the Vampire Slayer* and her favorite fabric. Rather than shifting anxiously to a Google window when one of her correspondents uses a term she doesn't understand – widdershins, for example, or athame – she has gained confidence in her command of Wiccan vocabulary, an important first step in establishing in-group identity. After a few weeks or months, she even begins helping other newcomers as they join the group, guiding them to what she considers appropriate websites, offering advice on topics ranging from spell casting to rituals of dedication to a particular goddess or god. In this way, through the Internet, she both risks performing her identity as a modern Pagan and receives the kind of feedback necessary for identity formation, maintenance, and/or modification. In Goffmann's terms, she has entered the dramaturgical space created online and presented her identity credentials for validation or refutation by the other actors on the same Internet stage.

As her confidence grows, she may even consider forming her own group and establishing herself in a leadership role. A quick Google search turns up a number of online covens, circles, magic "academies," and witch schools – all offering their wares for sale or trade. These offerings range from "shovelware" – readily available material that is simply cut-and-pasted from one site to another – to more developed educational ventures. Although some online Pagan schools, such as Cherry Hill Seminary,[8] strive for transparency and have sought accreditation through state educational agencies, relatively few conform to the principles of sound Internet disclosure practices, particularly in terms of authorship and authority. That is, potential subscribers, members, or "students" do not know who the people in leadership are or what their qualifications are. Many websites disclose Craft names only and operate in a somewhat opaque fashion. In *Cyberhenge*,[9] for example, I discuss the case of "Cougar Silvermoons [*sic*] School of Celtic Shamanism, Witchcraft & Magick" through which the eponymous Revd. Cougar Silvermoon offers among other things a three-year course of study leading to qualification as a "Certified Celtic Shaman Practitioner."[10] She lists her credentials:

> I have been a practicing Shaman for over 30 years. I was taught the ways of the Shaman by my Grandmother. I was raised in a "traditional" pagan family, and at the age of 12, I began practicing Ceremonial Magick (Qaballah & Babylonian systems) with my mentor who was a trained elder. I have also extensively studied Miyamoto Musashi's system of Zen (do not confuse with Buddhism).[11]

Online, however, though she also claims to have University of California degrees and a *juris* PhD, there is no information about who she actually is, nor what these qualifications actually mean. Her authority is a function of her statement of that authority. That is, on the Internet, you may be a dog, but no one else will know.

E-SPACE COMPETITION AND CULTURAL CONTROL: THE CHURCH OF SCIENTOLOGY

To say the Church of Scientology is controversial is a bit like saying J. K. Rowling has sold a few books. From the moment of its inception in the early 1950s, Dianetics, Scientology, and the man responsible for both, L. Ron Hubbard, have generated considerable debate among constituencies ranging from federal governments to local school boards, and from professional academic associations to self-styled anti-Scientology activists, both religious and secular. Though many people are familiar with the recent controversies surrounding celebrity Scientologists such as Tom Cruise and the anti-Scientology Internet campaign waged by a group calling itself Anonymous, few may be aware how long the Church of Scientology has been involved in the online struggle for perception control and information management. Indeed, evolution of the battle between Scientologists and its critics parallels in many ways the online transition from Web 1.0 to 2.0 to 3.0 – as we may expect it would. More particularly, the Church of Scientology demonstrates three important aspects of the new religious presence on the World Wide Web: the paradox of "ephemeral resilience"; the online battle of competing propagandas; and the inherent relationship between online and offline behavior.

The concept of "ephemeral resilience" is, of course, paradoxical, but it describes rather well both the fragility and the durability of one's electronic footprint, the information about one that exists on (and travels) the World Wide Web. While a severe thunderstorm can certainly knock out communications and bring an online chat to a sudden halt, just try deleting yourself entirely from Facebook or MySpace. The underpinning philosophy of the Internet (data must flow), its supporting architecture (packet communications transmitted through multiple nodes), and the easy replicability of online information (site-to-site-to-site hyperlinking) collude to make it virtually impossible to remove information once it has been uploaded – even more so when it has "gone viral."

In 1993, a former Scientologist named Steven Fishman included a number of confidential Scientology documents – theological esoterica and upper-level Church teachings – as part of his defense against a libel action launched by the Church of Scientology. As court documents these were now in the public domain and they were quickly copied and uploaded to the alt.religion.scientology discussion list. Despite the efforts of the Church of Scientology, these documents have remained available on sites around World Wide Web ever since. Citing the proprietary nature of their material, the Church of Scientology waged a running battle with Web service providers, Internet remailers, discussion groups, and, in some cases, individuals believed to have downloaded the documents to their own personal computers. In many jurisdictions, the Church sought injunctive relief against what they argued was clear and unambiguous copyright violation. In an attempt to limit the propagation of this material on electronic discussion boards, they used "cancelbots," programs that automatically seek out and delete messages containing particular words, phrases, or passages. The Church of Scientology discovered, though, that copyright legislation differs dramatically from jurisdiction to jurisdiction and did not always support their claims. In fact, their campaign to foreclose access to the material appears to have had precisely the opposite effect. The more they were perceived as attempting to forestall both information flow and online discussion of their activities, the more discussion participants, anti-Scientology activists, and interested others sought to republish the material across the World Wide Web. Ephemerally resilient, the Fishman documents might disappear from one site, but would reappear on multiple others. As the technology evolved, so too did the online battle for impression management.

Late one evening several years ago, I received a call from a high-ranking member of the Church of Scientology. He informed me that recent Google searches were returning results for anti-Scientology web-sites ahead of the official site and he asked whether there was anything I could do about it.[12] Would I contact Google, for example, and raise the issue with them? I pointed out that there was nothing I could do. It is not my role to advocate for one group over another in matters such as this, but more importantly he did not seem to understand how Google works. That is, online interest drives result popularity and ranking, interest that is calculated according to the number of links from one site to another. The more sites, blogs, or podcasts link to a particular webpage, the higher that page's ranking on Google. In the few years after the turn of the millennium, as online interactivity, website hosting, and general social penetration and cultural familiarity took the Internet away from the geeks, as it were, and offered it to the masses, offline critics of the Church of Scientology took their fight online in a big way. Indeed, among the Church of Scientology's various detractors, few have pursued their obsession more diligently than the critics who operate websites such as Operation Clambake[13] and the Apologetics Index.[14]

This is the move from Web 1.0 to Web 2.0 in the battle of com-peting propagandas. Each group is trying to get its message out to as many people as possible, both to ensure that the information reflects what they regard as correct and, just as importantly, to discredit coun-termovement information. Thus, for example, Heldal-Lund and Hein (the administrators of the sites mentioned above) regularly ridicule the Church of Scientology on their websites, aggregating any piece of infor-mation that can damage its credibility and disseminating that infor-mation through RSS feeds, subscriber services, and other automatic transmission protocols. Visitors to their sites are invited not only to comment on material, but to upload material of their own, a situation that has only exacerbated the issue of proprietary material with the popularity of social media sites such as YouTube. Now, anyone can embed an anti-Scientology video (or construct a "mash-up," a user-gen-erated over-dub or compilation usually designed for ridicule) email it to their friends (often in the thousands), or carry it with them on a variety of handheld devices (iPods and iPads, BlackBerries, and so forth). Rather than simply read content, as we move further from Web 1.0 they are participating in the creation of content.

The next technological shift – from Web 2.0 to Web 3.0 – is illustrated most remarkably by the Anonymous campaign against Scientology that began in January 2008. No longer are anti-Scientologists limited to their desks and hardline Internet connections. With the increasing availabil-ity of Wi-Fi, the advent of handheld computing and media consumption devices, and intuitive software that aggregates information according to increasingly personalized choices, online communication and offline protest become as one.

In January 2008, an internal Scientology video of Tom Cruise was leaked to the Internet and subsequently posted on YouTube. In a society that feeds on celebrity gossip, and following the much-debated 2005 *South Park* episode on Scientology,[15] the video became something of an overnight sensation, the more so since Cruise seems by turns incoherent and menacing as he discusses his devotion to the Church of Scientology.[16] Faced with threats of litigation, YouTube removed the video from its site, but in the viral nature of Internet content other sites had uploaded it and subsequently refused to delete it. Appalled at what they considered a blatant attempt by the Church of Scientology to censor Internet content, a group of Web users, many apparently highly sophisticated and technologically skilled, launched an online campaign to "expel Scientology from the Internet." Calling themselves "Anonymous," though also known as "Project Chanology," the group uploaded an initial video warning the Church of their intent. The first Anonymous video, voiced-over in the computer-generated manner of a protected witness, begins, in a passage worth quoting at length:

> Hello, leaders of Scientology. We are Anonymous. Over the years, we have been watching you, your campaigns of misinformation, your suppression of dissent, your litigious nature, all of these things have caught our eye. With the leakage of your latest propaganda video into mainstream circulation, the extent of your malign influence over those who trust you, who call you "leader," has been made clear to us. Anonymous has therefore decided that your organization should be destroyed. For the good of your followers, for the good of mankind, for the laughs, we shall expel you from the Internet and systematically dismantle the Church of Scientology.[17]

Anonymous made good on its threat and attacked the Church in ways designed specifically to disrupt its online presence. The most common of these was the "distributed disruption of service" approach, a range of techniques intended to overload target servers and either crash them or render them essentially inoperable. Reminiscent of the Church's own cancelbot campaigns more than a decade before, and its encouragement that followers jam discussion groups with multiple messages when material critical of Scientology was posted, the important technological differences here are twofold, and both reflect the evolution from Web

2.0 to 3.0. First, Anonymous members were no longer restricted either to desktop computing or hardwired Internet connections; the advent of laptops, notebooks, netbooks, and broadband, publicly available Wi-Fi, meant that these attacks could happen much more frequently and the locations from which they originated were more difficult to identify and, hence, to prosecute. Indeed, in the context of something like the Anonymous campaign, which participants describe as "ubiquitous," the concept of "location" seems to lose all meaning in the non-local phenomenon of the Net. Second, Anonymous participants were no longer limited to traditional computers at all, but could prosecute their attacks from iPhone and iPods, BlackBerries, text-messaging services, and other handheld devices. Riding on the bus, sitting in a university class, dining on a croissant somewhere – the non-locality of service and the mobile digital lifestyle continues to favor countermovements in their opposition to new religions.

In subsequent videos, the first of which appeared on January 28, 2008, Anonymous called for real-life protests outside Church of Scientology facilities around the world, designating February 10 as the date. News reports indicate that thousands of protesters in as many as a hundred cities responded to the Anonymous call – which, unlike Falun Gong's, was all but entirely Internet-based. In the weeks that followed, more protests were planned and carried out. The Church of Scientology's response was unsurprising. In addition to calls that various service providers either remove Anonymous videos or delete accounts altogether, Scientology put out its own YouTube video (later distributed as a DVD) labeling the Anonymous group "terrorists" – surely the most emotionally loaded term in the combative lexicon today, but one that resonates with at least part of the Anonymous movement. Many of the Anonymous protestors, both to protect their identities and to call attention to what they consider the oppressive nature of Scientology, took to wearing the Guy Fawkes mask affected by the protagonist in Alan Moore's and David Lloyd's *V for Vendetta* as he battles for freedom in a (future) totalitarian Britain.[18]

To date, Anonymous has not been successful in its attempts to "expel" Scientology from the Web and, however incensed it is by the attacks, the Church of Scientology maintains a solid Internet presence. The Anonymous campaign does demonstrate, however, one of the patterns of Internet usage that has shown some stability over the years: the move between online and offline environments, from the virtual world to real life. That is, commercial and enthusiast rhetoric notwithstanding, online and offline behavior remained inextricably linked.[19]

E-SPACE AND WEB 3.0: NEW RELIGIOUS MOVEMENTS AND THE CHALLENGE OF THE "DAILY ME"

To this point, many predictions about the future of the Web and new religions have been offered more in the spirit of naïve technophilia or uncritical technophobia than dispassionate analysis and empirical observation. The Internet has not, for example, proved to be the new religious recruiting tool many hoped (or feared) it would. Unlike Falun Gong, which claims as many as 100 million members worldwide, both modern Paganism and the Church of Scientology remain relatively small movements. Notwithstanding occasional claims to the contrary, there has been no significant emergence of new religions that are solely Internet-based. Those that begin as online groups, if they prove at all durable inevitably incorporate offline activity.

Social penetration of Internet technology and access has slowed slightly in recent years, but in areas of the world where it has penetrated – even a little – it has quickly become the first line of inquiry for information on just about anything. Whatever the drawbacks of a user-supported online encyclopedia, for example, the ubiquitous nature of Wikipedia (and its numerous offspring) speaks to this clearly. Although, as I note above, the Internet has not proven to be the almost magical recruiting tool many new religious movements hoped (and counter-movements feared) it would, if new religious movements want exposure at all, an online presence is unavoidable. This is especially the case for new religions, such as modern Paganism, that are geographically dispersed and theologically diverse. For Louise, there may be no Wiccan coven within easy distance of her home, or it may be resistant to new initiates. The opportunity to participate in an online ritual – however well or poorly that works out in practical terms – both supports her exploration of modern Paganism as a religious lifeworld and reinforces the development of her emerging modern Pagan identity, something not available in the same way from, for example, books or newsletters. The Internet is not so much changing the fact of religious participation, but it is changing the manner in which people participate and the network of coreligionists in which they participate.

Thus, what is also changing in the move to the more personalized Web 3.0 is the way in which Web users customize their online activity to select, filter, and receive information. First suggested by MIT's Nicholas Negroponte, this filtering process has become known as "the daily me," content that is automatically attuned to an individual user's preferences, dispositions, and prejudices.[20] In many cases, this creates what Web critics have begun to call the "echo chamber effect," the software-driven version of our own social psychological bent toward confirmation bias. That is, we tend both to privilege and to regard as more accurate information with which we agree, and now we can tailor our computer equipment and media consumption habits to support that bias. Many commentators, both academic and popular, have suggested that the "wealth" of information and diversity of opinion available through the Internet will lead inevitably to greater tolerance both online and off. (Similar arguments, it should be noted, were made for the telegraph, the telephone, and television.) A pleasant prospect, perhaps, but so far there is little to substantiate it empirically. Indeed, the emerging concept of the "daily me," the "echo chamber," the individually tailored information experience suggests quite the opposite.

It is axiomatic, for example, that much (perhaps most) of what non-practitioners know about new religious movements comes through media – whether mainstream or alternative, print, televisual, or computer-delivered. And, in this regard, it is no secret that mainstream Western media have rarely been kind to new religions. Indeed, new religions have more often provided sensationalist fodder for the increasingly voracious news cycle than they have been the subjects of responsible, in-depth reporting. Because the first principle of newsworthiness is still the negative character of an event, the occasional human-interest story that treats new religious adherents as anything other than dangerous social deviants is generally overwhelmed by the flood of journalistic opprobrium.

When considered in the context of the "daily me" phenomenon, little of this bodes well for new religions in the continuing battle of competing propagandas. As more and more people turn to the Web for media consumption, and as more and more of them restrict the range of those media products according to preference and taste, alternative and contradictory viewpoints will be bounded out both by our wet-wired bias toward confirmation and the emerging architecture of Web 3.0. Moreover, as news aggregators and search engines begin to operate more intuitively – running in the software background of our previous online choices rather than under the deliberate control of our current online behavior – perspectives that explicitly challenge our own views may be automatically excluded when feeds, blogs, podcasts, tweets, and whatever else lies just beyond the electronic horizon are downloaded to us. Rather than a multifarious environment in which many voices compete equally to be heard, as it were, for many users Web 3.0 will become an increasingly homogeneous series of information enclaves.

Thus, those who follow the adventures of Anonymous will not only receive information about that group, but, in the manner of the "customers-who-bought-this-also-bought-*this*" macros that run on many online shopping sites, aggregators and feed services will search other anti-Scientology Web content as well. While it will certainly not be the case for all Web users, for many confirmation bias coupled with the validity effect – our propensity to give credence to information we encounter more frequently over that we see only occasionally – will actually limit our knowledge about new religions rather than expand it. Finding alternative viewpoints and expanding our understanding will require more dedicated, proactive engagement with the online environment, not less. In the Web 3.0 world, there will be more information out there than ever before, but the battle to be informed will be harder than ever.

Notes

1 On Falun Gong, see David Ownby, "The Falun Gong: A New Religious Movement in Post-Mao China," in James R. Lewis and Jesper Aagaard Petersen (eds.), *Controversial New Religions* (New York, 2005), pp. 195–214.

2 Mark Landler, "Chinese Sect Protests Government Crackdown," *New York Times*, July 22, 1999.

3 M. R. Bell and T. C. Boas, "Falun Gong and the Internet: Evangelism, Community and Struggle for Survival," *Nova Religio* 6:2 (2003), pp. 277–93.

4 See www.falundafa.org. All Web references in this chapter were accessed in September 2011.

5 Stephen O'Leary, "Falun Gong and the Internet," posted on June 15, 2000 at www.ojr.org/ojr/ethics/1017964337.php.

6 Barbara Crosette, "The World: Out of Control; The Internet Changes Dictatorship's Rules," posted on August 1, 1999 at www.nytimes.com/1999/08/01/weekinreview/the-world-out-of-control-the-internet-changes-dictatorship-s-rules.html?pagewanted=all&src=pm.

7 Statistics are available on the China Internet Network Information Center's home page www.cnnic.net.cn/en/index/0O/02/index.htm.

8 See www.cherryhillseminary.org.

9 Douglas E. Cowan, *Cyberhenge: Modern Pagans on the Internet* (London and New York, 2005).

10 See celticshamaness1.tripod.com.

11 Quotation from celticshamaness1.tripod.com/bio.html.

12 The Church of Scientology has a number of official sites; the movement's primary Internet presence is www.scientology.org.

13 Andreas Heldal-Lund; www.clambake.org.

14 Anton Hein; www.apologeticsindex.org.

15 This episode of *South Park*, "Trapped in the Closet," is introduced by the producers: "When Stan is identified as the reincarnation of L. Ron Hubbard [the founder of the Church of Scientology], Scientologists converge on his front lawn and ask him to lead them. When Stan criticizes the acting skills of a prominent Hollywood actor, the actor locks himself in Stan's closet and refuses to come out." See www.southparkstudios.dk/full-episodes/s09e12-trapped-in-the-closet.

16 See www.youtube.com/watch?v=UFBZ_uAbxS0&feature=related.

17 The video-text message is available on YouTube in more than one version. See for instance www.youtube.com/watch?v=JCbKv9yiLiQ.

18 See vforvendetta.warnerbros.com.

19 On conflicts pertaining to the Church of Scientology, see various chapters in James R. Lewis (ed.), *Scientology* (New York, 2009) and James T. Richardson's chapter in this volume. On the Tom Cruise controversy, see Hugh A. Urban, *The Church of Scientology. A History of a New Religion* (Princeton, 2011), pp. 139–40.

20 The phrase was coined in Nicholas Negroponte, *Being Digital* (New York, 1996).

Further reading

Campbell, Heidi, *Exploring Religious Community Online: We Are One in the Network* (New York, 2005).

Castells, Manuel, *The Internet Galaxy: Reflections on the Internet, Business, and Society* (Oxford and New York, 2001).

Cowan, Douglas E., *Cyberhenge: Modern Pagans on the Internet* (London and New York, 2005).

Dawson, Lorne L. and Douglas E. Cowan (eds.), *Religion Online: Finding Faith on the Internet* (London and New York, 2004).

Højsgaard, Morten T. and Margit Warburg (eds.), *Religion and Cyberspace* (London and New York, 2005).

3 Major controversies involving new religious movements

JAMES T. RICHARDSON

INTRODUCTION

New religious movements (NRMs), although relatively small in absolute numbers of participants, have been controversial almost from when they began attracting public attention in the late 1960s in America. Controversy developed in many nations, sometimes in somewhat different ways, over how to manage and exert social control over the NRMs that were attracting some of the "brightest and best" youth in many societies.[1]

Controversies followed the NRMs as they spread around the Western world and into other nations, including former Soviet-dominated countries. Controversy derived from the competition with dominant religions in many nations, and particularly the fact that young people from middle and upper classes were drawn to the NRMs. Recruitment of these youth sometimes resulted in schisms within families, contributing to the politicization of the NRM phenomenon.

Controversies often centered on recruitment methods, fueling the "brainwashing" debate, with claims that some extremely powerful, heretofore unknown psychological techniques were being used to attract young people. The pseudo-scientific concept "brainwashing" was debunked by most scholars studying NRMs but not among the general public and some political and religious leaders.[2] "Brainwashing" became a basis for public policy in a number of nations.[3]

Another controversy involved how NRMs raised and used funds.[4] Efforts to exert social and legal control over NRM efforts to support themselves were made with some success in a number of societies. However, these efforts encountered difficulties in nations such as the United States, as a result of legal protections afforded fundraising activities of religious groups.

A third controversy focused on children within NRMs, as many encouraged the formation of families and the birth of children who became a major focus of attention from governmental authorities, the media, and others.[5] This was particularly the situation in groups that did not encourage birth-control techniques. The presence of children made NRMs particularly vulnerable to social control by governments, given recently developed concern about protecting children.

These three interrelated controversies will be discussed, with implications for the future of NRMs and societies in which they reside. Included will be discussion of governments using such controversies to promote their own agendas. NRMs may become pawns in much larger political machinations, and be used to justify broader social control and restructuring efforts.

RECRUITMENT CONTROVERSIES

Recruitment was the most controversial issue associated with NRMs bursting on the scene in the United States in the late 1960s, a time of great turmoil in American society. The Vietnam War was raging, causing considerable social unrest, and the rampant racism and sexism present in society were finally being discussed. Environmental movements were gaining momentum, as well. This social chaos contributed to various social movements seeking to address those perceived societal ills.

Out of this cauldron of unrest came a development that was surprising to many, including social scientists, public intellectuals, media representatives, and politicians. A significant number (in absolute terms) of America's most affluent and educated generation ever became involved in various new religions that seemed to spring up from nowhere. Among these groups were Christian-oriented ones, typically fundamentalist in orientation, but also some eclectic groups such as the Unification Church. Also included were Eastern-oriented groups (Hare Krishna, Divine Light Mission, Transcendental Meditation, and others), as well as "New Age" groups and movements such as est and Scientology. The voluntary opting out of their expected social location by young people to join an NRM attracted considerable media attention, and was of great concern to many parents and friends of the converts.

The rise of NRMs in America and other nations caused a media frenzy, in part because of the social location (middle to upper social classes) of most participants.[6] The sight of groups of young people being baptized in the Pacific Ocean, as happened with one major Jesus Movement group, and other reports of relatively affluent youth in various countries flocking to groups such as the Children of God,

Scientology, Divine Light Mission, or the Unification Church caused disquiet in many societies.[7]

That disquiet led to efforts at social control of the new religious phenomena, and to the adoption of the "brainwashing" myth.[8] Many parents and others, including a few mental health professionals, assumed that some powerful techniques must have been used to convince young people to join these strange new groups. This assumption undergirded efforts to exert control over the groups, and to "rescue" participants from them.[9] There were two types of such efforts: direct governmental actions and self-help measures where direct legal limitations precluded governmental action.

Direct government intervention

In modern democracies, including even some newer ones, if citizens have a concern they can petition their government, asking that the issue be addressed. The media frenzy that developed first in the United States and then elsewhere concerning NRM recruitment contributed to a "moral panic" about "cults." That moral panic led politicians and opinion leaders in various societies to issue a call to arms concerning NRMs.[10]

In some nations legal strictures precluded direct governmental action.[11] In Germany, however, governmental agencies developed curricular materials for schools that warned students (and teachers) of the dangerous new religions. Governmental agencies in Germany and elsewhere engaged in direct surveillance of NRMs, particularly Scientology, with such efforts being approved by the courts.[12] In France and Belgium official parliamentary panels issued quite critical reports concerning NRMs and minority faiths, and governmental entities were established to monitor them. In France and Russia private groups were allowed standing to sue NRMs in court, with assistance from officials in the justice system. Such suits could lead to dissolution of the targeted group and imprisonment of its leaders. In China a massive government-led campaign virtually eradicated the Falun Gong, forcing this several-million-strong NRM to go underground and operate mainly via the Internet.[13] In several countries governmental law enforcement and other agencies raided communal living settings of some NRMs. These raids will be detailed in the section dealing with control efforts involving children, since such raids were justified on the basis of protecting children.

These direct governmental actions varied considerably in severity and effectiveness, as well as the violence involved. In Germany actions were mainly educational in nature, although members of the Church of Scientology were subject to government harassment and problems getting jobs if "outed" as Scientologists. ("Outing" was often done through government-maintained lists of members.) In France and Belgium the listing by parliamentary bodies of unacceptable religious groups (both lists included nearly 200 groups) led to various forms of discrimination such as losing jobs, harassment, and the groups themselves being hindered in building or renting meeting places.

In Russia and some former Soviet nations in Eastern and Central Europe there were also overt efforts by governmental agencies, usually with encouragement by formerly dominant churches, to exert control over NRMs, especially "foreign" ones from Western nations.[14] In China the massive crackdown on the Falun Gong led to thousands being imprisoned, and nearly 3,000 deaths have been documented in prisons where Falun Gong practitioners were placed.[15]

Direct actions by governments to exert control over minority faiths often involved judicial systems. In the United States, the First Amendment of the Constitution afforded considerable protection for minority faiths, including NRMs. Such entities have, over the years, won a number of cases that allowed proselytizing and activities such as fundraising. Some limitations to such activities have been allowed, such as "time and place" restrictions based on safety concerns (see below). However, in the United States NRMs have generally enjoyed considerable freedom of action, even as they garnered negative attention from mass media, policy makers, and some parents.

In Germany a relatively autonomous Constitutional Court has issued rulings thwarting governmental efforts to exert social control over minority faiths such as Jehovah's Witnesses, but other German courts have allowed surveillance of Scientology.[16] In Russia and Hungary constitutional courts have also issued rulings that afford some protection for minority faiths and NRMs, even if those have been largely ignored in Russia, leading to strongly worded rulings against Russia in the European Court of Human Rights.[17] However, in countries such as Poland the Constitutional Court has ruled in a manner affirming the dominance of Catholic values, offering little solace to minority faiths. In many nations the courts do not have autonomy and typically follow the lead of political leaders. This can mean that NRMs suffer in such forums and become pawns in political games, as has been the case in Russia. In China efforts to make use of the judicial system to protect religious freedom are fruitless, as the court system functions as an arm of the Chinese Communist Party. Efforts to take Falun Gong cases to court have even resulted in severe sanctions against attorneys making such efforts.[18]

Self-help actions

Self-help remedies to perceived personal and social problems are ubiquitous. Indeed, as Donald Black notes, most social control on human societies is done informally, and without any governmental help.[19] And quite often such self-help remedies are not "extra-legal." This is certainly the case with many efforts to exert control over NRMs, especially in nations where most direct governmental action against religious groups is precluded by legal protections. In some nations where the government has engaged in direct actions the negative posture of the state towards NRMs may encourage other extra-legal self-help activities. Attacks by mobs against Jehovah's Witnesses and adherents of Hare Krishna in some former Soviet-dominated countries such as Georgia are examples of such actions. Government officials and the police did nothing to stop such attacks, which led to destruction of buildings and injury to a number of people, with no charges filed against the perpetrators.

In the United States an entirely new quasi-profession of "deprogramming" developed because of a demand for assistance with self-help remedies of parents attempting to "rescue" their children from NRMs. Deprogramming is a term coined by Ted Patrick, who claimed to have deprogrammed 1,600 young people during his career.[20] Patrick focused initially on the Children of God group in California, but then branched out to other groups and areas of the country. He and other self-defined deprogrammers operated with impunity for many years, kidnapping thousands of young people, nearly all of whom were of legal age, and putting them through a grueling resocialization process that often included use of force and imprisonment against the person's will.

Deprogramming of participants in a few NRMs continued unabated for years in America, but was eventually limited by court decisions recognizing the right of American youth of legal age to choose their religion. A few successful civil actions against deprogrammers also demonstrated that they were potentially liable for civil damages for such extra-legal activities.[21] After a series of negative (for deprogrammers) court decisions the new profession faded from public attention, to be replaced by a less coercive "exit counseling" process that sometimes involved the same individuals and organizations from the deprogramming industry.

Deprogramming also spread to other countries,[22] especially Japan,[23] where thousands of deprogrammings have taken place starting in the 1970s and continuing to this day. The frequency has dropped considerably, from a high of nearly 400 in 1993 to about 10 per year in 2010. The major focus of deprogramming in Japan has been the Unification Church (UC), although there are reports that others also have undergone deprogramming.

Whereas in America the deprogramming industry was made up of a few mental health professionals, some former members of NRMs, and other opportunists,[24] in Japan the industry was organized with different sorts of personnel and much more open institutional support.[25] Protestant ministers have been major players in the Japan deprogramming industry, and actually conduct most of the deprogrammings, working with some mental health professionals and establishments. Also in Japan the Japanese Communist Party (JCP) played an effective role, as did the legal profession. The JCP, a viable minority political party that puts up candidates for office and wins some seats, took umbrage with the strong anti-communist stance of the UC when the UC worked to defeat some JCP candidates in a few political races. Thus the JCP led attacks on the UC in the Japanese Diet (parliament), and afforded some cover to those involved in deprogramming through its continued public attacks on the UC. The organized legal profession in Japan also openly and regularly attacked the UC, and did considerable pro bono legal work when someone (usually a parent of a member) wanted to sue the church for money damages. Many such suits were successful, causing financial problems for the UC in Japan.

Self-help actions against NRMs include more than deprogrammings and exit counseling, however, as demonstrated in Japan, but also the United States and other nations. Media treatment of NRMs and other minority religious groups has been nearly totally negative, both in print and electronic news media, as well as in the popular mass media, which regularly uses as a theme someone being trapped in a terrible cult and needing to be rescued from their predicament.[26] These negative media treatments have fomented the moral panic about NRMs, as have actions by some politicians who have opportunistically taken on the "cult" issue for political purposes.[27]

FINANCIAL CONTROVERSIES

All NRMs have to learn to exist within the laws, rules, and norms of the societies within which they exist. This means that the organization structure, the ways they raise and spend funds, and other concerns, even including theological developments, must take into account these mundane considerations.[28] The imposing of a society's laws and regulations concerning raising and managing money can, therefore, be the site of much controversy and have dramatic effects on the life and culture of NRMs.[29] I will discuss controversies about how NRMs raise money, how they manage their funds, and how they spend them.

Raising money

Closely related to recruitment controversies have been concerns about how NRMs raise and spend money.[30] Indeed, part of the concern about recruitment was that young people joining one of the controversial NRMs might be put to work raising money, sometimes by peddling trinkets and books on the city streets or in airports around the world. Also, some of the NRMs expected or required that those who joined would dedicate their assets to their new membership group, or that they would pay sometimes large fees to experience the training and socialization processes of the group. These developments were upsetting to some parents of recruits, who had assumed that their children would stay in college and even attend professional school. Instead the parents learned that their children were living communally somewhere, peddling goods for money, and/or that they were turning over personal assets to the group they had joined.

The voluntary opting out of their expected social location by these young people attracted considerable attention from the mass media in America and other countries, and also was, as noted in the previous section, of great concern to parents and friends of the convert. Observing converts soliciting money in airports or on the streets of major cities or spending large sums for courses offered by some NRMs seemed clear evidence that something was amiss, and that the convert must have been "brainwashed." This "brainwashing" assumption contributed a crucial justification for social control efforts, as has been noted.

Spending money

Concern developed as well over expenditures made by some of the NRMs. Part of the animus toward NRMs of Western origin in former Soviet-dominated nations derived from concern about the infusion of funds from outside these countries by NRMs and other minority faiths. Accusations were made by politicians and representatives of formerly dominant churches (such as the Russian Orthodox Church) that these Western groups were attempting to buy influence and converts through the large amount of funding they were bringing into the countries. Funding from external sources for some religious groups operating in the newly freed former Soviet nations might even be viewed as threats to the autonomy of the countries, adding to the concern.

Similarly, the Unification Church bought major properties in some areas of America, and also in countries such as Brazil. There was concern that large amounts of money were being brought into these countries by the UC to fund the purchases, and questions were raised about the origin of the funds, and the purpose for which they were being spent.[31] The Bhagwan Rajneesh group purchased virtually an entire town in Oregon, built many communal buildings, and also bought a fleet of Rolls Royce automobiles that attracted much media attention. Again, questions were raised about where the money was coming from, and why it was being spent as the Rajneeshes were doing.[32]

Efforts to control financial dealings

Many attempts were made to exert control over the finances of NRMs in the United States, but also in other nations, such as France, which launched a major effort to exert control over NRMs through taxation policies.[33] There was considerable effort in the United States to stop solicitation for money in airports, on the streets, or other locations. Efforts were also made, usually unsuccessfully, to legislate against such activities, or to force the groups to return funds that had been given to them for training courses or other things.[34] Street solicitation when combined with proselytizing was protected in America by previous court decisions that had been rendered in a series of cases that had been brought by the Jehovah's Witnesses and other religious groups decades earlier. Thus the many attempts by local authorities to stop UC members from selling goods on the streets by requiring a solicitation permit usually failed in America, and members were allowed to continue doing so without a permit.[35]

The Hare Krishna (HK), famous (or infamous) for their solicitation in the 1970s and 1980s by "selling" books in airports and other public places in America, were less fortunate, however. The courts eventually issued a series of rulings that limited such activities, using "time and place" restrictions justified by somewhat questionable concerns about public safety. Also, in a number of states the HK were challenged on the basis that their fundraising activities were not focused on proselytizing. Thus it was argued that the HK should not be afforded First Amendment protections, and instead could be regulated as a commercial activity. Thus HK practitioners ended up being forced to do their book promotion from fixed booths instead of being able to "work the crowd." Such decisions contributed to their moving into other methods of group support.[36]

Similar accusations have been made in a number of countries that Scientology is a commercial enterprise bent on profit.[37] Many legal battles have been fought in the United States and other countries over Scientology's methods of raising money, which involves various training regimes and tests offered by the organization for fees charged to participants. Scientology finally won its major fight with the Internal Revenue Service in the United States, and is now considered a religion for tax purposes. This has also been the case in some other nations such as Australia, but in a number of other countries this issue is still unsettled, or has been decided against Scientology.

As indicated above, the raising of funds to maintain NRMs also made other groups vulnerable to social control efforts via tax authorities in the United States and elsewhere. The Jesus Movement groups studied in depth by this author and others was dealt a fatal blow when the Internal Revenue Service (IRS) changed its position on the organization's tax status (they were initially given a tax-exempt status), sending them a bill for over 1 million dollars.[38] The IRS claimed, in effect, that the organization was a "tax dodge" developed to avoid paying taxes on "unrelated business income." The legal battles that ensued cost the group dearly, as they eventually lost the case in federal tax court, and then lost their main communal property as a result.

How groups managed their funds also sometimes came under scrutiny. The Unification Church leader, Reverend Moon, was charged with tax evasion, was eventually found guilty, and spent time in a federal prison after a much-publicized trial and appeal all the way to the Supreme Court.[39] The issue concerned some stocks that the group controlled but that were held in the name of Reverend Moon; the IRS claimed that he should have declared the dividends as income. This much-criticized case led, however, to much sympathy for Reverend Moon from other religious groups, with representatives of a number of religious organizations filing amicus briefs on his behalf with the court since they held assets in a similar manner to Reverend Moon and the UC.

CONTROVERSIES INVOLVING CHILDREN

Controversy initially encompassed NRMs simply because they were attracting youth from relatively affluent families. Even though nearly all such early recruits were of legal age, they were still the offspring of parents who had other plans for them. Hence some NRMs gained a reputation for being something of a Pied Piper, attracting young people and "stealing" them from their families in order to have them follow some heretofore unknown guru. Hence the controversy erupted over recruitment of these "children" discussed above.

However, NRMs became even more embroiled in controversy when a second generation was born into the groups.[40] The "child saver" movement had gained considerable momentum in many nations, contributing directly to the passage of laws designed to protect children and guarantee them an education that would allow them to function in society and become productive citizens.[41] These laws have been used very effectively by detractors of NRMs, who quickly learned that making accusations about child abuse, particularly sex abuse, would mobilize government authorities to take action against the accused group.[42]

Another way of describing this development is to note that in the United States and a number of other nations, concern about the health and welfare of children trumps concerns about religious freedom and even family autonomy. Thus the barrier of constitutional or other legal protections that existed for minority religions could be breached quickly if a claim of child abuse was made. This occurred around the world with NRMs that had produced a second generation, particularly if they were living communally and away from the public eye.[43]

A number of NRMs have found themselves in a defensive posture concerning their children, including the Twelve Tribes, and The Family (formerly known as the Children of God), both of which did not usually practice birth control, thus leading to the presence of a number of children in the groups. Some older NRMs such as Jehovah's Witnesses, Christian Science, the Branch Davidians, the Fundamentalist Church of Latter Day Saints, and others have also seen a focus on their alleged treatment of children,[44] as has the Catholic Church itself.[45] Here the focus will be on the Twelve Tribes' experience and that of The Family, both of which have experienced major controversies in different countries based on allegations concerning how they cared for their children.

The Twelve Tribes groups experienced a major raid at their communal home setting in Vermont in 1984 when state law enforcement and child care officials descended on them and took away 112 children, arresting some of the parents.[46] The raid had been based on allegations of child abuse made against the group by some ex-members, some of whom were involved in custody disputes after leaving the group and their families who remained members. Some anti-cult movement leaders also figured prominently in advising government authorities about the group and in assisting the planning of the raid. However, a courageous judge ordered the 112 children to be released back to the group's care, claiming that there was insufficient evidence to warrant the state taking custody of the children.

Thus this dramatic effort at social control by the State of Vermont child protection agency was aborted. However, allegations of child abuse were also lodged against the groups communal homes in France and Germany by North American anti-cultists who wanted to alert authorities to the group's childrearing practices, which included home schooling and corporal punishment for misbehavior. Since home schooling is not legal in Germany or France, the group's decision to home school the children led to considerable difficulty with authorities in both countries.

The Family, another controversial communal NRM, encountered difficulties in even more countries from its very beginning in the late 1960s.[47] The lifestyle of the group was always unorthodox and even bizarre in the eyes of some. Their very open approach to sexuality, which for a few years early in the group's history included "flirty fishing," where young women engaged in sex as a recruitment method, attracted a huge amount of negative attention.[48] This rather lurid past has haunted The Family ever since, and made them vulnerable to efforts at social control involving allegations of child sex abuse. Former members who had left the group, sometimes acrimoniously, some people associated with the anti-cult movement, and others involved in custody disputes have used the historical openness of the group toward matters of sex as a weapon, and have accused members of the group of involving children in sexual activity.

Such accusations have resulted in action by authorities in a number of countries.[49] There have been raids of Family communal homes in Australia, France, Argentina, and Spain, and the group has been placed on the defensive in many other nations where they have had communal homes. In all instances the children have eventually been returned to The Family, and in Australia the government was even forced to pay damages to the group in the State of Victoria. However, sometimes it took months or even years before the situations were resolved, and custody of children was sometimes retained for months by state authorities while some parents languished in prison, as occurred in Argentina.

CONCLUSIONS

These interrelated controversies have resulted in considerable pressure on NRMs to change their behaviors, and to accept the norms and rules of the societies in which they exist. This movement toward more normative behavior has been given impetus by political pressures and legal cases on all three major fronts of controversy involving NRMs.[50] The controversies have also raised some quite significant questions in the arenas of human and civil rights, as well as religious freedom.[51]

The controversies discussed above may serve as proxies, or justifications, to exert control over NRMs for other reasons as well. The three major issues outlined above can be exploited by governments seeking to control NRMs that are viewed as threatening to political dominance, or by dominant churches who want to suppress competition from newer faiths. NRMs can be treated as pawns in larger political games and used just to make a point about who has ultimate control in a given society. The Chinese reaction to the Falun Gong, Germany's efforts to control Scientology, Russia's major change of heart toward NRMs and its use of them in efforts to assist the Orthodox Church regain a position of influence, France's campaign to force minority faiths to acquiesce to government control, and the State of Oregon's campaign to drive out the Bhagwan Rajneesh group from Antelope are examples of such broader battles. Others involving NRMs and other minority religions could be listed as well.

Such controversies are inevitable in modern societies where governments expand their role in ways that involve more pervasiveness in the lives of citizens. At the same time religious groups, especially communal ones, also take on more functions formerly relegated to the family or other mediating structures. Some religious groups are engaging in activities such as use of mass media that involve them quite predictably and understandably in governmental regulation. Thus we see more governments engaged in monitoring and even surveillance of religious groups, particularly new ones, and this increased scrutiny can lead to clashes over control of the lives of participants in the NRMs.[52] Hence recruitment strategies of NRMs, how they raise and spend money, and how they care for their children all become areas of considerable interest to the societies in which NRMs attempt to function. And that interest can lead to controversy, a situation that seems certain to continue and even increase in future years.

Notes

1   James A. Beckford, *Cult Controversies* (London, 1985); James T. Richardson (ed.), *Regulating Religion: Case Studies from around the Globe* (New York, 2004); Eileen Barker, *New Religious Movements*

(London, 1984); Anson Shupe and David Bromley, *Anti-Cult Movements in Cross-Cultural Perspective* (New York, 1994); Elisabeth Arweck, "Globalisation and New Religious Movements," in Peter Beyer and Lori Beaman (eds.), *Religion, Globalization and Culture* (Leiden, 2007), pp. 253–80.

2   David Bromley and James T. Richardson (eds.), *The Brainwashing/ Deprogramming Controversy* (New York, 1983); Dick Anthony, "Religious Movements and Brainwashing Litigation," in Tom Robbins and Dick Anthony (eds.), *In Gods We Trust* (New Brunswick, NJ, 1990), pp. 295–344; Dick Anthony, "Pseudoscience and Minority Religions: An Evaluation of the Brainwashing Theories of Jean-Marie Abgrall," *Social Justice Research* 12 (1999), pp. 421–56; James T. Richardson, "The Active versus Passive Convert: A Paradigm Change in Conversion/ Recruitment Research," *Journal for the Scientific Study of Religion* 24 (1985), pp. 163–79; James T. Richardson, "Cult Brainwashing Cases and the Freedom of Religion," *Journal of Church and State* 33 (1991), pp. 55–74; James T. Richardson, "A Social-Psychological Critique of Brainwashing Claims about Recruitment to New Religions," in Jeffrey Hadden and David Bromley (eds.), *Handbook of Cults and Sects in America* (Greenwich, CT, 1993), pp. 75–97.

3   James T. Richardson, "'Brainwashing' Claims and Minority Religions outside the United States: Cultural Diffusion of a Questionable Legal Concept," *Brigham Young University Law Review* 1996, pp. 873–904; James T. Richardson and Massimo Introvigne, "'Brainwashing' Theories in European Parliamentary and Administrative Reports on 'Cults' and 'Sects'," *Journal for the Scientific Study of Religion* 40 (2001), pp. 143–68.

4   James T. Richardson (ed.), *Money and Power in the New Religions* (New York, 1988).

5   Susan Palmer and Charlotte Hardman (eds.), *Children in the New Religions* (New Brunswick, NJ, 1999); James T. Richardson, "Social Control of New Religions: From 'Brainwashing' Claims to Child Sex Abuse Accusations," in Palmer and Hardman (eds.), *Children in New Religions*, pp. 172–86.

6   James T. Richardson and Massimo Introvigne, "New Religious Movements, Countermovements, Moral Panics, and the Media," in David Bromley (ed.), *Teaching New Religious Movements* (Oxford, 2007), pp. 91–111.

7   James T. Richardson, Mary White Harder, and Robert Simmonds, *Organized Miracles: A Study of a Contemporary Youth Communal Fundamentalist Organization* (New Brunswick, NJ, 1978).

8   Bromley and Richardson, *The Brainwashing/Deprogramming Controversy*.

9   Brock Kilbourne and James T. Richardson, "Psychotherapy and New Religions in a Pluralistic Society," *American Psychologist* 39 (1984), pp. 237–51; James T. Richardson and Mary White Stewart, "Medicalization and Regulation of Deviant Religions: An Application of Conrad and Schneider's Model," in Richardson (ed.), *Regulating Religion*, pp. 507–34.

10 Richardson and Introvigne, "New Religious Movements."
11 Beckford, *Cult Controversies*; Shupe and Bromley (eds.), *Anti-Cult Movements in Cross-Cultural Perspective*; James T. Richardson and Barend van Driel, "New Religions in Europe: A Comparison of Developments and Reactions in England, France, Germany, and The Netherlands," in Shupe and Bromley (eds.), *Anti-Cult Movements in Cross-Cultural Perspective*, pp. 129–170; Richardson (ed.), *Regulating Religion*.
12 James T. Richardson and Thomas Robbins, "Monitoring and Surveillance of Religious Groups in the United States," in Derek Davis (ed.), *Handbook of Church and State in the United States* (Oxford, 2010), pp. 353–69.
13 James Tong, *Revenge of the Forbidden City: The Suppression of the Falungong in China 1999–2005* (New York, 2007).
14 Marat Shterin and James T. Richardson, "Effects of the Western Anti-Cult Movement on Development of Laws Concerning Religion in Post-Communist Russia," *Journal of Church and State* 42 (2000), pp. 247–72.
15 Tong, *Revenge of the Forbidden City*.
16 Hubert Seiwert, "The German Enquete Commission on Sects: Political Conflicts and Compromises," in Richardson (ed.), *Regulating Religion*, pp. 85–101.
17 James T. Richardson and Jennifer Shoemaker, "The European Court of Human Rights, Minority Religions, and the Social Construction of Religious Freedom," in Eileen Barker (ed.), *The Centrality of Religion in Social Life: Essays in Honour of James A. Beckford* (Aldershot, UK, and Burlington, VT, 2008), pp. 103–16.
18 Bryan Edelman and James T. Richardson, "Imposed Limitations on Freedom of Religion in China and the Margin of Appreciation Doctrine," *Journal of Church and State* 47 (2005), pp. 243–67.
19 Donald Black, *The Social Structure of Right and Wrong* (New York, 1999).
20 Ted Patrick with Tom Dulak, *Let Our Children Go* (New York, 1976); Anson Shupe and David Bromley, *The New Vigilantes: Deprogrammers, Anti-Cultists, and the New Religions* (Beverly Hills, CA, 1980).
21 John LeMoult, "Deprogramming Members of Religious Sects," *Fordham Law Review* 46 (1978), pp. 599–634 (reprinted in Bromley and Richardson [eds.], *The Brainwashing/Deprogramming Controversy*); David Bromley, "Conservatorships and Deprogramming: Legal and Political Prospects," in Bromley and Richardson (eds.), *The Brainwashing/Deprogramming Controversy*, pp. 267–94.
22 The entertaining movie *Holy Smoke*, directed by Jane Campion and starring Kate Winslet and Harvey Keitel, was about a deprogramming in Australia by an American deprogrammer brought over just for the deprogramming on one young female participate of an Eastern-oriented new religion.
23 James T. Richardson, "Deprogramming: From Private Self-Help to Governmental Organized Repression," *Crime, Law, and Social Change* 55 (2011), pp. 331–36.

24 Shupe and Bromley, *The New Vigilantes*; Anson Shupe and Susan Darnell, *Agents of Discord: Deprogramming, Pseudo-Science, and the Anti-Cult Movement* (New Brunswick, NJ, 2006).

25 Richardson, "Deprogramming: From Private Self-Help to Governmental Organized Repression."

26 Barend van Driel and James T. Richardson, "Print Media Coverage of New Religious Movements: A Longitudinal Study," *Journal of Communication* 38 (1988), pp. 37–61; Laurel Rowe and Gray Cavender, "Cauldrons Bubble, Satan's Trouble, but Witches are Okay: Media Constructions of Satanism and Witchcraft," in James Richardson, David Bromley, and Joel Best (eds.), *The Satanism Scare* (New York, 1991), pp. 263–71; James T. Richardson, "Manufacturing Consent about Koresh," in Stuart Wright (ed.), *Armageddon in Waco* (Chicago, 1995), pp. 153–76.

27 Richardson and Introvigne, "New Religious Movements"; Shupe and Bromley, *The New Vigilantes*.

28 David Tabb Stewart and James T. Richardson, "Mundane Materialism: Economic Survival and Theological Evolution within Jesus Movement Groups," *Journal of the American Academy of Religion* 67 (1999), pp. 825–47.

29 James T. Richardson, "The 'Deformation' of New Religions: Impacts of Societal and Organizational Factors," in Thomas Robbins, William Shepherd, and James McBride (eds.), *Cults, Culture, and the Law* (Chico, CA, 1985), pp. 163–76.

30 Richardson (ed.), *Money and Power in the New Religions*.

31 David Bromley and Anson Shupe, "Financing the New Religions: A Resource Mobilization Approach," *Journal for the Scientific Study of Religions* 19 (1979), pp. 227–39.

32 Lewis Carter, *Charisma and Control in Rajneeshpuram* (New York, 1990); Richardson and Stewart, "Medicalization and Regulation."

33 See several chapters on France's effort in Richardson (ed.), *Regulating Religion*.

34 Burke Rochford, "Movement and Public in Conflict: Values, Finances, and the Decline of the Hare Krishna," in Richardson (ed.), *Money and Power in the New Religions*, pp. 271–303.

35 Note that efforts to control the raising of funds in other countries were sometimes more successful, as was the case in Japan, where the courts, not bound by constitutional structures, allowed a number of successful suits to regain funds raised by the UC. See Richardson, "Deprogramming: From Private Self-Help to Governmental Organized Repression."

36 Rochford, "Movement and Public in Conflict."

37 James T. Richardson, "Scientology in Court: A Look at Some Major Cases from Various Nations," in Lewis (ed.), *Scientology*, pp. 283–94.

38 Richardson, Harder, and Simmonds, *Organized Miracles*.

39 James T. Richardson, "Public Opinion and the Tax Evasion Trial of Reverend Moon," *Behavioral Sciences and the Law* 10 (1992), pp. 53–65; Herbert Richardson, *Constitutional Issues in the Case of*

Rev. Moon (New York, 1984). Also see David Bromley, "The Economic Structure of the Unificationist Movement," and "Economic Structure and Charismatic Leadership in the Unificationist Movement," both in Richardson (ed.), *Money and Power in the New Religions*, pp. 305–63.

40 Palmer and Hardman (eds.), *Children in New Religions*.
41 Joel Best, *Threatened Children* (Chicago, 1990).
42 Jean Swantko, "The Twelve Tribes Messianic Communities, the Anti-Cult Movement, and Governmental Response," in Richardson (ed.), *Regulating Religion*, pp. 179–200; Richardson, "Social Control of New Religions."
43 Vanessa Malcarne and John Burchard, "Investigations of Child Abuse/ Neglect Allegations in Religious Cults: A Case Study in Vermont," *Behavioral Sciences and the Law* 10 (1992), pp. 75–88.
44 Christopher Ellison and John Bartowski, "'Babies Were Being Beaten': Exploring Child Abuse Allegations at Ranch Apocalypse," in Wright (ed.), *Armageddon in Waco*, pp. 111–49; James T. Richardson and John DeWitt, "Christian Science Healing, the Law, and Public Opinion," *Journal of Church and State* 34 (1992), pp. 549–61; Carolyn Wah, "Religious Freedom and the Best Interests of the Child: The Case of Jehovah's Witnesses in Child Custody Litigation," in Pauline Côté (ed.), *Frontier Religions in Public Space* (Ottawa, 2001), pp. 193–234; Stuart Wright and James T. Richardson, *Saints under Siege: The Texas State Raid on the Fundamentalist Latter Day Saints* (New York, 2011).
45 Anson Shupe, *Rogue Clerics: The Social Problem of Clergy Deviance* (New Brunswick, NJ, 2008).
46 Susan Palmer, "Frontiers and Families: The Children of Island Pond," in Palmer and Hardman (eds.), *Children in New Religions*, pp. 153–71; Swantko, "The Twelve Tribes"; Malcarne and Burchard, "Investigations of Child Abuse."
47 James R. Lewis and Gordon Melton, *Sex, Slander, and Salvation: Investigating The Family/Children of God* (Stanford, CA, 1994).
48 James T. Richardson and Rex Davis, "Experiential Fundamentalism: Revisions of Orthodoxy in the Jesus Movement," *Journal of the American Academy of Religion* 51 (1993), pp. 397–425.
49 Richardson, "Social Control of New Religions."
50 James T. Richardson, "Law, Social Control, and Minority Religions," in Coté (ed.), *Frontier Religions*, pp. 139–68; James T. Richardson, "Discretion and Discrimination in Cases Involving Controversial Religious Groups and Accusations of Ritual Abuse," in Rex Ahdar (ed.), *Law and Religion* (Aldershot, UK, 2004), pp. 111–32.
51 James T. Richardson, "The Sociology of Religious Freedom: A Structural and Socio-Legal Analysis," *Sociology of Religion* 67 (2006), pp. 267–94: James T. Richardson, "Religion, Law, and Human Rights," in Peter Beyer and Lori Beaman (eds.), *Religion, Globalization, and Culture* (Leiden, 2007), pp. 407–29.
52 Richardson (ed.), *Regulating Religion*; Richardson and Robbins, "Monitoring and Surveillance."

Further reading

Barker, Eileen, *New Religious Movements* (London, 1984).

Beckford, James A., *Cult Controversies* (London, 1985).

Palmer, Susan and Charlotte Hardman (eds.), *Children in the New Religions* (New Brunswick, NJ, 1999).

Richardson, James T., *Money and Power in the New Religions* (New York, 1988).

Richardson, James T. (ed.), *Regulating Religion: Case Studies from around the Globe* (New York, 2004).

Shupe, Anson and David Bromley, *Anti-Cult Movements in Cross-Cultural Perspective* (New York, 1994).

Part II

Themes

4 History and the end of time in new religions

GARRY W. TROMPF

FRAMING THE PAST AND FUTURE

Members of new religious movements (NRMs) typically share a heightened sense of cosmic significance by believing their activities are crucial for human history ("macro-history"), even its very culmination ("the End Times"). The term macro-history denotes the writing and envisaging of the past as a whole, and doing so usually entails explaining present conditions and presaging momentous events in the future. NRM leadership usually encourages adherents to locate themselves in (sacred) time and look forward to group vindication, renown, and salvation. Sometimes earthly events are viewed as incidental to huge cosmic processes, stressing a descending hierarchy of spiritual powers before matter and human beings appear, or conceiving us in a vast succession of worlds, in which cases we talk of cosmo-history. At other times myth or story dominates, to explain how current predicaments have arisen, making the denotations "myth-history" or "mythological macro-history" most appropriate. The most basic frames of macro-historical reference are progress; regress; recurrence; and unfolding towards eschatological consummation. Teachings or freer-floating ideas within NRMs respond to these paradigms in varied, often complex ways. When movements stress their own role in reclaiming some past glory, for example, they can at the same time lament decline yet optimistically believe that what has been lost can be recovered (by rebirth, reform, final progress, or apocalyptic perfection). When social movements seek to make up for some cultural declension one can read them as revitalizing, or, if it is a question of indigenous peoples hoping to save their traditions, as nativistic. When the stress is on finality, totality, perhaps also on the imminence of a great future outcome resolving persistent human problems, the term "millenarian movement" can be employed. Emergent millenarian activities mostly spawn NRMs or distinctly religious social forms, whereas many reform(ist) and revitalizing agitations possess less religious qualities (class action, protest, rebellion, insurrection, etc.).

Macro-history among NRMs is not sophisticated in the manner of critical or philosophical history (found with Gibbon, Hegel, Spengler, Toynbee, etc.), for it rarely conforms to expected standards of doing history and apparently takes liberties with facts. NRM macro-histories are group-specific or sectarian in implication, even if adapting longer-received models of sacred history (*kalpa* theory, *Heilsgeschichte*, dispensationalism, etc.). In older religions, founder-figures did not normally attempt the (re-)writing of history; it was their followers who endowed these great ones with significance in the flow of temporalities. By contrast, it is a characteristic of NRMs, within the modern competition over grand narratives, that their leaders show a panoramic grasp of events to unveil the group's role in humanity's destiny. Accepting their leader's command over time usually involves adherents discarding or deliberately altering conventional interpretations, along with selective memory, antagonism toward contrary viewpoints (e.g., anti-evolutionism), not to mention forgetfulness of any facts giving the leaders an ambiguous or banal image. There will always be NRMs, admittedly, tending to render history quite irrelevant, eternalizing scripture, for instance, to shield it from being contextualized by critical commentators, as did the Indian Arya Samaj (founded in 1875) for the Vedas, or rendering their teacher timeless, as with the Sannyasins' (established in 1971) recent rewriting of the controversial Bhagwan Rajneesh into a domesticated entity called Osho whose earthly birth and death become inconsequential. Whatever the variations, though, big pictures of past and future are distinctly modern generators of both collective visions and cohesive membership in today's increasing plurality of religions.

Several older NRMs are well known for recasting both world history and *Endzeiten* in novel ways. To illustrate, consider how the key scripture of the Mormon religion, the *Book of Mormon*, amounts to a reopening of heavenly revelations after 1,400 years of apostasy and divine silence (from the time the angel Moroni buried his sacred records in America in AD 421 down to their disclosure to Prophet Joseph Smith, Jr. in 1823). Through this new text, now supplementing the Bible, we learn inter alia that Adam, co-creator with Christ, was the founder of the true Priesthood (in America as Eden), primordial President of the Church, and director over all dispensations in history; that the so-called Lamanite people, fleeing descendants of Lehi, crossed the ocean to propagate most American Indian tribes and prepared for the latter-day saints in America; and that Christ will return on American soil (ruling over the true Zion) and go on to sanctify worlds other than our own.[1]

RESTORATIONISM AND DISPENSATIONALISM

In this macro-historical outlook we can detect motifs found in other new developments arising out of an already complex Christian background. One is *restorationism*, the claim that the Truth has been lost for ages (since near the time of Jesus); and another is *dispensationalism*, the confident plotting of the course of the sacred successive (st)ages of God's guiding hand in time. Integral to these motifs is prophetic *adventism*, and in American Christian-originated NRMs this is usually traceable back to the teachings of William Miller, who in the 1830s preached the imminent Second Coming of Christ. In the 1870s, American founder-figure of the Jehovah's Witnesses Charles Russell propounded his own restorationist theology (that the true Christian way was at last re-established after eighteen centuries of apostasy, and that the Jews should return to Israel), and also a dispensationalist model (of sacred Ages running from Adam, through Noah and Moses to Christ's second coming, based on the Bible and the ascending and descending passages in the great pyramid, for Russell a Hebrew construction). Christ's Advent, a near event (set at 1874), would shock a depraved and environmentally changing world that brought tribulation on the faithful, before the return of Eden on earth (by 1914).[2]

The restoration of lost true practice or truth is crucial for other Christian groups, Seventh-day Adventism (established in 1863) insisting on the return of true (Saturday) Sabbath-keeping, modern British Israel(it)ism (est. 1884) revealing the descent of British (even American) rulers from ancient tribes of Israel, and Christian Science (est. 1866) rediscovering Christ's healing power. Apropos dispensationalism, Adventists like documenting Sabbatarian remnants through Christian history, and British Israelites various stepping-stone covenants. With Jehovah's Witnesses, these two movements are pre-millennialist in their eschatologies (suggesting that Christ will return to start his thousand-year reign or Millennium). In recent times the Children of God (est. 1968), through pamphleteering by Moses David (pseudonym of Californian David Brandt Berg), combined simplified messages about Advent, restoration, and dispensations. The Children were the true communists, with believers being equal, joyfully poor, and no longer controlled by human leaders, but by the Spirit. Their cosmic role was to remove the debris and dust of centuries that obscured the Plan and Goal God has given to history. When the Rapture arrives soon and suddenly (e.g., Matt. 24:40–41), God's true community will be miraculously completed, and only Berg's straightforward writings, without "churchy garbage," would be needed. This pre-millennialist Rapture theme formed a strong current among American Fundamentalists, producing a cross-denominational Rapture movement.[3]

Recently publicized pre-millennialist Christian NRMs have been offshoots of Seventh-day Adventism, especially the Davidian groups centred in Waco, Texas. The leader of the original Leviticus of Davidian sect (established in 1942), Bulgaro-American Victor Houteff, declared himself Elijah at Mount Carmel Center, announcing Christ's coming, at "the eleventh hour," would precede a 100-year probationary Time of the Harvest. The Branch Davidians, a Center that broke away in 1960 under Benjamin Roden, went on to identify "The Seven Seals of Revelation" before Christ's coming: the Seventh-day Adventist Church being the first, the Davidians the second, and "the Branch" (the 144,000 of Rev. 7:4) being the third. Sacred chronology confirmed the latter's crucial role: 430 years from Abraham to Moses, 1,500 years from Moses to Christ (placed centrally); 1,500 to the Reformation's Augsburg Confession (1530); and 430 to the budding of the Branch (from Houteff's prophecies in 1930). When Vernon Howell (aka David Koresh) purloined the group's dream of a new Davidic Kingdom of Christ by taking over New Mount Carmel, as a king with rights over women to start a new humanity, outside authorities acted extremely negatively with the disastrous 1993 Waco Siege.[4]

COSMIC CYCLING AND GREAT AGES

Returning to Mormonism's motifs, we should remark on a neo-gnostic feature found in various older NRMs. This is the idea that humans originate from higher planes or actual celestial bodies (for the Mormons the star Kolob) and that we go back at death to our divine Home(s), whether to the divine Unity, ethereal states, or actual supra-terrestrial bodies. This so-called cosmic U-curve is typically envisioned as a descent of spirits or souls, sometimes from decidedly prior worlds of cosmic history, into the necessary materialization of our current humanness before ascending back to re-spiritualization. The Theosophical Society (founded 1875) is the most famous older NRM disseminating such a vision, although it combines this model with the Indian view of enormous time cycles (*kalpas*) proceeding endlessly, involving lost civilizations and reincarnating souls. In a species of restorationism, Theosophy announces the happy recovery of lost wisdom, which in our current history originated in fabled India. Reflected in messages of different religions this wisdom is now best accessed in esoteric communication with ethereal Masters, spiritually elevated beings, who enable information about such lost civilizations as Lemuria and Atlantis in the far distant past from the so-called Akashic records believed to contain traces of all events. Despite the strong cyclicism, and the overall sense of man as a divine Unity only at his origin and his end, progress occurs enough for most souls to escape from the eternal rounds. To founder-Theosophist Helena Petrovna Blavatsky's mind, this is not like earthly progress, for everything on earth starts, not from savagery, but from supra-mundane etheric developments and with the truest wisdom, while any cosmo- or macro-historical spiraling on our globe is between so-called Root Races almost completely removed from each other over vast time distances.[5] As for Theosophy's Adventism, it involves an occult rather than external event, and a mystical shift of spiritual consciousness; although there was one striking messianic moment (in 1922), when young Jiddu Krishnamurti was welcomed as the coming world teacher, to initiate the dispensation of a new Christ and a new Root Race. But to the leaders' disappointment he reneged and went his own way.

Theosophy's cluster of neo-gnostic motifs was relayed yet modified in NRMs deviating from it, such as Alice Bailey's Arcane School in the USA (founded 1923), and the Anthroposophical Society which separated in 1912/13 from the parent organization under Austrian Rudolf Steiner. These movements derive lessons for the present from Lemurian and Atlantian civilizations for present humanity (Alice Bailey claiming the former collapsed from homosexuality and the latter through cancers; and Steiner instructing how the superior spiritual gifts of prior civilizations might be regained). Steiner, affected by Goethe and Hegel, made more of the civilizations in our order (from ancient India to the Graeco-Roman-Christian complex) to help retrieve the lost sense of seeing invisible worlds; and for Steiner Christ regained centrality after his displacement by Buddhist-inspired Blavatsky.[6]

As a separate motif, the view that all profound wisdom derives from the mystic East is a mark of the European Romantic movement, when newly discovered Indian texts presented a new source of divine truth to supplement, even replace, the Bible. The tendency to graft Christianity on to the Eastern (Indian and Hermetic) tree of wisdom soon manifested, as in American transcendentalism and New Thought. Given this background, including Bailey's influence, the penchant for recovering lost wisdom for today has become a key characteristic of the New Age profile, although some groups want to add contributions of the (pre-Lemurian Hyperborean) North (as in neo-Druidism) or give channeled reassurances that we can avoid the fate befalling Lemuria (Mu) or Atlantis, as offered by the Californian I AM Movement in the 1930s and 1940s. Another impressive Californian affair, the Brotherhood of the Sun (established in 1968) – a most syncretic religion – adopted Indian yogic worship practice, while elaborating a Theosophically affected macro-history to reveal how all primordial wisdom derives from the submerged Pacific continent of Mu. Leader Norman Paulsen, who teaches that the four races (white, blue [black], yellow, and red) derive from Mu, and that early modern explorers' reports of California's "white Indians" refer to white remnants that fled east with the reds. Paulsen also claimed a pre-existent role as one of the ancient rulers of Mu who flew a spaceship (*mu*) on the side of Melchisedec-Christ, a figure crucial in every cosmic conflict who will head the Return of the Ancients (or the space-master-ing Lemurians) when they arrive to establish "God's Empire of the Sun" in the battle of Armageddon. The Brotherhood and the I AM movement share the notion of returning Lemurians in their eschatologies, along with an expectation of space visitations (a motif considered below).[7]

By comparison, certain NRMs of Indian origin yet popular in the West can appeal to classical Hindu theories of time – to *kalpa*s, *manvantara*s, and the four *yuga*s – independently of Theosophical influences. They emphasize the superior spiritual condition of those in prior and future ages, especially the perfection of the golden age (*satya* or *krta yuga*), and warn of the need for spiritual preparedness in our own time (the worst age or *kali yuga*), which will become increasingly unbearable. This is the position of Bhaktivedanta Prabhupada of the Hare Krishna movement (founded 1966), who propounded mainstream *vaisnavite* Hindu teaching that the won-drous *krta* or *satya* age would bring the *kali yuga* (or Age of Iron) to a dramatic, millennium-like end. He thereby presents himself as founder-*acharya* of a dawning period of bliss, when his founder-*guru* Chaitanya Mahāprabhu (1486–1534), the last incarnation of Krishna, will return as long-awaited deliverer. In other views this classical model is modified. One of the earlier modern NRM leaders, Paramahansa Yogananda, bearing the Self-Realization Fellowship to California, construed all signs of a lingering *kali yuga* as the struc-tural equivalent of the Christian Time of Troubles, when money would become worthless and horrendous depressions arrive, accom-panied by natural catastrophes, wars, and famine. But he nonethe-less preferred to follow his *guru* Sri Yukteswar's teaching that the *yuga*s climb back up to the golden time in reverse order, and that in an overlap period we are now just entering the second (*dvapara*) age, which was mainly going to be a progressive 2,400-year period of atomic-energy developments.[8] In unusual fashion, the founder of Sahaja Yoga (established in 1970), Shri Mataji Nirmila Devi, distinguished the *satya* from *krta* as *yugas* and saw the *krta yuga* breaking in already as the Last Judgment and an Aquarian time when people suffer in reaping the fruits of very bad actions – before a wondrous time ahead. Notice how the Hare Krishna movement's intense apocalyptic tendencies combine with a stress on the need to bear a current regress, while the respective Self-Realization and Sahaja optimisms have eventual adjustment prevailing over presages of doom. One implication here is that macro-histories in NRMs may differ because some leaders' attitudes to the current order are more strident than others', or simply because they inherit one interpretation of traditional texts as against others.

Another macro-historical motif is found within the (basically neo-gnostic) Theosophical current: the image of humanity originating from a celestial Home, descending to earth and (re-)ascending to heaven in a cosmic U-curve. Although popularly associated with Theosophy, this schema has a rich lineage, going far back to ancient gnostic and Hermetic speculation, and reappearing in modern neo-gnostic churches.[9] The Church of Scientology (incorporated in 1953) is pertinent for its stress on humanity's original shared divinity that can be recovered through an NRM practice. Scientology's founder, L. Ron Hubbard, taught exoterically a gnostic version of the fall of perfect man into imperfection, conceiving us to start as primordial spirits called Thetans, who, in their non-material, massless, immortal state, co-created the universe along with the Supreme Being, but who got caught in their own trap and got stuck in their own creation. Losing their old power and omniscience, these spirits have become vulnerable human beings, and have returned, life after life by reincarnation over millions of years; yet their forgotten origin has been reawakened at last and their ascension to Survival now made possible by Hubbard's cosmically significant practices of Dianetics, for Scientology wants to bring man close to the state of the original Thetan as the culmination of all religious quests. In the esoteric account, though, past galactic ruler Xenu trapped Thetan spirits on earth 75 million years ago after a space war; as leftovers they came to enter our bodies by the thousands after humans began inhabiting the earth. Through so-called auditing programs, a therapeutic process, Scientology's object is to get rid of them and the false realities they create, so that members can become "clear" and progress on "The Road to Total Freedom."[10]

COSMIC RETURN AND OUTER-SPACE CONNECTIONS

One can expect among NRMs that beliefs in humanity's heavenly origins and return will be interpreted in distinctly physical terms, as with various UFO religions. In these cases macro-histories involve commitment to the view that actual visitors from other planets have dramatically affected our past and will return to connect with us in the future. This view was popularized by Erich von Däniken to explain the astounding technical achievements of the ancients, and the discrepancy between biblical accounts of beginnings and the evolutionists' stress on plodding Stone Age cultures. For von Däniken UFO technical expertise and insemination changed the human course forever, and the biblical Genesis could remain true because Adam and Eve were the first two new (i.e., post-visitation) humans on our planet. One can see how UFO religions seek to solve the same conundrums in different ways. A strong line taken in the Raëlian movement (founded in 1975), for example, is that evolution by (random) natural selection is a false myth, and that the Bible's account of the human story, though eventually overlaid by vain poetic babblings, is correct – but on the understanding that the name for God in the Hebrew texts (*Elohim*) should be taken literally as plural and referring to extra-terrestrials from a distant planet. Under criticism for their genetic experiments on a far-off planet, teams of research scientists (the Elohim) chose earth for their special work, and, after generating matter and different life forms, the most talented team (in today's Israel, where a veritable paradise had been made) started to create humans in their own image (see Gen. 1:26–27). But the new humans had to be driven out because they themselves wanted the superior scientific knowledge of the creators (see Gen. 3:5), even if a family of humans had to be saved later (in a spaceship, or the Ark, that was "lifted above the waters," see Gen. 8:17b) when the rulers of the distant planet tried to destroy earth with nuclear missiles.

The utterly alternative reading of the Bible goes on, and the Raëlian cosmic view turns out to be an openly atheistic set of beliefs (of an anti-evolutionary kind), through which science replaces religion. The movement's founder, Frenchman Claude Vorilhon (in his prophetic role known by the name Raël), is the one entrusted to build an Embassy to receive returning aliens, who will bring with them the best of the humanitarian prophets of old – Jesus, Moses, Buddha, and Muhammad – who had been deliberately cloned and watched over by the creators for an Aquarian apocalypse (when the church will die unless it reforms, Israel will prosper, and a humanitarian order, indeed world government, will prevail).

All this is part of a cosmic chain, because the creators themselves had been created by those on another planet, and they themselves may disappear one day, leaving us to continue something like the Theosophists' eternal cycle, but one thoroughly secularized and given only a physicalist meaning. Other UFO-inspired NRMs handle puzzles comparable to these. The Urantia Foundation, to illustrate, which holds custodianship of *The URANTIA Book*, takes the previously unimagined magnitude of the cosmos itself to be calling for a new religious reckoning. The huge *URANTIA* text of revealed or channeled data allows a panoramic *voyance* into a vast array of unseen worlds, with the worlds being like those one might expect to meet as a science-fiction-type space-time traveler. We encounter an enormous flat-disk heaven (*Havona*), along with local universes fathered by "God's Creator Sons" and monitored by ranks of angels (*supernaphim, omniaphim*, etc.), the planet *Jerusalem* (whence Adam and Eve were sent to our world to stop the Lucifer rebellion), and so on. Predictably, although Christ's work is honored, there is no talk of a dramatic Second Coming, but only the heaven's mediation of cosmic consciousness to humanity through *The URANTIA Book* itself, an approach much less radical than with other UFO coteries expecting dramatic salvation from a doomed earth at the last moment.[11]

The strikingly different end-time scenarios projected within UFO religions raise questions about diversity in NRM eschatologies or millennial expectations. So-called millenarian movements await imminent, total, ultimate *this-worldly* collective salvation, and thus the typical millennial projection is of a consummate reordering of affairs on *our* planet. Hence in their anti-establishment way the Jehovah's Witnesses have expected not only that Jews would return to their homeland, but also that the ruling class (Egypt as the commercial and military class, the Assyrians as the political rulers) would have to repent under a literal-political Restitution, as would the bigger churches for their falsities, all such parties then subjected to the new Covenant of Christ's earthly Davidic rule. The Branch Davidians, of course, would go so far as to say that they were part-*creators* of such a rule; while in the Raëlian case, there is no Kingdom of God, but a scientific surrogate of it nonetheless, with the imminence of alien salvific governance on this planet. In contrast, NRMs with the kinds of cosmic outlook we find in Theosophy and Urantia look to a long-term Return of all souls to the divine Home well beyond terrestrial conditions – a non-millenarian outlook – although we should note that our return to the stars can be represented to be a transformative end-of-cycle apocalyptic moment, as in the original 2012 Prophecies based on an imaginative interpretation of the so called Mayan calendar. Certain meditation movements can aspire to influence nations or create world government "down here" in our world (e.g., Transcendental Meditation), while others, as illustrated by the followers of Da Free John (aka Adi Da Samraj), now with head-quarters on an island in Fiji, insist on ascent "up there" (in this last case, only through devotion to their founder Samraj). neopaganism move-ments, in their fashion restorationist, want to see age-old indigenous beliefs re-established in particular (very earthly!) nations, as with the Latvian Dievturi movement (established in 1935), a European nativism in a country where widespread Christian allegiance is fairly recent.

THEMES IN NON-WESTERN MOVEMENTS

Continuing to explore separate motifs from our (Theosophical) clus-ter, a special one concerns access to the Masters and their teachings about past, present, and future. In the West it is common to find followers of those claiming to channel special Masters (e.g., Seth enthusiasts) or have information about their presence on other planets (e.g., the Aetherius Society). But there are other, more respectable-looking ideas with non-Western impetuses. Consider *The Work* initiated by Georges Gurdjieff in 1912: although related to Theosophy and always extolling the most ancient wisdom as best, it only has need of plainly historicized Masters and has no resort to speculation about a lost Atlantis or Lemuria, let alone Akashic records. As Pyotr Ouspensky argued, it suffices to know that esoteric schools and their Masters have persisted uninterruptedly in history, guarding knowledge from ancient civilizations that left no visible traces, and able to restart civilized life "after races ... have lapsed into a barbarous state." Referring to *The Work*, with its Armenian ori-gins, helps to remind us of Middle Eastern ideas of Masters. One per-haps thinks immediately of Shiite and heterodox Islamic imamology. In Persian Shaykhism (fl.1822–45), to exemplify, an alleged direct access to the occult Twelve Imams allowed its leaders to predict the arrival of *al-Bab* ("the Gate") in 1845, heralding the physical return of the twelfth and eschatological Imam or *al Mahdi* (the Director at the End of Time) exactly one thousand lunar years after his occultation. While some such Shiite NRMs concentrate on the future (including the Hojjatieh sect to which Iran's President Ahmadinejad belongs), others find the very pres-ence of the divine in a living figure (as do the Khodja Isma'ilis in the person of the Aga Khan). In the latter grouping lie collective responses to the Sufi "Perfect Masters" (*Harzrats/Qutbs*) as embodiments of the Divine. Behind the Meher Baba movement (1922–), for example, we find influential Pakistani *Hazrat* Inayat Khan's teaching that the founders of the great religions are always one and the same person through many cycles, the God-man or the same One Being (re-)incarnated; and so Indo-Persian Meher Baba, with his multi-faith lineage of prior Masters, presents himself as the same God, as another Jesus, incarnating himself for our current situation. For our time, however, it was important that straight after his great Silence (he stopped talking in October 1954), three-quarters of the world would be destroyed, and he would return 700 years later to preside over a time of prosperity and happiness, his governance guided by a newly disclosed *mantra* of love.[12]

In expanding coverage of NRMs originating from non-Western *Weltanschauungen*, researchers should expect representations of past and future that reflect interesting culture-specific concerns. Even in the Chabad-Lubavich claims about the late Rebbe Menahem Schneerson's messiahship, taking a Jewish movement, his rich Hasidic lineage remains important for his heavenly sanctioning because of its alleged cumulative effect in hastening the Endtime.[13] In Indian cases, *guru* lineages form an aspect of macro-history. Prabhupada's chain of authority is to the point, with the ten *avatara*s of Vishnu, the five establishers of Vedic culture in the Kali Yuga – Krishna, Vyâsa, Buddha, Shankara, and Chaitanya – and then ten spiritual masters in succession passing down Chaitanya's teaching to Prabhu and the Hare Krishnas. By comparison, there are claims by some gurus to direct divine authority without any immediate teaching lineage. It suffices in Sahaja Yoga (1970–), for instance, that Shri Mataji self-identified with Adi Shakti, Mother of Ganesha and Mary, Mother of Christ, and is thus ultimately behind the primordial guru Dattatreyâ and his ten incarnations in Raja Janaka, Abraham, Moses, Zarathustra, Lao-Tze, Confucius, Socrates, Nanak, Muhammad, and Shirdi Sai Baba (the last being the same figure whose reincarnation the recent guru Sathya Sai Baba claimed to be).[14]

In any non-Western-originated NRM, further, we should also expect the historical significance of the leader's own nation to be accentuated. Okada Yoshikazu, founder of Japan's Mahikari movement, taught that the Japanese were the leading beneficiaries of the sunken continent Mu, yet they must be further purged through coming eschatological earthquakes. Other leaders from previously colonized lands make much of the demeanors of the West – a chief theme in Shri Mataji's book *Meta Modern Era*. If Mataji, who early experienced Mahatma Gandhi's ashram and non-violent program, accepted positive change by slow and peaceful means, it was different with Prabhat Sarkar or Sri Sri Anandamurti ("Baba"), founder of the Ananda Marga (established in 1955). His complex social theory (called PROUT, Progressive Utilization Theory) was partly inspired by Subhas Chandra Bose, who responded to British domination of India in Gandhi's time with violent revolutionism. On Anandamurti's reading, socio-political affairs proceed cyclically, and in successive Ages the four great social types or "colors" (*varna*s) – the warriors, intellectuals, merchants, and toiling masses – each have paramountcy in turn. The object of PROUT is to forestall this cycling by achieving a perfect balance, an equilibrium also between capitalism and communism; but this social solution may require revolutionary action to secure the needed rule of philosopher-kings (*sadvipra*s).[15] Here India is imaged as a centerpiece for sorting out world conflict, the kind of patriotic attitude found with other Asian NRM leaders. Two clear cases are the Vietnamese Cao Dai (1926–) movement, and Tong Il Kyo (1954–) of South Korea, that is, the Unification movement.

Caodaists see their movement opening up the Third Era of Salvation or Religious Amnesty, which makes Vietnam ultimately significant for worldwide peace. Caodaist doctrine, then, revolves around a three-staged macro-history (a general framework not uncommon in the West and especially associated with the medieval Joachim of Flora). In the first Era came Moses, Buddha Dipankara, and such Chinese divine sages as Kuan Dao; in the second Buddha Shakyamuni, Confucius, Lao Tze, Jesus, and Muhammad.[16] As for Tong Il Kyo, or the so-called Unification Church, Reverend Sun Myung Moon stresses the sacred role of Korea. In his *Divine Principle* he parallels ancient Israel divided into north and south (disputing over idolatry and monotheism) with modern Korea as divided between north and south (godless communism versus freedom), declaring South Korea to be history's final frontline against Satan. Of all NRM texts Moon's *Divine Principle* is the book most littered with historical patterning, its author legitimating his procedures by evoking Hegel, Spengler, and Toynbee. Among his posited stages of time, there are 400-year periods in ancient biblical history (of slavery in Egypt, of judges, a united kingdom, a divided one, captivity, and of preparation for the coming of the Messiah) in symmetry with 400-year periods of the church (of persecution, patristic rule, royal control, divided kingdoms, papal captivity, and preparation for the second advent of the Messiah). A Third World War (over collective atheism and belief and focused on Korea) is inevitable, but – on the basis of the reference to "the rising sun" in Revelation 7:2–4 – (South) Korea will be where the Second Advent occurs (it cannot be in godless China or greedy Japan!). According to the Unification doctrine of indemnity (based on a culture-specific sense of keeping up reciprocity [Kor. *jeong*; Mand. *shu*]), it is a requirement of humans themselves to pay back God positively for falling out of reciprocal relations with Him. Macro-history becomes a rich arena in which laws of give-and-take, not only periods and recoveries, pertain; and history's worst messes, with much loss of life, eventually prove providential, resolved in the final "great Restoration." The effects of the human Fall, moreover, can be mitigated through group marriages based on the messianic pairing of Sun Myung Moon and his wife.[17]

Unification thought projects the promise of a new unfallen race on earth, and this points to the motif of genetic or laboratory changes in humans posited by other NRMs, whether for past or future. It appears in various black (African American, African, Melanesian) NRMs, with liberation from colonial racist oppression written into their macro-histories. Elijah Muhammad, founder the African American Nation of Islam (founded in 1930), is fabled for propagating a mythological macro-history about "white devils." Some 6,800 years ago, one evil Jacub, of the black tribe of Shabazz in Arabia, was exiled to the Aegean for his utter divisiveness in Mecca. On (apocalyptically associated) Patmos, he crossbred and genetically grafted humans and produced "the white devils," part-animals who escaped after 600 years and harassed Arabia, later exiled to the caves of Europe. There they evolved to be more like humans, and Allah granted these white cavemen 6,000 years to perpetuate their follies and evils, until 1914, when their time was up. Even with some reprieve, Allah saw no repentance in them, especially in the USA, so that by AD 2000 at the latest, Allah was to annihilate all white Americans, and black people choosing to live with them in their modern Babylon. The black Muslim movement has had to wear this strident prophetism as it has tried to normalize its relations with other Muslims, but Louis Farrakhan, on the radical fringe, has utilized Elijah's broader notion that all non-whites have been oppressed for six millennia, and that all the populations of Africa and Asia, and all brown, red, and yellow peoples, can make up a single global, supra-"Black Nation" in protest.[18]

Black NRMs are multiple, though, and it is not easy to generalize about trends in their macro-historical visioning, because so many fissures have occurred through minor squabbles and doctrinal or ritual differences. In Africa, later-coming sectarian and Pentecostal missionaries saw some of the legitimating macro-histories already discussed (of Jehovah's Witnesses, for a start) entering the African scene. Concerning more indigenous developments, Bengt Sundkler has documented the Ethiopic and Zionist motifs in the plethora of independent churches in South Africa.[19] The former picks up long-term African/Ethiopian

connections to the biblical story to give credence to Africans' independence from colonially associated missions, and has been capable of generating millenarian hopes, nowhere more interestingly than across the
Atlantic with the Jamaican Rastafarians, with their irredentist dreams
of returning to Ethiopia. As for their Zionisms, African churches take
on culturally relevant Old Testament practices (water cleansing, circumcision, polygyny, abstaining from pork) absent in introduced
Christianities.[20] Sometimes a church or its prophet/messiah believe
they have received a revelation or decree fulfilling the biblical ones, yet
poured out over and above them; thus the call of the Nigerian Olumba
Olumba Obu of Calabar – the arrived messianic Comforter (see John
15:26) and head of the Brotherhood of Cross and Star (1964–) – to "love
God, love your fellow human beings, and love the *Earth*" – the latter
plea somewhat crucial considering today's environmental stress.

In Melanesia, renowned cargo cult outbursts have been set in train
by many a novel version of the true course of things, prophets revealing
in narrative why their local followers lack access to "the Cargo" (i.e.,
modern commodities dominated by outsiders). In some cases, myth-
histories combine stories of culture heroes with versions of post-contact
events. In the story circulated by the short-lived Tagarab cult (1941–44),
of Madang, New Guinea, the local culture hero Kilibob long ago offered
the Cargo to "the natives," but they refused it as useless for their lifestyle. Kilibob angrily went to Sydney and became the god of the whites.
He eventually saw through them, though, and discerned the missionaries' failure to tell the truth about the Cargo in the Bible, and he would
soon return to Madang to drive out all the Europeans with a ship full
of munitions and new goods, backed by the ancestors in the guise of
Japanese servicemen and signaled by unparalleled storms and earthquakes. Such smaller movements as this gave way to bigger ones, with
higher expectations, after the presence of extraordinary quantities of
cargo witnessed during the Allied campaign to halt Japanese expansion.
In some cases Melanesian local messiahs played surrogates to Christ,
proclaiming their apocalyptic dreams that returning ancestors can by a
mere wish create huge cities. Various independent churches have also
recently arisen, crinkling mainstream Christian discourse. A novel
dispensationalist Age theory is taught by the Seven Church (Misima,
Papuan Islands) with its members set to join the eschatological nation of
the seventh Age of the Great Week of history. The righteous people from
the past and the Misima ancestors will return at the End to inherit the
island's gold mine, these dreams being very locally focused after all.[21]

Ideally, we are all supposed to share the same past, but NRMs are often bent on moving time itself with idiosyncratic (most will add imaginative) shifts and turns. The arresting new versions of past and future are crucial ingredients in NRMs that attract attention and a following, especially also when prospective joiners agree with a new movement's attitudes as to who in this world should be rewarded and punished. These ingredients give initial freshness to a social experiment, but they can be overtaken by events (by the delay of the Apocalypse, let us say, or by the group's tarnished reputation, or as in Theosophy's case by being too hard to fathom, or in the Unification case by communism's unexpected deterioration). When their force deadens or becomes habitually applied, story materials will shift more towards anecdotes of the great founder, with colored pictures of L. Ron Hubbard's life-episodes, for example, or anecdotes of Madame Blavatsky's magic, or "diamond days" with Osho. In the life of NRMs, after all, these materials were already temporally, if not cosmically central. If, as a member of the Peace Mission (1932–), one believes in Father (and Mother) Divine, obviously the divine presence will always remain, even after they leave the earth, and there is thus always the possibility of literally escaping physical death. Unfortunately, in some cases, a leader's need for self-adulation consumes all and requires destructive actions in the intensity of the Present, as the Manson murders, Jonestown, and Aum's subway gas attacks painfully demonstrate.

Notes

1   John Bracht, "The Americanization of Adam," in Garry W. Trompf (ed.), *Cargo Cults and Millenarian Movements: Trans-Oceanic Comparisons of New Religious Movements*, Religion and Society 29 (Berlin, 1990), pp. 97–141.

2   George D. Chryssides, "How Prophecy Succeeds: The Jehovah's Witnesses and Prophetic Expectations," *International Journal for the Study of New Religions* 1:1 (2010), pp. 27–48.

3   Stephen Hunt, *Christian Millenarianism: From the Early Church to Waco* (Bloomington, 2000), parts 3–5.

4   Kenneth Newport, *Branch Davidians of Waco: The History and Beliefs of an Apocalyptic Sect* (Oxford, 2006).

5   Garry Trompf, "Macrohistory in Blavatsky, Steiner and Guénon," in Antoine Faivre and Wouter J. Hanegraaff (eds.), *Western Esotericism and the Science of Religion*, Gnostica 2 (Louvain, 1998), pp. 269–96.

6   Garry Trompf, "Theosophical Macrohistory," in Olav Hammer and Mikael Rothstein (eds.), *Handbook of the Theosophical Current* (Leiden, forthcoming); Robert A. McDermott, "Historical Vision: Introduction," in McDermott (ed.), *The Essential Steiner* (San Francisco, 1984), pp. 171–75.

7   Garry Trompf, "The Cargo and the Millennium on Both Sides of the Pacific," in Trompf (ed.), *Cargo Cults and Millenarian Movements*, pp. 42–56, 80 n. 28.

8   Reender Kranenborg, "Hindu Eschatology within Modern Western Religiosity," in Mikael Rothstein and Reender Kranenborg (eds.), *New Religions in a Postmodern World* (Aarhus: 2003), pp. 141–42.

9   Richard Smith, "The Revival of Ancient Gnosis," in Robert Segal (ed.), *The Allure of Gnosticism: The Gnostic Experience in Jungian Psychology and Contemporary Culture* (Chicago, 1995), pp. 204–23.

10 Mikael Rothstein, "'His name was Xenu. He used renegades ...' Aspects of Scientology's Founding Myth," in James R. Lewis, *Scientology* (Oxford, 2009), pp. 365–87.

11 For variations, see Christopher Partridge (ed.), *UFO Religions* (London, 2003); Paul Boyer, *When Time Is No More: Prophecy Belief in Modern American Culture* (Boston, 1994), pp. 207, 293–339.

12 Charles B. Purdom, *The God-Man: The Life, Journeys and Work of Meher Baba with an Interpretation of His Silence and Spiritual Teaching* (London, 1964), pp. 272–75, 400–1.

13 Elliot R. Wolfson, *Open Secret: Postmessianic Messianism and the Mystical Revision of Menahem Mendel Schneerson* (New York, 2009).

14 J. Thomas, "Looking Forward, Looking Back: Mother Figures in Contemporary Hinduism" (unpublished BA hons. sub-thesis, University of Sydney, 1994, pp. 58–78); see also the chapter by Tulasi Srinivas in the present volume.

15 Eric J. Sharpe and Garry Trompf, *The New Sects*, special issue of *Current Affairs Bulletin* 58:4 (Sept. 1981), pp. 18–19.

16 Sergei Blagov, *The Cao Dai: A New Religious Movement* (Moscow, 1999), pp. 11–17.

17 M. Darrol Bryant, "Unification Eschatology and American Millennial Traditions," in M. Darrol Bryant and Herbert W. Richardson (eds.), *A Time for Consideration: A Scholarly Appraisal of the Unification Church* (New York, 1978), pp. 261–74.

18 Dennis Walker, "The Black Muslims in American Society: From Millenarian Protest to Trans-Continental Relationships," in Trompf (ed.), *Cargo Cults and Millenarian Movements*, pp. 343–90.

19 Bengt Sundkler, *Bantu Prophets in South Africa*, 2nd edn. (London and New York, 1961).

20 See Harold Turner, *Religious Innovation in Africa* (Boston, 1979).

21 Garry Trompf, "Pacific Movements," in Catherine Wessinger (ed.), *Oxford Handbook of Millennialism* (Oxford, 2010), part IV, ch. 23.

Further reading

Hesselgrave, David J. (ed.), *Dynamic Religious Movements: Case Studies of Rapidly Growing Religious Movements around the World* (Grand Rapids, MI, 1978).

Partridge, Christopher, *UFO Religions* (London, 2003).

Rothstein, Mikael and Reender Kranenborg (eds.), *New Religions in a Postmodern World* (Aarhus, 2003).

Sharpe, Eric J. and Garry W. Trompf, *The New Sects*, special issue of *Current Affairs Bulletin* 58:4 (Sept. 1981).

Trompf, Garry W. (ed.), *Cargo Cults and Millenarian Movements: Trans-Oceanic Comparisons of New Religious Movements*, Religion and Society 29 (Berlin, 1990).

5 Charismatic leaders in new religions

CATHERINE WESSINGER

Charismatic leadership is a common, but not a necessary, characteristic of a "new religious movement," understood here as a religion that is either emergent or alternative in a given cultural context. Emergent movements arise from within old traditions, or represent innovative combinations of characteristics from different traditions. Alternative religions include old religious traditions, which are revived, rediscovered or transplanted to a new cultural context. Although charismatic leadership is often associated with new and unconventional movements, charismatic religious leadership and charismatic political leadership go back to the origins of human religious creativity.

Charismatic religious leadership appears to be unconventional in cultures where religious authority has been channeled into offices obtained through authorization by institutionalized bodies and/or leaders. Some cultures have devised means to recognize charismatic religious authority within established institutions, but these expressions of leadership look exotic and alternative when the religion is transplanted to a new context.

"Charisma" may be understood as referring to a characteristic attributed by believers to an individual, scripture, place, or other social construct. Usually the term is used to refer to qualities possessed by a leader. In these instances, the belief is that the leader has access to an unseen source of authority. If charisma is attributed to a scripture or a place, likewise, it is regarded as imbued with the qualities of a source of authority that is normally unseen, but which reveals itself to particular individuals. That unseen source of authority may be understood by believers to be God, gods, Jesus, the Virgin Mary, the Holy Spirit, celestial buddhas and bodhisattvas, saints, angels, masters, spirits, ancestors, or extraterrestrials – all are beings who are not normally visible or tangible to most persons. The unseen source of authority may be a quality of enlightened or awakened awareness attributed to a leader, such as nirvana or *prajñā* (wisdom) in Buddhism, or *moksha* (liberation) in

Hinduism. It may also be an even more abstract understanding of the unseen authority, such as "Nature" or "Progress," or some other principle regarded as ultimate.

Charisma takes varied expressions, and the charismatic careers of individuals and groups have different trajectories. Charisma serves many purposes for the members of a movement – the leaders as well as the followers. Charisma may be the means by which talented but marginalized people – such as women, men of low social status or education, and children – gain authority, respect, and often a fulfilling religious career. Charisma may be the means by which a leader gives hope to members of a demoralized group or nation, and motivates them to recreate their collective entities and engage in self-sacrificing acts – including warfare and genocide.

Charisma can inspire new religious movements that may remain small, or that become worldwide religious traditions. Charismatic leaders may devise movements that empower others to charismatic authority, or they may seek to restrict charisma to the leader only. Leaders may mismanage their charisma to cause disasters resulting in deaths,[1] or they may exercise "responsible charisma"[2] to benefit their followers and others. Similarly, religious institutions that promote the charisma of a revered deceased leader may utilize that authority to instigate persecutions and wars, or to work for social justice and peace.

DEFINITIONS

Charisma

"Charisma" is a Greek word meaning "gift," understood as bestowed by a divine source. The pioneering sociologist Max Weber (1864–1920) provided a social scientific definition of charisma as:

> a certain quality of an individual personality by virtue of which he [or she] is set apart from ordinary [people] and treated as endowed with supernatural, superhuman, or at least specifically exceptional powers or qualities. These are such as are not accessible to the ordinary person, but are regarded as of divine origin or as exemplary, and on the basis of them the individual concerned is treated as a leader.[3]

Weber distinguished charismatic authority from "traditional authority" granted by custom, and "rational-legal authority" obtained through legally constituted offices. Stephen Feuchtwang and Wang

Mingming have defined charisma as involving the "expectation of the extraordinary."[4]

It is not unusual for the roles of charismatic religious leader and political leader to overlap. Weber's reference to charisma as "exemplary" was his way of indicating that political leaders are often attributed with either vague or specific access to divine authorization, until they fall out of favor with the populace. Charismatic religious leaders may become political leaders. Political leaders with various types of authority invoke the sacred ultimate reality revered in their cultural and religious contexts.

Here I define "charisma" as the belief that an individual, scripture, place, object, or other socially constructed entity has access to and is imbued with the qualities of an unseen source of authority. Since the believed source of authority is normally unseen, the attribution of access to that authority is a matter of faith on the part of the followers and also the leader(s).

If people do not believe the claim of access to an unseen source of authority, then that individual, scripture, place, or social construct does not have charisma. When a person claiming charisma gains followers, then she or he can be said to be a charismatic leader. If a scripture, place, sacred object, or other socially constructed entity is believed to be imbued with the qualities of the unseen source of authority, then it, too, has charisma. Since charismatic authority on all these levels is determined by the faith of followers, that authority will be lost whenever people lose faith in the claimed access to the unseen source of authority.

Prophet and messiah

A prophet is an individual who is believed to receive messages from the unseen source of authority. A prophet is not necessarily a messiah. The Hebrew term *messiah* (anointed) is used by scholars to refer to individuals who are believed to be empowered by an unseen source of authority to create a collective salvation. In other words messiahs are associated with millennial movements. Since the messiah is believed to have access to the unseen source of authority, the messiah is also a prophet, but the attributed functions of a messiah go beyond those of a prophet.

SOCIAL CONSTRUCTION OF CHARISMA

Shamanism

Phenomena that scholars have termed "shamanism" appear to be the earliest expressions of charisma in prehistoric and indigenous religions, and these forms continue today and often produce new religious movements. Cultures will have different names for this type of religious specialist. In general a shaman is an individual who is believed to have the ability to communicate with beings in the unseen spirit world, and can mediate between these beings and humans.

There are several types of shamanistic expressions. The first type can be termed "psychic shamans," to refer to persons who receive visions or messages with no trance or out-of-the-body experiences. Psychic visions or messages may be induced by a variety of means, such as dancing, drumming, chanting, or ingesting psychotropic plant substances. But these well-known methods of inducing altered states of awareness are not necessary for psychic shamanism to occur.

Persons who may be termed "traveling shamans" report experiences of leaving their bodies to soul-travel through the spirit world and communicate with beings there. "Possession shamans" experience having their bodies taken over by a spirit being or beings, who then act and speak through their bodies.[5] The altered states of traveling or possession shamans may be induced by the same means associated with psychic shamanism, or they may occur spontaneously.

The attribution of charisma is as old as humanity, and it continues to inspire and manifest in new religious movements.

Falling in love with the charismatic figure

Judith Coney, in her study of Sahaja Yoga and its female guru Sri Mataji Nirmala Devi (1923–2011), who is regarded by her followers as being an incarnation of Adi Shakti (Primordial Mother), highlights that developing faith in a charismatic leader is often like falling in love. A context is created by the movement in which an attitude of love toward the leader is encouraged.[6] To cultivate and maintain that love, the charismatic leader must be responsive to the needs of followers. If the charismatic leader fails to respond adequately to the needs of believers, they may lose faith and withdraw attribution of charisma.

Multiple claims of charisma

When one individual attracts a following through claims of messages received from an unseen source of authority, often other individuals in the movement will begin to make similar claims.

This phenomenon can be discerned in the history of the Theosophical movement. After Helena P. Blavatsky (1831–1891) claimed to receive the teachings of "ancient wisdom" from "masters," described as enlightened human beings who communicated with her via psychic means, other people asserted leadership in the Theosophical Society and its offshoot movements, by claiming that the normally unseen masters communicated with them, also.[7] Eventually the broad Theosophical movement came to regard the masters as "ascended" beings communicating from higher planes. Theosophical belief in masters – human and ascended – led to the appropriation of the concept by UFO religious groups from the 1950s on, whose leaders claim to receive messages from extraterrestrials.[8]

The Latter-day Saint movement initiated in the United States, based on the revelations received by Joseph Smith, Jr. (1805–1844), similarly led to other individuals claiming to receive messages from divine and angelic beings, thus leading to a number of offshoots from the Church of Jesus Christ of Latter-day Saints.[9] The same phenomenon has been observed in relation to Catholic apparitions of the Virgin Mary.[10]

Thus the containment of charisma becomes a problem for charismatic leaders who do not wish to share their authority, or for followers who do not wish to contend with competing claims within the movement.

Shared charisma

Some religious traditions, old and new, promote what can be called "shared charisma," when numerous individuals have access to the source of charismatic authority.

For instance, in the early Christian movement, the Pentecost event reported in Acts 2 is described as occurring when the sound of the Holy Spirit, like "a rush of violent wind," filled the house and "divided tongues of flame," "as if of fire," rested on each of the men and women there. They were all filled with the Holy Spirit and went out into the streets of Jerusalem to speak to pilgrims in their own languages. When bystanders accused the followers of Jesus of being drunk, Peter defended them by quoting a passage from the prophet Joel:

> In the last days it will be, God declares,
> that I will pour out my Spirit upon all flesh,
> and your sons and your daughters shall prophesy,
> and your young men shall see visions,
> and your old men shall dream dreams.
> Even upon my slaves, both men and women,
> in those days I will pour out my Spirit;
> and they shall prophesy. (Acts 2:17–18, New Revised Standard
>   Version)

This shared access to the Holy Spirit remains important throughout the Christian tradition. Despite the institutionalization of charisma in church structures, there remains in Christianity the concept that a person is "called" by the Holy Spirit to ministry. This concept of a "calling" has given numerous Christian women the "holy boldness" to ignore the restrictions imposed by patriarchal cultures and church organizations in order to preach and minister.[11] Pentecostal movements around the world continue to promote the concept and experience of "shared charisma."

Shared charisma is seen also in the movement known since 2004 as The Family International, which was founded as the Children of God in the United States in the late 1960s by David Berg (1919–1994). After Berg's death, charisma has been available through messages sought from beings in the spirit world, including Jesus and Berg himself, by residents of The Family's homes and by employees within the central administrative unit known as World Services. Gary Shepherd and Gordon Shepherd describe The Family International as promoting a "culture of prophecy" at the grassroots, in which residents of Family homes are encouraged to receive spiritual messages daily and discuss these to achieve consensus about issues of concern.[12]

Shepherd and Shepherd argue that The Family International has become a mature religious organization. The World Services staff members are encouraged to utilize prayer and prophecy in the administration of the organization. Charisma is shared, but it is not uncontrolled, since Maria (Karen Zerby, b.1946), Berg's widow, is credited with having the gift of discerning true spiritual direction from mistaken or false messages.[13] Members of The Family International make extensive use of laptops and Internet communications to record, share, and communicate with each other and Maria about messages received from the spirit world.

Restricted charisma

When a movement manifests multiple claimants to charisma, the possibility arises that the additional claims to charismatic authority can detract from the original revelation disseminated by the founder. Some movements take steps to restrict charisma to the founder only, and perhaps transfer that charisma to a scripture.

For instance in Islam, Muhammad, as the recipient of God's Word, is considered a prophet, and even more he is considered to be the "seal of the prophets." While Islam acknowledges that prophets appeared in the preceding Jewish tradition, and that Jesus is a prophet, it is asserted that since in Islam the revelation of God's Word has been recorded perfectly, there is no need for prophets to come after Muhammad. The Qur'an is the uncompromised Word of God and thus is filled with charisma.

When new prophets have arisen in Muslim lands, such as the Báb (1819–1850) and Baha'u'lláh (1817–1892) in Iran, giving rise eventually to the Baha'i Faith, they are promptly silenced by arrest, exile, or execution. Governments affiliated with all dominant religious traditions have a vested interest in maintaining the status quo, which charismatic leaders threaten to upset.

In the Sikh movement initiated by Guru Nanak (1469–1539) in the Punjab in the fifteenth century, a lineage of nine gurus was established after him. The tenth guru, Gobind Singh (1666–1708), declared that after his passing the Sikhs' eternal guru would be a scripture, which is a collection of hymns composed by the first five Sikh gurus and other Indian saints. Sikhs respectfully call this scripture the Guru Granth Sahib or Adi Granth (Primordial Book). In a Sikh Gurdwara, the Guru Granth Sahib is venerated with expressions of worship and devotion similar to those in a Hindu temple directed toward images believed to manifest the Divine.

After Mary Baker Eddy (1821–1910) founded the Church of Christ, Scientist in 1879 in the United States to promote her "discovery" of the metaphysical cause of illness and how it can be overcome, she attracted a number of talented female preachers who established early Christian Science churches. However, Eddy became concerned that her message was being changed by these popular teachers. She therefore created bylaws for all the Christian Science churches stipulating that in a service two Readers will read passages from the Bible and her own book, *Science and Health, with Key to the Scriptures* (1875),[14] in addition to a Lesson-Sermon written by a committee with the Mother Church in Boston, Massachusetts. Hence Eddy's charisma was transferred to her own book, which in the Church of Christ, Scientist has scriptural status alongside the Bible.

Post-life charisma
The charisma attributed by a small group of disciples to a spiritual leader may become amplified after his or her death, and the movement may grow well beyond its size when the leader was alive.

One example is Shirdi Sai Baba (c. 1838–1918), a wandering holy man who settled in the village of Shirdi in Maharashtra, western India around 1858.[15] His dress did not identify him as either a Hindu or Muslim, and he took up residence in an old mosque. He gained a small following of people from all castes, both Hindu and Muslim, due to his teachings from the Bhagavad Gita and the Qur'an and his reputation for being able to heal illnesses, grant children to childless couples, and perform other miracles. Disciples were impressed with his holiness. After his death, his reputation spread in India due to the dissemination of a printed hagiography, published memoirs of disciples who knew him firsthand, and the work of a key disciple who founded the Shri Shirdi Sai Heritage Foundation Trust to build Shirdi Sai Baba temples in India and throughout the world. Devotion to Shirdi Sai Baba is expressed by the display of bumper stickers and amulets bearing his image in and on vehicles, and through posters and images on a variety of buildings and altars all over India.

Shirdi Sai Baba's devotees regard him through a variety of lenses colored by their respective religious traditions. In general they believe that Shirdi Sai Baba partakes in a universal divine nature, continues to be active in the world today, and is responsive to the needs of his devotees. He is also seen as encouraging a unified Indian spiritual identity that counters sectarian tensions.[16]

The enhancement of the charisma of a deceased prophet or messiah as the movement grows and gains members, and also changes in history and different contexts, is well known in the history of religions. The study of contemporary new religious movements elucidates the dynamics by which a leader may have a post-life charismatic career. Such post-life charisma will become routinized into structures conveying that charisma to representatives of religious organizations.

Routinized charisma

Following Weber, sociologist Meredith McGuire defines the "routinization of charisma" as "the transformation of charismatic authority into some other basis of authority, such as tradition or the authority of office."[17]

Charisma may become institutionalized into an authorized priesthood and higher religious offices. Charismatic authority has been institutionalized and conveyed to the Catholic priesthood, to which a person is ordained through receiving sacred power when a bishop, who is judged to be a valid participant in "apostolic succession," lays hands on the candidate. Catholic priests, bishops, and the pope possess charisma derived from Jesus and men recognized as "apostles" by the Roman Catholic Church. While the Roman Catholic Church has for centuries recognized the charisma of individuals designated as saints and visionaries, it makes certain that only individuals who uphold the authority of the Catholic hierarchy are so recognized.

In Hinduism a guru considered to be enlightened may claim to pass on that quality of enlightenment to a successor, thus establishing a *paramparā*, a lineage of gurus. A similar lineage can be seen in Zen sects, in which the awakening of individuals is acknowledged by a respected teacher, thus authorizing them to teach the Buddha Dharma.

Loss of charisma

Since charisma is dependent on having followers who believe that a leader, scripture, location, or other social construct has access to an unseen source of authority, social scientists have pointed to the inherent instability of charismatic leadership.[18] Charismatic leaders must make constant efforts to manage their followers' impressions of them. If followers withdraw their faith, the individual is no longer a charismatic leader. Typically a person claiming charismatic authority is strongly invested in keeping that role and identity. Thomas Robbins and Dick Anthony assert that a charismatic leader may seek to resist routinization of his or her charisma by unexpectedly changing the message and demands on followers, as well as by engaging in "continual crisis-mongering," to keep the movement agitated so it will not begin to institutionalize authority.[19]

One example of loss of charisma illustrates also that a location can have charisma. Nancy Fowler was a Catholic housewife in Conyers, Georgia, who received visions from the Virgin Mary through the 1990s. A Marian apparition movement, attracting up to 100,000 pilgrims at the final gathering involving Fowler in 1998, developed on the basis of her visions and a sacred site known as The Farm. Fowler reported that the Holy Mother wanted a church built there, but Fowler opposed the fundraising practices of the organization called Our Loving Mother's Children (OLMC). In 1998 Fowler distanced herself from OLMC and The Farm, thus marginalizing herself in relation to the devotion of the faithful who continue to come to worship at The Farm. Deborah Halter reports that the pilgrims visiting The Farm in the late 2000s did not mention Nancy Fowler.

Halter points out that in the case of Catholic Marian apparitions, charismatic authority is attributed to the Virgin Mary and to the locations where she speaks and manifests miracles, not to the visionary. By removing herself from The Farm where miracles are believed to have occurred, Fowler distanced herself from the source of charisma. Other women who have been pilgrims to The Farm have become visionaries leading their own Marian apparition movements in Florida and Bolivia.

Our Mother's Loving Children has taken steps to affiliate the apparition site more closely with the Roman Catholic Church. In 1998, two days before the announced last apparition that appeared to Fowler at

The Farm, the local bishop made the site a Byzantine Rite parish called Mother of God Church under papal authority. The charisma manifested at The Farm is following a trajectory moving from visionary to apparition site to church.

Halter points out that the charisma of Marian apparition visionaries is tied to the charisma of a location, whereas the charisma of leaders of other new religious movements is not necessarily tied to a particular place.[20] For instance, in the case of Jim Jones (1931–1978) of Peoples Temple, followers relocated with him to several locations before moving to Jonestown, Guyana in the 1970s.

The post-life charisma routinized in a religious organization and conveyed to its representatives is also socially constructed. If a sufficient number of people lose faith in the institution's representatives, then it has lost charisma.

CHARISMATIC EMPOWERMENT OF THE SOCIALLY DISADVANTAGED

In highly patriarchal contexts where it is required that women maintain silent and uncomplaining roles within the home, access to charismatic authority is an important means by which women gain voice and status. Charisma similarly can promote the religious authority of men who are marginalized and ill equipped to succeed in society.

Often women in oppressive patriarchal circumstances become mentally or physically ill, and when medical treatments do not work, they may be diagnosed as possessed by a spirit or spirits. In Christian contexts, the woman may report that she has been called by the Holy Spirit to preach. In both types of scenarios, often the woman and some of the people around her believe that if she does not obey the divine command, she will be killed by the sacred power. She has no choice but to serve the possessing spirit(s), and in doing so, she permits the spirit or spirits to speak through her. In this way she may begin to articulate her grievances and get them resolved within her family.[21] She may take on "masculine," assertive characteristics, which are understood as originating from the possessing spirit, since women are not supposed to have those characteristics. Such a woman may become a religious leader, a shaman, and/or diviner or spiritual guide, and receive payment from clients.

A number of charismatic women have founded new religious movements, such as Mother Ann Lee (1736–1784) of the Shakers, Mary Baker Eddy of Christian Science, Nakayama Miki (1798–1887) of Tenrikyō, and Kitamura Sayo (1900–1967) of Tenshō-kōtai-jingu-kyō.[22]

Men who lack educational and social qualifications for rational-legal forms of leadership may also rely on charisma to exercise religious leadership. David Koresh (originally Vernon Howell, 1959–1993) was a high-school dropout who was an intelligent individual with learning disabilities. His demonstrated talent for memorizing passages of the Bible and weaving them together to create a complex theological system appeared to the Branch Davidians to be divinely inspired. Koresh was initially regarded by the Branch Davidians as a prophet in the tradition of Ellen G. White (1827–1915) of the Seventh-day Adventists and the subsequent prophets of SDA offshoots in and near Waco, Texas known as the Davidians and later the Branch Davidians. But since Koresh interpreted the symbolism of the "Seven Seals" of the New Testament book of Revelation (Apocalypse) in a manner that the Branch Davidians found persuasive, and since Revelation states that only "the Lamb," understood as Christ, can "open" the Seven Seals, Koresh and his followers concluded that he was Christ returned to initiate the Endtime events, making him a messiah in a millennial movement.

Koresh's charisma gave him great authority over the lives of his committed followers, which permitted him to rearrange their sexual lives and marriage bonds, so that their affections were directed foremost toward him. This expression of charismatic influence in the intimate and family areas of life has been seen in other leaders and movements, such as Jim Jones of Peoples Temple and Jonestown, Marshall Herff Applewhite ("Do," 1931–1997) of Heaven's Gate, as well as in earlier movements, such as the radical Anabaptist leaders at Münster in 1534–35.

QUALITIES OF CHARISMATIC LEADERS

Despite the diverse personalities of individuals who have been regarded as charismatic leaders, Lorne Dawson suggests that case studies and biographies indicate that these leaders have certain traits in common. Charismatic leaders tend to be energetic persons, who manifest complete commitment to their message. They lead by example, and they often make the same sacrifices demanded of their followers. In the early stages of the movement, they are likely to be directly involved in the daily life of the group and they are responsive to members' concerns. They are talented communicators who know how to manage the impressions they make on their followers. They are able to interpret the problems of the human condition and present the solutions they espouse in compelling terms. Lastly, charismatic leaders are able to "create the impression that they are extraordinary, and that they possess uncanny powers, by audaciously inserting themselves into the great historical and mythical scripts of their cultures."[23] They may present themselves as saviors, often by associating themselves with the lives of earlier revered savior figures.

CHARISMA AND MILLENNIALISM

A millennial movement is one that expects an imminent transition to a collective salvation, in which the limitations of the human condition are overcome for an elect group. Some millennialists expect the transition to be accomplished catastrophically (catastrophic millennialism). Others teach the expectation that human cooperation with a divine or superhuman agent can bring about the collective salvation as part of the ongoing operative principle of "progress" (progressive millennialism). Some movements teach believers to wait for divine or superhuman intervention. In some movements believers are told that they have to be prepared to defend themselves during the anticipated turmoil of the transition period. And in other movements (either progressive or catastrophic) believers are revolutionary, seeking to destroy the old order to create the new.[24]

New religious movements are often, but not necessarily, millennial movements. A millennial movement may have a prophet and/or a messiah, or it may not. When a prophet or messiah receives a new revelation, heightened millennial or apocalyptic beliefs help to create a sense of urgency that can motivate people to convert to the new movement and radically change their faith and lives.

Charismatic leaders, such as Jesus and Muhammad, may initiate movements that are explicitly millennial or apocalyptic. Some charismatic leaders of millennial movements are political leaders, such as Adolf Hitler (1889–1945) or Mao Zedong (1893–1976), who are committed to carrying out a radical change to accomplish a collective salvation for their respective constituencies.[25] The latter two are examples of charismatic leaders who instigate and encourage violent revolutionary millennial movements.

MISMANAGEMENT OF CHARISMA

Dawson points out that episodes of violence may occur when a charismatic leader mismanages his or her charisma. It is critical to note that in many cases, violent episodes involving the leader's mismanagement of charisma occur in contexts where there is also "the breakdown of communication and understanding between the groups and the agencies of social control in the surrounding society."[26] According to Dawson, when charismatic leaders "make the wrong choices in the face of structural challenges to the continued legitimacy of their leadership, they can set off a cycle of deviance amplification that destabilizes groups, greatly increasing the likelihood of violent behavior."[27]

This appears to have been the case with David Koresh and the Branch Davidians living at Mount Carmel Center outside Waco, Texas in 1993. Based on his interpretations of the Bible's prophecies, Koresh taught that the Mount Carmel community would be attacked by agents of "Babylon," a metaphor in Revelation for the corrupt earthly government aligned with Satan, which Koresh identified as being the United States. Koresh taught that the Bible's prophecies indicated that there would be an initial assault in which some members of the godly community would be killed, followed by a waiting period, and then a final assault in which he and other members of the community would die. Subsequently, they would be resurrected to carry out the final apocalyptic chastisement of sinful humanity. There was also a prediction that the Branch Davidians would have to undergo a baptism into new life by fire.[28] Based on Jesus' words reported in Luke 22:36, in which he instructed his disciples to purchase a sword, Koresh taught that he and his followers needed to be armed to defend themselves against the anticipated assaults.

Thus, when the Branch Davidians were assaulted on February 28, 1993 by agents with the Bureau of Alcohol, Tobacco, and Firearms, there was a shootout that caused the deaths of six Branch Davidians and four ATF agents. The deaths of federal agents led to Federal Bureau of Investigation agents taking control of the site. The FBI's surrounding of the residence with tanks and the application of "stress escalation" tactics during the fifty-one-day siege made it appear to the Branch Davidians that Koresh's prophecies were being fulfilled. To be able to resolve the siege peacefully and maintain Koresh's charisma in the eyes of his followers, Koresh needed to develop an exit strategy that conformed to a biblical prophecy.

On April 14 Koresh announced such a strategy through his attorney. He would write his interpretation of the Seven Seals in "a little book" to fulfill what he regarded as a prophecy in Revelation, and then they would all come out of the residence. But the FBI tank and gas assault on April 19 prompted Koresh and the Branch Davidians to revert to their original understanding that the Bible's prophecies indicated that most of them were destined to die at Mount Carmel at the hands of "Babylon."[29]

During the FBI assault, adults put on gas masks, dodged the tanks and ferret rounds coming into the building, and the mothers and small children were put in the safest location in the heart of the building, a concrete vault. But after a tank drove through the building to insert gas directly into the vault, an order went out inside the residence to light the fires.[30] Seventy-six Branch Davidians of all ages died, including twenty-one children and two infants in utero.

Research in government and media sources indicates that FBI decision-makers were cognizant of the Branch Davidians' apocalyptic theology of martyrdom, thus prompting the question of the extent to which government decision-makers were committed to the safety of the Branch Davidians when ordering the implementation of the assault.[31] On Koresh's side, his intense commitment to maintaining his charismatic identity cost the lives of fourteen of his children, other children and young people, and most of the adults in the residence, in addition to his own life.

RESPONSIBLE CHARISMA

Ji Zhe's study of a new Buddhist movement in Taiwan indicates that it is possible for charisma to be exercised responsibly by the leader to benefit followers.

Li Yuansong (1957–2003) founded a lay Buddhist group called the Modern Chan Society (Xiandaichan) at the end of the 1980s. Li claimed to be an *arhat*, someone who has attained awakening, and he was regarded as such by his followers. By 1994 there were about 12,000 members. From 1994 until his death, Li focused on building a communal lifestyle for the intensive training of 500 to 700 bodhisattvas. Li devoted himself particularly to the education of the community's children. Members throughout the movement expressed strong love and respect for Li, since he lived his life according to the Buddha Dharma that he taught.

When Li felt that his life would soon end, he judged that his followers would not be successful in living a lay Chan lifestyle without his presence as a model. In 2003 Li began encouraging his followers to shift to Pure Land Buddhism, which encourages devotion to Amitabha Buddha (Amituofo) to attain rebirth in his "Pure Land." Li converted formally to Pure Land Buddhism and the members of his organization followed his example. Li's larger organization was renamed Amitabha Society for

Collective Practice (Mituo gongxiuhui) and the community was renamed Amitabha Village. Shortly before his death, Li asked a Pure Land monk to serve as the organization's teacher. According to his wishes, after his death Li's head was shaved and he was buried as a Pure Land monk.

Li was aware that he was the charismatic leader of his religious organization. Due to his concern for the well-being of his followers after his death, he divested himself of charisma. He instructed his followers to cease calling him Supreme Master, and instead call him "the one who recites the Buddha's name," and later "the one who believes in the Buddha." Li's parting gift to his followers was leading them to convert to an easier method of Buddhist practice under the guidance of a Pure Land monk.[32]

CONCLUSION

Charisma, the belief that a person, scripture, place, or other social construct has access to an unseen source of sacred power and authority, has many manifestations. Charisma may be attributed to communities, groups, and nations, as well as to specific organizations and their leadership. Charisma, like other sources of authority, may be put to benevolent uses that people – not only the leader – find empowering and liberating. Like other sources of authority, charisma may also be abused.

Since charisma is socially constructed through the faith and affection of followers, it is important that people think critically about to whom and to what they attribute charisma.

Notes

1   Lorne L. Dawson, "Psychopathologies and the Attribution of Charisma: A Critical Introduction to the Psychology of Charisma and the Explanation of Violence in New Religious Movements," *Nova Religio* 10:2 (2006), pp. 3–28.
2   Ji Zhe, "Expectation, Affection, and Responsibility: The Charismatic Journey of a New Buddhist Group in Taiwan," *Nova Religio* 12:2 (2008), pp. 48–68.
3   Max Weber, *The Theory of Economic and Social Organizations*, ed. and trans. A. M. Henderson and Talcott Parsons (New York, 1964), p. 358.
4   Stephen Feuchtwang and Wang Mingming, *Grassroots Charisma: Four Local Leaders in China* (New York, 2001).
5   Traveling shamans and possession shamans are discussed in Robert S. Ellwood, *Many Peoples, Many Faiths: An Introduction to the Religious Life of Humankind*, 4th edn. (Englewood Cliffs, NJ, 1992), p. 41. I have added the term "psychic shaman."

6 Judith Coney, *Sahaja Yoga* (Richmond, UK, 1999), pp. 93–118.

7 Catherine Wessinger, "Democracy vs. Hierarchy: The Evolution of Authority in the Theosophical Society," in Timothy Miller (ed.), *When Prophets Die: The Postcharismatic Fate of New Religious Movements* (Albany, NY, 1991), pp. 93–106.

8 Robert Pearson Flaherty, "UFOs, ETs, and the Millennial Imagination," in Catherine Wessinger (ed.), *The Oxford Handbook of Millennialism* (New York, 2011), pp. 587–610.

9 Steven L. Shields, "The Latter Day Saint Movement: A Study in Survival," in Miller (ed.), *When Prophets Die*, pp. 59–77.

10 George H. Tavard, *The Thousand Faces of the Virgin Mary* (Collegeville, MN, 1996), p. 175.

11 Catherine Wessinger, "Women's Religious Leadership in the United States," in Wessinger (ed.), *Religious Institutions and Women's Leadership: New Roles inside the Mainstream* (Columbia, SC, 1996), pp. 7–10; Susie C. Stanley, *Holy Boldness: Women Preachers' Autobiographies and the Sanctified Self* (Knoxville, 2004).

12 Gary Shepherd and Gordon Shepherd, "Grassroots Prophecy in the Family International," *Nova Religio* 10:4 (2007), pp. 38–71.

13 Gordon Shepherd and Gary Shepherd, "World Services in The Family International: The Administrative Organization of a Mature Religious Movement," *Nova Religio* 12:3 (2009), pp. 5–39.

14 Ann Braude, "The Perils of Passivity: Women's Leadership in Spiritualism and Christian Science," in Catherine Wessinger (ed.) *Women's Leadership in Marginal Religions: Explorations outside the Mainstream* (Urbana, IL, 1993), pp. 59–61.

15 Shirdi Sai Baba should not be confused with Sathya Sai Baba (1926–2011), who is better known in the West.

16 Karline McLain, "Be United, Be Virtuous: Composite Culture and the Growth of Shirdi Sai Baba Devotion," *Nova Religio* 15:2 (2011), pp. 20–46.

17 Meredith McGuire, "Key Terms in the Sociology of Religion," in *Religion: The Social Context*, 5th edn. (Long Grove, IL, 2002), available at www.religionthesocialcontext.net/Resources/Glossary.htm, accessed November 17, 2011.

18 Thomas Robbins and Dick Anthony, "Sects and Violence: Factors Enhancing the Volatility of Marginal Religious Movements," in Stuart A. Wright (ed.), *Armageddon in Waco: Critical Perspectives on the Branch Davidian Conflict* (Chicago, 1995), pp. 244–49.

19 Ibid., pp. 247–48.

20 Deborah Halter, "Field Notes – Charisma in Conyers: A Journey from Visionary to Apparition Site to Church," *Nova Religio* 14:3 (2011), pp. 108–14.

21 Janice Boddy, *Wombs and Alien Spirits: Women, Men, and the Zar Cult in Northern Sudan* (Madison, WI, 1989); Martha B. Binford, "Julia: An East African Diviner," pp. 3–14; Youngsook Kim Harvey, "Possession Sickness and Women Shamans in Korea," pp. 59–65, both in Nancy Auer Falk and Rita M. Gross (eds.), *Unspoken Worlds: Women's Religious Lives*, 3rd edn. (Belmont, CA, 2000).

22 Kyoko Motomochi Nakamura, "No Women's Liberation: The Heritage of a Woman Prophet in Modern Japan," in Falk and Gross (eds.), *Unspoken Worlds*, pp. 168–78.

23 Lorne L. Dawson, " Charismatic Leadership in Millennial Movements," in Wessinger (ed.), *Oxford Handbook of Millennialism*, pp. 116–17, at p. 117.

24 Catherine Wessinger, "The Interacting Dynamics of Millennial Beliefs, Persecution, and Violence," in Wessinger (ed.) *Millennialism, Persecution, and Violence: Historical Cases* (Syracuse, 2000), pp. 3–61.

25 Scott Lowe, "Western Millennial Ideology Goes East: The Taiping Revolution and Mao's Great Leap Forward," pp. 220–40; and Robert Ellwood, "Nazism as a Millennialist Movement," pp. 241–60, both in Wessinger (ed.), *Millennialism, Persecution, and Violence*; David Redles, "National Socialist Millennialism," in Wessinger (ed.), *Oxford Handbook of Millennialism*, pp. 529–48.

26 Dawson, "Psychopathologies and the Attribution of Charisma," p. 4.

27 Ibid., p. 5.

28 Kenneth G. C. Newport, *The Branch Davidians of Waco: The History and Beliefs of an Apocalyptic Sect* (Oxford, 2006).

29 James D. Tabor and Eugene V. Gallagher, *Why Waco? Cults and the Battle for Religious Freedom in America* (Berkeley, 1995); Catherine Wessinger, "Deaths in the Fire at the Branch Davidians' Mount Carmel: Who Bears Responsibility?" *Nova Religio* 13:2 (2009), pp. 25–60.

30 Wessinger, "Deaths in the Fire," pp. 40–44.

31 Wessinger, "Deaths in the Fire."

32 Ji, "Expectation, Affection, and Responsibility."

Further reading

Barker, Eileen, "Charismatisation: The Social Production of an Ethos Propitious to the Mobilisation of Sentiments," in Eileen Barker, James A. Beckford, and Karel Dobbelaere (eds.), *Secularisation, Rationalism, and Sectarianism* (Oxford 1993), pp. 181–201.

Dawson, Lorne L., "Charismatic Leadership in Millennial Movements," in Catherine Wessinger (ed.), *The Oxford Handbook of Millennialism* (New York, 2011), pp. 113–32.

    "Psychopathologies and the Attribution of Charisma: A Critical Introduction to the Psychology of Charisma and the Explanation of Violence in New Religious Movements," *Nova Religio* 10:2 (2006), pp. 3–28.

Feuchtwang, Stephan, "Suggestions for a Redefinition of Charisma," *Nova Religio* 12:2 (2008), pp. 90–105.

Galanter, Marc, *Cults: Faith, Healing, and Coercion*, 2nd edn. (New York, 1999).

Ji Zhe, "Expectation, Affection and Responsibility: The Charismatic Journey of a New Buddhist Group in Taiwan," *Nova Religio* 12:2 (2008), pp. 48–68.

6 Rituals in new religions

GRAHAM HARVEY

New religions can appear novel because they involve unfamiliar rituals. However, these same rituals can be presented as proof of a group's
authentic participation in time-honored traditions. Novelty and
antiquity can be either attractive or threatening, legitimizing or repel-
lant. This tension between new and old – expressed in polarizations
between tradition and innovation, or authenticity and adaptation – is
at the heart of both religious and scholarly interest in ritual. Doing a
ritual "the way it has always been done," but performing it with appropriate attention or enthusiasm (remembering that "appropriate" might
mean either "almost casually" or "with restraint"), is often intimately
related to the depth or shallowness of a person's involvement in a religion or group. Scholarly theorization of the category of "ritual" is rife
with debate about the definitive centrality or marginality of repetition,
redundancy, structure, formality, archaism, understanding, and their
possible opposites. There can also be contention among religious people
about the expected outcomes of ritual practices: while some insist
that only "spiritual" results are appropriate others gladly anticipate
"material" rewards.

This chapter discusses ritual in relation to four new religions:
Paganism, ISKCON, the Soka Gakkai, and Santo Daime. It does not
insist on a particular definition of ritual, nor does it present a new theory of ritual. Rather, it assumes that a range of religious actions (including verbal and literary communication) are usefully considered to be
examples of this polyvalent but contested category. It recognizes that
rituals are not all alike functionally, structurally, formally, socially,
epistemologically, or experientially. Indeed, some people vehemently
object to the identification of particular acts or events as rituals. This

I am grateful for the advice of Amanda van Eck, Duymaer van Twist, Andy Dawson,
Anna King, Eileen Barker, Helen Waterhouse, and Sarah Harvey in their areas of
considerable expertise. Any errors are, of course, due to my not paying attention
adequately.

too is a common feature of religious and scholarly discourse about ritual. This contributes to polemics about the "fit" (or its lack) between particular new religions and their wider "traditional" and "modern" milieux.

Furthermore, tensions between tradition and innovation in ritual are precisely paralleled by tensions indicated by labeling particular movements as "new" and "religions." If religion is sometimes defined in relation to "tradition,"[1] in practice religions remain relevant by engagements with contemporary activities and ideas. Religious practitioners can be required (by coreligionists, scholars, journalists, or other observers) to tread a precarious path between heritage and relevance. Looking backwards and forwards at the same time is perhaps the best way of not having to keep looking sideways at one's neighbors and critics in those sometimes messy, sometimes subtle contests for legitimacy marked by the term "new religions."

PAGANISM

Rituals are frequently in the foreground of the ethnographic literature about Paganism. Sabina Magliocco, for instance, begins a chapter by stating that "Ritualization lies at the heart of modern Paganism" and then discusses "how it became the central form of religious expression" for and of Pagans.[2] Undoubtedly, as all other researchers among Pagans recognize, rituals are the most common shared and individual experiences of Pagans. Rituals that celebrate cosmic events (solstices, equinoxes, and other moments in the relationship between earth, sun, moon, stars, and other planets), often treated as markers of phases in the changing seasons, might not be the entirety of Pagan practice, but little happens that is not related to them. Initiations into groups are often braided into rituals honoring the full moon or a particular solar festival. Rites of passage weave the participants into larger cosmic relationships that they are deemed to match to some degree. Weddings during the rites of summer and memorialization of the dead during winter nights are exemplary.

The actual acts of Pagan rituals vary considerably. Some are formal, regulated by traditions integral to initiatory lineages, and precisely replicated in each performance. Others are more ecstatic and innovative. The same people may participate in both kinds of rituals: conducting initiations in carefully prepared and prescribed ceremonies but then drumming wildly. It seems likely that few if any Pagans participate only in the more formal or the more anarchic events. The precise balance between the two styles may customize Paganism for the Pagan or it may shape each Pagan in their chosen variety of Paganism.

It is unlikely that someone deliberately decided to make rituals and ritualizing central in or definitive of Paganism. There is no evidence of a debate about whether this new religion might be better practiced or disseminated by participative ritualizing, preaching, or publishing leaflets. Pagans rarely set up debates with members of other religions to demonstrate the veracity or rationality of their practice. It is equally indicative that Pagans do not commonly identify Paganism as a "faith" or talk much about "beliefs" (unless they are joining in interfaith events where the discursive ground rules are set by Christian "believers"). Paganism is a religion of praxis, performance, doing, but it is also radical in not stressing orthopraxis, the performance of "correct practice" in preference to innovative or individualist heteropraxis. There is a structure or pattern but Pagan ritualizing tends to diversify prolifically. That the structure of Pagan rituals is derived from the older European esoteric milieu is well established and uncontentious among Pagans and scholars.[3] The widespread formation of circles of participants, the orientation to cardinal directions, and much of the language of ceremonies is held in common with other movements that continue within or have developed from esotericism (e.g., the Order of the Golden Dawn or the diffuse phenomena often labeled "New Age"). The blending of popularized, democratized esotericism with emergent Romantic or radical engagements with "nature" (another polyvalent term in Paganism and in scholarly debate) unsystematically evolved into the varying styles of Paganism today.[4] That Pagans identify some, at least, of these variations as "traditions" or "paths" refers to recognizable commonalities and also to preferences and differences. While Pagans might celebrate every solstice with a ritual, the precise form of each ritual evolves and is refreshed with at least small changes. An adaptable structure or expected improvisation marks Pagan ritual and religious experience.

However, what is most intriguing about ritual among Pagans is (a) that it is so prevalent and (b) that it is about physicality. Both of these contrast strongly with the tradition of Protestant Christianity and its successor Enlightenment that is the larger milieu in which esotericism and therefore Paganism emerged. The dominant denigration of ritual as "vain repetition" (as opposed to either knowledgeable faith or rational experimentation)[5] and of physicality (as opposed to either spirituality or rationality) is implicitly contested by Pagans when they do ritual. Within the putatively modern world,[6] increasing numbers of people affiliate themselves with a counter-modernist trend by positively valuing rituals made edgy by an alluring tension between non-ordinary ceremonial and entirely everyday matters like sunrises and bodies. Transcendence and transgression meet, imbuing immediate and contemporary concerns with archaizing and indigenizing flavors, radicalizing what might otherwise have become just another Romantic environmentalism.

ISKCON

The International Society for Krishna Consciousness (ISKCON) has had a presence on many streets worldwide for over forty years. As Graham Dwyer and Richard Cole say, "One of the most prominent features of the tangible presence of the Hare Krishna movement during its early days in the West was its practice of chanting in public locations, the physical appearance of its members – with their shaven heads and exotic saffron robes – equally being conspicuous in the public domain."[7] They note that these public rituals of *sankirtan*, blended devotion and evangelism, are less common now than they once were. Temples have gained increasing prominence as the venues of ISKCON ritual life. Still, however, devotees can be heard and seen drumming, chanting, and processing through festivals and streets. Some offer literature to strangers, sometimes requesting monetary donations in return. References to "Hare Krishna" in the media or other public domains will evoke images of saffron-robed, entranced devotees. Ritual is, thus, a prime marker of the exoticism or strangeness of the movement to observers. Spectacle rather than devotion attracts attention.

For devotees, ritual practice has different resonances, but different tensions too. ISKCON may be post-charismatic,[8] but it has not developed significantly diverse local variants. What can be said of ISKCON in the UK is almost entirely applicable to ISKCON globally. The changes that have taken place since ISKCON's formation by Swami Prabhupada in 1966 are particularly visible in ritual practice within certain boundaries. While these boundaries are contested, they are nonetheless recognizable as defining a Gaudiya or Chaitanyite Vaishnava Hindu denomination. Many religions problematize the relationship between interior states, feelings, thoughts, desires, and intentions on the one hand, and outward acts, deeds, practices, and performances on the other. ISKCON evidences a "dialectic between the esoteric *bhakti* of love and the exoteric *bhakti* of ritual."[9] This dialectic is unceasing, never entirely collapsing even when particular devotees or events highlight one dynamic above the other. Someone, some text or event will encourage an alternative way or a redress towards balance. There have been tensions between those devoted to individual devotion and those insisting on the necessity of public rituals of outreach and invitation to commit to devotion. But the common ground of *bhakti*, devotion, seems firm as devotees seek the means of raising and enacting their Krishna-focused, Krishna-encountering consciousness. There is a parallel to Protestant-derived problems with ritual that is, for *bhakti*-devotion-acculturated devotees at least, indigenous to the logic of the originating tradition. Thus, here "ritual" may be problematized as "directed at 'fruit' (i.e., material ends) [rather than concerned with] what a traditional anthropologist might see as ritual but the devotees see as *seva*, the blissful mode of living which is directed to Krishna alone."[10] This is not to suggest that all Hindus object to ritually requesting divine help with the problems of life, or seeking material benefits from religious acts. This very tension does, however, emphasize ISKCON's Gaudiya context. Along with an insistence on the singularity and uniqueness of the godhead, ISKCON's recent history can be considered as a series of struggles to remain and grow as a devotional movement rather than any other kind of Hinduism.

Even some of those who have left the movement have done so in order to develop their devotion, developing their ritual repertoire to match what they perceive to be the core trajectory of the larger tradition. ISKCON may well have been a prime exemplar of "Easternization," "Indianization," or even "Hinduization" in its first decades of global expansion. As devotees danced, drummed, and chanted in Western cities and festivals, they expressed and/or illustrated a wider tendency to conceive of "the East" as spiritual in contrast with the decadence, materialism, and hedonism of "the West." But trends internal to ISKCON and the contemporaneous migration of Hindus from India and East Africa have provoked an alternative trajectory: the Hinduization of ISKCON. Struggles about gender roles and the place of families in the movement coincided with the development of congregations interested in the services of ISKCON temples and devotees. The resulting developments can be evaluated differently. The large numbers of people attending ISKCON temples to participate in major festivals may mark the success of a movement that seeks to attract people to express devotion to the supreme deity. Alternatively, such events may illustrate the transformation of ISKCON devotees into providers of clerical services to a wider population. Indeed, many congregants and festival participants are less interested than ISKCON devotees in theological niceties, happily honoring other manifestations of the divine. But rituals are not only affected by theology, the impact of sociological changes are vital too. Burke

Rochford's examination of ISKCON's American experience and history focuses on the rising importance of householders and families within ISKCON and among the new congregations.[11] If the movement left its Indian birthplace to encourage renunciation and the transcendence not only of materialism but especially of the round of birth and death, it has largely adjusted to serving those maintaining worldly lives. Those who seek more radical and rapid transcendence, rejecting accommodation in the world, and insistent on ritual as permanent devotion, have begun to form communities outside of ISKCON. In doing so, they and their ritualizing may be seen as innovating within the same tradition. Maybe the chief innovation within ISKCON is the full acceptance of its role as the provider of rituals and ritual expertise required by tradition.

THE SOKA GAKKAI

As with many "new" religions, Soka Gakkai has an ancient lineage, claiming direct descent from the Japanese Buddhist monk Nichiren (1222–1282). The movement also claims to be, if not the only true Buddhism, certainly the best teacher of the proper understanding of the Buddha's teaching. Simultaneously, Soka Gakkai has a clear organizational establishment dating to tensions among Nichiren and other Buddhists, and between Buddhists and the Japanese state in the 1930s and 1940s. Organizational and authority patterns have continued to develop in relation to internal and external pressures ever since. In particular, the relationship between this lay movement and the priestly authorities and ritual experts of Nichiren Shoshu Buddhism have been traumatic for many members. As Soka Gakkai rapidly expanded globally, the tensions that exist in modernity between "traditionalism and modernism, hierarchy and egalitarianism, objective knowledge traditions and subjective understanding, mysticism and rationalism, collective authority and individualism, sacredness and secularism, faith and skepticism"[12] have been played out in the relationship between Nichiren Shoshu and Soka Gakkai and subsequently within the internal working of the Soka Gakkai.[13]

However, the practice of the movement is that established by Nichiren: the chanting of a mantra in honor of the core text of the originating style of Buddhism (the Tendai sect) and the recitation of that scripture, the *Lotus Sutra*. The purposes and understanding of this practice too have not diverged from those of the founder, but they have found new resonances in the process of globalization.

Members of Soka Gakkai, like the Nichiren-lineage priests, are supposed to chant the phrase *nam-myoho-renge-kyo*, "homage to the *Lotus*

Sutra," frequently. Typically, they sit in front of an enshrined official photographic reproduction of a legitimate, priest-authorized copy of an inscribed version of the mantra surrounded by various other significant names (all in Japanese calligraphy). This mandala representation of the sacred chant is called a *gohonzon* and is placed in a shrine, recognizably a version of a Japanese household shrine or *butsudan*, emphatically privileging the text and elevating it above any potential distraction. In addition to chanting *nam-myoho-renge-kyo* (a practice called *daimoku*), members are supposed to recite two chapters of the *Lotus Sutra* every morning and evening in front of the *gohonzon*. Japanese members may have little more advantage than others in learning this practice given the classical Japanese style that is expected of all chanters. However, members are provided with transliterated versions of the *gongyo* (*Sutra* text/chant) book to guide them – and frequent repetition may lead to recitation without this aid. The holding or rubbing of a string of prayer beads between the hands, along with incense burning, candle lighting and bell ringing, is standard. In addition to doing these things because they are supposed to be done (which might be a concise definition of ritual), they may facilitate the maintenance of attention while chanting for periods of an hour or more.

Chanting, then, is the core ritual practice of Soka Gakkai members. I have noted a number of Japanese terms that are common coinage in the movement because they demonstrate the blending of new and old not only to outside observers but also to members. The learning of words (and ways of speaking) is both traditional to a long-established mode of Japanese ritual and novel to many new members internationally. As in most religions, an orientation to the world includes specific terms and ways of talking that express and influence ways of understanding, experiencing, and/or expressing things more adequately than other words might enable. Similarly, having noted that chanting takes place sitting down, it is noteworthy that the specific position now varies. "Tradition" indicates the normative position that involves sitting on the floor, but adaptation to cultural norms beyond Japan (and for at least some Western-acculturated Japanese) involves the provision of chairs.

Many basic textbooks purport that the chief purpose of Buddhists is to achieve enlightenment and that the chief means of doing so is meditation. This categorization is powerfully challenged by significant numbers of studies of both popular and elite practice among many kinds of Buddhist. That Soka Gakkai's fundamental practice is chanting is implicit in at least one response to research about why some people cease to identify with the movement. This is simply expressed: "I just kind of slowly decreased. It wasn't a total stopping point ... I just [found myself] doing it less and less."[14] This could not be said about religions in which either believing or guru-devotion were central (where words like "doubt" are more likely than "decrease" to appear in departure or decommitment narratives). This interviewee identifies *daimoku*, chanting, as what it is to be in Soka Gakkai, and ceasing to do it is implicated in finding oneself leaving. Perhaps this is a somewhat simplistic analysis, after all, "once one has learnt to chant, there is no necessary reason for participating in [Soka Gakkai International-]sponsored group activities."[15] So, even people who leave the organization may continue chanting. Indeed, the official teaching of Soka Gakkai might even encourage this. An insistence that people should chant to improve themselves, to receive worldly and spiritual benefits (to the limited extent that this dichotomy is operative or generative here), and to work towards world peace by self-improvement and the increase of happiness does not require much more than the learning of the correct mode of chanting. Once achieved, the individual might be better advised to go it alone than to risk the potential distractions of organizational activities and group events. While this may look like both Western individualization and acquisitiveness of a modernist, secularizing, and consumerist kind, Soka Gakkai's invitation to chant for personal benefits is, again, quite traditional and quite within the bounds of this Buddhist heritage.

There is, however, a tension here. The organization of the movement is "orientated, foremost to individual spiritual growth" but that growth may be recognized in the readiness to "practice for others [by those who link] their personal practice with the great goal of world peace."[16] The tension here is not between personal benefit and altruistic practice. In common with the norms of Japanese religious culture,[17] Soka Gakkai members seem to have no problem with chanting for material and physical benefits. These are, indeed, taken as elements of the fulfilled happy life that is at least a valued goal. Furthermore, what one chants for others to receive may also be happiness and material benefits. The gaining of such benefits can be used to demonstrate the effectiveness of Soka Gakkai practice – and speaking about them may parallel the use of personal "testimony" or "witness" in evangelical Christian missionizing. Perhaps all this is implicit in the common Buddhist rhetoric about the beautiful lotus flowering in muddy swamps (although this might suggest an uneasiness about involvement in the murky material world). But if material and spiritual benefits are not dichotomized into a hierarchical dualism privileging transcendence, neither is the tension exactly one between individuals and groups. While Soka Gakkai is, clearly, an organization – and one related to other Buddhist communities – both its core practice (individual chanting) and its difficult relationship with Nichiren Shoshu mean that it is not exactly an "identifiable community" as Jim Cox requires any phenomenon to be that deserves to be labeled a "religion."[18] Even members at the core of the organization of Soka Gakkai chant for their own well-being and benefit. Nonetheless, the ritual practice of the movement contains an invitation to think that the benefit of others may well be served by the further spread and numerical growth of the organization. Thus, although everything else that looks like tensions between tradition and modernity may in fact exemplify a resonance between traditional and modernist notions of individuality, it is the thoroughly modern difficulty with institutionalization which contrasts with the more traditional balance between group and individual practice and belonging that is most significant. There is irony in the fact that the modern bureaucratic structure of this religious movement (seemingly utilizing successful business models) is found to be problematic because of the modernist logic that institutions are contrary to spirituality. Sandra Ionescu illustrates this in writing about the way that German members of Soka Gakkai identify chanting as the heart of Buddhism while both contesting some Soka Gakkai practices as merely Japanese culture and at the same time seeking to acculturate the movement as a German expression of Buddhism.[19] As illustrated by shifting evaluations of group membership and institutions, ritual serves both tradition and innovation.

AYAHUASCA PSYCHONAUTS AND SANTO DAIME

This fourth example of ritual practice of a new religion also dabbles with a tension between organization and individuality. It is not really about Santo Daime but about the consumption of this new and evolving Brazilian religious movement by Europeans who could not possibly participate regularly and fully in its ritual and cultural life. Instead, in performing the rituals of spiritual seekers, tourists, or shoppers, they extract elements that fit the existing if sometimes inchoate practices and cosmologies of psychedelic seekership. Such psychonauts do this not only with Santo Daime but with a shifting selection of other ritual and cultural practices. Santo Daime may be of interest largely because it is a provider of access to *ayahuasca*, but perhaps a sense of legitimation (religious and legal) is sought in the company of *daimistas* too.

Ayahuasca is one blend of a range of psychotropic and emetic stimulants derived from Amazonian plants. It has gained popularity beyond its original indigenous ritual usage within two related complexes: what we might call "shamanism" and what we might call "psychedelia." Andy Dawson traces the origins of "Brazil's non-indigenous ayahuasca religions" to Raimundo Irineu Serra (1892–1971) and the people he met as he traveled around the region, and those upon whom he had a considerable influence.²⁰ Ayahuasca-induced or -enhanced visions coincided with the influences of various forms of Christianity, Spiritism, indigenous, and African-diasporic religions to make up a movement now identifiable as Santo Daime. Literally, this draws attention to the holiness ("Santo") of the ayahuasca brew ("Daime") that is prepared and drunk ceremonially.

The ritual life of Santo Daime groups is a rich and quite bounded one. In a dramatic contrast with the effect ayahuasca has on the body's boundaries (inducing both vomiting and visions that are interpreted, at least, as purifying the body and enabling the soul to fly), lengthy rituals establish and control borders. Separations based on gender, age, and marital status are pervasive. Men and women, for example, might be in the same room, performing the same dance steps, but they do not mingle in ceremony. Physical movements are restrained, often in a dance that involves mostly swaying, with some steps forwards and backwards. Even when the music suggests a waltz, rituals do not slip towards much conviviality. A corpus of hymns is authorized for singing in the stages of the ceremonies. While these may seem to promiscuously blend elements from religions that are putatively discrete (in the understanding of those who believe "syncretism" to usefully label something other than the ordinary practice of every culture and religion), they are also rhythmically repetitive. There is little encouragement of the wilder flights of ecstasy that accompany much that defines spirit possession or shamanism in popular imagination.²¹ This is, then, perhaps a corporate shamanistic practice that has been performatively shaped by Brazilian inflections of Christianity and esotericism (largely in the form of Spiritism) more than by more dramatic repertoires of indigenous animistic engagements.

Some Santo Daime groups have outposts in Europe: an Internet search suggests that the Netherlands and Ireland are more attractive than England. There are also other ayahuasca-using groups or individuals outside of Amazonia (its spread among urban Brazilians coinciding with a more global reach). Many of these people draw ayahuasca into their pre-existing practice, sometimes making it their main psychotropic, more often using it occasionally alongside other chosen plants or derivative concoctions. Thus, for example, a number of people who consider psilocybin mushrooms to be the initiator of visionary, animistic, or cosmic wisdom have at least experimented with ayahuasca.[22] An Internet search for "ayahuasca" provides considerable evidence of a thriving spiritual tourism of a kind paralleling that previously devoted to mushrooms like those containing psilocybin, cactus derivatives like mescaline, and/or various opiates. Groups like the Hozho Foundation for Wellbeing present an eclectic array that they identify as "ancient indigenous healing practices." Although privileging West African origins, they seem to make nothing of the psychoactives that are indigenous there, but devote significant attention to ayahuasca and its rituals. In this broader context, the question is not why people imbibe ayahuasca, but why some do it in the context of Santo Daime rituals and others elevate the movement as a prime exemplar of the influence of this great inspirer of spirituality and holistic well-being.

Santo Daime is hardly the kind of movement to encourage unbounded experimentation. It may be eclectic – or, at least, various elements of its practice can be identified as deriving from distinct sources – but it does not typically advertise itself as something to add to a mix of possibilities. It has a complex but established repertoire of rituals and an agreed cosmology within which their performance makes sense. Websites and blogs, however, demonstrate that Santo Daime groups are one aisle, or maybe just one shelf, in the spiritual supermarket of some neo-shamans (cyber-shamans, perhaps[23]) and some psychonauts. Some of these people explicitly say that they are unlikely to become committed practitioners or devoted members within the group: Santo Daime is just "too Christian." Possibly, too, the ritual practice demands too many hours and days of structured ritual "work." Certainly it is attractive to the more psychedelic wing of the New Age movement because of a recognition of elements expressive of esotericism. Among other things, this is a place to find and elevate one's "higher/inner self." Certainly, too, Santo Daime's growth throughout Brazil (not just in Amazonia) and internationally demonstrates that it is attractive to many people. There are groups in various European countries who have devoted themselves to the whole of the Santo Daime project. But the people of interest in this discussion are those who seem primarily interested in making use of the movement because it makes available a powerful stimulant (although it is illegal in many countries). In religious contexts, tests suggest, powerful effects occur which are valued not merely for "altering consciousness" but also for their contribution to recognizably psychonautic goals. Ayahuasca ritual experiences are re-embedded and recontextualized in various broadly shamanic and broadly esotericist contexts. That is, the use and effects of ayahuasca are meaningful to people who understand the cosmos and life in various ways.

It is, then, necessary to return to the cliché of the supermarket. Too many studies of new religions or contemporary spirituality allege that there is a novel situation in which contemporary consumer capitalism has spilled over into religiosity so that now people "shop" for religion. It is implied, at least, that eclecticism or bricolage are both modern and foolish. Modern(ist) spiritualities do not match the grandeur or authority of established traditions. What the tired metaphor of the spiritual supermarket misses is that people do not shop randomly. Whether seeking food, clothes, or religious activities, people do not wander blindfold among the possibilities, only ever gathering what is most immediately available, or what is most aggressively marketed. Even if people shop for French bread to eat with Italian pasta to be accompanied by German beer and American music, they do usually set out with an idea of what kind of meal they wish to enjoy. At the least, dietary rules and needs influence their actions (explicitly or implicitly). Just so, the religious supermarket is a place where people select elements that fit together in patterns that make good sense. People who want to use ayahuasca and find a provider in Santo Daime might not fully appreciate the "traditional" importance of vomiting – European history has rejected the notion of purification in favor of a stress on salvation. Consumers will, more likely, focus on the inspiring visions of an enchanted, larger-than-human world to which ayahuasca and its rituals provide an entry.

There is one more thing that seems likely to be enmeshed in this non-member interest in Santo Daime and related ritual groups. If there have been several globally widespread episodes of Orientalism, Indianization, or Hinduization (illustrated by the nineteenth-century Theosophists and the 1960s Krishna devotees), the late twentieth and early twenty-first centuries have seen a pervasive turn to the Amazon. Environmentalists, explorers, sympathizers with indigenous peoples, questers after healing plants and good chocolate, and seekers after psychoactive plants have found rich resources in the Amazon. Perhaps the fact that this is a threatened, endangered zone adds to the allure; certainly an air of urgency is imputed. Bruno Latour's use of the ethnology of Eduardo Viveiros de Castro to further his argument that "we have never been modern" similarly illustrates the powerful attraction and critical value of Amazonian ritually based, experienced, and conveyed ways of dwelling in the world.[24] Ayahuasca may be the sacrament, for some, of a current quest for salvation, enlightenment, or wisdom. If so, its rituals are one means by which people regain a sense of their participation in the larger-than-human, other-than-consumerist world. In imbibing the sacramental brew and in discovering some kind of ritual, even if not the full version of the *daimistas'* extensive practice, people contest the allegation that they are merely consumerists. The spiritual supermarket is a venue of selectivity and profound quest for meanings that, for some, require somewhat startling ritual experiences. Even as Santo Daime itself was undergoing both *umbandization* and "new-erization" (developing its spirit possession repertoire under the influence of another Brazilian esoteric-indigenous fusion and of global New Era preoccupations),[25] psychonauts have treated the movement as an initiator of a somewhat different version of cosmo-ritualizing. Selectivity between old and new, tradition and innovation, continues.

CONCLUSION

Academic interest in rituals parallels academic interest in new religions: most obviously in debates about the relationship between tradition and innovation. The groups selected in this chapter all evidence tensions between ancient origins and recent organizational structures, or resonances between old and contemporary acts. However one assesses the validity of claims by specific new religions to be the legitimate heirs of noble lineages, it is evident that other religious or cultural movements have had significant effects on them. Similarly, new religions provide material for reflection on the varied attractions, necessities, distractions, and rejections of both convention and change. Then there are vexed questions of how much members of new religions know about their originating tradition, its authoritative teachings and authorized practices, and the meaning of the rituals they are expected or encouraged to participate in and, perhaps, introduce to other people. As Robert McCauley and Thomas Lawson say of rituals, "Sometimes all the ethnographer gets is 'we do it because our ancestors did it'," alongside noting that informants frequently suggest that researchers should consult the greater expertise and knowledge of specialists.[26] In presenting their own theory, however, they do not bow to this pressure to find the meaning of rituals only among experts rather than in vernacular performance. The research and publications of too many scholars do favor elite, textual, or official traditions over vernacular ones.[27] Admittedly, scholars of new religions are more likely to attend to the actual practices of members – perhaps because most of them are sociologists or ethnographers – but there remains a tendency to judge a "new religion" against the standards of a literary or preached version of its (claimed) originating movement. These are just some of the leitmotivs in studies of new religions that resonate with studies of ritual and ritualizing.

Approaching matters from the other direction, ritual studies scholars are as committed as scholars of new religions to engage with what people do. Whilst "what people understand themselves to be doing" can be significant, it can also lead down the cul-de-sac marked by the warning sign: "we do it because we do it." It is not exactly that rituals have no meaning, more that their primary meaning is *in*, and inseparable from, their performance. Rituals are done (as Pagans and *daimistas* seem to implicitly note in calling their rituals "work," thereby echoing Hebrew ritual terminology that rejects a ghettoization of ritual). What has been termed a "performative turn" in the study of ritual (exemplified by Catherine Bell[28]) is matched in the study of religion – to the degree that Malory Nye invites us to talk about "religioning."[29] Religions and their rituals are modes of action, ways of actively being or living, and are only separate from other acts and lifeways when scholars or practitioners sometimes discuss them apart from more everyday acts.

Engaging with rituals (and religions) as performance may entail a recognition of the commonality of redundancy. Doing what has "always been done" not only indicates the marginality of "knowing why we do it" but also requires appreciation of why people do things without minding whether they are rationally meaningful. Noting that "what is done" shifts because contexts change suggests that contingency and innovation are necessary elements of tradition. Particularly helpful leads here are provided in the core insights of two leading scholars of ritual. Jonathan Z. Smith argues that ritual is principally a "mode of paying attention ... a process for marking attention."[30] Quite ordinary acts and objects can be utilized to direct, mark, and maintain attention to significant matters. The regular practice of rituals (drawn from the past but kept relevant by negotiation with the present) establishes and reinforces practitioners' belonging and "fit" with their group. Such reinforcements are, almost tautologically, mutually reinforcing. They make the world as they make the ritualist. Ronald Grimes demonstrates that ritual drives a way of being "deeply into the bone": "ordinary acts, when extraordinarily practiced, break open, transforming human conventions and revealing what is most deeply desirable, most cosmically orientating, and most fully human."[31] In doing ritual, members of new religions are transforming conventions, revealing desires, reorientating themselves, and demonstrating what they wish to be. To do ritual is to be a member of a group. To be a member is to be shaped by the doing of ritual.

Notes

1 For example, Danièle Hervieu-Léger, *Religion as a Chain of Memory* (Cambridge, 2000).
2 Sabina Magliocco, "Reclamation, Appropriation and Imagination in Modern Pagan Ritual," in James R. Lewis and Murphy Pizza (eds.), *Handbook of Contemporary Paganism* (Leiden, 2009), pp. 223–40, at p. 233.
3 For example, Wouter J. Hanegraaff, *New Age Religion and Western Culture: Esotericism in the Mirror of Secular Thought* (Leiden, 1996).
4 Graham Harvey, *Listening People, Speaking Earth: Contemporary Paganism* (London, 2006).
5 Jonathan Z. Smith, *To Take Place: Toward Theory in Ritual* (Chicago, 1987).
6 Bruno Latour, *We Have Never Been Modern* (New York, 1993).
7 Graham Dwyer and Richard J. Cole (eds.), *The Hare Krishna Movement: Forty Years of Chanting* (London, 2007), p. 1.
8 Anna S. King, "For Love of Krishna: Forty Years of Chanting," in Dwyer and Cole (eds.), *Hare Krishna Movement*, pp. 134–47, at p. 134.
9 Ibid., p. 135
10 Anna King, personal communication.
11 Burke Rochford, *Hare Krishna Transformed* (New York, 2007).
12 Brian Bocking, "Of Priests, Protests and Protestant Buddhists: The Case of Soka Gakkai International," in P. Clarke and J. Somers (eds.), *Japanese New Religions in the West* (Folkestone, 1994), pp. 118–32, at p. 119
13 Helen Waterhouse, "Soka Gakkai Buddhism as a Global Religious Movement," in John Wolffe (ed.), *Global Religious Movements in Regional Context* (Aldershot, 2002), pp. 109–55, at p. 134; citing Bocking, "Of Priests, Protests and Protestant Buddhists."
14 Cited in Phillip E. Hammond and David W. Machacek, *Soka Gakkai in America* (Oxford, 1999), p. 56.
15 Ibid., p. 59.
16 Ibid., pp. 59 and 63.
17 Ian Reader and George Tanabe, *Practically Religious: Worldly Benefits and the Common Religion of Japan* (Honolulu, 1998).
18 James Cox, *From Primitive to Indigenous: The Academic Study of Indigenous Religions* (Aldershot, 2007), p. 85.
19 Sandra Ionescu, "Adapt or Perish: The Story of Soka Gakkai in Germany," in Peter B. Clarke (ed.), *Japanese New Religions in Global Perspective* (Richmond, UK, 2000), pp. 182–97.
20 Andrew Dawson, *New Era – New Religions: Religious Transformation in Contemporary Brazil* (Aldershot, 2007). Also see Dawson, "Taking Possession of Santo Daime: The Growth of Umbanda within a Brazilian New Religion," in Bettina Schmidt (ed.), *Spirit Possession and Trance: New Interdisciplinary Perspectives* (London, 2010), pp. 134–50. For more discussion of the ritual use of ayahuasca in Brazil, see the special issue of the journal, *Fieldwork in Religion* 2:3 (2006).

21 Schmidt (ed.), *Spirit Possession.*
22 Andy Letcher, *Shroom: A Cultural History of the Magic Mushroom* (New York, 2007).
23 Graham Harvey and Robert J. Wallis, *Historical Dictionary of Shamanism* (Lanham, 2007), pp. 64–65.
24 Bruno Latour, "Perspectivism: 'Type' or 'Bomb'?" *Anthropology Today* 25:2 (2009), pp. 1–2.
25 Dawson, "Taking Possession," pp. 145–48.
26 Robert McCauley and E. Thomas Lawson, *Bringing Ritual to Mind: Psychological Foundations of Cultural Forms* (Cambridge, 2002), p. 36.
27 Leonard N. Primiano, "Vernacular Religion and the Search for Method in Religious Folklife," *Western Folklore* 54:1 (1995), pp. 37–56. Also see Graham Harvey (ed.), *Religions in Focus: New Approaches to Tradition and Contemporary Practices* (London, 2009).
28 Catherine Bell, "Performance," in Mark C. Taylor (ed.), *Critical Terms for Religious Studies* (Chicago, 1998), pp. 205–24.
29 Malory Nye, *Religion: The Basics* (London, 2004), p. 8. Compare the anthropological suggestion of "culturing" rather than "culture" by Nigel Rapport and Joanna Overing, *Social and Cultural Anthropology: The Key Themes* (London, 2004), p. 97.
30 Smith, *To Take Place*, p. 103.
31 Ronald Grimes, *Deeply into the Bone: Re-inventing Rites of Passage* (Berkeley, 2000), p. 346.

Further reading

The Ritual Studies website is an invaluable resource for those interested in all aspects of ritual and ritual studies; in particular see its regularly updated "publications" page at http://ritualstudies.com/category/publications/ (accessed July 29, 2011).

The *Journal of Ritual Studies* (also available as an e-journal through many libraries) publishes articles from many disciplines, and includes articles about new religions. The following are important foundations for any study of ritual:

Bell, Catherine, "Performance," in Mark C. Taylor (ed.), *Critical Terms for Religious Studies* (Chicago, 1998), pp. 205–24.
Grimes, Ronald, *Rite Out of Place: Ritual, Media, and the Arts* (Oxford, 2006).
Schechner, Richard, *Performance Theory* (London, 2003).
Smith, Jonathan Z., *To Take Place: Toward Theory in Ritual* (Chicago, 1987).

7 Canonical and extracanonical texts in new religions

OLAV HAMMER AND MIKAEL ROTHSTEIN

INTRODUCING THE THEME

Texts devoted to religious matters can be categorized in various ways. One common way of doing so is to divide the corpus according to genre. The terminology of religious genres is extensive and includes categories such as myth, legend, creed, homily, apology, hagiography, commentary, eschatology, theological tract, hymn, psalm, and prayer. Founders of and spokespersons for new religions have produced all of these well-known types, confirming one of the main points made in the Introduction to this volume: there is nothing extraordinary or strange about new religions.

A cross-cutting distinction of more immediate concern in the present context is based on the status accorded the writings within a given religious tradition. Most if not all traditions have selected a small subset of writings as being particularly sacred, effectively creating a canon. Thus, Hindu texts are divided according to status ranking the direct revelations from the divine – *shruti* – highest, while the recollections of sages since the dawn of time, the *smriti*, occupy a secondary position. And of course, Christian, Jewish, and Islamic traditions also set certain texts (Bible, Tanakh, Qur'ān) apart as canonical. Some religions go further and distinguish several levels of sacredness. Mahayana Buddhism grants canonical status to a large corpus of works, but suggests that certain texts present religious truth in its highest form, while others are formulated in a manner appropriate to the spiritually less astute, because the Buddha was a master at deploying skillful didactic means.[1] Outside of the core canon of each tradition there are vast numbers of other texts, with manifold purposes such as explicating the "true meaning" of the canon, presenting ritual means of approaching the canonical scriptures, recalling the lives of the sages who first recorded the sacred words, and so on. In this respect, as well, new religions function just like their older counterparts. Although few new religions have a distinct term for their core of canonical writings, they do in practice distinguish between a core of essential texts and more peripheral writings that comment on or supplement the key "scriptures."

The bulk of scholarship on religious texts, whether canonical or extracanonical, deals with writings from older traditions, and little research has been carried out specifically on the role of religious texts in new religions. Nevertheless, texts are ubiquitous also in NRMs, and are of key importance in many of these newer religions. The same questions can be asked of these as of texts in older religions: how are canonical or "sacred" texts perceived by members of NRMs? How do they relate to the social groups within which they are perceived as sacred? By what historical processes do such texts emerge? How is the process of according them canonical status carried out? What roles do such texts play in the ritual, intellectual, and organizational life of NRMs? How are they interpreted by the members of the movements to which they belong?

NRMs allow us privileged insights into such processes of production, distribution, revision, and selective use of texts. Christianity, Buddhism, and Islam were not born in the clear light of history, and considerable scholarly controversy surrounds the details of how the canonical scriptures of these religions were created and how they received the shape that they have today. In the case of religions with roots stretching back only some years or decades, the historical record is often more revealing, and sometimes the emergence of religious beliefs in terms of religious texts can be followed at very close range. In this sense, NRMs provide a living laboratory for the scholar of religions. We will in the course of the present chapter focus on texts in emergent religions, but in doing so we pursue questions that are relevant to understanding the role of texts in the formative period of any tradition.

THE NATURE OF CANONICAL TEXTS

One of the most commonly invoked criteria distinguishing noncanonical from canonical texts is their putative origin. Canonical texts are often believed to ultimately originate with various types of superhuman or transcendent agents, or at least with authors whose insights into a spiritual dimension set them radically apart from the mass of ordinary humans.[2] Extracanonical writings, by contrast, are understood to have human authors and more mundane origins.[3] This is clearly the case with scriptures familiar from older religions. Some of these are attributed verbatim to the divinity itself: the Qur'ān, for instance, is seen by most Muslims as an exact reproduction of the words of Allah.

Some are understood to represent a divine message, even if the wording may have been colored by its recipients: many Christians understand the Bible in this way. Yet others are attributed to individuals who, although they may have some human properties, are nevertheless described in a decidedly hagiographic literature as being set apart from all other human beings. This is the case with the *sutras* of early Buddhism, attributed to a being (the Buddha) whose biography abounds with miraculous events, and whose advice is sought out even by the gods.

Canonical texts in new religious movements are understood in structurally equivalent ways. *A Course in Miracles* is presented as an extra-Biblical message from Jesus;[4] the *Liber AL*, a foundational text for the religion of Thelema, is understood as the result of dictation by a suprahuman entity, Aiwass, to Aleister Crowley;[5] the *Mahatma Letters* of Theosophy were received from a group of spiritually advanced beings known as the Mahatmas or Masters.[6]

Yet other texts were penned by individuals believed to posses truly unique insights: the key texts of Scientology were written by L. Ron Hubbard, who is understood by Scientologists as an unsurpassed genius. The fundamental texts of Anthroposophy were written or dictated by Rudolf Steiner, whose abilities to clairvoyantly perceive spiritual truths are considered by his followers to be unparalleled. Similarly a host of texts have been written by enlightened or divine gurus of the many Hindu-inspired NRMs, and within Christian-based traditions, new prophets have produced large quantities of religious writings. Various groups that treat such texts as canonical have furthermore produced vast extracanonical literatures that explain and comment upon the foundational scriptures.

The attribution of texts to a divine source or a unique individual is a social phenomenon. Sacred texts are sacred, not because of some overt property of the texts themselves, but because a group of people bestows special meaning upon them. Texts and the community of people using these texts are thus interdependent. There are basically only a few ways in which a new religious organization or movement can emerge, and the texts that these movements use are vested with special status in matching ways.

A religious movement can be distinctly novel, and will typically form around a religious entrepreneur – say, a charismatic leader or successful writer – who formulates a distinctive new set of doctrines and practices. In some cases the sayings and writings of that individual can be promoted as essential to accessing religious truth, and in time, parts or all of these writings may acquire canonical status. If the novel religious movement is led by a charismatic individual, we may with Max Weber expect the role of texts to gain in importance once the founder is dead. As long as the founder is alive, his charisma is vested in his person, and guidelines to religious thinking and behavior can be obtained from him or her directly. When the founder is gone, only his or her words remain, and charisma is *routinized* in literature.[7] In some movements, this process is accentuated further by the decidedly uncharismatic role played by successors to the founder.

Other movements are more closely linked to an already existing family of religions, and will often adopt the canonical writings of that family as their own. In these cases, the distinct identity of the new group will often be constructed around the claim that previous translations or versions of the canonical text were faulty, or that earlier understandings of the sacred texts are flawed and should be replaced by those of the new group. Commentary, for many of these new religions, becomes essential: the key canonical text is provided by historical tradition, but commentaries dictate the appropriate way of reading and understanding that text. A sacred text may ultimately function as a palimpsest of interpretations: the new movement becomes the vehicle of an exegetical tradition that engages with generation upon generation of predecessors, approving of, eschewing, or improving upon already existing understandings of the canonical texts.

NOVEL MOVEMENTS AND RELIGIOUS ENTREPRENEURS

For many years, beginning in the late 1960s, the ritual activities and doctrinal stances of the Rajneesh or Osho movement were based on the day-to-day statements of its leader, Osho (aka Rajneesh), born in 1931 as Chandra Mohan Jain. Osho repeatedly shifted ideological focus over the years, for example going from a stance of encouraging sexual experimentation to one of advocating caution in view of the mounting threat of an AIDS epidemic. He changed his residence and his mode of living, and switched from a free and inclusive organization to a tightly regimented community. In life, the turns and twists in his views and actions were communicated to his followers, who with each new development could either choose to accept his new directions or to distance themselves from him and to leave the movement. Since his death, no prominent leader figure has come forward to take Osho's place.[8] Charismatic leadership has effectively ceased, and books by Osho have become instrumental in promoting a selection of his more liberal statements to audiences that might have been unsympathetic to the strict views and disciplined lifestyle advocated in his later years. A number of titles have been sold in New Age venues, or can be downloaded for free, allowing his texts to be promoted in a wider, non-affiliated "spiritual" milieu, years after the Osho movement in a stricter sense had passed its zenith.[9]

In the case of the Osho movement a body of writings has gradually emerged from an already existing religious group. In other cases, the production of religious texts is prior to, or concurrent with, the formation of a formalized social group willing to accept that text as sacred. Mormonism is a classic example. The *Book of Mormon* was produced by Joseph Smith in 1828–29 and published on March 26, 1830, as the result of what he described as a process of translation from a text written in "reformed Egyptian." The new scripture was at first accepted by a very small number of people, who have gone down in Mormon history as the "Three Witnesses" and the "Eight Witnesses," and whose approving statements are reproduced in every copy of the book. During 1829, as work on the volume progressed, converts were baptized, and on April 9, 1830, immediately after publication of the book, the Church of Christ (later renamed the Church of Jesus Christ of Latter-day Saints) was formally founded.

The relation between putative suprahuman origin, process of canon formation, and social organization can be complex and convoluted. The Theosophical Society, perhaps the most successful of all late nineteenth-century religious movements, was founded by a small group of people in 1875. Only after the movement had come into existence did a canon gradually emerge. The suprahuman authors said to be responsible for the key doctrines, the Mahatmas or Masters, communicated with the founders via correspondence that was much later published as the *Mahatma Letters*.[10] At first, these missives circulated privately, and were the raw material for Theosophist Alfred Sinnett's book *Esoteric Buddhism* published in 1883. The key ideologue of the Theosophical Society, Helena Blavatsky, countered by suggesting that her interpretation of the Mahatmas' messages was more accurate than Sinnett's, and composed a large work and a spate of articles that set out her understanding of these messages. Her magnum opus, *The Secret Doctrine*, furthermore referred to an ancient document in an otherwise unknown tongue, the *Book of Dzyan*, which she quoted and commented upon and which she claimed contained the perennial truths of the Mahatmas in condensed form. *The Secret Doctrine* was published in 1888, fourteen years after the foundation of the Theosophical Society, and is explicitly understood as the work of Blavatsky, not as a text channeled from a spiritual dimension, but it has nonetheless – not least due to Theosophical reverence for Blavatsky – achieved a status as a canonical writing of the movement of which she was co-founder.

Religious entrepreneurs as understood here need not be charismatic leaders of structured social movements. Key religious texts can take on the shape of literature, written by authors with no overt claim to leadership of any group and perused by readers with no institutional affiliation. The phenomenon of religious texts mainly reaching individual buyers on a market has been labeled "audience cult" by sociologists of religion Rodney Stark and William Sims Bainbridge.[11] Compared with the texts of tightly knit social groups, these works display a salient difference. Since there is no organization to promote certain works before others, there can strictly speaking be no canon of sacred writings. Books that do achieve a special status do so by appealing to the taste of readers, and compete on a market composed of two major segments. The first consists of books with only a loose affiliation with any institutionally organized religious tradition: writings often identified as "spiritual," "self-help" or "New Age." Characteristic examples include James Redfield's *The Celestine Prophecy* (1993) and *Conversations with God* by Neale Donald Walsch (a series whose first volume was published in 1995). The second is the Christian market, where the prime example is the immensely popular sixteen-volume series *Left Behind* authored by Tim LaHaye and Jerry Jenkins (published 1995–2007).

NEW RELIGIONS, EXISTING TEXTS, AND THE CRAFTING OF COMMENTARY

All the above examples deal with texts composed in connection with the development of a new religious movement or current (although, as in the case of the *Book of Mormon* and the *Book of Dzyan* purportedly underlying *The Secret Doctrine*, the novelty of these writings is denied by the movements themselves). Despite their recent date of composition, the texts disseminated in novel forms of religions live in an intertextual universe where older texts are already in place. The *Book of Mormon* is structured in books, chapters, and verses like a biblical text and uses language reminiscent of the King James Bible. The series *Conversations with God* was published in a social context where monotheism is the most familiar form of religion and where, as the book title implies, it can seem reasonable to readers to conduct a conversation with a personal divinity.

The similarity between old and new is often explicitly commented upon: positively by the emergent religion, negatively by the older tradition that it most closely resembles. The *Book of Mormon* can be perceived by the Church of Jesus Christ of Latter-day Saints as a "third Testament" that complements the Christian Bible, and *The Principle*, the canonical text of the Unificationist movement, can be understood similarly within that religious group. Traditional Christians will, on the contrary, see such writings as "false," "counterfeit," or "heretical." Animosity directed against the new texts can in fact contribute to the survival and success of NRMs. Members of new religions can interpret the hostility of outsiders as an encouraging sign that their own group is fighting a righteous struggle for truth.

The role of texts in creating an identity for a group is particularly evident where new religions break off from an already existing family of religions and use traditional sacred texts, recognizing that they share them with a host of other groups, but insisting that their own translations, interpretations, and commentarial traditions surpass those of their predecessors. This is, for instance, the case with Transcendental Meditation (TM), and the International Society for Krishna Consciousness (ISKCON), both of which have issued their own versions of the *Bhagavad Gita* with extensive commentaries by their gurus. The Sanskrit text is recognized as a revelation from a divine source, but it is only when interpreted and commented on by the guru that followers will make religious use of the text. On the bookshelf the volume may look like yet another version of the *Bhagavad Gita*, but in effect competing versions of the scripture will be carefully eschewed by followers of either movement.

In a Christian context the case of Jehovah's Witnesses displays a number of similarities. The Jehovah's Witnesses consider the Bible to be the absolute and unchallenged authority in all matters, but "the Bible" is to be understood within the interpretive framework of the movement. The translation from the original Greek and/or Hebrew has to be correct, and it is assumed that only the translation authorized by the leadership of the Jehovah's Witnesses is trustworthy. There are two reasons for privileging their own version of the text. Firstly, the "correct" translation confirms the tenets of the Jehovah's Witnesses' beliefs. Secondly, the very idea of being in possession of the only true version of the Bible, which to the Jehovah's Witnesses is equivalent to the only true manifestation of God's will, adds significantly to the self-perception and self-confidence of the group. Being a Witness means being a caretaker of "God's word." The text reaches beyond mere doctrinal issues and becomes the prime marker of social and religious identity.

In cases such as these new religions use primary texts that originate *outside* the context of the movement itself in order to develop and promote secondary texts (translations, commentaries) from *within* its own social and intellectual confines. The new religion offers something novel, but does so by disembedding traditional, authoritative texts from already existing contexts. The earlier text may in turn be a link in an even longer chain of texts. The sacred texts of Christian sects and new religious movements, for instance, are best contextualized as links positioned within the overall totality of Christian religious texts, with further links back to the Old Testament/Hebrew Bible (Tanakh). A good example of this process concerns Sun Myung Moon (b.1920), founder and leader of the Unificationist movement.

Referring to Moon as the Messiah, Unificationists consider his teachings to be a body of texts that completes and explains the Bible. Unificationists believe that the same god throughout history has tried to reach mankind with a message of redemption, but insist that salvation could only be attained when Reverend Moon stepped forward as the "Third Adam" or "The Lord of the Second Coming," that is as the savior who has re-established the proper relationship between humans and their god. Moon's massive textual corpus, as it appears, mirrors his attributed status as savior. On a personal level, Adam rejected the rules of God and failed to establish a divine family and raise children free from sin. Jesus was sent to accomplish this task, but his message was misunderstood by his disciples and thus Jesus also failed. Reverend Moon and his wife, however, have completed the task, and his teaching explains how and why. On a textual level, as seen from the viewpoint of Unificationists, the Old Testament holds the basic truths about God and his relationship with humankind. This theme is expanded in the New Testament, but not until Moon's theological expositions became available in 1966 in a volume known (in the original Korean) as *Wolli Kangron* and in English translation as *The Exposition of the Divine Principle* (1973), or simply *The Principle*, could the ultimate truth be known. The sacred text is thus intimately connected to the individual who provided it.

Of parallel importance are the speeches and talks delivered by Moon. Moon plays a unique role in the salvation history of mankind, and his statements will be understood in the light of this status. New sacred texts have come into being as transcriptions of his oral presentations and have been published. Whether they have done so intentionally or not,

Moon's followers have emulated the process that transformed sayings of other religious figures into sacred texts. In a Korean-Christian context, obvious parallels are the sayings attributed to Jesus in the Gospels, as well as the texts expounding the wisdom of Kongfuzi, Laozi, and other sages. The very structure of the texts recording Moon's pronouncements supports his claim to be a universal Messianic figure who will engage all major religious traditions in his soteriological project.

Commentarial traditions surrounding chains of texts of the kind we have been discussing typically interpret earlier texts in the light of newer ones. For Christians, the Old Testament is usually read through the lens of the New Testament, allowing them, for instance, to find portents of the coming of Christ in Old Testament passages. In the same way, Moon and his followers will read and interpret the classic Christian canonical texts according to the ideas and doctrines in Moon's own writings. Moon's followers find signs in the New Testament narratives concerning Jesus that they believe point to Moon.

Whether deployed consciously or not, this exegetical move is a very common element in the formation of new sacred texts. On the one hand the new text gains credibility by its numerous intertextual links to an older, well-established sacred text. On the other hand, the new text qualifies these links to the past by insisting on the uniqueness of its own specific message. Ultimate authority, the text as well as the commentarial tradition insists, lies in the new text, which completes and therefore in a sense supersedes the tradition upon which it builds. In our example, Moon positions his text (and himself) in a biblical tradition, that is, a sacred historiography that claims that a universal god has manifested his presence through these texts since ancient times. This perspective allows Unificationists to insist that newer texts shed light on the intention already embedded in older ones, rather than seeing newer texts as drawing on older ones (which is obviously the view of the historian of religions).

CANONICAL TEXTS AND RELIGIOUS LIFE

Not only do texts play key roles in the emergence of new religions, they continue to be of paramount importance in defining the doctrines and structuring the ritual life of novel traditions. In many religions access to the divine is primarily granted through authoritative texts: doctrines are formulated, rituals are specified in detail, the history of the movement, and the deeds of the founder are recorded in texts. Each religion will have its own version of this theme.

In Scientology, the movement's scriptures are considered a prolongation or even manifestation of the founder of the religion, L. Ron Hubbard (1911–1986). Any understanding of Scientology's sacred texts, consequently, has to include the hagiographic tradition of this religion. Every single piece of writing authored by Hubbard is considered scripture. Scientology's sacred writings amount to thousands upon thousands of pages. Some are more important than others, and in this sense Scientology is built on a tiered canon, but no single volume stands out as the sacred text above all others. Hubbard's first book on issues pertaining to religion, the self-improvement classic *Dianetics* (1951), is often described by Scientologists as the most important publication in the history of mankind, but it is never promoted as anything like "the Scientology bible." Hubbard himself is called "Source," as a sign of the conviction that all true knowledge and understanding derives directly from him. His texts, accordingly, may be interpreted as a manifestation of his intellectual and philosophical achievements, the foundation upon which Scientology rests: in a sense, they are an incarnation in words of his mind. All texts by Hubbard, consequently, are considered "scripture," but because many of these texts deviate considerably in genre and language from traditional religious writings, the organization has strategically developed a number of texts in the fashion of traditional sacred texts. These include, for instance, a composition known as *The Factors* that is structured as a series of numbered sayings in a recognizably "religious" style.[12]

The crucial role played by Hubbard's writings can also be seen from a piece of circumstantial evidence. It is almost inconceivable that Hubbard, the claims of Scientology notwithstanding, could have written or dictated all titles attributed to him. The bulk of writings carrying Hubbard's name is simply of such an overwhelming magnitude that he would have had to produce perhaps fifty, sixty, seventy or more pages on Scientology every single day.[13] The fact that Scientology officially insists that Hubbard is the author of all the books, treatises, pamphlets, reports, dictionaries, handbooks, and other publications that carry his name points to the underlying function of the texts: to maintain not only the legacy, but also the presence of the founder in his organization and among individual Scientologists.

The importance of the author does not mean that the contents of these texts are of minor importance. Scientology is in certain ways a very intellectually based religion, and the study of texts is a focal point in the religious life. Scientologists spend considerable time reading, going through manuals, checking dictionaries during courses and workshops and in therapy in an effort to proceed on "The Bridge," that is, to make progress in their individual religious development. Individual progress is closely monitored and proceeds in discrete steps in a way that shows how sacred texts in Scientology function in a highly ritualized context. Scientology is a religion based on control over information, where access to new levels of doctrinal insight is carefully guarded. A Scientological origin myth that has been hotly debated in the media concerns the role of the evil space ruler Xenu. This myth is kept secret to most Scientologists, who will only be allowed to hear of this incident in the mythic past during initiation into one of the higher, advanced initiatory levels (known as Operating Thetan III, or OTIII). In this way, core texts presenting basic information regarding Scientology's belief system are unavailable to most practitioners.[14]

Restricting access to texts is closely connected to issues of power: the leader or the highest echelons of a movement in this way monopolize the source of religious truth. This method of exerting control is brought to its ultimate consequence in movements where, besides actual texts that can be read and commented upon, reference is made to texts that exist only in a metaphysical realm, inaccessible to ordinary humans but of considerable importance nevertheless: virtual texts. According to Scientology executives, a library of ground-breaking texts by L. Ron Hubbard is stored in Church facilities, still awaiting the proper time for revelation. Another example of a text with (presumably) only a narrative existence is the *Book of Dzyan* that forms a basis of Theosophy. Purportedly composed in the ancient language of Senzar, this work – not known outside the Theosophical context – was, as mentioned above, quoted and commented upon by Helena Blavatsky, who structured much of her *Secret Doctrine* around this virtual text.

LEGITIMATING CANONICAL TEXTS

Warrant and legitimacy

As stressed at the beginning of this chapter, canonical texts are the result of a process of selection. Out of the mass of religious writings, some are set apart as sacred, divinely revealed, or permeated by unique insight. All of these attributes are, of course, social labels. A text cannot by itself be "sacred," "divine," or "uniquely insightful": concrete, historically and socially situated people decide to attribute such an extraordinary status to certain texts. This status needs to be constructed and supported by various means.

At times, canonical texts self-referentially claim particular status. This is, for instance, the case when the Second Letter of Paul to Timothy (3:16, King James Bible) affirms that "All Scripture is given by inspiration of God." More frequently, sacred status can be actively created by the deployment of various types of explicit arguments in the extracanonical literature of the religious tradition. Inspired by the argumentation analysis formulated by Stephen Toulmin, we suggest that these arguments are crucially backed up by one or more of a small set of warrants.[15] This clinching warrant can be the apparently unquestionable authority of tradition, for example the purported fact that the canonical writings go back to the dawn of mankind or to a golden age. The warrant can be the alleged unique characteristics of the sacred texts itself. Or it can be the extraordinary deeds and qualities of the individuals who have transmitted the text. Sacred status can also be created and sustained ritually and symbolically: the canonical texts are often not only (or even primarily) meant to be read: they are ritually displayed and recited, treated with extraordinary reverence, housed in visually striking shrines, or are aesthetically designed to be uniquely impressive. In older religions, examples of all of these "canonizing strategies" abound. As an example, the divine origin and unique status of the Qur'ān is supported by literature that relates that this sacred text is the final revelation of a message delivered to prophets ever since the days of the first human being, Adam; that its message and language are unsurpassed by that of any other book; that its recipient, the prophet Muhammad, was as a man of unique qualities, whose acts are worthy of emulation. Copies of the Qur'ān need to be treated with respect, worn-out tomes cannot be disposed of as other written materials, passages from the text are used for apotropaic purposes, are ritually recited, and so forth.

New religions similarly use a variety of means in order to construct the canonicity of their core writings, and it is to three of these status-inducing strategies that we shall devote the remainder of this section: invoking ancient tradition, stressing the unique qualities of the recipient of the message, and deploying symbolic and ritual means of promoting the canon.

Ancient tradition

Although the very term "new religious movement" implies that the religion in question is a relatively recent development, many NRMs insist on the ancient roots of their teachings. Theosophy, a religious current with roots in the nineteenth century, claims to be an expression of a perennial wisdom tradition. The Raëlian religion, based on purported encounters of its founder Raël with beings from outer space, can give the impression of being a hyper-modern religion, but supports its claims, inter alia, by referring to passages in Genesis. Books on the New Age market can present radically innovative claims, but nevertheless insist that these are in fact based on wisdom from Ancient Egypt, Tibet, or the Native Americas.

Privileged recipients

The key texts of these and other traditions were produced by individuals who are almost always described and promoted as very special people. The religious leader will often modestly claim to be nothing but a caretaker of a religious message or spokesperson acting on behalf of a higher authority, but proclamations of that kind remain discursive constructions. In reality, most leaders of new religious movements are regarded by their followers as truly extraordinary, or even divine. Maintaining this image of the leader involves presenting the life history of that person in a particular light, treating the leader (or images of him or her) with extraordinary respect, and deploying various other means of creating enthusiasm and devotion.

The role of Scientology's L. Ron Hubbard is – once again – a good illustration. As we have seen, Hubbard is believed to have penned Scientology's scriptures in their entirety. In order to make such a notion seem plausible, that is, in order to make acceptable the theological concept of "Source" (see above), Hubbard himself must be legitimized as a matchless individual. A substantial number of hagiographic books, pamphlets, websites, and audiovisual resources elevate Hubbard from the class of ordinary human being to that of a sage, saint, and savior. While the claims found in this literature can seem grossly exaggerated to the outsider, Scientologists perceive them as factual statements.[16]

Similarly, the canonical text of the Unificationists and the charismatic founder of the movement lend authority to each other. Moon's importance exceeds that of a prophet: Moon incarnates the divine power that is propagated in his own text, and a theological circle of argumentation becomes part and parcel of all aspects of Unificationist philosophy. How can we know that Moon is the Messiah? We know this because it becomes obvious when we study the truths expressed in *The Principle*. But how can we know that *The Principle* tells the truth? This is obviously the case, because it was conceived of and written by the Messiah, Sun Myung Moon.

Ritual and symbolic promotion

We noted earlier that older traditions often demonstrate the sacred quality of their canonical texts in ritual ways: scrolls or books are treated with respect, displayed prominently, produced lavishly, recited solemnly, and when worn and torn are disposed of ceremonially. New religions can employ similar symbolic and ritual means to promote the status of their sacred writings. Rituals in ISKCON temples involve reciting passages of the *Bhagavad Gita* in Sanskrit, a language that presumably none of the participants understands; Soka Gakkai members will gaze at calligraphically produced reproductions of key passages of the *Lotus Sutra* and will recite the name of this scripture; and Evangelical Christians will decorate their churches with posters depicting the Bible.

Some movements will mobilize considerable effort and resources to express the idea that their writings are sacrosanct. The Church of Scientology has gone to extraordinary lengths to preserve the writings of its founder L. Ron Hubbard. An underground base has been constructed in a remote spot at the outskirts of the town of Trementina, New Mexico. In deep vaults, hidden behind fences and protected by armed guards, beneath a luxury mansion, copies of Hubbard's texts are kept in order to preserve them for all time. The texts, meticulously cared for, have been transferred to special paper and platinum plates, and are stored in carefully designed titanium boxes with advanced locking systems. A gigantic version of a Scientology symbol has been etched into the ground, and is clearly visible on Google's satellite photos on the Internet. Hubbard's greatness and that of his texts are thus made manifest on the grandest of scales.[17]

THE RISE AND FALL OF RELIGIOUS TEXTS

Canon formation, and indeed, the very process of producing religious writings is, as we have seen, dependent on warrants such as those mentioned above. One approach to defining myths and legends is substantive: it sees such "sacred narratives" as, for example, set apart in terms of the persons appearing in them (beings with suprahuman abilities), and their setting in time and place (a realm outside everyday human history). We have here, however, suggested that "sacred narratives" become set apart by being supported by discursive and ritual means that provide legitimizing background.[18] Some stories depicting the adventures of beings with exceptional powers are understood by particular social groups as accounts of a sacred reality. Other narratives of exceptional beings, such as *The Lord of the Rings* trilogy or the *Star Wars* films, are promoted as fictional. Only when fictional literature becomes treated by some as the foundation of ritual activity, or as the repository of hidden truths or existential meaning, do such works meander over into the domain of the mythical. In the past, fictional accounts such as Plato's dialogue *Timaeus* were mined for their spiritual truths and hence were elevated to canonical status. In the contemporary period, *Star Wars*, or the adventures of Bilbo, Frodo, and their companions, can be similarly given special status, and their potential to become sacred text is actualized.[19] Conversely, when sacred texts are divested of their legitimizing warrants, they lose their status as lived religious texts and are used for mundane purposes such as entertainment or education. This has happened with Greek and Roman mythology, with the sacred texts of the pre-Christian and pre-Islamic Middle East, and with the religious narratives of pre-colonial Polynesia, to mention just a few examples. Most new religions are ephemeral creations, and the scholar of religion is again and again witness to the on-going processes that give rise to new texts, provide them with special status, divest them of that extraordinary position, and ultimately contribute to their demise.

Notes

1   Michael Pye, *Skilful Means: A Concept in Mahayana Buddhism* (London, 2003).
2   Einar Thomassen, *Canon and Canonicity: The Formation and Use of Scripture* (Copenhagen, 2010) mentions tradition as a second commonly shared attribute (pp. 10–11). This certainly is the case for literary canons, and for particular traditions such as the Confucian, but is less relevant for the present purposes.
3   These human authors can, of course, be described in hagiographic terms, but they are – unlike the authors or recipients of canonical texts – usually not seen as unique beings.
4   D. Patrick Miller, *The Complete Story of* The Course: *The History, the People and the Controversies Behind* (London, 1997), p. 4.
5   For an insider's account of the origin of this text, see www.thelema. org/aa/documents/the_book_of_the_law/index.html (all links referred to here were accessed November 22, 2011).
6   For a range of examples and discussions pertaining to Theosophy, see Olav Hammer and Mikael Rothstein (eds.), *Handbook of the Theosophical Current* (Leiden, 2012).
7   For the process of transferring the religious leader's authority into another medium (such as a text), *routinization*, see Max Weber, *Theory of Social and Economic Organization* (New York, 1997 [first published in German, 1922]), pp. 363–72.

8   For academic discussion of Osho and his movement, see, e.g., Hugh B. Urban, "Osho, from Sex Guru to Guru of the Rich: The Spiritual Logic of Late Capitalism," in Thomas A. Forsthoefel and Cynthia Ann Humes (eds.), *Gurus in America* (New York, 2005), pp. 169–92; Marion S. Goldman, "When Leaders Dissolve: Considering Controversy and Stagnation in the Osho Rajneesh Movement," in James R. Lewis and Jesper Aagaard Petersen (eds.), *Controversial New Religions* (New York, 2005), pp. 119–37.

9   Downloads are available at www.messagefrommasters.com/Ebooks/Osho_Books.htm.

10 Regarding the *Mahatma Letters*, see, e.g., Joscelyn Godwin, *Atlantis and the Cycles of Time: Prophecies, Traditions, and Occult Revelations* (Rochester, VT, 2011), pp. 69–73. An online edition of the *Letters* is available at theosociety.org/pasadena/mahatma/ml-hp.htm.

11 William Simms Bainbridge and Rodney Stark, "Client and Audience Cults in America," *Sociological Analysis* 41:3 (1980), pp. 199–214.

12 The text is available at www.bonafidescientology.org/Append/01/page03.htm.

13 Mikael Rothstein, "Scientology, Scripture, and Sacred Tradition," in James R. Lewis and Olav Hammer (eds.), *The Invention of Sacred Tradition* (Cambridge, 2007), pp. 18–37.

14 Mikael Rothstein, "'His name was Xenu. He used renegades ...' Aspects of Scientology's Founding Myth," in James R. Lewis (ed.), *Scientology* (New York, 2009), pp. 365–88.

15 Stephen Toulmin, *The Uses of Argument* (Cambridge, 1969).

16 See Dorthe Refslund Christensen, "Inventing L. Ron Hubbard: On the Construction and Maintenance of the Hagiographic Mythology on Scientology's Founder," in Lewis and Pedersen (eds.), *Controversial New Religions*, pp. 227–59.

17 The *Washington Post* was one of the first to run the story, see washingtonpost.com/wp-dyn/content/article/2005/11/26/AR2005112601065.html.

18 For a discussion of "substantive" accounts of myth versus perspectives on myth as a manner of privileging particular types of discourse, see Russell T. McCutcheon, "Myth," in Willi Braun and McCutcheon (eds.), *Guide to the Study of Religion* (London and New York, 2000), pp. 190–208.

19 See Carole Cusack, *Invented Religions: Imagination, Fiction, and Faith* (Farnham, UK, and Burlington, VT, 2010) for examples of such processes of converting fiction into lived religion.

Further reading

Assmann, Aleida and Jan Assmann, *Kanon und Zensur* (Munich, 1987).

Henderson, John B., *Scripture, Canon, and Commentary* (Princeton, NJ, 1991).

Hughes, Aaron, "Presenting the Past: The Genre of Commentary in Theoretical Perspective," *Method and Theory in the Study of Religion* 15 (2003), pp. 148–68.

Sawyer, John F. A., *Sacred Languages and Sacred Texts* (London, 1999).
Smith, Jonathan Z., "Sacred Persistence: Toward a Redescription of Canon," in *Imagining Religion* (Chicago, 1982), pp. 36–52.
Thomassen, Einar, *Canon and Canonicity: The Formation and Use of Scripture* (Copenhagen, 2010).
Ulrich, Eugene, "The Notion and Definition of Canon," in Lee M. McDonald and James A. Saunders (eds.), *The Canon Debate* (Peabody, MA, 2002), pp. 21–35.

Part III

New religious movements

8 Scientology: up stat, down stat

JAMES R. LEWIS

INTRODUCTION

Scientology has probably received the most persistent criticism of any church in America in recent years. But ... Scientologists bear some of the responsibility. "They turn critics into enemies and enemies into dedicated warriors for a lifetime."[1]

The Church of Scientology is a psychotherapeutically oriented religion founded in the mid twentieth century by L. Ron Hubbard (1911–1986). Hubbard's extensive writings and taped lectures constitute the beliefs and the basis for the practices of the Church. Hubbard was a talented fiction writer and adventurer deeply interested in the human psyche. Scientology grew out of Dianetics, a popular therapy movement founded by Hubbard in the early 1950s.[2]

Rather like ancient gnosticism, Scientology views human beings as pure spirits ("Thetans") trapped in MEST (the world of Matter, Energy, Space, and Time). Humanity's ultimate goal is to achieve a state of total freedom in which – rather than being pushed around by external circumstances and by our own subconscious mind – we are "at cause" over the physical universe. Unlike traditional gnosticism, achieving this exalted state of total freedom does not require that we distance ourselves from everyday life. Instead, the greater our spiritual freedom, the more successful we will be at the "game of life."[3]

Though other non-traditional religious groups that have been involved in dramatic incidents have attracted more public attention for short periods of time, the Church of Scientology is arguably the most *persistently* controversial of all contemporary new religious movements

During his tenure as organizational head, L. Ron Hubbard established the tradition of each branch of the Church sending in reports on Thursdays. He then spent Fridays reading them. This is the origin of the "Thursday Report" that is the bane of many staff members. The ideal Thursday Report embodies a measurable increase over the preceding week's report, which is referred to as being "Up Stat." A decrease is referred to as "Down Stat."

(NRMs). As a consequence of its involvement in numerous legal conflicts, Scientology has acquired a reputation as a litigious organization, ready to sue critics or anyone else who portrays the Church in
an unfavorable light. Partly as a consequence of this fierce reputation,
academicians have tended to avoid publishing studies about Scientology
outside the esoteric realm of scholarly journals.[4]

Thus, at present, there exist only a handful of scholarly, English-
language books about the Church, Roy Wallis' *The Road to Total Freedom*
(1976), Harriet Whitehead's anthropological study, *Renunciation and
Reformation: A Study of Conversion in an American Sect* (1987), J.
Gordon Melton's short (80 pages) treatment, *The Church of Scientology*
(2000), James R. Lewis' anthology, *Scientology* (2009), and Hugh B.
Urban's *The Church of Scientology* (2011). The Church has generally
not interfered with the publication of academic papers, and the bulk of
the scholarly literature on Scientology is in the form of articles.

THE FOUNDER AND THE EARLY HISTORY OF THE CHURCH

L. Ron Hubbard grew up mostly in Montana, but also lived in
Nebraska, Seattle, Washington, and Washington, DC. According to his
official biography, he informally studied psychology, philosophy, and
religion during his youth. In 1929 he enrolled in George Washington
University, studying mathematics and engineering. The Church of
Scientology often calls attention to the fact that Hubbard took one of
the first courses in nuclear physics, but neglects to mention that he
failed the course and dropped out of college before receiving a degree.[5]

He began a literary career in the early 1930s. He published numerous stories and screenplays in various genres, including adventure,
mystery, and science fiction. Hubbard served in the United States Navy
during World War II. He was injured during the war, and it is claimed
the he used some of his own theories concerning the human mind to
assist in his healing.

Scientology has its roots in the "cultic milieu"[6] of the industri-
alized West during the mid twentieth century (the milieu that later
evolved into the New Age movement) and draws on certain themes
in American popular culture. It clearly bears the imprint of American
culture's interest in self-help psychology and popularized psychoanaly-
sis. Though the Church asserts that its closest relative among the
world religions is Buddhism, Scientology is more indebted to the New
Thought movement for its focus on the solution of practical problems.

Hubbard was also influenced by Will Durant's popularized history of Western philosophy, *The Story of Philosophy* (1926),[7] particularly Durant's presentation of Spinoza's psychology.[8] Though critics have accused Hubbard of having been influenced by the controversial occultist Aleister Crowley, Hubbard's teachings bear little resemblance to Crowley's.

In 1950, Hubbard published *Dianetics: The Modern Science of Mental Health.*[9] This book presented techniques aimed at ridding the "reactive mind" (Scientology's term for the subconscious) of the residues of traumas that Hubbard postulated lie at the source of irrational behaviors and psychosomatic illnesses. *Dianetics* quickly became a best-seller, and groups were soon formed to practice Hubbard's techniques. He lectured extensively and wrote more books. In 1951 he announced Scientology, described as different from Dianetics because it dealt not only with the mind (the focus of Dianetics), but also with humanity's spiritual nature.[10]

In 1954, the first Church of Scientology was established in Los Angeles, California. In 1959 Hubbard moved to Saint Hill Manor, in Sussex, England, and the worldwide headquarters of Scientology was relocated there. In 1966, Hubbard resigned his position as Executive Director of the Church and formed the Sea Organization (often referred to as the "Sea Org"; upper-level Scientology Organizations are referred to as "Orgs"), a group of dedicated members of the Church who lived aboard large, ocean-going ships. In 1975 these activities outgrew the ships, and were moved onto land in Florida and California. From this time until his death in 1986, Hubbard continuously wrote and published materials on the subjects of Dianetics and Scientology, as well as a number of works of science fiction.

Hubbard has the distinction of being the world's most translated author. His publications number over a thousand (all of his lectures were recorded and later transcribed for publication). They cover a wide variety of subjects from communication and the problems of work to past lives. *Dianetics: The Modern Science of Mental Health* has continued over the years to be a best-seller.

Hubbard was a complex character. On the one hand, he was brilliant and charismatic. On the other hand, he was controlling and overly sensitive to criticism. He has often been accused of being a power- and money-hungry charlatan. In response to the oft-cited but probably apocryphal Hubbard remark about how, "If a man really wanted to make a million dollars, the best way would be to start his own religion," Harriet Whitehead offered the observation that:

Elements of hype and razzle-dazzle, however, do not necessarily a con artist make. Taken in the context of Hubbard's long-term commitment to the elaboration, promulgation, and defense of his idea system, even during financially unrewarding years, and also in light of the barricades of secrecy, conspiracy theory, and defensive litigation with which he surrounded his embattled organization (see Wallis 1976:190–241), these traits seem less indicative of greed for gain than part of an egoistic complex that often characterizes visionaries, cranky or not.[11]

BELIEFS AND PRACTICES

Up until the middle of the twentieth century, most people accorded science and science's child, technology, a level of respect and prestige enjoyed by few other social institutions. Thus any religion claiming to be *scientific* drew on the prestige and perceived legitimacy of natural science. The appropriation of the term "science" by groups such as Christian Science and Science of Mind embody this pattern. The Church of Scientology is in this same lineage, though Scientology takes the further step of explicitly referring to their religio-therapeutic practices as religious *technology* – in Scientology jargon, the "tech." In much the same way as the 1950s viewed technology as ushering in a new, utopian world, Scientologists see their psycho-spiritual technology as supplying the missing ingredient in existing technologies – namely the therapeutic engineering of the human psyche

The Church of Scientology believes that "Man is basically good, that he is seeking to survive, [and] that his survival depends on himself and upon his fellows and his attainment of brotherhood with the universe." This is achieved in Scientology by two methods, referred to as "auditing" and "training." Dianetics and Scientology auditing (counseling of one individual by another) consists of an "auditor" guiding someone through various mental processes in order to first free the individual of the effects of the "reactive mind," and then to fully realize the spiritual nature of the person. The reactive mind is said to be that part of the mind that operates on a stimulus–response basis, and is composed of residual memories of painful and unpleasant mental incidents (termed "engrams") that unconsciously exert control over the individual. When the individual is freed from these undesired effects, s/he is said to have achieved the state of "Clear," which is the goal of Dianetics counseling. An individual can then go on to higher levels of counseling dealing with his or her nature as an immortal spiritual being, referred to in Scientology as a "Thetan," and eventually achieve the state of "Operating Thetan" (usually abbreviated "OT"). Scientologists believe in reincarnation – specifically, that a Thetan has lived many lifetimes in a human body before this one and will live more lifetimes in the future.

Scientology training consists of many levels of courses about: (1) improving the daily life of individuals by giving them various tools (e.g., concerning communication), and (2) learning the techniques of auditing so that one can counsel others. Scientology teaches people enrolled in its courses a rather elaborate system of practical psychology, along with a new vocabulary involving such notions as the "tone scale" (which arranges various emotional states into a hierarchy), the "eight dynamics" (a hierarchy of increasingly more general levels of the urge to survive), the "e-meter" (a device based on lie-detector technology that helps auditors locate a client's psychological and spiritual issues), the "ARC" triangle (affinity, reality, and communication), and the like. Progress along the Bridge – Scientology's spiritual path – is also arranged into a hierarchy of levels, from pre-Clear, to Clear, to eight Operating Thetan levels (Hubbard actually delineated more than eight levels, but these higher levels were never released).

Unlike many other NRMs, its membership includes people of a wide variety of ages and backgrounds. There are also numerous community action and social reform groups affiliated with Scientology that concern themselves with literacy (the World Literacy Crusade), education (the Study Tech), drug rehabilitation (Narconon), the rehabilitation of criminals (Criminon), and other issues.

Scientologists refer to a Supreme Being, but do not worship any deity as such, instead focusing on the application of Scientology principles to daily life. One unusual aspect of the Church is that members are not discouraged from actively participating in other religions, though few upper-level Scientologists or full-time staff actually do so.

Many critics have focused on the so-called "space opera," which involves secret teachings only revealed to Scientologists at the OT III level. The reasoning behind these critics' focus appears to be that – as captured in Mikael Rothstein's words – it seems "so utterly stupid that it unwittingly provides the best argument why people should denounce L. Ron Hubbard's teachings and altogether avoid the organization he founded."[12] Another sore point for critics is that Scientologists who have reached the OT III level routinely deny the existence of these inner teachings (what has been referred to as the Xenu narrative) rather than simply stating that they are not permitted to discuss it.

Part of the problem appears to be that upper-level Scientologists take these teachings literally, as potent information that must be kept secret from the uninitiated. However, as Whitehead points out, "Hubbard was careful to emphasize that these accounts are specula-tion, not established fact,"[13] and often presented this information in a "tongue-in-cheek tone ... Hubbard's interest in the universal incidents was less in their character of unalterable revelation than in their useful-ness as a springboard for his technical abstractions."[14] In the case of the Xenu narrative, Hubbard's purpose was likely to provide an etiology for the "body thetans" that are exorcised during OT III processing rather than to reveal timeless truths.[15]

CONTROVERSY

One of the first new religions in the second half of the twentieth cen-tury to be embroiled in controversy, Scientology eventually prevailed in the majority of its legal suits in North America and played a leading role in destroying the Cult Awareness Network, the most important anti-cult organization in the United States. While earlier controver-sial religions like the Jehovah's Witnesses had attracted controversy as a consequence of their very public proselytizing, Scientology's initial point of friction with the larger society was its challenge to the medical and psychotherapeutic establishments.

During the initial stages of the Dianetics movement, Hubbard naïvely contacted medical and psychiatric associations, explaining the significance of his discoveries for mental and physical health, and ask-ing that the AMA and the APA investigate his new technique. Instead of taking this offer seriously, these associations responded by attack-ing him. The subsequent popular success of Dianetics did nothing to improve the image of Hubbard in the collective mind of the medical-psychiatric establishment, and was likely instrumental in prompting an FDA (Food and Drug Administration) raid against the Church.

On January 4, 1963, the Founding Church of Scientology in Washington, DC, was raided by United States marshals and deputized longshoremen, acting on behalf of the FDA. Five thousand volumes of Church scriptures, 20,000 booklets and 100 e-meters were seized. In 1971, after years of litigation, the US District Court for the District of Columbia issued the *Founding Church of Scientology* v. *United States* decision. The FDA was ordered to return the books and e-meters that had been taken in the 1963 raid. In its decision, the court recognized Scientology's constitutional right to protection from the government's excessive entanglement with religion. Though the raid was declared illegal, the seized documents remained in government possession and were open to public scrutiny. According to these documents, the Church was keeping files on people it considered unfriendly. The documents also revealed that there had been various attempts by Scientology to infiltrate anti-cult organizations.

After the raid, the Church's Guardian's Office sent a number of top officials incognito into selected government agencies that were collecting data on Scientology. Several members were eventually indicted and convicted for theft of government documents. The convicted members were released from their positions within the Church. The Church of Scientology then closed the Guardian's Office, which had been responsible for initiating illegal activities. It was thus made to appear that the Church of Scientology had disbanded a rogue office. However, the Church's Office of Special Affairs, which was the organizational successor to the Guardian's Office, has subsequently been accused of continuing most of the objectionable practices of the Guardian's Office.

In 1991, *Time* magazine published a front-page story attacking Scientology, which subsequently responded with a massive public relations campaign and with a lengthy series of full-page ads in *USA Today*. Early in 1992 the Church filed a major lawsuit against *Time*, after discovering that the maker of Prozac – a psychiatric drug Scientology had been active in opposing – had been the ultimate prompter of *Time*'s assault on the Church. This suit was eventually dismissed.

The Church of Scientology was also involved in extended conflicts with the Australian, French, and German governments, and problems with the IRS through the 1980s and 1990s. Hubbard was charged with criminal tax evasion, and the IRS often moved against the Church in ways that questioned its tax-exempt status. These problems terminated in a landmark decision in 1993, when the IRS ceased all litigation and recognized Scientology as a legitimate religious organization. Following this decision, the Church redirected its legal resources against the Cult Awareness Network, and managed to sue the group out of existence by 1996.[16] Scientology in North America then entered a period of relative calm, but more recently the Church has been in the news again because of the public activities of Scientologist Tom Cruise, a high-profile episode of the television show *South Park* that led to the resignation of the late Isaac Hayes (another celebrity Scientologist) from the show, and an exposé article that appeared in *Rolling Stone* in early 2006.

In 2008, an Internet group calling itself Anonymous began a campaign against the Church of Scientology that involved, among other strategies, picketing Church facilities and harassing Scientologists.[17] The most recent controversy involves Scientology's current leader, David Miscavige, who has been accused of abusing Church members. The source of these accusations has been numerous high-level defectors who have taken their stories to the press. A particularly notable series of articles based around interviews with these ex-members was published in the *St. Petersburg Times* in 2009. The *St. Petersburg Times* exposé subsequently prompted a number of television news programs – BBC's *Panorama* and CNN's *AC360* – to air special programs based around the physical and psychological abuse of these ex-members.

PATTERNS OF ORGANIZATIONAL SELF-SABOTAGE

In the majority of conflicts, the Church of Scientology has proven to be its own worst enemy. Thus, for example, the covert infiltration of US government agencies has been responsible for generating some of the Church's worst publicity. The Church has also frequently employed the strategy of attempting to block publications – both popular and scholarly – judged to be critical of Scientology. Once again, this aggressive tactic has produced far more negative publicity than if the Church had simply ignored these publications.

One of the more heavy-handed practices has been to declare anyone who criticized Scientology a "suppressive person" (S.P.). As originally formulated, suppressive persons were "fair game," meaning, among other things, that they could be "Tricked, sued or lied to or destroyed."[18] The fair-game policy was terminated only after Hubbard concluded that it resulted in "bad public relations," though he added that this does not "cancel any policy on the treatment or handling of an S.P."[19]

In more recent years, the Church of Scientology has waged a vigorous campaign against online critics, which has led Scientology to become one of the most attacked religions on the Internet. Church leaders appear to believe that they can use the same unproductive tactic they have used over and over again in the past to obtain a different result in the present. Whitehead observes that distortion often enters into the Church's conflicts as a result of its "overreaction to threat and its unwillingness to examine its role in provoking or exacerbating hostile reactions. Conflicts, rather than being defused, are often escalated."[20]

In addition to attacking the Church's critics, Hubbard also adopted harsh policies regarding ex-members. As part of declaring a former member to be an S.P., individuals who had been personally close to the ex-member (e.g., family members, close friends, or even a spouse) were required to cut off all communication. Though comparable to the Amish practice of "shunning," Scientology disconnections involve additional practices, such as former associates sending "disconnection letters" to ex-members.[21] In recent (2011) media interviews, current members of the Church of Scientology have adamantly denied the existence of the Church's disconnection policy.

This ill-advised policy has helped transform many otherwise neutral to moderately critical ex-members into devoted enemies of the Church. Research on apostates from other alternative religions has demonstrated that, on the whole, ex-members generally tend to be at least mildly positive about their membership years.[22] In my own research, I have also observed that many individuals who drop out of full-time involvement in a new religion would prefer to remain linked to the group as a part-time participant – if that option is available to them – and sometimes will later rejoin as a full-time member after a longer or shorter period of reflection outside of their former group. This scenario is obviously far less likely in a religious organization that adopts an attitude of sustained hostility toward former participants.

These policies help to explain the emergence and growth of the "Free Zone." The Free Zone refers to the large, but loosely organized community of people who consider themselves Scientologists, but who are not members of the Church of Scientology. Across the course of the sixty years of the Church's existence, tens of thousands of Scientologists have left the fold. Many of these former members left for personal or for organizational reasons, and continue to believe in Scientology as a religious philosophy. Because of Church policies toward ex-members, rapprochement with the Church of Scientology is extremely difficult, creating the conditions for the emergence of an independent Scientology community.

Over the years there have been numerous schisms and alternative organizations, some of which have been sued out of existence by the Church. At one point, Hubbard's own son left the Church to set up a more profitable private practice.[23] This led Hubbard to begin utilizing e-meter technology for "security checks" that identified potentially disloyal staff members. Hubbard also regularly sacked high-ranking Scientologists (most of whom subsequently left the Church) who he thought might one day challenge his authority.[24] One result of this pre-emptive policy – in combination with certain other ill-considered actions, such as the Mission Holder's Conference that led to the schism of 1982/83[25] – was to place numerous highly trained, upper-level Scientologists outside of Church control.

The emergence of the Internet within the past couple of decades has been a boon to the Free Zone. It has not only provided Freezoners with a forum for airing grievances against the Church, but the Internet has also provided more recent ex-members with points of contact for becoming affiliated with the Free Zone. Given the decline of the Church in recent years, it may well be that independent Scientologists will one day out-number members of the Church of Scientology.

NRM SCHOLARSHIP ON SCIENTOLOGY

The field of NRM studies as we know it in Western countries came into its own in the 1970s, though NRM studies had emerged several decades earlier in Japan in the wake of the explosion of religious innov-ation following the end of World War II. Even the name "new religions" is a direct translation of the expression *shin shukyo* that Japanese soci-ologists coined to refer to this phenomenon. Though the generation of new religious groups has been an ongoing process for millennia, the study of such groups and movements was the province of pre-existing academic specializations (e.g., social anthropology) in the West until the 1970s.

However, when a wave of non-traditional religiosity emerged out of the declining counterculture in the late 1960s and early 1970s, acad-emicians at first perceived it as representing a different phenomenon from prior cycles of religious innovation, and NRMs initially attracted scholars from a wide variety of disciplines interested in assessing the broader cultural significance of new religions. It was at this juncture that the study of NRMs began to develop as a distinct field of scholar-ship in Western countries.

This academic landscape changed over the course of the 1970s. By the latter part of the decade, it had become clear that new religions were *not* indicative of a broader social transformation – or at least not the kind of transformation observers had anticipated. During the 1970s, issues raised by the cult controversy – issues like conversion and "brainwash-ing" – gradually came to dominate the field. Because social conflict and social control are bread-and-butter issues for sociology, more and more sociologists were drawn to the study of new religions. By the end of the decade, the study of NRMs was a recognized specialization within the sociology of religion.[26]

The Church of Scientology was one of the first modern NRMs to be utilized as a case study in this new field. Some of the earliest ser-ious research was carried out by Roy Wallis. In his classic *The Road to*

Total Freedom, and in some of his articles,[27] Wallis used his research on Scientology as the basis for his theory of "sectarianization,"[28] which was a way of interpreting Scientology's transformation from an individualistic cult to an authoritarian sect. Wallis was also interested in developing a new typology for NRMs. In his schema, Scientology was a prominent example of a "world-affirming" (as opposed to a "world-rejecting" or a "world-accommodating") movement.[29]

In their "Of Churches, Sects and Cults," Rodney Stark and William Sims Bainbridge put forward another influential typology that classified cults into audience cults, client cults, and cult movements.[30] Comparable to Wallis' use of the cult–sect distinction, Stark and Bainbridge's tripartite classification was utilized by Paul Schnabel to describe the evolution of Scientology from the period of Hubbard as an audience cult leader (when his following was confined to readers of *Dianetics* and other early titles), to the formation of his fully blown cult movement – the Church of Scientology.[31] More recently, David G. Bromley has utilized the Church of Scientology to exemplify a "prophetic, contractual religion," which is a classification in his typology of religions.[32]

When new religious movements first became the subject of serious social-scientific inquiry in Western countries in the 1960s and 1970s, researchers initially focused on trying to understand how and why members became involved. Though the topic of conversion was gradually displaced from the center stage of NRM studies, it is still the single most discussed subject in the field. There is general agreement among researchers that such converts are disproportionately young. In Lorne Dawson's survey of NRM conversion studies,[33] he briefly covers the psychology of why people join alternative religions. Both of the studies he summarizes – Eileen Barker's study of the Unification Church[34] and Saul Levine's longitudinal study of NRM members[35] – portray involvement as a crisis of youth. However, data from James Lewis and Nicholas Levine's recent (2010) study of a high-demand group indicating that the average recruit is middle-aged calls this generalization into question.[36] There were, however, much earlier studies which should have prompted researchers to question the youth-crisis model decades ago, particularly the research reported in Wallis' *Road to Total Freedom*, which determined that the average age at which people joined Scientology was 32 years old.

As a major new religion that neither claims continuity with any prior religion (except for a tenuous parallel with Buddhism) nor asserts that it grows out of a special revelation, Scientology is an especially interesting case study for researchers analyzing this movement's claims to authority. Some observers have examined Scientology's appeal to the charismatic status of L. Ron Hubbard as a uniquely gifted individual.[37] A number of other observers have pointed out how Scientology appeals to the authority of science rather than to a religious tradition.[38] This mode of analysis has been brought to bear on the question, hotly debated in some countries, of whether Scientology should be regarded as a religion.[39] Additionally, the Church of Scientology is an obvious case study for the analysis of "invented traditions."[40]

Because it is so often embroiled in conflict, Scientology is also a useful case study for analyses of the "cult" controversy.[41] As part of a larger effort to discredit Scientology, critics have, as mentioned earlier, called attention to what they regard as the transparent absurdity of the Church's secret teachings. Scholars of religion normally feel bound to respect such prohibitions, but the fact that Scientology's "secret" teachings are now widely available on the Internet places them in a unique category. Mikael Rothstein has recently put forward an argument for why researchers should make the Church of Scientology an exception in this regard.[42] Additionally, the Church's efforts to control its own image have extended to academicians, which has provoked resentment and influenced at last some scholars to avoid researching Scientology – and even, in a few cases, to become dedicated critics of Scientology.[43]

THE FUTURE OF SCIENTOLOGY AND THE FUTURE OF SCHOLARSHIP ON SCIENTOLOGY

Prediction is always a problematic business, especially with regard to dynamic situations in which many variables can affect outcomes. Yet it is probably safe to assert that the quantity of scholarship on Scientology will increase. Scholars avoided undertaking extensive research projects on the Church for many years, in large part because of the kinds of interference Wallis and others encountered during their research. However, Church officials finally seem to have realized that their efforts to control what academicians write about Scientology does them more harm than good. Thus, for example, one of the most recent book-length treatments of the Church – my edited volume, *Scientology* (2009) – contained material judged to be "blasphemous" by members, yet neither I nor my publisher was threatened with legal action. This bodes well for the future of research on Scientology.

The future of the Church itself is less certain. I have observed this organization for over two dozen years. For most of that time, it seemed Scientology confronted every challenge, emerged victorious more often than not, and continued to grow and even thrive in the face of adversity. However, the relatively recent defection of large numbers of long-time, high-level Scientologists – some of the most experienced administrators and others with expertise in the highest levels of Scientology technology – bodes poorly for the future of the Church. In particular, the pattern of solid growth I analyzed just a few years ago seems suddenly to have ground to a halt.[44]

Based on the upgrading and expansion of its various worldwide centers over the past several years, the organization appears to be healthy from the outside. But funds for the upgrading of Church facilities (for the so-called "Ideal Orgs") have been generated almost entirely from new strategies for amplifying donations from current members.[45] For instance, new, slightly "corrected" editions of Hubbard's basic books have been issued, and Scientologists have been asked to purchase as many sets of volumes as they can afford so that complete sets can be donated to libraries across the globe. This has all been done in the name of the utopian ideal of "clearing the planet." But placing books in public libraries is a poor strategy for spreading any sort of message in a digital age.

Unless the Church is able to stop hemorrhaging top talent, stop burdening its congregants with increasingly heavy donations, and, more positively, develop better strategies for reaching new clients for Scientology services, it appears to be headed for a sharp decline in strength and numbers.[46]

Notes

1   Douglas Frantz, "Boston Man in Costly Fight with Scientology," *New York Times*, December 21, 1997, p. 24. Cited in Douglas Cowan, "Researching Scientology: Perceptions, Premises, Promises, and Problematics," in James R. Lewis (ed.), *Scientology* (New York, 2009), pp. 52–79, at p. 73. The quotation is from an interview with J. Gordon Melton.

2   For general information, refer to J. Gordon Melton, *The Church of Scientology* (Salt Lake City, UT, 2000); Lewis (ed.), *Scientology*; Dorthe Refslund Christensen, "Rethinking Scientology: Cognition and Representation in Religion, Therapy and Soteriology" (unpublished PhD dissertation, University of Aarhus, Denmark, 1999); Roy Wallis, *The Road to Total Freedom: A Sociological Analysis of Scientology* (New York, 1976); Harriet Whitehead, *Renunciation and Reformulation: A Study of Conversion in an American Sect* (Ithaca, NY, 1987).

3   Hubbard likely drew this expression from the title of Florence Scovel Shinn's 1925 popular New Thought book, *The Game of Life and How*

to Play It, though his notion was significantly different from Shinn's. For an overview of Hubbard's notion, refer to Harriet Whitehead, "Reasonably Fantastic: Some Perspectives on Scientology, Science Fiction, and Occultism," in Irving I. Zaretsky and Mark P. Leone (eds.), *Religious Movements in Contemporary America* (Princeton, 1974), pp. 547–87, and Whitehead, *Renunciation and Reformulation*.

4 Cowan, "Researching Scientology."

5 Wallis, *Road to Total Freedom*, p. 21n. 1.

6 Colin Campbell, "The Cult, the Cultic Milieu and Secularization," in *A Sociological Yearbook of Religion in Britain* 5 (London, 1972), pp. 119–36.

7 Will Durant, *The Story of Philosophy. The Lives and Opinions of the Greater Philosophers* (New York, 1926).

8 Gerald Willms, "Scientology: 'Modern Religion' or 'Religion of Modernity'?" in Lewis (ed.), *Scientology*, pp. 245–65.

9 L. Ron Hubbard, *Dianetics: The Modern Science of Mental Health* (New York, 1950).

10 Many critics, including certain national governments, have rejected Scientology's status as a religion. In part, this seems to be based on the "misunderstanding that once the label is granted to Scientology, then somehow one has approved of its basic goodness" as stated by Andreas Grünschloß in his "Scientology, a 'New Age' Religion?" in Lewis (ed.), *Scientology*, pp. 225–44, at p. 227. Once the "goodness" issue is set aside, it is obvious that Scientology is a religion – and it certainly functions as a religion in the lives of most members of the Church of Scientology (refer to the discussion ibid., p. 227). On the other hand, Hubbard regarded Dianetics-Scientology as a science rather than as a religion (as discussed in Willms, "Scientology"), meaning that Scientology was incorporated as a religion for pragmatic purposes.

11 Whitehead, *Renunciation and Reformation*, pp. 53–54.

12 Mikael Rothstein, "'His name was Xenu. He used renegades' Aspects of Scientology's Founding Myth," in Lewis (ed.), *Scientology*, pp. 365–88, at p. 383.

13 Whitehead, *Renunciation and Reformulation*, p. 170.

14 Ibid., p. 172.

15 Ibid., p. 185.

16 James R. Lewis, *Cults: A Reference Handbook* (Santa Barbara, 2005).

17 John Bowen Brown, "The Scientology Critic Group Anonymous: A Research Paper," paper presented at the CESNUR Conference, Salt Lake City, Utah, June 11–13, 2009.

18 L. Ron Hubbard, *HCO Policy Letter*, October 18, 1966. Cited in Wallis, *Road to Total Freedom*, p. 144.

19 Sir John G. Foster, *Enquiry into the Practice and Effects of Scientology* (London, 1971), p. 129. Cited in Wallis, *Road to Total Freedom*, p. 144.

20 Whitehead, *Renunciation and Reformulation*, p. 223n. 3.

21 As discussed in Wallis, *Road to Total Freedom*, pp. 144–45.

22 James R. Lewis, *Seeking the Light* (Los Angeles, 1998); James R. Lewis and Nicholas M. Levine, *Children of Jesus and Mary: A Study of the Order of Christ Sophia* (New York, 2010).

23 Wallis, *Road to Total Freedom*, p. 148.

24 Ibid., pp. 154–55.

25 Jon Atack, *A Piece of Blue Sky: Scientology, Dianetics and L. Ron Hubbard Exposed* (New York, 1990), part 7, ch. 1. It is generally agreed that it was the fallout from the Mission Holders' Conference that led to the emergence of Free Zone Scientology.

26 James R. Lewis (ed.), *Oxford Handbook of New Religious Movements* (New York, 2003).

27 Wallis, *Road to Total Freedom*; Roy Wallis, "Scientology: Therapeutic Cult to Religious Sect," *Sociology* 9:1 (1975), pp. 89–100; Roy Wallis "A Comparative Analysis of Problems and Processes of Change in Two Manipulationist Movements: Christian Science and Scientology," in *Contemporary Metamorphosis of Religion: Acts of the Twelfth International Conference for the Sociology of Religion* (Lille, 1973), pp. 407–22.

28 Inspired by Richard Niebuhr's theory of "denominationalism" as presented in Niebuhr's classic study, *The Social Sources of Denominationalism* (New York, 1929).

29 Roy Wallis, *The Elementary Forms of the New Religious Life* (London, 1984).

30 Rodney Stark and William Sims Bainbridge, "Of Churches, Sects and Cults," *Journal for the Scientific Study of Religion* 18 (1979), pp. 117–33.

31 Paul Schnabel, "Tussen Stigma en Charisma: Nieuwe Religieuze Bewegingen en Geestelijke Volksgezondheid/Between Stigma and Charisma: New Religious Movements and Mental Health" (unpublished PhD thesis, Faculty of Medicine, Erasmus University Rotterdam, Deventer, 1982, p. 82 and pp. 84–88).

32 David G. Bromley, "Making Sense of Scientology: A Prophetic, Contractual Religion," in Lewis (ed.), *Scientology*, pp. 83–101; David G. Bromley, "A Sociological Narrative of Crisis Episodes, Collective Action, Culture Workers, and Countermovements," *Sociology of Religion* 58 (1997), pp. 105–40.

33 Lorne L. Dawson, "Who Joins New Religions and Why: Twenty Years of Research and What Have We Learned?" in Dawson (ed.), *Cults and New Religions: A Reader* (Oxford, 2003), pp. 116–30.

34 Eileen Barker, *The Making of a Moonie: Choice or Brainwashing?* (Oxford, 1984).

35 Saul V. Levine, "Cults and Mental Health: Clinical Conclusions," *Canadian Journal of Psychiatry* 26:8 (1981), pp. 534–39; Saul V. Levine, *Radical Departures: Desperate Detours to Growing Up* (New York, 1984).

36 Lewis and Levine, *Children of Jesus and Mary*.

37 Dorthe Refslund Christensen, "Inventing L. Ron Hubbard: On the Construction and Maintenance of the Hagiographic Mythology on Scientology's Founder," in James R. Lewis and Jesper Aagaard Petersen (eds.), *Controversial New Religions* (New York, 2005), pp. 227–59.

38 For example, William Sims Bainbridge, "Science and Religion: The Case of Scientology," in David G. Bromley and Phillip E. Hammond (eds.), *The Future of New Religious Movements* (Macon, GA, 1987), pp. 59–79;

James R. Lewis, *Legitimating New Religions* (New Brunswick, NJ, 2003); Mikael Rothstein, "Science and Religion in the New Religions," in Lewis (ed.), *Oxford Handbook*, pp. 99–118; James R. Lewis, "The Science Canopy: Religion, Legitimacy, and the Charisma of Science," *Temenos* 46:1 (2010), pp. 7–29; Régis Dericquebourg, "Legitimizing Belief through the Authority of Science: The Case of the Church of Scientology," in James R. Lewis and Olav Hammer (eds.) *Religion and the Authority of Science* (Leiden, 2011), pp. 741–62.

39 For example, Willms, "Scientology."
40 Mikael Rothstein, "Scientology, Scripture, and Sacred Tradition," in James R. Lewis and Olav Hammer (eds.), *The Invention of Sacred Tradition* (Cambridge, 2007), pp. 18–37.
41 For example, Anson Shupe, "The Nature of the New Religious Movements – Anticult 'Culture War' in Microcosm: The Church of Scientology versus the Cult Awareness Network," in Lewis (ed.), *Scientology*, pp. 269–81; James T. Richardson, "Scientology in Court: A Look at Some Major Cases from Various Nations," in Lewis (ed.), *Scientology*, pp. 283–94; Susan J. Palmer, "The Church of Scientology in France: A History of Legal and Activist Responses to the Forces of Anti-cultism and the Government-Sponsored 'War on Sectes'," in Lewis (ed.), *Scientology*, pp. 295–322.
42 Rothstein, "His name was Xenu."
43 Cowan, "Researching Scientology."
44 James R. Lewis, "The Growth of Scientology and the Stark Model of Religious 'Success'," in Lewis (ed.), *Scientology*, pp. 117–40.
45 Geir Isene, a Norwegian OT VIII who left the Church not too many years ago, has been highly critical of the emphasis on new buildings that constitute the centerpiece of the Ideal Org program, accusing the new building program of being itself a covert strategy for enriching the Church. In Isene's words, "I find the Ideal Org program to be a scam where the church tries to add to its value of assets by pressuring its public for money with no exchange back." (www.isene.com/GeirIseneDoubtCoS. pdf [accessed December 2011]). He cites L. Ron Hubbard in support of his critique: "When buildings get important to us, for God's sake, some of you born revolutionists, will you please blow up central headquarters." Hubbard Tape: *The Genus of Scientology*, December 31, 1960 (from The Anatomy of the Human Mind Congress).
46 According to the pseudonymous "Plockton," who contacted the ARIS (American Religious Identification Survey) researchers directly, the ARIS estimate for the number of Scientologists in the USA for 2008 was 25,000. This contrasts sharply with the figure of 55,000 from the 2001 ARIS survey. ("2008 ARIS Study on Scientology Membership in US – Important Data." Posted March 28, 2009 at: http://ocmb.xenu. net/ocmb/viewtopic.php?t=30372.) The drop in total numbers was likely less dramatic than these figures indicate (due to sampling issues discussed by Plockton in his posting). The 2011 national censuses in the UK, Canada, New Zealand, and Australia will produce figures for total numbers of self-identified Scientologists. It will thus be relatively

simple to contrast these numbers with comparable data from the 2001 censuses (for Canada and the UK) and from the 2006 censuses (for Australia and New Zealand). The net figures derived from these comparisons should indicate decisively whether membership in the Church of Scientology is growing, declining, or stagnating.

Further reading

Lewis, James R. (ed.), *Scientology* (New York, 2009).

Melton, J. Gordon, *The Church of Scientology* (Salt Lake City, UT, 2000).

Urban, Hugh B., *The Church of Scientology: A History of a New Religion* (Princeton, NJ, 2011).

Wallis, Roy, *The Road to Total Freedom: A Sociological Analysis of Scientology* (New York, 1976).

Whitehead, Harriet, *Renunciation and Reformulation: A Study of Conversion in an American Sect* (Ithaca, NY, 1987).

9 Neopaganism

SABINA MAGLIOCCO

INTRODUCTION

Neopaganism, also called modern Paganism or simply Paganism, is an umbrella term for a number of new religious movements that strive to revive, reinterpret, and experiment with pre-Christian polytheistic religions. While the impulse to revive ancient forms of worship is widespread in the early twenty-first century, this term is usually reserved for those groups that focus on the ancient religions of Europe, the Near East, and North Africa, although they can also be inspired by the indigenous religions of Africa and the Americas. Necessarily, this group of religions is broad and eclectic; thus it is more correct to speak of modern Paganisms in the plural. Neopagans share a desire to reconnect with nature, community, and the sacred, a view of the divine as immanent, and a search for religious experience that is personal, direct, and embodied. They generally lack a single codified scared text or charismatic leader. Drawing heavily from traditional folklore in their creation of rituals, their goal is the re-enchantment of the world and the creation of a personalized relationship with divinity.

"Pagan" comes from the Latin word *paganus*, meaning "country-dweller." When Christianity became the dominant religion of the late Roman Empire in the fourth and fifth centuries, the word came to be used to designate those who were not Christian and identified with the *pagus*, or rural territory, rather than with the state. The word had also acquired the slang connotation of "civilian" among Roman soldiers, and was picked up by Christians to refer to those who had not joined the army of God.[1] The term "heathen," preferred by some modern Pagan religions inspired by Germanic and Scandinavian practices, is similarly problematic in its derivation. While often explained as designating those who lived out on the heath and continued to practice the older

Parts of this chapter are substantially similar to the chapter "Pagans" by the same author, in Graham Harvey (ed.), *Religions in Focus* (London, 2009), pp. 101–20.

religion, this may be a folk etymology. The *Oxford English Dictionary* does not link it to the word "heath," but to the Gothic term for followers of non-Christian religions. The term eventually spread to speakers of other Germanic languages. Regardless of the linguistic derivation of the terms, by the nineteenth century, both "pagan" and "heathen" had acquired nostalgic, Romantic associations with nature and the rural world left behind by the Industrial Revolution.[2] Romantic poets and literary authors saw in them a balm for the alienation brought about by the ills of urbanization, the domination of state structures, and monotheistic religions, in particular Christianity. The term "pagan" came to be associated with the celebration of nature and the sensuous, qualities which had long been distrusted as "feminine" and marginalized by science and the Enlightenment. The term "neo-pagan" originated as a critique of these literary tropes by authors such as W. F. Barry and G. K. Chesterton.[3] It was picked up again by American author Tim Zell in the 1970s to designate the character of his own branch of modern Paganism, the Church of All Worlds, and is now used by social scientists studying the movement in order to distinguish it from ancient paganism. Today, some modern Pagans reject the designation "neopagan," preferring to stress the continuities between their practices and those of ancient and indigenous peoples embodied by the use of the word "Pagan." This chapter will use both terms interchangeably.

THE DEVELOPMENT OF MODERN PAGANISMS

The roots of modern Paganisms lie in the notion of an enchanted universe common to all ancient and indigenous religions. But that link is indirect and complex, interrupted by a series of movements, both religious and secular, that separated Westerners from local, nature-based spiritualities for many centuries. Some of these traditional concepts and practices continued to exist in vernacular magic and in customs associated with seasonal festivals. Yet neopaganisms as practiced today are also new religious movements whose origins can clearly be traced to the late nineteenth and early twentieth centuries, a period of great religious and spiritual ferment in Europe and North America.

Scholars have studied modern Paganisms as revitalizations (social movements that emerge during periods of marked social transformation, and attempt to change society by introducing new worldviews),[4] as well as revived religions, a term that presupposes their link to past religions.[5] Modern Paganisms share the practice of reclamation, the revaluing and recasting of discarded or devalued traditions for the purpose of creating a new identity. Reclamation, part of the process of tradition, encompasses revitalization and revival as well as the creation of new cultural forms out of what was previously rejected.[6]

The revival of paganism can be traced to the European Enlightenment and its rediscovery of elements of Classical culture, including Greek and Roman art, literature and deities. England saw the emergence of various orders of druids, who reinterpreted the ancient priests of Britain and Gaul as keepers of secret wisdom and forces of resistance against Roman domination. While these early druid societies were not primarily religious in nature, they nevertheless had a strong spiritual component. They created a link in the popular imagination between the ancient Celtic order and prehistoric monuments by conducting rituals at Stonehenge, which was then thought to be a druid construction.[7]

The nineteenth-century Romantic revival contributed two additional discourses to the emergence of modern Paganisms: the revaluation of nature and its personification in the Greek god Pan and an earth mother goddess, and the revisionist interpretation of European witchcraft as the vestige of an ancient pre-Christian nature religion.[8] According to this explanation, the witch persecutions that had racked the early modern period were based on misinterpretations of what had been an ancient fertility religion that venerated a horned god and an earth mother goddess. Medieval clerics had mistaken the horned god for the devil, fertility rites for perversions, and healing philters for evil spells. While it originated with the Frenchman Jules Michelet, this interpretation was popularized by British folklorist Margaret Murray through her books *The Witch Cult of Western Europe* (1923) and *The God of the Witches* (1935). These in turn influenced Gerald B. Gardner, a British civil servant who had spent much of his life in Borneo and Malaysia, but returned to England in the mid 1930s. In 1954, he published *Witchcraft Today*, a book in which he claimed to have discovered a coven of witches practicing in southern England according to the pattern described by Murray, and made their practices known to the world.

Scholars disagree about the existence of such a group. Gardner was a member of several esoteric circles around Bournemouth in the 1930s and 1940s, and it is entirely possible that their members had formed a society devoted to practicing magic before Gardner came upon it and interpreted it as a witch cult. However, two things are certain: the first is that if such a group indeed existed, its history did not go back much further than the early twentieth century, as its early texts draw heavily from ceremonial magic books of the period. The second is that by the mid 1950s, Gardner had himself formed a witches' coven. He became a great promoter of his new religion, appearing on many popular radio and television programs and even founding a witchcraft museum on the Isle of Man (which has since been moved to Boscastle, Cornwall).[9] By the time of his death in 1963, numerous covens existed in England, some of which claimed to have independent origins, and a few of his followers had migrated to the United States, bringing with them what came to be called Wicca or "Gardnerian" Craft.[10]

The 1960s was a critical decade for the expansion of neopaganism. The counterculture, with its rejection of all that was staid, conventional, and mainstream, created an atmosphere in which people were eager to experiment with new ways of worship. Colleges and universities, as centers of learning, free speech, and liberal ideals, became hubs around which interest in modern Paganism flourished. A number of neopagan groups were formed originally by university students. Just as many of the foundational texts for the neopagan movement came out of early twentieth-century academic culture, the creators and practitioners of modern Paganism have strong ties with the academy.

Because of its emphasis on a feminine divinity and availability of key liturgical roles for women, revival Witchcraft appealed to feminists who were searching for alternatives to patriarchal religions. The second-wave feminist movement inspired authors Zsuzsanna "Z" Budapest and Starhawk (Miriam Simos) to create variants of Pagan Witchcraft that foregrounded feminist ideals and women's spiritual development. Budapest's Dianic Witchcraft featured women-only covens centered on the worship of the goddess Diana where women could experience freedom from male dominance and explore their personal spirituality. Starhawk, a key founder of the Reclaiming tradition, saw the oppression of women as linked to a patriarchal system of domination that included the exploitation of the earth. In Reclaiming covens, women and men work together to bring about political and social change, using ritual as an important tool to change consciousness.[11]

By the late 1980s, the definitive collapse of the myth of Wicca as a descendant of a pre-Christian pagan religion, and disillusion with the eclectic nature of modern Pagan Witchcraft, led to a yearning among some practitioners to reconnect with the historical religious practices of pre-Christian European peoples. This resulted first in the emergence of ethnically based modern Witchcraft practices, such as Raymond Buckland's "Seax Wicca," which is allegedly based on Anglo-Saxon practices,[12] Raven Grimassi's "Stregheria," based on Italian magical traditions,[13] and numerous strains of "Celtic" Witchcraft. By the 1990s, a number of traditions had moved away from modern Witchcraft altogether, seeking instead to reconstruct as accurately as possible the practices of specific ancient religions within the parameters of a modern sensibility. Among the earliest were the various branches of Heathen traditions focused on revitalizing the religions of Scandinavia and Northern Europe, based on practices in the *Elder Edda* and the Norse sagas. These were followed by reconstructionist Celtic, Kemetic (Egyptian), and Hellenic traditions. Celtic reconstructionism includes various types of modern Druidry. Around the same time, a number of Pagans began experimenting with methods of spirit communication inspired by shamanism, leading to an element of neo-shamanism that cuts across Wiccan and reconstructionist traditions. The arrival of the Internet in the mid 1990s further contributed to the expansion of modern Paganisms,[14] making them some of the fastest-growing religious movements of the early twenty-first century.

NEOPAGAN TENETS AND PRACTICES

Modern Pagans perceive sacredness in nature and the seasonal cycle, and believe ancient pagans lived in greater harmony with the earth than modern, post-industrial Westerners. On one level, neopaganism is a reaction against the excesses of modernity: Pagans tend to see contemporary life as alienating human beings from nature, the sacred, and a feeling of kinship to other human beings and life forms. Their rituals and other forms of religious practice attempt to heal this rift, re-creating the harmony and connectedness they imagine once existed in the religions of their ancestors. Yet neopaganism is itself a product of modernity, urbanization, the development of individualism and modern concepts of personal growth and self-realization. This paradox lies at the heart of modern Pagan religions.

Neopagan religions are unified by a set of attitudes and practices, but do not have common beliefs or sacred texts. The most widely shared outlooks are a feeling of connection to the natural world and a search for personal, ecstatic, and embodied spiritual experiences. The most important shared practice is ritual. Neopagans tend to ritualize many aspects of life, both as a way of sacralizing the everyday and as a pathway to religious ecstasy and embodied experiences of the sacred. Most celebrate a variety of seasonal festivals, and some denominations also mark the cycles of the moon. Many modern Pagan traditions also celebrate life-cycle rites for their members, including the birth of a child, a young person's coming of age, a formal union with a romantic partner, and the remembrance of life upon an individual's death. Some traditions of Paganism are mystery religions that require members to undergo initiation in order to fully participate; these constitute another type of rite of passage. Finally, at times of crisis, Pagans may either singly or in groups perform rites to address the situation and bring about a resolution.

Neopagans perceive the sacred as both immanent and transcendent. It is present in nature and in every living thing, including humans; yet it extends beyond the material world to include unseen entities such as gods and goddesses, elemental spirits, nature spirits and, for some Pagans, a single universal force that manifests through these other spirit forms. The idea of nature as sacred is central to modern Pagans; for this reason, neopagans sometimes refer to their traditions as "nature religions" or "earth-based religions." Most forms of Paganism recognize the sacredness of four Aristotelian elements: air, fire, water, and earth. Some see the planet itself as a living organism, the embodiment of a nurturing goddess. Humans are thought to partake of this sacredness; the body is perceived as holy, and human sexuality is a manifestation of the creative, generative force that lies at the center of existence. Modern Pagan religions generally celebrate all forms of sexuality and have few rules restricting its expression between consenting adults. This emphasis on the body extends to a search for an embodied spirituality: Pagans seek spiritual experiences they can feel in their bodies through such activities as dancing, drumming, chanting, song, sacred sexuality, and occasionally through the use of mind-altering substances. Neopagan religions also share a search for a direct, personal, individualized experience of the sacred, an emphasis on spirituality as a path to personal development and self-realization, a distrust of religious hierarchy and dogma, and a tendency to borrow elements from a variety of different cultural and religious sources in their quest to construct a spirituality that is personally meaningful.

Most Pagans believe that rituals can bring about transformations, though they differ in their interpretations of how this takes place. Commonly, the transformation is said to occur within the individual's consciousness, changing perceptions of reality and leading to greater spiritual development. Some think the rites themselves have power, while others see them as symbolic statements that work on the psyches of the individuals concerned as a form of spiritual therapy. This range of attitudes also applies to sacred figures such as goddesses, gods, and nature spirits: while some Pagans see them as having an independent existence, others interpret them as human projections, symbols, or aspects of the self. Neopagans share few beliefs about the afterlife; they emphasize life in the present, rather than life after death. Many Wiccans believe in a form of reincarnation: after a period of rest in a pleasant afterworld, sometimes called the Summerland, souls are reborn into healthier bodies in the company of those whom they loved in previous lives. Others believe that the dead become part of some greater spiritual force or energy, but lose individuality and personality. Still others have no particular beliefs about life after death, although many think that the dead can occasionally communicate with the living, particularly with loved ones and descendants. Neopagans generally do not believe in afterlife rewards or punishments for deeds done in this life. In these religions, the consequences of moral violations occur in the present world.

Folklore plays a significant role in modern Paganisms, in that it is regarded as a repository for bits and pieces of ancient religion that survived to the present day. Because neopagans locate authenticity in ancient religions, folklore becomes an important index of authenticity, and a way to reconnect with the past. Many modern Pagans are knowledgeable and well versed in folklore, especially European lore, which has been collected and documented since the late eighteenth century. Significantly, the Romantic, survivalist approach of the early collectors, who saw in folklore the remnants of knowledge and customs from ancient pre-Christian societies, appeals to neopagans because it allows them to use folklore to attempt to reconstruct the practices of ancient pagan religions and cultures.

WHO ARE MODERN PAGANS?

It is difficult to generalize about such a broad and individualistic group of religions, but studies have shown that in Europe and North America, neopagans are better educated than average, slightly more likely to be female than male (about 60 to 40 percent), and earn lower average incomes than their degree of education would warrant. This may be because modern Pagans tend to study subjects like the humanities, in which high-paying jobs are not easily available; because many prefer to make a living at creative endeavors, such as the arts, that do not provide high salaries; and because they often value creativity and service to others over high earnings. Although there are a few Pagan intentional communities, for the most part, Pagans do not separate themselves from the surrounding populace. While they may live in cities, suburbs, or the countryside, they are often concentrated in urban areas and university towns, where there is greater tolerance for nonconformism. More Pagans than average tend to identify as other than heterosexual. This may be in part because these religions lack the judgmental attitudes towards non-mainstream sexuality which characterize some established religions, and thus attract gay, lesbian, bisexual, and transgendered individuals searching for religious community; but it could also reflect the generally non-conformist and experimental nature of neopagans, who may have partners of both genders over the course of a lifetime. Some Modern Pagans also embrace alternative practices such as vegetarianism, naturism, holistic and herbal healing, astrology, yoga, and unconventional sexual practices such as polyamory and polyfidelity.

The first generation of modern Pagans were not born into these religions, but came to them as young adults, as a result of reading, political and social interests, friendships, and, increasingly, the influence of the Internet. Today, there are a growing number of second- and third-generation Pagans who grew up in Pagan families. The basic unit of Pagan social organization is the small group. These groups, called covens, circles, or groves, typically consist of between three and fifteen individuals, meet regularly to worship in each other's homes, public parks, or rented spaces, such as community halls and church basements. They may affiliate with larger denominational groups with whom they share a liturgy, practice, and ritual style. Pagan networking organizations bring together many different denominations to pursue common interests, engage in political and social activism, and do charitable work; three of the most prominent are the International Pagan Federation, the Pagan Alliance, and Covenant of the Goddess. Neopagans have also played an important role in the Global Interfaith movement, an association that strives for inter-religious understanding and cooperation.

Despite the existence of these groups, the majority of neopagans may choose not to affiliate with any group or organization, preferring to practice their spirituality individually. Occasionally, these "solitaries," as they are called, attend a ritual, festival, or camp organized by one of the larger groups or networking organizations. "Moots" are another feature of Pagan social networks; these informal but regularly occurring meetings in coffeehouses and pubs are generally open to all interested parties, and are a way for Pagans to get to know one another before committing to joining a particular group or denomination. The Internet plays a significant role in Pagan social interactions, as well, with over 20,000 websites and chat rooms devoted to Pagan topics.[15] Online Pagan groups on listservs and social networking sites such as Facebook and Twitter serve as important sources of information, community, and support. There is some evidence that younger Pagans are increasingly using the Internet to form communities rather than joining face-to-face groups, as early neopagans did throughout the twentieth century.

There is no single unifying authority or charismatic leader recognized by all neopagans. Modern Pagan religions are non-exclusive and informal; members may belong to a variety of groups and denominations with no apparent contradictions or conflicting loyalties. Some belong simultaneously to other religious communities; for example, it is not unusual to find Pagans of Jewish ancestry who feel culturally Jewish, but spiritually Pagan. At the same time, neopaganism often overlaps with a number of non-spiritual communities, including historical re-enactment societies, fantasy role-playing gamers, fans of science fiction and fantasy literature, folk musicians, feminists, environmentalists, the Goth subculture, and the New Age movement. Because of the fluidity and informality of the movement, it is difficult to estimate the exact number of practitioners. According to some estimates, there are about 1 million neopagans worldwide,[16] although some believe the actual number is far greater.

TYPES OF MODERN PAGAN RELIGIONS

Neopagan religions as a whole are eclectic and syncretic, combining material from a wide variety of sources, including Western occultism, Eastern religions, science fiction and fantasy novels and television programs, popular psychology, and academic research on anthropology, archaeology and folklore. Most, however, are inspired by one particular pre-Christian religion, or by the traditions of a specific national or regional group. Often, Pagans are attracted to traditions with which they feel a connection because of their own ethnic background.

In Europe, modern Paganisms can be tied to national and regional notions of identity and concepts of place. For neopagans in Latvia, Lithuania, and Russia, the revival of traditional folkloric and religious practices served as an important expression of national identity after the collapse of Soviet domination.[17] In Greece, the Ellinais, or Holy Association of Greek Ancient Religion Believers, successfully lobbied for state recognition of the ancient Greek religion by staging rituals and demonstrations at the Parthenon and other important national heritage sites. Stone circles and prehistoric monuments play an important role for British Pagans, many of whom consider the sites sacred and conduct both personal and public devotional rites there.[18] A small number of groups combine nationalism with racist ideologies, but they are far outnumbered by those that espouse liberal views and are open to members of any national or ethnic background. While European groups often draw inspiration from the ancestral religions of their own regions, even these are by necessity eclectic, drawing upon a variety of sources to reconstruct lost aspects of religious practice.

In the pluralistic societies of North America, Pagans are strongly influenced both by notions of ancestral religion and by surrounding cultures. There is a predominance of Celtic-inspired revival Witchcraft and Paganism, but those who live in cities with a large Afro-Caribbean population may incorporate elements of *orisha* worship into their work, while throughout California, the strong Latino presence makes itself felt in elaborate ancestor altars inspired by Mexican *Dia de los Muertos* observations. The borrowing or imitation of Native American sacred practices has caused friction between North American neopagans and many Native American groups, who perceive this as the ultimate form of disrespect and violation. As a result, the incidence of this type of cultural hybridity is decreasing as neopagans become more sensitive to Native American concerns. Specific ethnic traditions are also gaining popularity. North America too has its share of racist Pagan groups, some of which developed in prisons and espouse a white supremacist ideology.[19] However, the vast majority of ethnically based American neopagan traditions strongly oppose racism and are open to members of all ethnicities.

One of the most important distinctions Pagans make among themselves is between those who consider themselves Witches and those that do not. Witches, also called Wiccans, constitute the largest percentage of modern Pagans. While only a small percentage can trace their lineage directly to Gerald Gardner's covens, the majority have been strongly influenced by Gardnerian Craft in the structure of their rituals, their ritual year, and their general liturgical patterns. Witches generally recognize a goddess and a god as embodiments of the feminine and masculine principles in nature. Their symbolic union is celebrated at monthly coven meetings, which take place at the time of the full moon, and at eight yearly sabbats, which occur on the solstices, equinoxes, and on the days falling roughly between them: November 1, February 1, May 1, and August 1. Of all the modern Pagan groups, Wiccans are the most magic-oriented, in that they recognize magic as a natural force and regularly incorporate it into their rituals.

There are various denominations, or "traditions," of modern Witchcraft. British traditional Craft, which includes Gardnerian and Alexandrian Witchcraft, traces its ancestry directly back to either Gerald Gardner or Alex Sanders, promoters of the religion who lived in England in the mid twentieth century. There are also various ethnic varietals of Witchcraft, each claiming descent from the folk practices of a specific European ethnic or national group; for example, Seax Wicca draws from Anglo-Saxon religious practices, while Stregheria claims a connection to Italian, and ultimately Etruscan, polytheism. On the other hand, eclectic Witchcraft traditions may draw from the pantheons and folk practices of a variety of peoples, combining them according to their own aesthetic pleasure.

There are also a substantial number of non-Wiccan Pagan groups. While some, like the Church of All Worlds, are eclectic in their orientation, others center on the traditions of a specific culture area or ancient tradition. Thus, for example, the Fellowship of Isis focuses on an Egyptian pantheon; various Druid orders are inspired by the practices of the ancient Celtic priestly class; and Heathenry comprises a group of Pagan traditions reviving a Norse heritage. For these neopagans, ritual and magic are not synonymous. Instead, ritual may be seen as a way to connect with ancient pagan traditions, to experience the world as the ancients did, or it may be predominantly devotional. Among the fastest-growing neopagan traditions in the early twenty-first century are reconstructionist traditions. These practitioners seek as much authenticity as possible in their recreations of ancient pagan ceremonies, although they stop short of re-enacting rites that are violent or harmful to humans. Members may study ancient languages and texts to gain information about the organization and practice of ancient religions.

Finally, some modern Pagans pursue shamanic paths inspired by the healing traditions of indigenous peoples. Here, shamanism is broadly interpreted as any practice involving communication with the spirit world, usually in an alternate state of consciousness, for the purpose of healing. Neopagan shamans generally interpret healing to include personal spiritual growth and development, as well as larger goals such as healing the ecological damage humans have done to the earth. They may communicate with spirit helpers, who often take the form of animals, in their ceremonies.

PAGAN PRACTICES

Modern Pagans seek nothing short of the re-enchantment of the universe: to re-create the kind of relationship they imagine their ancestors had with the sacred, in which the universe was animated by forces that could be influenced through ceremonies, rituals, and prayers. Many traditions use magic, which they interpret as a natural force, to create and develop this sense of enchantment. Definitions of magic vary within the movement, but a commonly accepted one is "the art of changing consciousness at will." Modern Pagans believe that by changing human consciousness, the true, enchanted nature of the universe can be revealed, and humans can align themselves with it and live in greater harmony. Some believe that magic can directly affect the outcome of events, beyond just changing individuals' consciousness and perceptions. Most Pagans see everything in the universe as infused with a life force, or energy, which can be raised, manipulated, and directed by knowledgeable practitioners. Pagans may perform magic in order to enhance their chances of getting the results they want – for example, to help them find a job, sell their house, or undertake an important project, as well as to heal the sick or bring about planetary harmony and healing. The majority also recognize that magic alone is not enough to bring about results, and that actions must be taken in the material world in order to effect change. An ethical code governs the practice of magic in most traditions. It is often summarized by two principles: "Do what you will, but harm none"; and the Threefold Law, a principle whereby what one puts out into the world is believed to return threefold. Therefore, generous and caring actions will eventually bring positive consequences, while selfish and immoral ones will have serious negative repercussions. Nearly all modern Pagan religions forbid the use of magic to coerce or manipulate others.

Because Pagans see the universe as interconnected, they may practice forms of divination such as tarot-card reading and astrology, believing that larger patterns mirror smaller ones, and vice versa. Divination is sometimes interpreted as reflecting the will of the gods regarding some matter. A number of Norse Pagan traditions have revived an oracular practice known as *seidr*, in which a priestess answers questions and makes predictions in a trance state.[20] Her pronouncements are understood to be divinely inspired.

Ritual is central to the practice of most modern Pagans. Even those denominations that do not practice magic hold regular rituals or worship services. Much of the purpose of monthly and seasonal festivities is to help re-create a sense of connection between practitioners and the natural cycles around them, imparting a sense of mystery to natural processes and connecting them to human development and desires. Thus the cycle of the seasons, with its rhythms of birth, growth, fruitfulness, death, and regeneration, is equated to phases in the human life cycle, and to the natural progression of any project or undertaking. Rituals also connect modern Pagans with their predecessors in history, even if they understand that the rites were not practiced in exactly the same way. They form a bridge through time and space, connecting the modern world with the ancient, technology with nature, and human with divine.

The majority of modern Pagans do not have a specially designated place of worship, such as a temple or church; they hold rituals in private homes and gardens, in public parks and rented halls. Ordinary space must be consecrated for the spiritual work that will take place, so most rituals begin by creating sacred space. This may be done through purification, for example by sprinkling the perimeter of the location with salt water that has been blessed, then censing it. Pagans usually worship in a circle, and many traditions cast the circle by having a priestess or priest walk its perimeter bearing a sacred knife, sword, or staff and physically marking off the sacred space for all to see. Once the space has been purified and marked, the four elements (air, fire, water, and earth) and cardinal directions (east, south, west, and north) may be invoked, goddesses, gods, and other spirits may be called into the sacred space, and practitioners may interact with them in various ways, depending on the rite's purpose. The core of the ceremony usually involves what Pagans call "raising energy" and directing it towards a specific goal. That goal may be summarized in a statement of the rite's intent, such as "Today is Midsummer's Day, and we dance to celebrate the bounty of the earth at the peak of the growing season," or "We work today to send healing energy to [name of person] and to all others who need it at this time." Energy may be raised in a variety of ways: through body movement, dancing, chanting or singing, meditation, drumming, or some combination of these. All rituals have a strong participatory element, which often aims to personalize the rite's message and allow for individual input. Pagans greatly value this participatory, egalitarian aspect of their ceremonies; it is part of what connects them with the sacred. Once the work of ritual is done, and the energy has been directed towards a specific goal, the deities and other spiritual forces are thanked and released, the circle is opened, and all return to ordinary time and space. Many traditions, especially Wiccan ones, include a ceremonial meal of cakes and wine at the end of the rite.

The search for direct contact with the sacred is central to many rituals. To this end, rituals are frequently designed to bring about alternate states of consciousness in which participants enter the realm of their imagination and commune directly with gods and other spiritual entities. Rituals can be colorful, stimulating, and filled with music, dance, dramatic performances, storytelling, and other cues that transform the everyday world and encourage participants to enter into a mild trance state. At these times, Pagans may experience religious ecstasy, a feeling of being outside of the ordinary world and in touch with something sacred, mystical, and profound. Each individual experiences this differently, and experiences may likewise differ greatly from one ritual occasion to the next. They range from deep insights into the practitioner's life and spirituality, to messages perceived as coming directly from the gods, to states in which the individual becomes filled with divine spirit and embodies the divinity. Some Wiccan traditions practice deity possession: the spirit of the goddess or god is invoked into the body of a priestess or priest, and the practitioner then speaks and behaves as the deity for the duration of the rite. Ecstatic states are central to many Pagan rituals: while not everyone achieves religious ecstasy during every ritual, individuals yearn for and look forward to this aspect of ceremonies. Religious ecstasy makes beliefs real for practitioners; it also personalizes the religion, allowing each participant to be a priestess or priest and communicate directly with gods. Pagan rituals can also be light-hearted and imaginative, drawing inspiration from science-fiction television programs, comic-strip characters, and other elements of pop culture.

Many Pagans are extremely creative, artistic individuals, and modern Pagan rituals can be elaborate pieces of performance art, complete with costumes and props. For this reason, religious material culture is important to modern Pagans. This artistic impulse finds expression through the construction of temporary and permanent ritual altars, robes, and sacred objects used in ritual. Altars serve as portals between the human and divine worlds – places where relationships to the deities are imagined, negotiated, and maintained. Practitioners may leave offerings there for their tutelary spirits, work magic spells, meditate, pray, and perform other religious activities. Domestic altars are always changing, in that they reflect the current concerns of their makers. Some become quite elaborate; quite a few neopagans have transformed their entire homes and gardens into sacred spaces that reflect their personal spiritual paths.[21]

Like members of other modern subcultures, neopagans create identity through consumption, and may recognize one another through their jewelry, clothing, music, books, home décor, and other aspects of material culture. To keep Pagans supplied with the accoutrements for their religious practice, a large industry has sprung up providing everything from sacred statuary and jewelry to liturgical robes and music, not to mention necessary altar items such as incense, charcoal, candles, anointing oils (to bless candles and other items), pentacles, wands, and ritual knives. Much of this is produced by Pagans, for Pagans, and consists of hand-crafted objects; other items, such as music CDs and books, are mass-produced and marketed, but also originate as divine inspiration. Pagans buy these items through the Internet, at local occult and craft shops, and at Pagan festivals and camps, where the vendors' stalls are always popular destinations.

Most neopagans live surrounded by what they sometimes call "mundane" or "cowan" culture – people who do not share their practices and views, and who may not even know their neighbors, co-workers and associates are Pagan. In many cases, they must keep their religious identity concealed in mainstream settings because of intense prejudice: Pagans have lost jobs, child custody disputes, homes, and businesses because of their unconventional religion. However, they have recently won a number of court victories that illustrate their religions are becoming more accepted, or at least that the principles of religious freedom in modern liberal democracies are working in their favor.

Pagan festivals and camps serve as contexts in which they can freely express their religious identities in a setting that celebrates and glories in them. These events typically take place in the warmer months, and are usually outdoor events at primitive camping facilities. They feature daily workshops on a variety of topics, as well as scholarly lectures, musical performances, dances, and, of course, rituals. These events play a key role in the diffusion of ritual elements, chants, songs, and magical techniques, and act as important venues for networking. They are usually sponsored by Pagan networking organizations. Reclaiming's Witch Camps have now acquired a global presence, with branches all over North America, in Europe, and in Australia.[22] Away from the pressures of their workday lives and surrounded by the beauty of the natural world, Pagans are more able to fully experience religious ecstasy, spiritual growth, and communion with the sacred and with community. Camps and festivals are also places where Pagans can fully perform their religious identities, wearing elaborate robes and jewelry (or nothing at all, at clothing-optional retreats), decorating their campsites with altars and shrines to their tutelary deities, and using sacred names that connect them to their religious and spiritual beliefs.[23]

Ultimately, most Pagans believe religious convictions must be taken beyond the confines of the sacred circle, festival, and campsite and into the world in order to bring about real, lasting change. Some traditions include among their teachings a directive that members contribute to the world in proportion to what they have received. For this reason, a large number of Pagans participate in volunteer activities of various sorts, from community clean-ups in parks, reservoirs, and heritage sites, to political actions and demonstrations, to interfaith work that allows them to work with clergy from other faiths to achieve humanitarian goals. Many feminist and environmental organizations draw Pagan participation, as do community health-oriented projects such as soup kitchens and clean needle exchanges for drug addicts. Pagans who feel a strong connection to animals may work on animal conservation and welfare issues. For modern Pagans, there is no contradiction between the practice of magic and involvement in grass-roots causes; political action is in fact a form of magic, a way to change consciousness and reality, and an extension of religious expression.

Although they may practice magic and see the world around them as animated by spiritual forces, Pagans do not reject science; in fact, a large number are employed in the fields of technology and health care.[24] Pagan religions seek to recreate the magical universe they attribute to ancient and indigenous religions, but with a modern perspective that includes science. Spirituality becomes a vehicle for self-realization, personal growth, and perfecting the self, bringing humans closer to the gods and becoming one with them.

Notes

1   Robin Lane Fox, *Pagans and Christians* (San Francisco, 1986), pp. 30–31.
2   Ronald Hutton, *Triumph of the Moon: A History of Modern Pagan Witchcraft* (Oxford, 1999), p. 4.
3   Ibid., pp. 28–29.
4   Anthony F. C. Wallace, "Revitalization Movements," *American Anthropologist* 58:2 (1956), pp. 264–81.
5   See Loretta Orion, *Never Again the Burning Times: Paganism Revived* (Prospect Heights, IL, 1995), pp. 25–27; Margot Adler, *Drawing Down the Moon: Witches, Druids, Goddess-Worshippers, and Other Pagans in American Today* (Boston, 2007), p. 253; Catherine Albanese, *Nature Religion in America* (Chicago, 1990), p. 6; and Hutton, *Triumph*, pp. 415–16.
6   Sabina Magliocco, *Witching Culture: Folklore and Neopaganism in America* (Philadelphia, 2004), pp. 8–9.
7   See Ronald Hutton, *Blood and Mistletoe: A History of the Druids in Britain* (New Haven, 2009) and Prys Morgan, "From Death to a View: The Hunt for the Welsh Past in the Romantic Period," in Eric Hobsbawm and Terence Ranger (eds.), *The Invention of Tradition* (Cambridge and New York, 1983), pp. 43–100.
8   Hutton, *Triumph*.
9   See www.museumofwitchcraft.com, accessed June 19, 2011.

10 Chas S. Clifton, *Her Hidden Children: The Rise of Wicca and Paganism in America* (Boulder, CO, 2006).

11 See Cynthia Eller, *Living in the Lap of the Goddess: The Feminist Spirituality Movement in America* (Boston, 1995) and Jone Salomonsen, *Enchanted Feminism: The Reclaiming Witches of San Francisco* (New York and London, 2001).

12 See Raymond Buckland, *Buckland's Book of Saxon Witchcraft* (Newburyport, MA, 2005).

13 See Raven Grimassi, *Italian Witchcraft* (St. Paul, MN, 2000).

14 See Douglas Cowan, *Cyberhenge: Modern Pagans on the Internet* (London and New York, 2004).

15 Ibid.

16 www.adherents.com/Religions_By_Adherents.html.

17 See Michael F. Strmiska and Vilius Rudra Dundzila, "Lithuanian Paganism in Lithuania and America," in Michael F. Strmiska (ed.), *Modern Paganisms in World Cultures: Contemporary Perspectives* (Santa Barbara, CA, 2005), pp. 241–97, and Anne Ferlat, "Neopaganism and New Age in Russia," *Folklore* 23 (2007), pp. 40–48.

18 Jenny Blain and Robert Wallis, "Sacred Sites, Contested Rites/Rights. Contemporary Pagan Engagements with the Past," *Journal of Material Culture* 9:3 (2004), pp. 237–61.

19 See Mattias Gardell, *Gods of the Blood: The Pagan Revival and White Separatism* (Durham, NC, 2003).

20 See Jenny Blain, *Nine Worlds of Seidr Magic* (London and New York, 2001).

21 See Sabina Magliocco, *Neo-Pagan Sacred Art and Altars: Making Things Whole* (Jackson, MS, 2001).

22 See www.witchcamp.org/.

23 See Sarah Pike, *Earthly Bodies, Magical Selves: Contemporary Pagans and the Search for Community* (Berkeley, 2001).

24 Orion, *Never Again the Burning Times*, pp. 66–69.

Further reading

Drury, Nevill, *Stealing Fire from Heaven: The Rise of Modern Western Magic* (Oxford, 2011).

Greenwood, Susan, *Magic, Witchcraft and the Otherworld: An Anthropology* (Oxford, 2000).

Hutton, Ronald, *The Druids* (London, 2007).
     The Triumph of the Moon: A History of Modern Pagan Witchcraft (Oxford, 1999).

Magliocco, Sabina, *Witching Culture: Folklore and Neopaganism in America*. (Philadelphia, 2004).

York, Michael, *Pagan Theology: Paganism as a World Religion* (New York, 2005).

10 The International Raëlian Movement

SUSAN J. PALMER AND BRYAN SENTES

The International Raëlian Movement (IRM), founded in 1974 by Claude Vorilhon (who later became known as Raël), is arguably the largest "flying saucer cult" in the world, claiming over 60,000 members in 52 countries.[1] Vorilhon was born in Ambert (near Vichy, France) on September 30, 1946, and a brief narrative of his early life, mixing emic and etic perspectives, runs as follows.

Claude was the illegitimate child of a 15-year-old village girl and a married man, a Sephardic Jew named "Marcel" who was in temporary hiding from the Nazis. Marcel returned to his family and his lumber factory in Alsace at the end of the war, but he continued his relationship with his young mistress, Claude's mother.[2] Claude himself was never baptized, and was raised by his aunt and grandmother to be a staunch atheist. At the age of 9, he was briefly placed in a Catholic boarding school, where he naïvely opted to participate in the Mass, along with the other boys, not realizing that he was committing blasphemy (due to his not being baptized). This allegedly caused an uproar among the priests.[3] At 15 Claude was taken out of high school to work to help support his mother, but he ran away, hitch-hiking to Paris with a race car driver who introduced him to the pleasures of prostitutes and the race track. The teenager Claude was a fan of Jacques Brel, the Belgian singer, and wrote many songs imitating Brel's style and sang them in Paris cafés to support himself. He was discovered by an agent who set him up as a teen pop star named Claude Cellier, and he enjoyed a brief success on France's hit parade. But suddenly the agent committed suicide, and Claude's singing career ended abruptly. Vorilhon married a nurse,[4] and the couple had two children. He then founded a race car magazine called *Auto Pop* in 1973 and became well connected in the racing world, where he established a career as a test driver. This career was abruptly curtailed in November 1973 by a new French law that banned speeding on the highway and suspended car races. His career as a prophet or UFO contactee commenced soon thereafter.[5]

UFO SIGHTINGS IN FRANCE

Vorilhon's contactee career is illuminated by a study of the history of *soucoupe volante* ("flying saucer") sightings before his initial 1974 encounter. Arguably, sightings of unidentified aerial phenomena over the landmass of present-day France can be traced back to antiquity.[6] The modern UFO myth, however, begins with Kenneth Arnold's 1947 sighting over the continental USA, and in 1954 a wave of sightings began over France that supplied the first and classic stories of silver disks with transparent cupolas, cigar-shaped "mother ships," and so forth.[7] Closer in time to Vorilhon's encounter, between 1974 and 1975, there was a new wave of numerous UFO sightings. People who claimed to have seen UFOs were interviewed not only by gendarmes and ufologists, but also by distinguished scientists and astronomers, and the witnesses all proved to be solid and respectable citizens. The sheer volume of these sightings was impressive. Five thousand accounts of "close encounters of the second kind" were collected within six years.[8] Vorilhon's story needs to be seen in this context.

Two weeks after a significant Turin airport sighting, on December 13, Vorilhon experienced his own "close encounter of the third kind" – a face-to-face meeting with a space alien – during a walk in the Puy de Lassolas volcanic crater in the Clermont-Ferrand mountains of the Massif Central of France. As he describes the incident in his 1974 book, *Le livre qui dit la vérité* ("The Book That Tells the Truth"),[9] a spaceship descended through the mist and an "Eloha" (a representative of a particular kind of extraterrestrial, as we will see below) emerged from the hatch and invited him on board for a series of lessons in which the true meaning of the creation myths in the Bible was revealed.[10] Vorilhon was informed that the first humans were originally "implanted" on earth by a team of Elohim (plural of Eloha) scientists, who set up a laboratory on a barren planet and proceeded to create life from DNA. Thus, the very first "Adams and Eves" on our planet were created from the Elohim's own DNA. This narrative is a version of the "Ancient Astronaut" theory that was already well known in France when Vorilhon's first book was published. Along with the more famous Erich von Däniken, whose work first appeared France in 1970, French ufologists Jean Sendy (1969),[11] Serge Hutin (1970),[12] and Jacques Bergier (1970)[13] all advanced the theory that the earth was an ancient colonial outpost of an advanced extraterrestrial civilization. In the context of Vorilhon's narrative, it is particularly interesting to note that Sendy's *La Lune: clé de la Bible* points out that the Hebrew word "elohim" is the plural of "eloha," and that the word designating the god mentioned in Genesis should in fact be translated as "gods." Sendy also suggests that the Elohim were not immaterial beings, but rather gendered "physical angels." The "truth" communicated to Vorilhon by the Elohim is thus essentially an interpretation of the Bible informed by the Ancient Astronaut hypothesis. John A. Saliba sums up the Ancient Astronaut biblical hermeneutic as follows:

> God becomes an astronaut, a superior being who lives in a more advanced civilization in some other faraway galaxy. Divine revelations are nothing but teachings from space creatures and miracles are awesome interventions by intelligences who are technologically superior to the human race. The supernatural, in this view, is reduced to the super-technological. God is a superior humanoid creature living on another planet. He has made himself immortal through technology and has created the human race.[14]

The relation between Vorilhon's claims and Sendy's has become a hotly disputed topic among ex-members of the Raëlian movement and anticultists. At one extreme, Vorilhon has been accused of plagiarism by a former high-ranking member, Jean-Denis Saint-Cyr. On the other, given the ubiquity of flying saucers in global and francophone popular culture and the wide dissemination of Ancient Astronaut literature, it is equally possible to argue that Vorilhon's books rearticulate ideas that were widely available in contemporary popular culture.

BELIEF SYSTEM

The Eloha who awarded Vorilhon the honorific name Raël, which we shall use in the remainder of this chapter, charged him with the mission to be the prophet of the "Age of Apocalypse," the era that began with the detonation of the atomic bomb at Hiroshima. The prophet's role is to reveal the true origins and nature of human beings and by means of this revelation lead humanity from the destructive abuse of science and technology (which threatens us with nuclear annihilation and environmental catastrophe) to their use for our benefit. This will trigger the return of the Elohim to earth accompanied by thirty-nine immortal prophets (including Jesus, Buddha, and Muhammad) before the year 2035, at which time humanity's "fathers from space" will share their science and technology – which is "25,000 years in advance" of our own – and thereby usher in a utopian world. The two immediate goals of the IRM are to spread the message of humanity's true origins and to build an Embassy in order to welcome the Elohim upon their return. The Raëlians' initial intention to build an Embassy in Jerusalem came to nothing after their request for land was sent out to Israeli embassies worldwide in 1992 and met with no response. The Guides, Raël's closest associates, then began to investigate the possibility of Hawai'i as a site. In 1998 Raël gave his blessing to this change in plans, announcing a new revelation received from the Elohim that the Embassy did not have to be built in Jerusalem.[15] The Embassy project is explained on the movement's website as follows:

> Through their messenger, Raël, the Elohim have respectfully expressed a desire to come and meet with us. But since they wish to come only if their presence here is welcome, they ask that we first demonstrate our desire to invite them by building an appropriate Embassy in advance of their arrival. That Embassy would become the Third Temple as predicted in the ancient scriptures. According to specifications provided by the Elohim, it must be built in a neutral location that has been granted rights of extra-territoriality and guaranteed neutral air space. Providing such an Embassy and obtaining the necessary guarantees for the rights of its occupants will prove that humanity is ready for an official meeting with its creators.[16]

The Raëlian movement has similarly initiated various other projects to improve the future of humanity and hasten the return of the Elohim and the thirty-nine prophets. In 1998 Raël created an order of beautiful women, called Raël's Angels, in response to a revelation from the Elohim. These women were personally trained by Raël to please the Elohim and the prophets on their return: only Raël's Angels will be allowed into the Embassy when the extraterrestrials land on earth, to act as ambassadors and to negotiate between the Elohim and the world's politicians and journalists. The reason for this is that the male Elohim are extremely gentle, delicate, and sensitive, and therefore have special requirements. As Raël says, "the most feminine woman on earth is only 10% as feminine as the Elohim."[17]

"SCIENCE IS OUR RELIGION: RELIGION IS OUR SCIENCE"

In his role as the "Last Prophet," Raël claims to have founded the world's first atheistic and scientific religion, a religion purged of blind belief, superstition, or, in his words, "obscurantism and mysticism."

To this end he primarily draws on materials from the Bible, discarding much as superstition and reinterpreting select passages as primitive allegorical depictions of the technological achievements of the Elohim. Consistent with the unorthodox hermeneutic of Sendy (among others), the Raëlians deny the existence of a creator god, insisting, instead – as already mentioned – that the (plural) "Elohim" of Genesis refers to a humanoid, extraterrestrial race that terraformed earth and created all life by means of biotechnology. The Elohim are themselves the creation of a prior race, who are in turn a creation of another race, *ad infinitum*. Similarly, the cosmos extends infinitely, not only backward and forward in time, but so to speak in scale as well. The heavenly bodies, stars, and planets of our material reality are said to be the subatomic particles of a much larger macrocosmos, in the same way that the atoms in our world and their particles compose tiny universes, a pattern continued infinitely in both the micro and macro directions. This monistic and absolutely immanent cosmology, one without a metaphysical or supernatural "outside," heaven or hell, also dissolves the "soul" into matter. The individual human being is essentially the expression of his or her DNA and one's "self" or mind is nothing more, ultimately, than all the information stored in the person's physical brain.

The Raëlian motto is indicative of the movement's ideology: "Science is our religion: religion is our science." The phrase is often cited and sometimes appears on a banner draped over the stage, for instance during the monthly meetings of the Raëlian Movement in Montreal, Quebec. This provocative slogan highlights the centrality of "science" to the Raëlian worldview, a term that orients its metaphysics, psychology, ethics, and politics. "Science," here, is a richly suggestive term, encompassing a clearly atheistic, anti-clerical, secular rationality rooted in the Enlightenment, perhaps even in its specifically French version. The worldview expounded by the natural sciences and the technological achievements springing from scientific research receive an almost iconic status. Science and technology provide Raël with concepts and images with which he primarily reinterprets the narratives in the Bible and develops an interpretation of the world and human being, ethics, and politics suitable to modernity.

Consistent with his Enlightenment forebears, Raël mocks what he sees as traditional Christian concepts, such as a personal, creator god known as God, "with a white beard, perched upon a cloud, omniscient and omnipotent."[18] Raël thus posits a monistic, immanent, and purely material cosmology, with specific claims such as the infinite micro- and macroverses noted above, based on a picture of the atom and matter borrowed from popularizations of physics. Raëlian optimistic reifications of science and technology also resonate with popularized Enlightenment views. Raëlians have been informed by the Elohim that science and technology are "natural" to intelligent life. All societies develop in a manner parallel to the life cycle of an organism, and they do so in an equally predictable way. At a crucial point, society's technological abilities become sufficient for self-annihilation, at which point the species in question either self-destructs or overcomes its own misuse of technology in order to reach a cultural sophistication ultimately equal to that of the Elohim when they first created life on earth and made humankind "in their own image." The view that science and technology are natural, predictable, and universal, and are capable of overcoming the dire problems that they themselves have created, is a tenet of fundamental importance in the Raëlian philosophy.[19]

Concerning life, the Raëlian view is rigorously materialistic as well, but with a twist when it comes to life's origins. As noted, Raël espouses a kind of Intelligent Design theory, but with the important difference from other versions of the theory that his designer is not a god or gods, but the extraterrestrial race of the Elohim. Consistent with other proponents of Intelligent Design, Raël rejects Darwinian theories of evolution, claiming that chance mutation coupled with natural selection is insufficient to explain the development of complex organisms. The Raëlian doctrine that all life is artificial leads, according to Raël, to an appreciation of the variety and beauty of all organisms and a respect for all living beings. As long as our species cannot create complex life, humans are expected to respect the techno-artistic achievements of their creators.[20] Respect, in the Raëlian view, includes empathy for the potential suffering of animals and even plants. Though meat-eating is allowed, the imposition of pain is condemned.

The Raëlian advocacy of human cloning (see below) is just one aspect of a more general enthusiasm for all forms of reproductive technology and informs the Raëlian approach to sexuality. Since "life was made to be enjoyed,"[21] heterosexual sex is freed from the obligation to procreate. Raël advocates the use of contraceptives and abortion. As Raël declares in his book *Let's Welcome Our Fathers from Space*, "each individual has the right to do with their body as she or he sees fit."[22] Those with more unusual sexual preferences may seek pleasure from biological robots designed as sex slaves, a practice that Raël assures us is normal on the Elohim's home planet. Moreover, Clonaid, a company set up by Raël, offers its services to homosexual couples who wish to have children. We shall return to this issue below.

Raëlian scientism goes even further: faith in the scientific method extends even to Raëlian political philosophy. The ideal political system is, according to the movement's ideology, a system known as Geniocracy, the rule by the most intelligent, a quality affirmed to be unproblematically determinable by means of "scientific testing." The material basis of this ideal society is guaranteed by technology. Onerous labor is carried out by robots, whether mechanical or biological (i.e., clones). Healthy, plentiful food is available in the form of genetically modified organisms (GMOs). Eternal youth and health are available via the cloning technology mentioned above.

THE EARLY MOVEMENT

On receiving an enthusiastic response to his first book, reverently referred to by Raëlians as *Le livre* ("The Book"), in 1974 Raël founded the Movement to Welcome the Creators of Humanity (MADECH).[23] In response to internal power struggles and schisms, Raël called an emergency meeting in April 1975, when he dismissed MADECH's executives and replaced them with seven disciples of his choice. By 1976 MADECH was dissolved, and the Raëlian Movement was born out of its ashes. A strict hierarchy was set up whereby all members must accept the authority of the "Guide of Guides," Raël, the "Last Prophet." Two ranks of membership were established: the core group of committed "Guides" who made up the "Structure" and assisted Raël in his mission and the more loosely affiliated "Raëlians" who embraced the Message when they were initiated or "baptized" (see below), paid their annual dues, and received the newsletter, *Apocalypse*. New dietary rules were imposed that banned alcohol, coffee, tea, and recreational drugs as damaging to the genetic code.

RAËL'S CHARISMA

In 1975 Raël experienced a second "close encounter of the third kind," as described in his 1976 book, *They Took Me to Their Planet*.[24] On October 7, 1976, Raël allegedly embarked on a marvelous journey. He reports that he suddenly awoke in the middle of the night, overcome with the desire to return to Puy de Lassolas. There, an alien ship was waiting, which took him to the planet of the Elohim. Raël recounts his adventures of how he became initiated into Elohim customs: First, he was welcomed by six biological (female) robots who made love to him in a bath; then he was shown his own body being cloned in a vat from a particle of his DNA; and he was given a class in sensual meditation, a sensory awareness technique that activates psychic abilities and stimulates the growth of new neural pathways – a technique he shared with his followers in his 1980 book, *La méditation sensuelle*.[25] Raëlians are advised to engage in the ritual of "sensual meditation" daily by means of an instruction tape in order to cultivate telepathic communication with the Elohim and to cultivate a state of harmony with the universe. This practice evoked some controversy in France because it includes a hedonistic exercise in sexual stimulation. However, the high value the Raëlians place on sexual stimulation reflects their belief that new brain cells will be generated and improved neural pathways will result. Moreover, sexual activity and a more general cultivation of sensuality are perceived as a path to mystical awareness of, or oneness with, the universe and telepathic communication with the Elohim.[26] Raël also studied the Elohim's political system – an elitist oligarchy not unlike Plato's Guardians – the Geniocracy or "rule of geniuses" described above.

Upon his return to earth, Raël introduced the symbol of the Raëlian Movement that he first observed on the hull of the Elohim's craft, a swastika inside the Star of David. This connotes, according to Raël, the unity of infinity and eternity and is worn on a medallion by the members. Raël also attempted to found a political party in France modeled on the geniocratic system of the Elohim. After he and his Guides, who were suspected in France of forming a neo-Nazi "fascist" cell, became the target of police raids and investigations, Raël decided to abandon the project. In 1992 he announced that "out of respect for the victims of the Nazi holocaust and in order to make the building of the Embassy in IsRaël easier," it was decided to revise the symbol of the Raëlian Movement, replacing the swastika with a swirling galaxy symbol which represents the cycle of infinity in time.[27]

Three years after his journey through space, Raël finally revealed his messianic identity. In his book *Let's Welcome Our Fathers from Space. They Created Humanity in Their Laboratories* (first published 1979), he describes an intensely emotional encounter with an Eloha named Yahweh.[28] Yahweh, the same individual who, according to Raël, is misconceived as God in Judeo-Christian religion, revealed himself to be Raël's biological father, who for centuries has been selecting earthly women to impregnate whenever the planet needed a new prophet to point humanity in the right direction. The mothers (including Mary, the mother of Jesus) would be chosen for the purity of their genetic code ("virgin DNA"), and beamed up into a UFO, impregnated, and then released with their memories erased. Allusions to the myth of the immaculate conception are obvious and serve to position Raël as the equal of Jesus. Raël (who grew up illegitimate, fatherless, an only child) also describes a joyous meeting with his half-brothers Jesus, Muhammad, and Buddha on the alien planet.

As can be seen, Raël's charismatic persona has escalated in the course of his writings. In his first book (published in 1974) he presented himself as a contactee entrusted with a message. In his 1976 book he reports how he was taken aboard the Elohim's starship and flown to their planet, outside our solar system but within the same galaxy.[29] In 1979 his messianic role was revealed,[30] and in 2003 Raël published *The Maitreya*,[31] in which he explains his new charismatic persona as the Maitreya, an incarnation of the Buddha.

ESSENTIAL RITUALS

Raëlians participate in four annual festivals that commemorate important encounters with, or revelations from, the Elohim. The initiation ritual or "baptism" ceremony of new members is performed on these occasions. The Raëlians' initiation ceremony is called the "transmission of the cellular plan." Raël himself, or one of his highest-ranking associates, the so-called "Bishop Guides," will dip his hand in water and place it on the initiate's forehead in order to telepathically transmit his or her genetic code to the Elohim's computers, where it is stored for a future cloning process, if the aspirant is deemed worthy. For that very purpose Raëlians must also sign a contract with a local mortician so that their "third eye" (a chunk of frontal bone considered an essential ingredient for the recreation process) can be cut out upon their decease, packed in ice and stored in a bank vault in Switzerland. The initiates must, however, first sign an "Act of Apostasy" renouncing their baptism in their former church, and also make a will bequeathing their assets to their local Raëlian community. Thus, monistic materialism and biotechnology are synthesized in the Raëlian version of the afterlife. Furthermore, Raëlians are encouraged to practice sensual meditation on a daily basis, and newcomers have the opportunity to try out some of the phases of this meditation, "oxygenation" and guided relaxation, at the monthly meetings.

SOCIAL ORGANIZATION AND LEADERSHIP

There are, as indicated, two levels of membership in the IRM. First, there are the rank-and-file "Raëlians" who make up the majority; the loosely affiliated, baptized members, who comprise various degrees of commitment and engagement. The higher level is, as we have seen, the "Structure" who make up the six-tiered leadership, descending from Raël, who is the "Guide of Guides," through the Bishop Guides, the Priest Guides, the Animators, the Assistant Animators, and the Probationers at the bottom. Three bishops sit on the "Council of the Wise" that monitors heresy and sanctions rule breakers. Some of the most prominent career apostates have been punished by "demarking" or the cancellation of their transmission of the cellular code by Raël (at the bequest of the Elohim) which at once excommunicates them and revokes their potential for immortality through cloning.[32] Usually, however, the "excommunication" expires after seven years, which is the time it takes to regenerate the body's cells, and the penitent Rëalian is then offered a second chance.

RAËLIAN VALUES

Raëlians congregate on the third Sunday of the month in every city where there is a Raëlian presence. They have always made it a policy to rent rooms rather than purchase property, thus there are no Raëlian centers, although the movement has owned country estates, the first in Alby, France, and the second in Valcourt, Quebec, where the summer seminars are held. These "Stages of Awakening" seminars are held at camps in rural settings in various countries. These feature daily lectures by Raël, sensual meditation, fasting and feasting, testimonials and avant-garde therapies. The campers discard clothing, in emulation of the Elohim, who are nudists on their planet, but wear name tags and white togas. In 1997 the Raëlians opened UFOland in Valcourt, Quebec, which functioned as a museum of ufological lore to raise funds for the eventual building of the Embassy, and as a shrine to Raëlian beliefs. The museum featured a fiberglass model of the UFO that took Raël to the planet of the Elohim, a large replica of a DNA structure, and a small donut-shaped *maquette* of the Embassy the Raëlians aspire to construct. UFOland was closed to the public in 2001, but it continued to house Raël and several of his leaders and was used as the location for the summer seminars until it was sold after an act of vandalism in November 2002 which caused damage estimated at more than $81,942.47 CAD. The Raëlian Church (another of the IRM's names) of Canada is today an officially recognized religion in Quebec, but has been unable to claim tax deductions since the federal tax department rejected the Canadian Raëlian Movement's application for status as a religion – on the grounds that their "gods" did not meet the standards of the *loi d'impôt*, since they were material beings, not transcendent deities. All Raëlians are expected to donate a tenth of their income to the fund for the construction of the Embassy, as well as 1 percent to support their "Beloved Prophet," but this rule is not actually enforced. Members are encouraged to pursue sexual pleasure with many partners of either sex, since pleasure is believed to increase the individual's intelligence, but rape and pedophilia are strongly censored and punished by excommunication. In the year 2000 Raël founded NOPEDO, dedicated to counteract pedophilia. On the organization's homepage pedophilia is deemed a "plague" and Raëlians are exhorted to report any incidents of child molestation to the authorities. Raël even recommends that pedophiles should be castrated or incarcerated in mental institutions.[33]

In the Raëlian Movement marriage contracts are rejected, and members of the "Structure" must choose between breeding or gaining personal immortality through the cloning process. Raël himself has been married twice. His first wife bore him two children before he encountered the Elohim. She left him and his movement in 1985. Sixteen years later, Raël, at the age of 47, married a 16-year-old ballet student, with the consent of her mother (who is a Raëlian). Although marriage is against Raël's philosophy, he found it expedient in this case, because he had been questioned by customs officials when he traveled across borders with her. The couple filed for divorce on August 28, 2000, but they continue to live together as a couple.

The Raëlian culture is not particularly sentimental concerning motherhood, nor child-friendly. Members of the core group rarely procreate. As mentioned earlier Raël strongly recommends birth control and, if necessary, abortion, so that the individual can achieve his or her full potential through the "fulfillment of the body," which leads to the "blossoming of the mind," and he even gives women permission to discard their children: "If the child becomes a nuisance, however slightly [she should] entrust him to society."[34]

SOCIAL ACTIVISM, HUMAN RIGHTS, AND LEGAL ISSUES

The Raëlians are known for their political and social activism. Among their causes are women's rights, gay rights, anti-racism, the promotion of genetically modified foods, and a ban on nuclear testing. Raël also founded ARAMIS, the Raëlian Association of Sexual Minorities, an association of persons on all five continents who are homosexual, bisexual, transsexuals, or transgendered. Raël proclaims that sexual orientation is genetic, rather than a lifestyle choice, and, as mentioned above, encourages his people to live their sexuality openly, as an essential condition to a full blossoming. Since 2009 the Raëlians have been raising funds for the "Adopt a Clitoris" project, which focuses on the issue of female circumcision. They claim to be constructing a hospital in Africa where a French surgeon will restore women's mutilated clitorises.

In 1992, shortly after the assassination of Raël's friend and follow ufologist Jean Miguères, Raël wrote a book, *Le racisme religieux financé en France par le gouvernement socialiste*,[35] condemning France's government-sponsored anticult group, UNADFI, which Raël claims organizes "witch hunts" against philosophical minorities,[36] and in October 1992 he founded a human rights organization called FIREPHIM: la Fédération Internationale des Religions et Philosophies Minoritaires. In the wake of the Solar Temple's mass suicides/homicides in Switzerland and Quebec in October 1994,[37] the National Assembly appointed a commission to study the "problem of sects" in France. This commission produced the so-called Guyard Report with its "blacklist" of "dangerous sects" in 1995, at which point the Raëlians found themselves subjected to ever more stringent measures of social control and discrimination. Many Raëlians were fired from their jobs and lost custody of their children, or were deprived of visiting rights, due to their affiliation with a known "sect." FIREPHIM staged demonstrations protesting the Guyard Report, and many Raëlians were arrested and taken in for questioning on the grounds of *trouble à l'ordre publique* – disturbing the peace. FIREPHIM was disbanded in the wake of a new resistance movement formed in 2000 as CAP (Coordination des Associations et Particuliers pour la liberté de Conscience), created with a broader base of supporters.

In France the movement has officially disbanded and gone underground due to pressure from *le Fisc français* (the French tax department). Between 1977 and 1981, the French branch had enjoyed the tax-exempt status of an *association*. But in 1981, the government voted in a law requiring that all *associations* pay tax on their commercial sales, and the French Raëlian Movement was suddenly presented with an enormous bill on the sale of Raël's books. Raël, outraged by what he considered a "biased new tax," refused to pay, claiming his movement was a real religion, unable to gain recognition as such in France. But then the TVA (*taxe sur la valeur ajoutée*), or indirect tax, began to accrue. The government sent a notice to the Raëlian Movement telling them they owed *le Fisc* 80,000 francs. Raël refused to negotiate and the French Raëlian bishops feared it would double every year and cripple the movement. Thus, they resorted to the drastic solution of disbanding and going underground.

In 1995, a parliamentary commission issued a report through the National Assembly of France that categorized the Raëlian Movement as a *"secte"* (the French word for "cult").[38] Similarly, in 1997 a parliamentary inquiry commission issued a report through the Belgian Chamber of Representatives that categorized the Belgian Raëlian Movement (Mouvement Raëlien Belge) as a *"secte."* Glenn McGee, the Associate Director of the Center for Bioethics at the University of Virginia, states that part of the Raëlian sect is a cult while the other part is a commercial website that collects large sums of money from those interested in human cloning. However, the Bureau of Democracy, Human Rights, and Labor of the United States Department of State have classified the International Raëlian Movement as a religion.[39]

THE CLONE CONTROVERSY: BABY EVE

In 1997, shortly after Dr. Ian Wilmut announced the successful cloning of a lamb called "Dolly," Raël set up a cloning company called Valiant Venture. Grieving parents, and infertile and gay couples could already wait in line for Clonaid for $200,000, and special services storing the DNA of loved ones were also available, as in the case of the untimely death of beloved children, through Insuraclone. A furious international debate ensued among world religious leaders including the pope, eminent scientists, and distinguished ethicists concerning the ethics and philosophical implications of human cloning, and thus of Raël's projects. One of the top female Raëlian bishops, Dr. Brigitte Boisselier (b.1956), became the co-founder, director, and leading spokesperson for Clonaid. Formerly the director of research for a French chemical company, Air Liquide, she "came out" as a Raëlian in the French media in support of human cloning, was promptly fired and moved to Quebec. Raël and Boisselier participated vigorously in the debate over human cloning and even attended President Clinton's congressional hearing on the topic in the US Capitol on March 28, 2001.

On December 27, 2002, Boisselier held a large press conference in Miami where she announced that Clonaid had successfully produced a cloned human, delivered by cesarean section, and that the parents had named her "Eve." However, no scientific evidence was provided, and nobody was presented with the child. In January 2003 it was announced that Eve's parents had gone underground, after deciding to protect their baby from media exposure and scientific testing. Boisselier then continued to announce periodically the advent of more cloned babies in Holland, Japan, Australia, and South Korea. At that point, the international journalists decided they were unwitting participants in an embarrassing hoax and began to boycott the Raëlian press conferences and ignore their new human rights projects. On January 19, 2003 Raël spoke at the monthly meeting in Montreal, stating that he had "informed the entire planet of [his] message" and thus his mission was "50% complete" – thanks to the international media blitz following the Baby Eve announcement. Next, he appointed Boisselier as his successor, expressing his appreciation of the effective means she had found for spreading the message.

To this day, the significance of the "Baby Eve announcement" is unclear. Internal Raëlian opinions range from agreeing it was a hoax to claiming there are clandestine cloned babies who will step forth some day. Another theory is that the purpose of the "Baby Eve announcement" was to "raise the public's awareness so they will be ready for human cloning when it happens in the future." For Raëlians, human cloning is apocalyptic, even Nietzschean, for it means that man has become "god," a proof that humanity is undergoing "elohimization."

THE CULTURAL SIGNIFICANCE OF THE INTERNATIONAL RAËLIAN MOVEMENT

The centrality of science and technology to the Raëlian worldview is revelatory because of its peculiar mirroring from the margins of the values that arguably stand at the centre of contemporary world civilization. Arising in the late twentieth century, it is no surprise that a new religious intuition would seek to articulate itself in terms proper to the cultural matrix of its own appearance. As Herbert Marcuse and Jürgen Habermas have observed, science and technology constitute the ideologies of the advanced societies.[40] David F. Noble goes so far as to characterize the present scientific research establishment as a religion with its own dogma, priesthood, and rites.[41] That intelligent life "naturally" develops from superstitious beliefs to science and technological sophistication is a belief reified in traditional talk of "primitive"

and "advanced" societies and even in the assumptions of researchers engaged in the search for extraterrestrial intelligence (systematized in a network organization of that very name, SETI). Raël's views are inspired and shaped by a crucial moment in human history, when our intelligence and ingenuity seem to outstrip our wisdom, leading to potential species-suicidal scenarios. The Raëlian worldview is seized by and seizes this moment of crisis, taking up and reflecting back in a hyperbolic form the key assumptions and values that underwrite the earth's "advanced" societies.[42]

Notes

1 This figure is probably inflated. The movement's main homepage refers to a number of countries, but in effect only very few people may represent the Raëlians in the areas mentioned. In 2008, Denmark, for instance, had one representative, who was only reached through a French contact.

2 Emmanuelle Chantepie in *Le Journal du Dimanche* (January 5, 2003).

3 Interview with Raël in Montreal by the author[s], December 18, 1994.

4 The ex-Mrs. Vorilhon wishes to remain anonymous.

5 Claude Vorilhon, *The Message Given to Me by Extraterrestrials* (Slough, 1993 [first published 1975]), p. 14.

6 Jacques Vallee and Chris Aubeck, *Wonders in the Sky* (New York, 2010).

7 Jacques Vallee, *Anatomy of a Phenomenon* (Chicago, 1965).

8 Jean-Claude Bourret, *Ovnis 1999: Le contact?* (Paris, 1997), pp. 100–7. "Close encounters" of the I, II, and III kind are expressions denoting the quality of UFO-observations, level III being direct contact with the beings believed to pilot them.

9 Raël [Claude Vorilhon], *Le livre qui dit la vérité* (Clermont-Ferrand, 1974).

10 Ibid.

11 Jean Sendy, *La lune: clé de la Bible* (Paris, 1969).

12 Serge Hutin, *Hommes et civilisations fantastiques* (Paris, 1970).

13 Jacques Bergier, *Les extraterrestres dans l'histoire* (Paris, 1970).

14 John A. Saliba, "Religious Dimensions of the UFO Phenomenon," in James R. Lewis (ed.), *The Gods Have Landed* (New York, 1995), pp. 16–54, at p. 34.

15 See also Mikael Rothstein's analysis of the Embassy strategies in his "Institutionalised Anticipation: Architecture and Religious Symbolism in the Raëlian Religion," in James Lewis (ed.), *Encyclopedic Handbook of UFO Religions* (New York, 2003), pp. 281–98.

16 www.rael.org/embassy (accessed September 2011). See also: www.ElohimEmbassy.org/.

17 Susan Palmer, *Aliens Adored: Raël's UFO Religion* (New Brunswick, NJ, 2004), p. 140.

18 Vorilhon, *Message*, p. 90.
19 This point was made in Bryan Sentes and Susan Palmer's "Presumed Immanent: The Raëlians, UFO Religions and the Postmodern Condition," *Nova Religio* 4:1 (2000), pp. 86–105.
20 See also George D. Chryssides, "Scientific Creationism: A Study of the Raëlian Church," in Christopher Partridge (ed.), *UFO Religions* (London, 2003), pp. 45–61.
21 Claude Vorilhon [Raël], *Let's Welcome Our Fathers from Space. They Created Humanity in Their Laboratories* (Tokyo, 1986), p. 61.
22 Ibid., p. 86.
23 The acronym refers to the French name: le Mouvement pour l'accueil des createurs de l'humanité.
24 Raël [Claude Vorilhon], *Les extraterrestres m'ont emmené sur leur planète* (Brantôme, 1977).
25 Raël [Claude Vorilhon], *La méditation sensuelle* (Vaduz, 1980).
26 Ibid.
27 Raëlian information pack, February 1992. Stickers with the new symbol were subsequently placed over the old on printed materials, posters, hand-outs, etc.
28 Vorilhon [Raël], *Let's Welcome*.
29 Raël [Claude Vorilhon], *Les extraterrestres*.
30 Vorilhon [Raël], *Let's Welcome*.
31 Raël [Claude Vorilhon], *The Maitreya* (Vadux, 2003).
32 See Palmer, *Aliens Adored*, for examples of "demarking."
33 www.nopedo.org/français/pages/position.html (accessed September 2011).
34 Raël [Claude Vorilhon] *La méditation*.
35 Raël [Claude Vorilhon], *Le racisme religieux financé en France par le gouvernement socialiste* (Geneva, 1992).
36 See www.unadfi.org/.
37 See Jean-François Mayer, *Les mythes du Temple solaire* (Genève, 1996).
38 The website http://en.wikipedia.org/wiki/Ra%C3%ABlism-cite_note-fr99annex-137 provides further information.
39 In Palmer, *Aliens Adored*, it is argued that the International Raëlian Movement is a religion.
40 Jürgen Habermas, *Toward a Rational Society* (Boston, 1970).
41 David F. Noble, *The Religion of Technology* (New York, 2001).
42 See Sentes and Palmer, "Presumed Immanent" for a more detailed discussion of this point.

Further reading

Palmer, Susan J., "The Raëlian Movement: Concocting Controversy, Seeking Social Legitimacy," in James R. Lewis and Jesper Aagaard Petersen (eds.), *Controversial New Religions* (New York, 2005), pp. 371–85.
"Women in the Raëlian Movement," in James R. Lewis (ed.), *The Gods Have Landed* (New York: 1995), pp. 105–35.

Partridge, Christopher (ed.), *UFO Religions* (New York, 2003).

Rothstein, Mikael, "Institutionalised Anticipation: Architecture and Religious Symbolism in the Raëlian Religion," in James Lewis (ed.), *Encyclopedic Handbook of UFO Religions* (New York, 2003), pp. 281–98.

"The Myth of the UFO in Global Perspective: A Cognitive Analysis," in Rothstein (ed.), *New Religions and Globalization*, Renner Studies on New Religions 5 (Aarhus, 2001), pp. 133–49.

11 The Sathya Sai Baba movement

TULASI SRINIVAS

The Sathya Sai Baba movement (SSB) is a transnational religio-cultural movement and social phenomenon.[1] Approximately sixty-five years old, the movement had a single identifiable charismatic leader, Shri (honorific) Sathya Sai Baba, who was, until his death, the titular and acting head of a large global organization and a privately funded religious trust – the Sathya Sai Seva Organization and the Sai Charitable Trust. According to news reports, Sathya Sai Baba, god-man, guru, mystic, saint,[2] "passed away" on April 24, 2011, Easter Sunday, at 7.40 a.m. Indian Standard Time, at the Sathya Sai Seva Institute for Higher Medical Sciences in his home town of Puttaparthi in rural Andhra Pradesh in south India after a month-long critical illness in which he was diagnosed with "multiple organ failure."[3]

On April 27, 2011, Sai Baba was given a state funeral, with a twenty-one-gun salute and a flag-draped coffin, attended by the President of India, Manmohan Singh, along with other prominent political figures, dignitaries, and celebrities. According to BBC reports, over half a million devotees are believed to have attended the public funeral ceremony, and a million-plus to have paid their last respects as his body lay in state in a crystal coffin for three days in the Sai Kulwant Darshan (sacred witnessing) Hall, where he would give his devotees *darshan* of himself (i.e., allowing his followers to behold him) twice daily. Sai Baba was buried, as is sometimes the custom for religious leaders, though most Hindus are cremated, and traditional Hindu rites were performed after the state funeral.[4]

The Sathya Sai movement, before Sai Baba's death, attracted a self-reported 50 million followers worldwide (though the Indian news magazine *India Today* estimated the SSB following to be 20 million in 2007 and their net worth to be US$6 billion). In a more recent financial estimate after Sai Baba's death, the Sathya Sai Trust suggested the figure was closer to US$9 billion;[5] it is known that he had several powerful devotees including P. N. Bhagwati, a retired justice of India, Isaac Tigrett, the founder of the Hard Rock chain of restaurants, and Sunil Gavaskar, India's most famous cricket star. Through a message of universal values of truth, righteousness, peace, love, nonviolence, and charitable and philanthropic service, Sai prospective devotees were remade into a community of believers and moral stakeholders who engaged in charitable acts worldwide.

Sathya Sai Baba's distinctive appearance – his long saffron robe, his graceful gliding walk, and his electrically charged hair-style (which Americans and some Westernized Indians call an "Afro") make his image instantly recognizable across the world. The story of Sathya Sai Baba's life from peasant boy in a remote town in rural India to global god-man/guru, has been recorded in over 600 texts, some devotee-based and others scholarly.[6] Sathya Sai Baba's many prophesies, miracles, epiphanies, and moments of reinvention in apostolic accounts serve to transform the meanings of the mundane into the supernatural. Apostolic and apologetic accounts of Sathya Sai Baba's life make riveting reading, woven through with magical interludes, self-proclaimed revelations of divinity, and dramatic contestations and confessions.[7] These accounts of Sathya Sai Baba's life and the Sai paradigm of faith cover a range of media including audio, blogs, and traditional texts.

FROM PEASANT BOY TO GOD-MAN

Sathya Sai Baba's birth in a rural, peasant family on November 23, 1926, as Sathyanarayana Raju (his given name) in the remote village of Puttaparthi in the Rayalseema district (a name meaning "boundaries of kings") of the south Indian state of Andhra Pradesh was, according to apostolic texts, accompanied by divine signs heralding the birth of a great soul such as the sounds of divine music, the appearance of divine lights, and so on. His childhood attributes of compassion for all living beings, his intelligence, musical and compositional skill, his magical materializations of food and sweets and his healing abilities were all seen as signs of future greatness.[8] After suffering a series of seizures and falling into trances, he declared his greatness in a series of revelatory episodes[9] at the age of 13 and proclaimed: "I am Sai, I am of the Bharadwaja Gothra [lineal descent from the Hindu sage Bharadwaja]; I am Sai Baba [i.e., a reincarnation of a Muslim holy man]; I have come to ward off all your troubles; and to keep your houses clean and pure,"[10] thereby creating an Indic, syncretic religious tradition and claiming reincarnation from Shirdi Sai Baba, a Muslim *faqir* (saint) from Maharashtra who had died in 1918.[11]

Sathya Sai Baba, as he came to be known, was believed to regularly materialize healing *vibhuti* (sacred ash) and other sacred items.

Devotees imbibe the ash and/or apply it to their foreheads. These magical materializations of sacred and healing ash established Sathya Sai Baba's connection to Shirdi Sai Baba, who had apparently distributed healing *vibhuti* to his followers from a sacred fire he kept lit in a mosque.[12] Sathya Sai Baba is called *Bhagawan* (God) by devotees, or, fondly, Baba or *Swami* (Lord). He, in turn, addressed them as *bangaru* (Telugu for "golden ones"). Between 1940 and 1950 Sathya Sai Baba's following grew slowly within India from south to the north, creating a pan-Indian movement.[13]

In 1963 Sai Baba is believed to have suffered another seizure, which left him unconscious and unable to communicate. After a few days he appeared before his followers in a hemiplegic state and stated that not only was he Shirdi Sai Baba reincarnated but also the Hindu gods Shiva and Shakti (Shiva's consort, embodied divine feminine power). Accordingly, Sathya Sai Baba is most frequently associated, iconographically and in *bhajans* (devotional music), with Shiva. However, drawing from the widespread Hindu belief that all gods and goddesses are but manifestations of one divine principle, Sai Baba and his followers claim that all names creatively include many other divine and semi-divine figures, in *avatar* form.[14] And so Sathya Sai Baba is thought by some to be a charismatic *guru* (teacher) and by others to be a reincarnated Muslim seer (*faqir*), a saint, or an *avatar* (incarnation) of God.

In his discourses, which number in the thousands, Sathya Sai Baba divided his life into four phases, each of sixteen years: during the first sixteen he engaged in mischief and playful pranks (*balalilas*), during the second he performed miracles (*mahimas*), for the third sixteen-year segment he dedicated himself to general teaching (*upadesh*), while still performing miracles, and in the last segment (which would have begun around 1984) he dedicated his life to teaching select devotees his spiritual discipline (*sadhana*). He predicted his own death at the age of 96, but his body, it is said, would remain young until then.[15] This prediction has been the source of much revisitation and reinterpretation in the light of his recent death at the age of 84, with some devotees claiming that Sai Baba intended an accounting of time in lunar calendar months, and others claiming that the prophesy merely meant that he would return in another form at some point in time.

TRADITIONAL WAYS AND SYNCRETISTIC CHANGES

Sathya Sai Baba and his movement drew philosophical and theological strands seamlessly from several great religious traditions of the subcontinent – Sufi mysticism, popular Vaishnavite Hinduism, Shaivite Hindu iconography, Vedanta philosophy, contemporary Christian teachings, and indigenous healing rituals – to weave a constantly evolving Indic urban syncretism in which the problems of dogma, creed, and literature appear to magically fade into the background, as did problems arising from divisions of caste, class, nationality, and religion.[16] Devotees from various cultures and nation-states abide by what Sai Baba said in his sermons and talks, and it is his articulation of any intention, problem, or solution that is important in the devotee's mind. Devotees believe Sathya Sai Baba was and is "omniscient, omnipotent, and omnipresent." They also claim that he was capable of teleportation, mind reading, healing, materialization, and telekinesis.

The mission of the Sai movement is the "establishment of Dharma (righteousness)" on earth primarily articulated through a philanthropic mission.[17] There is no formal doctrine for the movement, though thousands of books have been published detailing Sai Baba's many discourses and established and recommended practices to encourage *dharmic* behavior (i.e., a balanced lifestyle according to religious ideals). So while scholar Lawrence Babb describes the Sai doctrine as having "relatively little to dwell upon, or at least nothing very distinctive. His philosophical views are simplistic, eclectic and entirely unoriginal,"[18] in fact, as Kent suggests, the "lack of doctrinal originality" allows for the contention that Sai faith "rekindles awareness of eternal truths not to invent new ones."[19] This simplicity makes the teachings accessible to a broad audience and their eclecticism makes them appealing to people of many cultures.

An early emblem of the Sathya Sai Organization consisted of a five-petaled lotus flower displaying on its petals symbols from five "world religions" (Hinduism, Christianity, Islam, Zoroastrianism, and Buddhism) and at its center the lamp of knowledge. More recently, it would appear that Jewish devotees asked for their religious symbol to be included and so in some cases the Zoroastrian fire is replaced by the Star of David. The symbol of the ecumenism of the Sai faith (the Sarva Dharma image) is found on all official communiqués of the Sathya Sai movement and in iconic form in every Sai center in the world. Doctrinally, as well, the Sai faith is ecumenical, drawing ideas from all major world religions. In 1995 to that emblem was added another, also with five petals, on which are written the Sai faith's five central values: truth, nonviolence, love, peace, and right conduct, and the two symbols are used interchangeably. The universalism of the Sai faith and its enactment through an institutional edifice that links hundreds of Sai centers all over the globe is central to any analysis of a successful global religious movement.

THE LOCAL AND THE GLOBAL

In 1950 the movement funded the building of a 100-acre ashram called Prasanthi Nilayam ("abode of supreme peace") in Sai Baba's birth village of Puttaparthi in southwestern rural Andhra Pradesh, about 150 kilometers (100 miles) from the city of Bangalore.[20] The movement then became international, primarily through the efforts of a few individuals from California. The American (and international) counterculture movement of the 1960s produced a wave of spiritual seekers who rejected what they saw as the ill effects of Western rationality and greed and came to India in order to find a guru. A few became devotees of Sai Baba in the mid 1970s and wrote the first devotional books, and soon a flood of devotional literature was available to introduce Sai Baba to the larger world. This effort was matched by the now fully functional Sai organization, the Sathya Sai Seva Organization (SSSO), composed of many subsidiary institutions that issued volumes of translations of Sathya Sai Baba's many discourses, created a newsletter called *Santhana Sarathi* ("The way of the charioteer," an analogy with the *Mahabharata*'s divine charioteer, Krishna), and launched several journals.

Sathya Sai Baba lived in Prasanthi Nilayam, so devotees had to travel to the ashram to experience *darshan* (sacred witnessing of the deity) and be close to him. Sathya Sai Baba left India only once, visiting devotees in Uganda in 1968. In the summer Sathya Sai Baba resided in another ashram called Brindavan (in homage to the home of the Hindu god Krishna) in Kadugodi, a locality in the town of Whitefield on the outskirts of Bangalore. Occasionally, he visited the Sai Shruti ashram in Kodaikanal in the highlands of the state of Tamil Nadu as well. Besides the three ashram locations there are also three primary Sai mandirs (temples) in India; the first center, "Dharmakshetra," in Mumbai, the second center, "Shivam," in Hyderabad, and the third, "Sundaram," in Chennai. Several hundred smaller temples and shrines have been erected by devotees in major metropolitan centers in India and abroad.

The architecture of the ashrams and of Puttaparthi city is unique, incorporating as it does elements of the south Indian Hoysala style with Islamic domes, Mughal landscapes and modern touches, and devotees who travel there often say they find it "beautiful" and "awe-inspiring." The architecture is, according to sociologist Smriti Srinivas, metonymical of Sathya Sai Baba's charisma.[21] The central devotional space of Puttaparthi and the network of Sai transnational spaces of devotion and worship – devotees' altars in Bethesda, Boston, Bangalore, and London, Sai centers in Tokyo, Singapore, Wimbledon, and Hollywood,

Sai bookstores in Tustin and Puttaparthi, Sai temples in Toronto and Mumbai, Sai schools in Puttaparthi and Guadalajara – link together in a network of postmodern devotional enspacement which devotees believe Sai Baba occupies and inhabits.

According to officials in the Sai movement today there are about 9,000 official centers of devotion in India and about 2,000 in over 137 countries outside India, most of them urban sites. Two hundred centers exist in the USA alone, the earliest being set up in 1969 in California. A World Council with its headquarters in Puttaparthi was and still is the center of the organization though the flood of devotees has slowed to a trickle since Sai Baba's death. Estimates vary widely and depend at least in part on definitions, but Sai Baba is said to have somewhere between 5 million and 50 million followers worldwide, with perhaps half to a third of those followers located in India and the rest elsewhere. The Sai international following is thus not confined to the Indian, primarily Hindu diaspora,[22] though they form a significant part of the devotional base, but has expanded to include the middle classes of many different countries and cultures.[23]

During the first half of the movement's life (between approximately 1950 and 1975) the devotees appeared to be largely lower middle class and rural, with a smattering of very wealthy urban devotees, but in the past three decades the devotional base has changed to become largely middle class and urban, though one could, until recently, still see in Puttaparthi vestigial groups of lower-middle-class and rural devotees. The devotees – professional, technocratic, "Westernized,"[24] or what Smriti Srinivas calls an "urban following"[25] – are characterized by their mobility, their affluence, and their focus on creating a healthy union between body, spirit, and mind;[26] Sai Baba was what Weiss calls "a prophet of the jet-set more than he is a guru of peasants."[27] Socially, they strive for a "better society" defined as less poverty, cruelty, inequality, and other forms of repression. Politically, they are relatively inactive, but their beliefs appear to include a politically liberal, environmentally conscious viewpoint. They believed they lived their lives in exile away from Sathya Sai Baba's magical presence[28] and they are "called" to him at his pleasure through divine means, in dreams, and through various other modes of divine communication.[29] Devotees made the pilgrimage to Puttaparthi to see and be seen by Sathya Sai Baba in *darshan* during which they communicated their cares and worries to him through handwritten letters which they gave to him. Devotees hoped to be asked into a smaller room for "private *darshan*" where they got to speak to Sathya Sai Baba one to one.[30]

ASPECTS OF THE RITUAL LIFE

Twice a day, every day, at dawn and nearing dusk, Sathya Sai Baba gave *darshan* of himself to devotees who came from all over the world to gather in the ornate Sai Kulwant Darshan Hall at Prasanthi Nilayam. Devotees witnessed his *anubhava* (divine grace), as he walked through the crowds of gathered devotees, and a few "lucky" ones received his blessings or communicated their hopes to him through letters, whilst the rest waited in hope for another day. For this *darshan* devotees spent the better part of the day queuing around the ashram to obtain "good" seats close to where Sai Baba might sit or walk. This twice-daily *darshan* accommodated roughly 5,000 to 9,000 devotees every day. Part of the ritual included magical materializations for devotees of sacred gifts such as images of Sathya Sai Baba, sacred healing *vibhuti*, which devotees consumed, and healings of devotees at Sai Baba's touch.[31] Devotees often waited many months in order to interact with Sai Baba and saw this wait, with its daily emotions of expectation and rejection, as part of the work of becoming a good Sai devotee. The Sai liturgical tradition is strong, with distinct local contextualized manifestations, such as the singing of *bhajans* in Spanish in the Sai temple in Madrid. Since his death it has been suggested that Puttaparthi and the ashram have become a ghost town, and Indian television programs have aired news pieces with Puttaparthi vendors speculating about the future of the town and the ashram.

Devotees often stayed for extended time at the ashram participating in the community life there. Within the ashram, encoded bodily ascetic prescriptions, including powerful daily liturgical practices of recitation of prayers, naming and remembering of the Sai divinity (*namasmarana*), of attending *darshan*, of dressing modestly, eating a *sattvic* (pure) diet, singing devotional *bhajans*, reading sacred texts (such as Sai Baba's discourses), engaging in Sai worship, and prayer, dominated the everyday experience of devotees. The "everyday" or mundane, repetitive daily praxes of eating, sitting, praying, singing, dreaming, working, and other unnamed sensory, extrasensory, somatic, kinetic, tactile, and aural receptors and prophylactics became ritualized as embodied hermeneutic pathways for devotees, creating "new ways of being" and erasing the self through discipline, a central ingredient of self-transformation.[32]

ORGANIZATION AND SOCIAL STRUCTURE

The communitarian ideal is held in high esteem in the Sai movement; devotees refer to each other in familial terms as "Brother" and

Sister" to encourage a sense of community. Sathya Sai Baba exhorted the value and importance of a devotional community, encouraging communal practices of worship and charity.[33] Socially, this translates into an institutionalized program where devotees do defined charitable work (*seva*) in hospitals, schools, colleges, and shelters all over the world, catering to those less fortunate. The Sathya Sai Seva Organization (SSSO), the organizational arm of the World Council, consists of local chapters (*samhiti*) that act as spiritual centers, where devotees come together for worship and singing of *bhajans*, and loci for educational, charitable, and spiritual services for the benefit of the community. The activities of the SSSO are divided into three wings: the educational, the spiritual, and the service. The spiritual wing conducts the liturgical activities of *bhajans* and hymn singing, *sadhana* (meditative practices) camps, and so forth. The service wing deals with hospital visits, village/slum adoption, medical camps, blood donation camps, and so on. The educational wing conducts the education in human values (EHV) program in schools and Bal Vikas spiritual education for children. It is too early to tell how this structure might change in the future, though the Sai Trust has claimed it will not change much.

This faith-based development model is successful, as Sathya Sai Baba inspired millions of his followers around the globe to take on charitable works in education, health, and healing initiatives, and in infrastructural and social development for charitable giving, philanthropy, and charitable work. Some have suggested that the Sathya Sai movement's capacity for mobilizing human resources to do good works is the most admirable part of the phenomenon. Homeless shelters, food banks, clothing drives, festival dinners, hospital visits, free clinics and other participatory social services are performed by Sai devotees in urban areas all over the world. For example the Hollywood Sai temple in California has a standing request on its website for donation of clothes and blankets to homeless shelters in the Los Angeles region. Devotees who wish to work for the Sai movement in any country are organized into local groups of volunteer workers run by a centralized body, the World Council in Puttaparthi, which has several organizational and infrastructural elements within it at every location, to run the many Sai centers, charitable endeavors, health care initiatives, educational ventures, and public good citizenry efforts under its umbrella. Devotees all over the world spend a considerable amount of time doing *seva* as part of their mission to heal the world of its problems and to transform themselves into better people. In contemporary understandings, faith-based stakeholding and citizenship are seen as mutually exclusive. Using the

Sathya Sai example, we can examine how religious actors operate in the social realm within plural democracies, their activities, valorizations, and objectives, and the consequences of their involvement.

Sai temples and centers all over the globe are set up with the cooperation of the Sai movement in India. Leadership within the movement is organized by territory and the hierarchy of leadership is complex and confusing, with some appointments made "by divine will" (i.e., by Shri Sathya Sai Baba himself) and others by democratic process. The levels and organizations within the SSSO are numerous and the entire structure is linked together in a complex way. Sai Baba's followers have created an international institutional edifice, which is managed by the Shri Sathya Sai Central Trust (also known as the Sai Central Trust, or by the acronym SCT), and are active through various branches of the International Sai Organization (or International Sathya Sai Baba Organization). The International Sai Organization (ISO) is, according to them, involved in service to humanity – distributing aid to the poor (especially those in war-torn or natural-disaster zones)[34] and other participatory social services. Some, though not all of this activity takes place in India, concentrated around Prasanthi Nilayam, where the ISO runs top-notch schools and universities and manages state-of-the-art medical facilities staffed by doctors from all over the world who provide health care free of charge and have brought potable water to this dry region.

The ISO also projects Sai's mission abroad, largely through a network of Sai Baba Centers all over the world. The Sathya Sai Baba Central Council of America's website (www.sathyasai.org) includes information on nearly two hundred US Sai centers in forty-three states.[35] Local chapters and centers emphasize education in the Sai faith's five central values: truth (*sathya*), right conduct (*dharma*), nonviolence (*ahimsa*), love for God and God's creatures (*prema*), and peace (*shanti*). Since Sai Baba's death it has come to light that most of the financial decisions were taken by a core of devotees, the six male members of the Sai Charitable Trust, including Sai Baba himself. The position of the trustees and the composition of the Trust is currently (2011) being debated in the Indian media, though the Trust itself, in many joint announcements and news briefings, has claimed no internal strife or any wrangling for power between members.

MEDIATED PRESENCE

Sai bookshops worldwide run by the Sai movement stock newsletters, journals, magazines, and keepsakes. The bookshops were central to the globalizing efforts of the early movement, and they remain integral to the institutional structure of the movement even today. Devotees know by rote bite-sized popular, often rhythmic, sayings attributed to Sathya Sai Baba. Calligraphic graffiti of these sayings and his image adorn all sorts of unexpected places, signifying a devotional space that others of the faith recognize. One of his sayings, "Love all, serve all," is etched behind the cash register at the Hard Rock Café in central London, and another, "Help ever, hurt never," adorns the plastic tops on Seven Stars yogurt containers from the biodynamic dairy farm in Pennsylvania. They decorate the backs of autorickshaws (three-wheeled vehicles) in India and are popular on electronic greeting cards that devotees send one another.[36] Satya Sai Nag Champa incense (said to be Sathya Sai Baba's favorite incense) is to be found in venues around the world and in the West, primarily in New Age-style shops; DVDs featuring various bands that dedicate their songs to him are available in airport bookshops all over India and the Middle East; and small pictures of him can be seen in homes and commercial establishments from Manchester to Tokyo.

The proliferation of Sathya Sai Baba's image, and through them the extension and growth of his power, is enabled through these many net-worked portals – the Internet, music, radio, books, and television. His presence proliferates in every kind of media.[37] Websites constructed by technophile devotees feature photographs of him, both historical and contemporary; music; events at centers around the world; maps; useful tips about traveling to India; books; merchandise; and links to other sites that deal with his life and work. His audio sermons play endlessly on a global radio channel owned by the Sai Central Trust (Sai Global Harmony), as a "news" bulletin and commentary on the Internet (Heart 2 Heart), and in videos, news items, documentary movies (both pro and anti).[38] Sai Baba is the central character in a comic book, *Sai Baba for Beginners*. His image graces a huge array of items, from jewelry gifted by him to devotees, and sculptures and life-size photographs worshipped by devotees, to sundry paraphernalia such as calendars, snowglobes, incense boxes, and cushions that are eagerly purchased in Puttaparthi and Sai centers all over the world. The growing cultural and religious self-awareness of Sai devotees as consumers of religious objects trans-forms markets, distribution strategies, and consumer behavior.

CONTROVERSY AND CRITICISM

The Sai movement and Sathya Sai Baba have attracted their fair share of controversy and criticism. In the 1970s active groups of Indian skeptics and scientists focused on Sathya Sai Baba's materializations and launched a newspaper "investigation" which devotees termed an attack on him. A BBC documentary, *The Secret Swami*, aired in 2004, focused on the materializations, which have been seen by critics as nothing more than skillful prestidigitation, which angered devotees, who believe them to be miraculous. More recently anti-Sai Baba sentiment has gone global (since 2000). Allegations of corruption, fiscal mismanagement, conspiracy, abuse, and even murder, have been leveled at the Sathya Sai movement and emphasized by a significant, though small, global anti-Sai movement, made up of a union between disaffected "former devotees" who were keen to expose some troubling practices at the ashram and Indian skeptics and rationalists such as Basava Premanand and others who were keen to debunk Sai Baba's magical illusions. Former devotees run a wide network of cyber accusations of sexual "healings" including oiling of the genitals of young male devotees, profiteering, and other unsavory activities,[39] raising discussions of tantric practice. The accusations pit the ex-devotees against current devotees in a cyber war over the nature of truth and disclosure. Indian and non-Indian news journals including *India Today*, *The Week*, and *The Telegraph* have published critical pieces about Sathya Sai Baba, but despite his critics' claims of malfeasance, Sai Baba was never accused (much less convicted) of wrongdoing in an Indian court of law though since his death the calls for transparency have gotten louder and louder.[40] In the months after his death, ex-devotees have made claims of conspiracy around the circumstances of Sai Baba's death and money found in the ashram, all of which are deeply troubling to devotees but have not yet been disproven.

In fact in the months after Sai Baba's funeral, allegations of financial mistrust have been leveled at the members of the Sai Charitable Trust by the national news media. In June 2011 over 150 kilograms of gold and 1,000 kilograms of silver, a treasure trove of currency, precious stones, and jewelry, estimated to be worth tens of millions of US dollars, was found in a search of Sai Baba's private rooms in his ashram.[41] In the aftermath there have been myriad calls for the government to take over the private Sai Charitable Trust and to render a transparent accounting of the assets of the Trust.

The many controversies notwithstanding, the Sathya Sai movement is seen by scholars as a significant example of an emergent transnational religious movement with a well-established organization and a wide range of activities in civil and urban society with a global devotional base and an ecumenist philosophy.

Notes

1 Most of this text was written and cleared for publication while Sathya Sai Baba was still alive. It has been amended to reflect recent events in the ashram.
2 Tulasi Srinivas, *Winged Faith: Rethinking Religion and Globalization through the Sathya Sai Movement* (New York, 2010).
3 *Times of India*, June 7, 2011.
4 BBC News, April 28, 2011, www.bbc.co.uk/news/world-south-asia-13205086 (all websites referred to in this chapter were accessed on November 25, 2011).
5 Ibid.
6 Lawrence A. Babb, *Redemptive Encounters: Three Modern Styles in the Hindu Tradition* (Berkeley, 1986); see also Lawrence Babb, "Sathya Sai Baba's Magic," *Anthropological Quarterly* 56:3 (1983), pp. 116–24; Morton Klass, *Singing with Sai Baba: The Politics of Revitalization in Trinidad* (Boulder, CO, 1991); Alexandra Kent, "Divinity, Miracles and Charity in the Sathya Sai Baba Movement of Malaysia," *Ethnos* 69:1 (2004), pp. 43–62; Smriti Srinivas, *In the Presence of Sai Baba: Body, City and Memory in a Global Religious Movement* (Leiden and Boston, 2008); Tulasi Srinivas "A Tryst with Destiny: The Indian Case of Cultural Globalization," in Peter L. Berger and Samuel P. Huntington (eds.), *Many Globalizations* (New York, 2002), pp. 89–116; T. Srinivas, *Winged Faith*; D. A. Swallow, "Ashes and Powers: Myth, Rite, and Miracle in an Indian Godman's Cult," *Modern Asian Studies* 16 (1982), pp. 123–58; Hugh B. Urban, "Avatar for Our Age: Sathya Sai Baba and the Cultural Contradictions of Late Capitalism," *Religion* 33 (2002), pp. 73–93.
7 S. Srinivas, *In the Presence of Sai Baba*, pp. 67–75.
8 Chad Bauman, "Educating the God Man's Children: The Sai Baba Center of Indianapolis," paper presented at the American Academy of Religion Annual Meeting, San Diego, November 17–20, 2007, pp. 1–2. See also R. Padmanabha, *Love Is My Form: The Advent, 1926–1950* (Puttaparthi, 2000).
9 S. Srinivas, *In the Presence of Sai Baba*; T. Srinivas, *Winged Faith*.
10 Narayan Kasturi, *Sathyam Sivam Sundaram. The Life of Bhagavan Sri Sathya Sai Baba*, 4 vols. (Prasanthi Nilayam, 1961–80), vol. 1, p. 39.
11 Kevin R. D. Shepherd, *Gurus Rediscovered: Biographies of Sai Baba of Shirdi and Upasni Maharaj of Sakori* (Cambridge, 1986); Howard Murphet, *Sai Baba Avatar: A New Journey into Power and Glory* (San Diego, 1977).
12 Bauman, "Educating," pp. 1–2; see also S. Srinivas *In the Presence of Sai Baba*, pp. 40–42, 76–77.
13 T. Srinivas, *Winged Faith*.
14 Michael J. Spurr, "Sathya Sai Baba as Avatar: 'His Story' and the History of an Idea" (unpublished PhD dissertation, University of Canterbury, 2007).
15 Bauman, "Educating," pp. 5–6; Norris Palmer, "Baba's World: A Global Guru and His Movement," in Thomas Forsthoefel and Cynthia Humes (eds.), *Gurus in America* (Albany, NY, 2005), pp. 97–122.

16 T. Srinivas, *Winged Faith.*
17 Samuel Sandweiss, *Sai Baba: The Holy Man and the Psychiatrist* (San Diego: 1975), p. 89.
18 Babb, "Sathya Sai's Magic," p. 117.
19 Alexandra Kent, "Divinity, Miracles, and Charity in the Sathya Sai Baba Movement of Malaysia," *Ethnos* 69 (2004), pp. 43–62, at p. 57.
20 Padmanabha, *Love Is My Form,* pp. 20–22; Swallow, "Ashes and Powers," pp. 123–58.
21 S. Srinivas, *In the Presence of Sai Baba.*
22 Klass, *Singing with Sai Baba*; see also Babb, *Redemptive Encounters.*
23 T. Srinivas, "A Tryst with Destiny."
24 Alexandra Kent, *Divinity and Diversity: A Hindu Revitalization Movement in Malaysia* (Copenhagen, 2005).
25 S. Srinivas, *In the Presence of Sai Baba.*
26 Paul Heelas and Linda Woodhead, *The Spiritual Revolution: Why Religion Is Giving Way to Spirituality* (Oxford, 2005), pp. 75–79.
27 Richard Weiss, "The Global Guru: Sai Baba and the Miracle of the Modern," *New Zealand Journal of Asian Studies* 7:2 (2005), pp. 5–19; see also Agehananda Bharathi, *The Ochre Robe* (Seattle, 1962).
28 T. Srinivas, *Winged Faith.*
29 Murphet, *Sai Baba.*
30 The issue of globalization is discussed later in this chapter.
31 Howard Murphet, *Sai Baba: Man of Miracles* (London, 1971); see also T. Srinivas, *Winged Faith.*
32 T. Srinivas, *Winged Faith.*
33 Kent, "Divinity, Miracles and Charity."
34 Palmer, "Baba's World," p. 117.
35 Bauman, "Educating," pp. 5–9.
36 S. Srinivas, *In the Presence of Sai Baba,* pp. 5–7.
37 Meredith Feike, "Logging on to Sai Baba" (unpublished PhD dissertation, Louisiana State University, 2007).
38 Ibid., pp. 48–60.
39 Alexandra Nagel, *De Sai Paradox: Tegenstrijdigheden van en rondom Sathya Sai Baba* ("The Sai paradox: Contradictions of and Surrounding Sathya Sai Baba"), Religieuze bewegingen in Nederland/Religious movements in the Netherlands 29 (Amsterdam,1994)
40 Bauman, "Educating," p. 7.
41 *Times of India,* July 20, 2011, http://articles.timesofindia.indiatimes.com/2011–06–17/india/29669449_1_sathya-sai-central-trust-nephew-and-trust-member-valuables.

Further reading

Babb, Lawrence A., *Redemptive Encounters: Three Modern Styles in the Hindu Tradition* (Berkeley, 1986).
Kent, Alexandra, *Divinity and Diversity: A Hindu Revitalization Movement in Malaysia* (Copenhagen, 2005).

Klass, Morton, *Singing with Sai Baba: The Politics of Revitalization in Trinidad* (Boulder, CO, 1991).

Srinivas, Smriti, *In the Presence of Sai Baba: Body, City and Memory in a Global Religious Movement* (Leiden and Boston, 2008).

Srinivas, Tulasi, "A Tryst with Destiny: The Indian Case of Cultural Globalization," in Peter L. Berger and Samuel P. Huntington (eds.), *Many Globalizations* (New York, 2002), pp. 89–116.

Winged Faith: Rethinking Religion and Globalization through the Sathya Sai Movement (New York, 2010).

12 Neo-Sufism

MARK SEDGWICK

Sufism is a long-established phenomenon in the Muslim world, where Sufi orders emerged in the twelfth century, and thereafter fulfilled a range of important religious, social, political, artistic, intellectual, and economic functions. It has been present in geographical Europe – in Russia and the Balkans – for centuries, but did not attract much attention in Western Europe until the eighteenth century, or in America until the nineteenth century. At the end of that century, Sufism began to emerge in modified form in the West, as neo-Sufism. The forms that neo-Sufism have since then taken were determined partly by the forms taken by Sufism in the Muslim world, and partly by preceding developments in Western Europe.

Sufism in the Muslim world can be identified either in terms of its doctrines and religious practices (many of which are in some sense mystical and some of which go back beyond even the twelfth century), or in terms of its classic organizational structure, the *tariqa* or order. The Sufi order is, in a sense, the classic NRM.[1] Every Sufi order originates with a *shaykh* or spiritual guide possessed of great charisma, generally claiming a privileged connection with the Prophet Muhammad or with God, to whom miracles are ascribed. The death of such a *shaykh* produces the classic problem of the routinization of charisma, made especially difficult by Sunni Islam's general distrust of formal hierarchical organization in religion. The most successful Sufi orders have spread very widely, but lost all organizational coherence. A number of Sufi orders named after *shaykhs* from the thirteenth and fourteenth centuries are now to be found everywhere from Morocco to Indonesia, but these invariably fragmented long ago into totally independent sub-orders started by later charismatic *shaykhs*, which themselves have also fragmented into yet more sub-orders in the same way, in a continual process of reinvention. Looked at in terms of organization, the average Sufi sub-order had a life cycle of perhaps only two or three generations.[2] Sufism in the Muslim world, then, can be understood as a swarm of

NRMs, constantly in motion, but generally staying within established – if contested – limits. These limits will be used in this chapter to distinguish Sufism from neo-Sufism. Sufism in the Muslim world can also be understood in terms of "glocalization." The general rule is that the order, main doctrines, and practices are global (in terms of Muslim parts of the globe, at least), and have been for centuries, while the sub-order, organization, and some doctrines and practices are local.

The term "neo-Sufism" was first used by scholars to describe an unusually fertile wave of new orders and sub-orders in the eighteenth-century Muslim world.[3] The term is now increasingly used, however, to describe various forms of Sufism found in the West since the nineteenth century. The main difference between these and Sufism as found in the Muslim world is that the limits within which Sufism operates in the West are much looser, and the influence of the local is much greater. The local context in which the global finds concrete expression matters a lot for Sufism, and until recently local contexts in the West have been very different from those in the Muslim world, especially in their limits, or the lack of them. When the limits of the acceptable are tested in the Muslim world, they are tested against a well-established social and intellectual consensus that is not uniform, but is agreed on certain essential points. Until recently, this has not been the case in the West.

Local contexts in the West today are very different from those in the eighteenth century, when Sufism first came to Western public attention. Despite this, as this chapter will show, the impact of earlier contexts is still felt today. The chapter will therefore cover earlier contexts as well as current ones, and to do so will consider not just classic NRMs – that is to say, organized groups of people – but also what will be called NRIMs, new religious intellectual movements. An NRIM is a loose movement of thought that is not organized, but expresses new religious ideas and interpretations, and in so doing often paves the way for future organized groups, NRMs in the classic sense. NRIMs are to be found within the "cultic milieu," but are more internally consistent than is the cultic milieu as a whole.

The chapter will first consider two Western European NRIMs, the Theist neo-Sufism originating in the eighteenth and early nineteenth centuries, and the Romantic neo-Sufism originating in the high nineteenth century. It will then consider Theosophical neo-Sufism, which was the beginning of neo-Sufism as an NRM rather than an NRIM. Finally it will consider interwar neo-Sufism, a group of Western European NRMs that also had a presence in America, many of which still exist, and transregional neo-Sufism, which is found equally in

America and Europe. Given the number of NRMs involved, the chapter
will sometimes consider the general characteristics of groups of NRMs
rather than individual NRMs, placing the emphasis on the regional context and its consequences.

THEIST NEO-SUFISM

Eighteenth-century neo-Sufism was a small NRIM that emerged
against the background of another small NRIM, Theism. The local
regional context of seventeenth-century Western Europe included what
Richard Popkin has called a "sceptical crisis" resulting from the growing availability of information about both the chronology of human history and the variety of human religions.[4] Popkin's seventeenth-century
"sceptical crisis" is an early echo of Peter Berger's "heretical imperative" – Berger famously uses "heretical" in the sense of its lexical root,
haireisthai, to choose. For those who know only one version of something, there is no real choice. Multiple versions make choice imperative.[5] Berger did not locate this phenomenon in the seventeenth century,
but that is when his imperative started, as Jonathan Irvine Israel has
shown.[6] At first it affected only a small number of intellectuals, linked
by private correspondence, who only occasionally dared to publish their
conclusions.

The seventeenth-century heretical imperative resulted sometimes
in Atheism, sometimes in Deism, and sometimes in Theism. Atheism
does not concern us, and was probably anyhow very infrequent. Deism
and Theism both discarded much Christian doctrine, but retained certain basic points, including for example Creation and Judgment. They
are sometimes hard to distinguish, but Popkin uses "Theism" to identify
the current that emphasized the origin of these basic points in revelation, and "Deism" to identify the current that emphasized the compati-
bility of these basic points with reason, thus de-emphasizing revelation
and divine authority,[7] a distinction that this chapter will follow.

Theism's emphasis on divine revelation as the source of basic points
common to all religions might logically imply a number of independent
revelations, but might also imply a single original revelation that has
subsequently been embellished and confused. This second understanding was popular among eighteenth-century Theists, and was that of Sir
Isaac Newton, who identified the original revelation with the religion
of Noah, and with the *prisca theologia*,[8] essentially the *philosophia
perennis* of pre-Enlightenment Hermeticism. This was a popular view
at the time, but alternative identifications were also made. In 1671, a

Latin translation of the Arabic classic *Hayy ibn Yaqzan* created a sensation across Europe and was widely read as showing the quasi-Sufi Ikhwan al-Safa (Brothers of Purity) to have been Deists.[9] This seems to have been the first origin of an idea that still remains influential today: that Sufism is a surviving form of the *prisca theologia*. Voltaire seems to have held this view, to judge from his treatment of a Sufi in *Candide* in 1759,[10] though he did not make the point explicitly. The earliest explicit identification of Sufism in general (not just the Ikhwan al-Safa) as a form of the *prisca theologia* rather than as a form of Islam is to be found in a French encyclopedia of 1767.[11] Unfortunately, little is known about its author.

Although the first expressions of the NRIM that understood Sufism as *prisca theologia* are found in France, it was in British India and England that they then developed, initially under the impulsion of Sir William Jones (1746–1794), the son of a friend of Newton's. Jones was an accomplished scholar and, like Newton, a theist. In 1792 he identified Sufis in much the same terms that the 1767 French encyclopedia had, but with more detail.[12] Jones' work was then expanded by a younger scholar working in the same environment, James Graham, who in 1819 published what is probably the Western world's first in-depth study of Sufism.[13] The idea that Sufism is the survival of a pre-Islamic Theistic religion was then propagated by a scholar-diplomat who wrote for the general educated public, Sir John Malcolm (1769–1833), who drew extensively on Graham's work.[14] The NRIM that this chapter will call Theist neo-Sufism thus became well established, and can be traced throughout the nineteenth century and into the twentieth century.

ROMANTIC NEO-SUFISM

Although it was at the start of the nineteenth century that Theist neo-Sufism became firmly established, the Western context of the high nineteenth century was a different one, and produced a different type of neo-Sufi NRIM. The high nineteenth century saw not a skeptical crisis but a crisis of rationalism, conventionally ascribed to reaction against the excesses of the French Revolution and the Industrial Revolution. One of the consequences of this crisis was the Romantic movement, a "movement" that is hard to define, perhaps because the phrase really describes an era. Among its causes was the growth of a middle class with the wealth and education to appreciate new literary forms, notably the novel and the epic poem. Among the characteristics of Romanticism were an emphasis on feeling and the soul, and on

Sehnsucht, a German word that indicates a feeling that was famously understood by C. S. Lewis as the "inconsolable longing" for "we know not what."[15] *Sehnsucht* was not specifically religious, but blends into the spiritual. Romanticism generally shifted the focus from doctrine – which had preoccupied Europe since at least the Reformation – to religious experience.

Also characteristic of Romanticism was a rejection of classical models and an interest in the alternatives offered by indigenous and national cultures, often at their pre-Christian roots. A further alternative was provided by exotic Oriental models, which inspired a considerable output of "Orientalist" poetry, fiction, music, and painting. Some felt that as the discovery of classical Greek civilization had produced the original Renaissance, so the discovery of Oriental civilization could produce a new renaissance.[16] That this new renaissance did not in fact materialize owed something to the fact that Muslim philosophy shares much with classical Greek philosophy, and thus was not so new, and something to the fact that the diffusion of Oriental knowledge happened not so much at the hands of scholars – though the successors of Newton and Jones grew in number and learning – as at the hands of poets and novelists. Poets and novelists read the works of scholars, and even consulted them in person, but in the view of Jean Bruneau, "the contribution of specialists seems limited essentially to the Oriental décor."[17] The nineteenth-century Oriental tale and Oriental travelogue, of which there were great numbers, often examined philosophical and spiritual themes of interest to Western writer and readers, but bore little relation to Oriental realities beyond a romanticized "décor." Samuel Taylor Coleridge's "Kubla Khan" of 1798 tells us much about Romanticism, but nothing about the actual Orient. Edward Said has argued that this Orientalism not only bore no relation to reality, but also created stereotypes that justified, and still justify, Western imperialism and oppression of "Orientals." While there is clearly truth in this, Orientalist literature also created some positive stereotypes of the Orient, including one of the Orient as innately spiritual, in contrast to a Western materialism.

Sufism did not occupy a prominent place in the mass of Romantic Orientalist writing. Sufis did make occasional appearances, but usually as generic wise men, following (consciously or not) the lead of Voltaire. The impact of occasional mentions of dervishes in these terms was presumably no more than to establish a loose association between Sufism and wisdom, an association strengthened by the overall stereotype of Oriental spirituality.

Sometimes, however, Sufism played a more prominent part. As well as poetry and fiction, translations of original Oriental texts reached a wide public. One of the first was the 1812 German translation of the Sufi poems of Hafez.[18] Without doubt the most widely read was the 1859 English "rendering" of the *Rubaiyat of Omar Khayyam* by Edward Fitzgerald (1809–1883), which became one of the most popular works of the entire century, retranslated from English into many other languages.

Widespread enthusiasm for authors such as Hafez, Rumi, and Umar Khayyam constitutes the dominant form of the NRIM that is Romantic neo-Sufism. It raises the problem of reception, of how all the enthusiastic readers of these Sufi poems understood what they read. Sufi poetry was presumably mostly read as literature, but to some extent must have also been read with a focus on spiritual experience, if not on doctrine.

THEOSOPHICAL NEO-SUFISM

The Theosophical Society (henceforth TS), founded in New York in 1875, was *the* NRM of the nineteenth century, and some connection with it is to be found in very many subsequent developments, if only because for a while it was really "the only show in town." Anybody with any interest in alternative religion was thus likely to gravitate towards it. It offered a very nineteenth-century mixture of Oriental religion, Western esotericism, and faith in progress,[19] enlivened by an attempt at charisma that eventually backfired, depending as it did on mechanical tricks that were ultimately exposed. Its views on the relations between different religions were essentially Theist, and its views on the great authority of Oriental religions were essentially Romantic. The TS, then, reflects the same Western context as Theist and Romantic neo-Sufism.

The coming into being of the TS is the immediate context for the development of Theosophical neo-Sufism, and itself reflects a change in the limits set by Western states and societies that was part of the context for later neo-Sufism. Christian sects and denominations had risen and fallen more or less freely since the Reformation, but there had been no public space for avowedly non-Christian organizations, save latterly for Jewish ones. Others had existed only in secret, if at all. The TS was very public. It was also run by a woman, which marked a further change in Western limits. Previous Western organizations, Christian and public or non-Christian and secret, had generally been led by, and sometimes composed exclusively of, men. The TS anticipated the Protestant churches by many decades in having women in senior positions.

The Oriental religions that interested the TS's Helena Blavatsky (1831–1891) were Buddhism and Hinduism, and she mentions Sufism only in passing in her books.[20] Her earliest mention repeats the Theist view,[21] as does a short article published in 1882 in *The Theosophist*, a journal published in Bombay – an article that is actually an unattributed abbreviated version of Graham's 1819 study,[22] neatly linking Blavatsky to Newton. In New York, however, a series of six articles on Sufism were published in the first volume of another TS journal, *The Path*, in 1886.[23] The author of these articles, the Danish-American librarian Carl Bjerregaard (1845–1922), later published an edition of Fitzgerald's *Omar Khayyam* with his own "Sufi" interpretation facing each page,[24] inserting Theist neo-Sufism into Romantic neo-Sufism. His expensively printed book does not seem to have sold well, however.

Romantic and Theosophical neo-Sufism together created the beginnings of a neo-Sufi NRM within the overall NRIM. In 1899 or 1900, the Russian-French travel writer Isabelle Eberhardt (1877–1904) joined the Rahmaniyya Sufi sub-order in Algeria.[25] In 1907, the Swedish-French painter Ivan Aguéli (1869–1917) joined the Arabiyya sub-order in Cairo.[26] In the same way, in 1924, the French painter and satirical cartoonist Gustave-Henri Jossot (1866–1951), who had converted to Islam without reference to Sufism in Tunis in 1913, joined the Alawiyya sub-order, also in Algeria.[27] All three of these people had a connection to the TS,[28] and all three had elements of the Romantic in their creative work, which emphasized the exotic, the freedom of the remote desert, and other such (by then well-established) motifs. They did not form an NRM, however, as they were not connected other than by their associations with Romanticism, France, and Theosophy.

A similar individual, the French Orientalist painter Etienne Dinet (1861–1929), also joined the Rahmaniyya (in 1913),[29] but is not known to have any connection to Theosophy and – from the limited information known – seems to have become a Sufi rather than a neo-Sufi, despite his Romantic background. The other three, however, became individual neo-Sufis rather than Sufis. Nothing is known of Eberhardt's views on doctrine, but her continued (and immoderate) use of alcohol and hashish and her continuation of her highly promiscuous sex-life all severely transgressed the limits that constrained Sufis and Sufism in the Muslim world.[30] Aguéli was deeply interested in Sufi doctrine, and took it seriously, but also continued to take non-Sufi doctrine seriously, including that of the TS and that of an informal "esoteric" circle to which he belonged in Paris. He also seems not to have followed normal

Sufi practice.[31] He too, then, transgressed the limits of Sufism in the Muslim world.

Jossot's account of his conversion to Islam reveals both Deist and Romantic elements. His characterization of Islam as "without mystery, without dogma, without clergy, almost without worship," and as "of all religions the most rational," [32] corresponds with eighteenth-century views rather than reality – Islam does not lack dogma, clergy, or worship, except perhaps in comparison with Catholic Christianity. Among the reasons he gave for his conversion was that "the beauty of oriental life long fascinated my artistic imagination: my love of reverie, my disgust with civilization, all encouraged in me a total transformation."[33] This is distinctly Romantic. His later account of his participation in the Alawiyya sub-order, in contrast, lacks these elements,[34] and suggests Sufism rather than neo-Sufism, but something other than Sufism is suggested by his abandonment of the Alawiyya in 1927.[35]

Though these three Theosophical and Romantic neo-Sufis did not constitute an NRM, one of them, Aguéli, did establish the West's first neo-Sufi group, in Paris in 1909, "giving" the Alawiyya to other members of his esoteric circle. This consisted of men who had previously been members of a Parisian offshoot of the TS, from which they had broken off to form a so-called "Gnostic Church," and who were more interested in Hindu and Chinese religion than in Sufism.[36] Were it not for these interests, and for the apparent total absence of any Sufi or even Islamic practice in the group, Aguéli might have been considered to have founded a Sufi sub-order in the way that has happened many thousands of times in the history of the Muslim world. Given that the doctrines and known practices of the group transgressed the limits that constrained Sufism in the Muslim world, however, it must be considered neo-Sufi rather than Sufi. It was not, however, an NRM in the normal sense, because it does not seem to have actually done anything. It did not expand, and soon vanished.

INTERWAR NEO-SUFISM

One new local context during the interwar period was the collapse of the TS, which had shown what was possible, and then left a vacuum. Another was the impact of World War I, which reinforced the changes in Western limits that had assisted the original rise of the TS. The war also created a new context by challenging the nineteenth century's optimistic faith in science and progress, producing a new crisis, this time of faith in Western civilization.

The interwar period saw the establishment in Western Europe of at least five neo-Sufi NRMs,[37] all of which responded to the perceived crisis of Western civilization, all save one of which were public organizations, and all save two of which involved women in senior positions. The first, the "Sufi Society" (later the "Sufi Order," SO) founded in London by Inayat Khan (1882–1927) in 1914, still exists in various forms and countries today, and remains one of the most important neo-Sufi NRMs. The second, the Thulegesellschaft, was founded in Munich in 1918 by Rudolf Freiherr von Sebottendorf (1875–1945?), and lasted less than a year. The third, the "Fourth Way" founded in Paris in about 1921 by Georges Gurdjieff (1866–1949), also still exists today and is probably of even greater importance. The fourth, of which the European branch was founded in 1931 by Meher Baba (1894–1969), lasted only until its founder's death. The fifth, the Alawiyya (later Maryamiyya) founded in Basel in about 1934 by Frithjof Schuon (1907–1998), also survives, and is important, if not large.

Sebottendorf's unsuccessful Munich group is known only because it had an incidental relationship with the foundation of the Nazi Party. Without this, it would have been forgotten, and there may also be other such unsuccessful or small neo-Sufi groups from the interwar period that are not known today. The overall Western neo-Sufism of which the NRMs mentioned above were expressions may, then, have been even bigger.

The Sufi content in these neo-Sufi NRMs varied. At one extreme lies Sebottendorf, who claimed a Sufi provenance for certain numerological exercises that he combined with Freemasonry, and Meher Baba, who claimed initiation from a Sufi saint, but otherwise was much more neo-Hindu than neo-Sufi.[38] At the other extreme lies Schuon's Alawiyya, which saw itself as Sufi rather than neo-Sufi, and might be classed as Sufi were it not for the presence of elements in its doctrine, drawn and developed from the *philosophia perennis*, that transgressed the limits constraining Sufism in the Muslim world.[39] In between lie the SO, which described itself as Sufi, and the Fourth Way, which did not. Both claimed a Sufi provenance for their doctrines and practices, exclusively in the case of the SO and non-exclusively in the case of the Fourth Way. In fact, the Fourth Way's practices owed more to Sufism than did the SO's, but the SO's doctrines owed more to Sufism than did the Fourth Way's.[40]

Sebottendorf's NRM was atypical, and will be ignored, save to observe that it was one of the two NRMs that did not involve women. The other NRM that did not involve women was the Alawiyya, which was also the exception in not being public. On the other hand, it was the NRM that most emphasized the perceived crisis of Western civilization, incorporating the anti-modernist Traditionalism of René Guénon (1886–1951).[41]

All four NRMs reflected Theosophical (and so also Theist) neo-Sufism in their conception of relations between Sufism and other religions, most clearly in the case of the Alawiyya, which specifically identified the core of Sufism with the *philosophia perennis*,[42] and almost equally clearly in the case of the SO, which presented Sufism as an ancient truth that had long existed secretly within various religions.[43] The Fourth Way did not refer to divine revelation or to reason, but rather to experience – the golden standard with which Romanticism had replaced the Enlightenment's reason. According to Gurdjieff, Sufism consisted of doctrines and practices of varying origins that had been successfully "realized."[44] All these three thus, in effect, presented themselves as encompassing all religious paths of value, which Meher Baba also did, though rather differently: by presenting himself as an *avatar*, a divine incarnation, a position that he took to the lengths of publicly reminiscing about his time on the cross when he was Jesus. God, by definition, encompasses all religious paths of value. In addition, the SO and the Alawiyya had a direct relationship to Theosophical neo-Sufism. It was the TS which published Khan's first and most important book, in 1914. In 1915, Bjerregaard, who had written on Sufism in the Theosophical journal *The Path* in 1886, and who had met Khan in New York,[45] published a new book on Fitzgerald's *Omar Khayyam*, declaring his support for the SO.[46] The Alawiyya's debt was less direct, running through René Guénon to Aguéli.[47]

All four NRMs also reflected Theosophical and Romantic neo-Sufism by seeing the Orient as uniquely spiritual, and also by using the Muslim world as many Romantic writers had (and as Blavatsky had used the Orient as a whole) as décor for their own ideas, in effect taking advantage of their Western audience's ignorance of the realities of the Muslim world. Khan did this because he thought he would otherwise never be able to penetrate Westerners' prejudices against Islam.[48] Schuon did not consciously or deliberately present anything as other than what he knew it to be, but he interpreted what he found in Sufism in the light of what he considered the *philosophia perennis* to be, on the basis of other sources, thus to some extent making Sufism a décor for non-Sufi doctrines. Gurdjieff used "teaching stories" set in the Muslim world (in his case, Central Asia) that have sometimes been taken literally, but which are certainly often fictional,[49] thus again using the

Muslim world as décor. To the extent that Meher Baba was neo-Hindu rather than Hindu, he was perhaps doing something similar.

Three of the four NRMs also reflected central traits of Theosophy and Romanticism in emphasizing individual experience and, as an extension of this, the individual spiritual quest and freedom from the restrictions of established religion. Individual self-realization was especially stressed by Khan (as the development of "personality") and by Gurdjieff (as "self remembering"), and was at least accepted by one of Meher Baba's English spokespersons, if less emphasized by Meher Baba himself. Schuon, in contrast, condemned typical Romantic traits, and in this was the odd NRM out in not being public, in not involving women, and in drawing much more on Sufism.

That the Alawiyya was the odd NRM out partly explains why, in the post-war period considered below, it remained distinct from the other three neo-Sufi NRMs, while branches of the Fourth Way and the SO became somewhat entangled, as did branches of the SO and of Meher Baba's group, as important individuals shifted from one NRM to another.[50] Although further research is required to confirm this, an important later (post-war) neo-Sufi NRM, that founded by Idries Shah (1924–1996), seems to derive partly from the SO and partly from the Fourth Way.

TRANSREGIONAL NEO-SUFISM

The Western context for neo-Sufism changed again after World War II, especially from the 1970s, as travel between the West and the Muslim world became much easier and cheaper than ever before. Migration from the Muslim world to the West led to the establishment there of significant Muslim minorities. Short trips to one region from the other became affordable and even routine. The West and the Muslim world were no longer really separate.

Migration and Sufi *shaykhs* visiting from the Muslim world brought classic Sufism to Western Europe and America, where it took forms little different from those it had taken among Muslim communities in the Balkans and Russia in earlier centuries. The limits within which neo-Sufism operated in the West became less loose as knowledge of classic Sufism became easier to acquire, and the influence of the purely Western context thus declined. Although interwar neo-Sufi NRMs survived and in some cases prospered, new neo-Sufi NRMs were (with a few exceptions, including Idries Shah) far closer to classic Sufism, maintaining ties with sub-orders in the Muslim world, and operating increasingly within much the same limits as Sufis in the Muslim world. Some branches of interwar origin also established such ties and became much closer to classic Sufism.

Transregional neo-Sufism is very different from the varieties of neo-Sufism that preceded it, except in often retaining interwar neo-Sufism's emphasis on the crisis of Western civilization and in being as public as interwar neo-Sufism was, which is anyhow the norm in the Muslim world. Theism is generally absent, save for individuals with a previous association with surviving interwar NRMs, and Romantic neo-Sufism is also generally absent, save for individuals with a previous interest in translations of Sufi poets, which continue to sell remarkably well, often being bought by readers who also read Rilke, Hermann Hesse, and Paulo Coelho.[51]

The development of routine intercontinental travel has also brought the beginning of the end of the long-established rule that the order, main doctrines, and practices are global, while the sub-order, organization, and some doctrines and practices are local. Today, there are sub-orders that are transregional and some that show signs of becoming truly global. One effect of this is that, to the extent that a sub-order is neo-Sufi rather than Sufi, the neo-Sufi elements are now becoming present in the Muslim world, as well as in the West that gave rise to them.

Recent transregional neo-Sufi NRMs have been relatively well studied,[52] so this chapter will consider only one example, the Haqqaniyya, founded in London in 1974 by a Turkish Cypriot, Muhammad Nazim (b.1922).[53] In fact, this is much more a classic Sufi sub-order rather than a neo-Sufi NRM. It is certainly new, its leader is certainly charismatic, and it certainly plays a role of overwhelming importance in the lives of its adherents – but that is completely normal for a new Sufi sub-order in the Muslim world. The Haqqaniyya operates within the limits set by the context from which many of its followers come – Turkey and Muslim communities in the West. In fact, it is probably only considered an NRM because many of its followers are Western converts. As a result, it does transgress some of the limits of the Muslim world by making certain concessions to the Western context, especially at its branch in Glastonbury, a New Age town in England. It also transgresses established limits by its unusual emphasis on apocalyptic predictions,[54] but this transgression pales into insignificance when compared with the transgressions of Theist, Romantic, Theosophical, and interwar neo-Sufism.

Some other transregional neo-Sufi NRMs reflect the contemporary Western context more than this, and so transgress the limits of the Muslim world more, notably with regard to gender and, sometimes, the requirement that a Sufi formally convert to Islam. Even so, they are in a different category from earlier varieties of neo-Sufism.

CONCLUSION

Neo-Sufism, the reception and adaptation in one region of a religious form from another region, is naturally affected by the extent to which the two regions are separate. Transregional neo-Sufism, the most recent form the phenomenon has taken, is very different from earlier forms of neo-Sufism. To the extent that the West and the Muslim world have become entwined, transregional neo-Sufism operates in the West within much the same limits that Sufism has long observed in the Muslim world. The impact of the local Western context is limited, and generally relates to matters such as gender, where Western limits are very hard to transgress. If transregional neo-Sufi sub-orders sometimes still look like NRMs despite this, that is to some extent because the Sufi sub-order in the Muslim world is itself in some ways a classic NRM.

Despite the growing similarity between transregional neo-Sufism and Sufism, neo-Sufi NRMs of interwar origin still prosper, sometimes adapting to current circumstances by becoming more Sufi and less neo-Sufi, but sometimes not. Interwar neo-Sufism was and is very different from transregional neo-Sufism, much more Western, and much more affected by earlier European NRIMs, Romantic and Theist.

The history of neo-Sufism mirrors the history of Western religiosity. It starts with the "sceptical crisis" of the seventeenth century as an NRIM in an age when Christian doctrine was questioned only by a few intellectuals, and could hardly be questioned in public. It takes a new form as Romanticism shifts the emphasis from doctrine to experience, benefiting from Romanticism's use of the exotic Orient, but is still an NRIM rather than an NRM, in a period when Christian doctrine could be questioned publicly, but non-Christian religious organizations remained beyond the limits. Only when the West changed enough to allow the existence of the TS could and did neo-Sufism become an NRM rather than an NRIM – or rather a group of NRMs that had some things in common, usually inherited from Theist and Romantic neo-Sufism, often via Theosophical neo-Sufism.

In this, there was some similarity between neo-Sufism in the West and Sufism in the Muslim world. In the Muslim world, Sufism as a whole is not an NRM. Sufism as a whole has no organizational existence, however, and is made up at the operational level of a swarm of sub-orders, all of which are in a sense NRMs. Likewise, neo-Sufism as a whole is not an NRM, and consists at an operational level of a number of individual local (or transregional) NRMs, some of which have been mentioned in this chapter, and some characterized in terms of their general characteristics.

Sufism and neo-Sufism, then, do not fit entirely comfortably into the standard understanding of what an NRM is. They fit closely enough, however, for this chapter's examination of neo-Sufism in terms of the NRM to have revealed something about the nature of neo-Sufism, and also, perhaps, to have extended somewhat the understanding of what an NRM is, or might be.

Notes

1 For more details, see Mark Sedgwick, "Establishments and Sects in the Islamic World," in Phillip Lucas and Thomas Robbins (eds.), *New Religious Movements in the 21st Century: Legal, Political, and Social Challenges in Global Perspective* (New York, 2004), pp. 283–312.

2 Mark Sedgwick, "Upper Egypt's Regional Identity: The Role and Impact of Sufi Links," in Nicholas S. Hopkins and Reem Saad (eds.), *Identity and Change in Upper Egypt* (Cairo, 2004), pp. 97–118.

3 Rex S. O'Fahey *Enigmatic Saint: Ahmad ibn Idris and the Idrisi Tradition* (London, 1990), pp. 1–4.

4 Richard Popkin, "Polytheism, Deism, and Newton," in James E. Force and Richard Henry Popkin (eds.), *Essays on the Context, Nature, and Influence of Isaac Newton's Theology* (Berlin, 1990), pp. 27–42, at p. 27.

5 Peter L. Berger, *The Heretical Imperative: Contemporary Possibilities of Religious Affirmation* (Garden City, NY, 1979), p. 50.

6 Jonathan Irvine Israel, *Radical Enlightenment: Philosophy and the Making of Modernity 1650–1750* (Oxford, 2001). Israel shows how that which is known as "the Enlightenment" was in many ways the fruition of earlier events. Those earlier events, however, did not lead only to the Enlightenment.

7 Popkin, "Polytheism, Deism, and Newton," p. 31.

8 C. de Pater, "An Ocean of Truth," in T. Koetsier and Luc Bergmans (eds.), *Mathematics and the Divine: A Historical Study* (Amsterdam, 2005), pp. 459–84, at pp. 470–71.

9 G. A. Russell, "The Impact of the *Philosophus autodidactus*: Pocockes, John Locke and the Society of Friends," in Russell (ed.), *The 'Arabick' Interests of the Natural Philosophers in Seventeenth-Century England* (Leiden, 1994), pp. 226–28.

10   Voltaire, *Candide* (London, 1759), pp. 160–61.
11   Jacques-Philibert Rousselot de Surgy, *Mélanges intéressans et curieux* (Paris, 1767), vol. VII, pp. 118–19.
12   William Jones, *Dissertations and Miscellaneous Pieces Relating to the History and Antiquities, the Arts, Sciences, and Literature of Asia* (London, 1792), pp. 197–98 and 202.
13   James Graham, "A Treatise on Sufiism, or Mahomedan Mysticism," *Transactions of the Literary Society of Bombay* (London, 1819), pp. 89–119.
14   John Malcolm, *The History of Persia* (London, 1825), pp. 382–409.
15   Although Lewis used both phrases quoted, he does not actually seem ever to have used them in the same sentence. The formulation, however, is well established, and probably owes more to Lewis than to anyone else.
16   Jean Bruneau, *Le 'Conte Oriental' de Flaubert* (Paris, 1973), pp. 23–25.
17   Ibid., p. 19.
18   Joseph von Hammer-Purgstall, *Der Diwan von Mohammed Schemseddin Hafis* (Stuttgart, 1812).
19   Nicholas Goodrick-Clarke, *The Western Esoteric Traditions: A Historical Introduction* (New York, 2008), pp. 211–26.
20   Once in *Isis Unveiled* (New York, 1877), and even more briefly in *The Secret Doctrine* (London, 1888), vol. II, p. 431. Available online at www.theosociety.org (accessed December 2011).
21   Blavatsky, *Isis Unveiled*, vol. II, p. 306, quoting the Theist view of Charles King.
22   As "A Treatise on Sufism: Or, Mahomedan Mysticism," no author given, *The Theosophist* 3 (August 1882), pp. 265–66.
23   Tables of contents and actual articles available at www.theosociety.org (accessed December 2011).
24   C. H. A. Bjerregaard, *Sufi Interpretations of the Quatrains of Omar Khayyam and Fitzgerald* (New York, 1902).
25   Julia Clancy-Smith, *Rebel and Saint: Muslim Notables, Populist Protest, Colonial Encounters (Algeria and Tunisia, 1800–1904)* (Berkeley, 1994), pp. 245–49.
26   Mark Sedgwick, *Against the Modern World: Traditionalism and the Secret Intellectual History of the Twentieth Century* (New York, 2004), pp. 61–62.
27   AbdulKarîm Jossot, *Le sentier d'Allah* (Tunis, 1927). Text from al.alawi.1934.free.fr/modules.php?name=Content&pa=showpage&pid=50 (accessed August 19, 2010).
28   For Aguéli, see: Sedgwick, *Against the Modern World*, p. 60. For Gustave H. Jossot, see: Henri Viltard's "Biographie" (January 2008), gustave.jossot.free.fr/biographie.html (accessed December 2011). For Eberhardt (less certain): K. Paul Johnson, *Initiates of Theosophical Masters* (Albany, NY, 1995), pp. 167–68.
29   Clancy-Smith, *Rebel and Saint*, p. 226.
30   Ibid., p. 248.

31 Sedgwick, *Against the Modern World*, pp. 62–63.
32 Abdul Karim Jossot, "J'ai accompli, hier soir, un acte d'une extrême gravité," 1913, available at gustave.jossot.free.fr/polemique_tunisienne.html (accessed December 2011).
33 Ibid.
34 Jossot, *Sentier d'Allah*.
35 Viltard, "Biographie."
36 Sedgwick, *Against the Modern World*, pp. 62–63 and *passim*.
37 Information concerning these is taken from Mark Sedgwick, "European Neo-Sufi Movements in the Interwar Period," in Nathalie Clayer and Eric Germain (eds.), *Islam in Inter-war Europe* (London, 2008), pp. 183–215.
38 Ibid. Sedgwick, *Against the Modern World*, pp. 122–23.
39 Sedgwick, *Against the Modern World*, pp. 122–23.
40 Sedgwick, "European Neo-Sufi Movements," pp. 190–97 and 207–13.
41 Sedgwick, *Against the Modern World*, pp. 122–23.
42 Ibid.
43 Inayat Khan, *Sufi Message of Spiritual Liberty* (London, 1914), p. 26.
44 A. T. Challenger, *Philosophy and Art in Gurdjieff's Beelzebub: A Modern Sufi Odyssey* (Amsterdam, 2002), p. 16.
45 Inayat Khan, *Biography of Pir-o-Murshid Inayat Khan* (London, 1979; ebook edn.), p. 86.
46 Khan, *Sufi Message*; C. H. A. Bjerregaard, *Sufism: Omar Khayyam and E. Fitzgerald* (London, 1915). The support for the SO appears on p. 4.
47 Sedgwick, *Against the Modern World*.
48 Inayat Kahn, Journal (1923), available at wahiduddin.net/mv2/bio/Journal_1.htm (accessed December 2011).
49 Sedgwick, "European Neo-Sufi Movements," p. 208.
50 Hülya Küçük, "A Brief History of Western Sufism," *Asian Journal of Social Science* 36 (2008), pp. 292–320, at pp. 306 and 309–10.
51 Mark Sedgwick, "The Reception of Sufi and Neo-Sufi Literature," in Ron Geaves, Markus Dressler, and Gritt M. Klinkhammer (eds.), *Sufis in Western Society: Global Networking and Locality* (London, 2009), pp. 180–97, at p. 190.
52 See the further reading for this chapter.
53 Jørgen S. Nielsen, Mustafa Draper, and Galina Yemelianova, "Transnational Sufism: The Haqqaniyya," in Jamal Malik and John Hinnels (eds.), *Sufism in the West* (Abingdon, 2006), pp. 103–14, at p. 104.
54 Ibid., pp. 106–7.

Further reading

Dressler, Markus, Ron Geaves, and Gritt Klinkhammer (eds.), *Sufis in Western Society: Global Networking and Locality* (London, 2008).
Goodrick-Clarke, Nicholas, *The Western Esoteric Traditions: A Historical Introduction* (New York, 2008).

Küçük, Hülya, "A Brief History of Western Sufism," *Asian Journal of Social Science* 36 (2008), pp. 292–320.

Malik, Jamal and John Hinnels (eds.), *Sufism in the West* (Abingdon, 2006).

Sedgwick, Mark, "European Neo-Sufi Movements in the Interwar Period," in Nathalie Clayer and Eric Germain (eds.), *Islam in Inter-war Europe* (London, 2008), pp. 183–215.

13 Satanism

JESPER AAGAARD PETERSEN AND
ASBJØRN DYRENDAL

On June 6, 2006, representatives of the Church of Satan convened in the Steve Allen Theatre in Los Angeles to celebrate a fortieth anniversary High Mass.[1] About a hundred specially invited guests met in a highly mediated affair, showing the world that Satanism was alive and able to push the buttons of the establishment even after forty years of existence. Other groups also took advantage of the apocalyptic date 06–06–06; Twentieth Century Fox, for example, leant heavily on the demonic symbolism of the date when they released the highly anticipated thirtieth-anniversary remake of *The Omen* worldwide, and many Christian fringe groups speculated on the coming of the Antichrist.[2]

In short, Satan and Satanism constitute a significant presence in popular culture of the Western world. This is hardly inexplicable – Christianity is a powerful cultural presence worldwide, theories of secularization notwithstanding.[3] What is important for the present discussion, however, is the fact that *Satanism* is not simply inverted Christianity or bloodthirsty Devil worship. As we can see from the various offerings on June 6, 2006, contemporary Satanists are both mythological Christian bogeymen, narrative elements in movies, books, music and other expressions of popular culture, and self-declared individuals and groups claiming to be in league with "Satan" in some way.

In effect, both Satan and Satanism have been transformed through *cultural processes of dis- and re-embedding*, taking traditionally Christian elements out of their framework of values and meaning and inserting them into other contexts.[4] Today, Satan represents a variety of things to different people: mankind's carnal self, the adversary, supreme evil, a Hebrew angel, or Romantic anti-hero. Similarly, "Satanism" connotes a range of different things: a belief in and worship of Satan; the practice of nonconformity; a tragic resistance to oppression; or even bloody sacrificial rituals. What is meant by the use of "Satan," "Satanism," and "Satanist" is therefore in large part determined by practices of ascription – and it is very important whether these words are ascribed to oneself or someone else.

What we offer in this chapter is a *framework for studying* the milieu and the new religious movements that constitute modern Satanism, rather than a study of the phenomenon itself; for in-depth studies, see the suggested further readings at the end. After briefly surveying the history of modern religious Satanism in relation to other cultural narratives, this chapter will propose a typology of Satanism, present selected groups and influential formulations in the wider territory of what we call the "satanic milieu," and discuss identity construction and recruitment through various gateways to and from popular culture.

SATANISMS THEN AND NOW: A HISTORICAL PICTURE

Satanism manifests in two discrete cultural ways: on the one hand *discourses on the satanic* in the media and public sphere, most often based on the Christian mythology of evil, and on the other hand self-declared *satanic discourses* that take a variety of forms. Although these two ways of narrating "Satanism" borrow from each other, and point to one another as individual agents construct and reconstruct what they actually mean, they are quite distinct: the typical discourses on the satanic on the one end of the spectrum are narratives of the evil Other from whom the narrator is absolutely different (or if there are likenesses, this is due to possession or seduction); in contrast, typical satanic discourses at the other end of the spectrum are stories and practices about self-identity – the narrator *is* satanic, and even more so *by telling* us about and *doing* Satanism, in essence enacting the ideological framework.

Discourses on the satanic are most clearly found in modern demonologies and related moral panics, where claims of what "the Satanists" actually do to the community are calls for collective action.[5] These discourses construct an imagined negative satanic counterpoint from which to establish a positive identity, for example as devout Christian fighting evil, sympathetic psychologist treating traumatized victims, traumatized victim blowing the conspiracy open, as social worker providing the children with a voice, or as police officer taking on "cults." Aside from this markedly demonological discourse, we also find discourses on the satanic in popular culture, where Satan has an *ambiguous* role as both absolute evil and sensual anti-hero.[6]

In contrast to the discourses of imaginary Satanism as the Other of Christian or secular culture, satanic discourses use the orthodox establishment as a negative Other while extending the positive connotations of the figure of Satan. Although a contemporary phenomenon, satanic discourses have their roots in Enlightenment modernity, and have a complex relationship to historical discourses on the satanic.

Even if the common view on the Devil in the Middle Ages was ambiguous, associated with mastery over the earth as well as with carnival folk-culture, he was the Prince of Darkness and hence the author of sin, illness, and other bad things, not least the vice of woman. Nevertheless the somewhat educated, destitute, or desperate individual occasionally sought out the Devil for a bargain. All of this was of course understood under the sacred canopy of Catholic and later Protestant Christianity that associated witchcraft with Satan.[7]

The stories and beliefs surrounding the Devil gradually lost their prominence and changed in content. The end of the early modern witch craze and the wars of religion changed the arena, and with the Enlightenment and later Romanticism a cultural and political climate for critique of religion and sovereign power opened up the symbol of "Satan" for new, anti-traditional uses and readings. Satan became a symbol of, among other things, the human psyche and of resistance to tyrannical power. From John Milton's *Paradise Lost* (1674) this reading was strengthened by nineteenth-century Romantic poets invoking Satan as involved in a tragic-but-heroic fight against mediocrity, injustice, and established religion.[8]

Romantic literary Satanism, while contributing to the pool of cultural artefacts and stories used today (not least its reading of Milton) was still defined by Christian tradition.[9] The same can be said about other important sources for modern Satanism, such as Friedrich Nietzsche's *Genealogy of Morals* (1887), and the widespread bohemian interest in Satanism in decadent *fin de siècle* Europe and America.[10] The twentieth century witnessed new gnostic and mystical uses of Satan (often identified with Lucifer or Pan), usually formulated as anti-Christian but pro-spiritual views. New religious movements incorporating this in different ways range from Theosophy to Aleister Crowley's Ordo Templi Orientis. The German esoteric group Fraternitas Saturni is another case in point, associating Satan with Saturn as a source of power and knowledge; in America, Herbert Sloane's Our Lady of Endor Coven combined Satanism and gnosticism.[11]

Thus, discourses actively using Satan and Satanism as positive markers of identification definitely existed, but they did so primarily, indeed almost exclusively, within a literary context. The first substantial, official manifestation of Satanism as the identity of choice in a new religious movement occurred within the occult revival or "explosion" of the 1960s. Anton Szandor LaVey's founding of the Church of Satan, in San Francisco in 1966, is *the* seminal event. The group evolved out of LaVey's Magic Circle, one of many occult alternatives in California, then a hotbed of alternative religiosity and "seekership."[12]

From 1966 on, we may speak of roughly three phases of modern Satanism. From 1966 to 1975 the Church of Satan was established first as a local, then national and international phenomenon. Centered on the charismatic figure of LaVey, the church quickly gained media attention and attracted recruits. Far fewer stayed active, however, than dropped out of active participation, and internal strain showed ever more clearly once local groups were out of immediate contact with LaVey. In 1975 a combination of factors led to a second phase with new schisms. New groups, such as the Temple of Set, made sure that there was always a multiplicity of new religious movements with different conceptualizations of the satanic. At the same time the Church of Satan and LaVey himself changed tack and became less actively public. The 1980s satanic panic made Satanism a theme of media discourse, but at the same time the mythology presented kept most *real* Satanism closeted. In the third phase, that is, since the 1990s, a much wider range of satanic "groups" have formed. With the widespread availability of the World Wide Web various discourses on what Satan and Satanism may be have found more areas in which to be disseminated, and have provided more easily accessed arenas for those wanting to embrace the designation Satanist.[13]

MODERN SATANISM: A TYPOLOGY

As a consequence of this historical development, contemporary Satanism should be conceived of as satanic discourses in a "satanic milieu," which again shares traits with all contemporary fringe religions and currents on the "alternative margins." This decentralized network is called the "cultic milieu" or "occulture" and exists more as individual "self-religion," as virtual networks, and as ways of producing and consuming religion, than as specific groups with a physical address.[14] Authority is vested in the individual, and the goals are tied to success, self-development, or personal meaning. In parallel, the satanic milieu consists of world-affirming, often hyper-consumerist self-religions manifesting the common "pick-and-mix" practices of individual meaning-making.[15] Socialization into this milieu is dependent upon popular culture, understood as materials from which to synthesize "Satanism" and as identity markers with which to demonstrate a satanic position.[16] In this sense, popular culture and "occulture" are pathways to and from the satanic milieu, considerably blurring the boundary between margins and mainstream, a point we will return to below.

The satanic milieu may be understood in a broad and a narrow sense. In the *broad* sense, modern Satanism consists of all self-identified discourses appropriating the figure of Satan. As discussed above in the context of historical dis- and re-embedding processes, an alignment to the values attributed to the Prince of Darkness does not necessarily entail an association with traditional Western demonologies. It should be considered a *positive* appropriation, which is produced, distributed, and consumed through a variety of cultural products in a milieu conducive to adopting a satanic stance.[17] In the *narrow* sense, modern Satanism consists in the ideologies, worldviews, and practices of organized satanic groups with specific texts, spokespersons, and interpretations. Self-religion, antinomianism, the use of certain "S"-words (Satan, Satanism, etc.), and a formulated ideological genealogy have been suggested as the main traits in a minimum definition of organized Satanism within the satanic milieu.[18]

In order to avoid the error of blindly adopting emic typologies, we here use a simple ideal-typical categorization of self-declared Satanism in the satanic milieu: *rationalist, esoteric,* and *reactive.*[19] These should be understood as narratives of self-image and as dynamic categories, not as absolutes or reified roles. The typology is based on four distinct elements: the conception of Satan, the primary modes of legitimization, the general collective ethos, and the advocated goal.

The first category, *rationalist Satanism,* is an atheistic and philosophical Satanism often associated with Anton LaVey and the Church of Satan, although it has developed beyond the specific formulations found there. Nevertheless, all rationalist Satanisms acknowledge their roots in LaVey's work and the practice of explicitly using Satan as a symbol for the human condition as a carnal, emotional, and rational being. Hence Satan is an ideal figure of adversarial practice, the critical practice of "the accuser," and a name for the self expressing itself rather than being dominated by something or someone else. This materialistic outlook is expressed in the goals of "rational self-interest" and "indulgence," and support is found in rationalist, secular, and individualist arguments based on science, philosophy, and the arts.[20]

The second category is that of *esoteric Satanism,* a more mystical and initiatory formulation of Satanism as self-deification. Thus Satan is associated with traditional Left-Hand Path conceptions of magical practices and mystical experiences, whether he is considered a literal entity or a symbolic being. The gnostic or esoteric outlook is supported by ritual experience, widespread syncretism, and scientism.[21]

The final category, although somewhat residual, is still important in order to understand the satanic milieu: *reactive Satanism*.²² This is the Satanism previously dubbed "adolescent," "pseudo-Satanism," "inverse" Christianity, and so forth. Instead of using these purely negative concepts (of age, seriousness, complexity, or dependence on other creeds) we should attempt to define it in a positive or at least non-antagonistic way. By "reactive" we are alluding to the fact that this Satanism is firstly a *reaction* against society, but in a way that is secondly dependent upon and thus *paradigmatically conforms* to the context of which it is a part.²³ It is a form of "transgression from" rather than a "transgression to" different ideal norms, and thus conforms to existing stereotypes. In contrast to the two other types, reactive Satanism rarely distances itself from inverse Christianity and popular conceptions of Satan and Satanists, but is actually an appropriation of these stereotypes in the construction of individual and collective identity. It is thus mainly a "living out" or *ostension* of a mythical frame.²⁴

But reactive Satanism is more complex than that: it is always an *appropriation*. It is not a passive reception devoid of any possibility or interest in interpretation and combination. Indeed, whether it constitutes a phase or a longer engagement it can be perceived as deeply meaningful, and is not *necessarily* criminal or shallow, as media reports on phenomena such as "teenage Satanism" might make us believe.²⁵ This makes reactive Satanism a borderline phenomenon between the satanic milieu and the broader cultural narratives on Satan. It is too fluid in ideology, practice, and community to be contained: when these appropriations condense into a more coherent worldview with explicit practices, a community, and institutions, the phenomenon has often moved into one of the other two categories. All in all, these Satanists exist, but should be considered on the margins between modern Satanism and an ostensive display of the cultural narratives of the enemy.

When we discuss modern religious Satanism in the *narrow* sense outlined earlier (the antinomian self-religion of organized satanic groups with specific texts, spokespersons, and interpretations), we mainly refer to rationalist and esoteric Satanism.

SATANIC COMMUNITIES: AN ORGANIZATIONAL PICTURE

In what follows, brief snapshots of two satanic organizations are offered. These are but examples of organized groups, taken from those that have proved to be most long-lived. As discussed above, the easy availability of satanic discourse, model organizations, and relevant cultural products has facilitated the growth of a much larger satanic milieu with many different, mostly local and short-lived, groups.

Rationalist Satanism

Rationalist Satanism is non-theistic, self- and life-centered. Freedom, responsibility, leading a good life on one's own terms, and striving towards self-defined goals are among its central values. The distinction between black and white magic is rejected, but many accept a separation between lesser magic, which is seen as using psychology and material tricks, and higher magic, which by some is seen as also relying on unknown forces of nature. Collective ritualizing is rare, but a substantial minority practices some form of magic that is not seen as merely a kind of applied psychology.

The paradigmatic example of rationalist Satanism is the self-declared Epicurean, skeptical atheist version professed by the Church of Satan. Having evolved through different phases and gone through several processes of winnowing and the transition following the death of its charismatic founder, the current organization is run by a High Priest (Peter H. Gilmore) and a High Priestess (Peggy Nadramia). Membership is reserved for legal adults only and falls in two main categories: registered member and active member. Passive registered members fill in a form, apply for membership, and pay a one-off fee that is currently (2011) set at US$200. These members fall outside the formal degree system of the church and may have no further contact with the organization. Those who are accepted for active membership pay variable further annual dues to cover administration and other costs. The Church of Satan is not an initiatory order, but from early on, it has had a degree system structurally based on that of esoteric orders. New active members constitute the first degree.[26] Further levels are conferred on those members that the leadership chooses to elevate to higher degrees. In order to qualify, it is suggested, the applicant should have achieved a further understanding of theoretical and practical aspects of Satanism, but the precise qualifications remain unspecified by the organization's leaders. In addition to the degree system, there are administrative roles bearing their own titles.

The Church of Satan has had changing attitudes towards establishing formal groups on the local plane. Currently, its attitude is that local sections, called grottos, are no longer chartered, and the Grotto Master's administrative duties have ceased. Members who for various reasons wish to form groups are expected to find other suitable individuals via the Internet, rather than by asking the Church of Satan to set up local grottos.

Esoteric Satanism

Organized esoteric Satanism first arose out of the tension inherent in LaVey's construction of modern Satanism, since he borrowed extensively from popular scientific and philosophical material, and from various esoteric and occult treatises. In this sense, esoteric Satanism, although antedating rationalist Satanism as a historical phenomenon, only makes sense in relation to the "outing" of Satanism performed by LaVey in the late 1960s and the concomitant change in the satanic milieu.

In 1975, complex internal issues and ideological differences led several members of the Church of Satan to leave and, under the leadership of Michael Aquino, found the Temple of Set.[27] Basic elements of LaVeyan thinking are still visible in many texts, but the temple adds an esoteric dimension. From the start, symbolic interpretations of Satan were replaced by a more mystical idea of a deity related to the Egyptian god Set as the inspiring force behind "Satan" and, indeed, human intelligence and aspirations.

The Temple of Set is devoted to personal development, *xeper*, "to come into being," through a balanced development of rational, intellectual, experiential, and magical faculties.[28] The Temple places emphasis on learning and experimenting with the tools and texts of the occult tradition. Ritual performance is central, but this is mainly a personal rather than collective activity, related to the goal of self-deification.

The Temple of Set is organized as an initiatory order with six degrees.[29] Applications for membership at the first degree must be approved by members of the priesthood (third degree and above), either on the basis of personal acquaintance with the applicant or following a more thorough written application. Like the Church of Satan, the Temple accepts only members over 18 years of age. Once admitted, the member must progress to the second degree within two years, or affiliation will be terminated. Further degrees are formally conferred when esoteric achievement is recognized by peers. With the second degree comes full membership, which then excludes similar memberships elsewhere.

The social organization has two sides: Pylons are a reworked form of the Grotto system of the Church of Satan, but fitted to a reality where members are often too few and far between to meet regularly and where the Internet removes the need for geographical proximity; some are "correspondence Pylons." In addition to the Pylons, the Temple has different Orders, functioning as working groups delving into particular areas of study, often for a limited period. Members are expected to take an active part in both Pylons and Orders.

INDIVIDUAL, GROUP, MILIEU, AND OCCULTURE: A DISCURSIVE PICTURE

So far we have used historical, typological, and sociological approaches to Satanism. A more anthropological or ethnographic approach may focus on the individual practices of constructing viable identities and worldviews in negotiation with the multitude of available choices offered through variable *gateways* into Satanism. In an important study by James R. Lewis, the following "statistical caricature" of the modern religious Satanist is offered:

> [A]n unmarried, white male in his mid-twenties with a few years of college. He became involved in Satanism through something he read in high school, and has been a self-identified Satanist for seven years. Raised Christian, he explored one non-Satanist religious group beyond the one in which he was raised before settling into Satanism. His view of Satan is some variety of non-theistic humanism and he practices magic. His primary interaction with his co-religionists is via e-mail and internet chat rooms.[30]

From our experience this picture seems generally correct.[31] But even though the answer to the question "Who serves Satan?" may seem clear, this clarity is in part an artefact of viewing Satanists through the statistical lens. In real life, there is a bewildering variety of Satanist identities.

First, we have met quite a lot of female Satanists in the last ten years of study. There *is* a distinct masculine tendency in ideology and demographics, but Satanism is not solely a male club. Women also occupy leading positions, like High Priestesses Peggy Nadramia of the Church of Satan and Patricia Hardy, who leads the Temple of Set. Second, the average career given in the above quotation is in many ways nothing but an average. There are Satanists of both rationalist and esoteric persuasions, and many older Satanists started as reactive adolescents.[32] Similarly, one can encounter Satanists that are both much younger and much older than the mid twenties. In other words, when actually studying Satanists in the satanic milieu, statistics primarily serve as a first impression.

We could profitably describe the satanic milieu and the individual vectors within it through ever-widening circles of analysis: the individual participant; local affiliations and "scenes"; the NRMs proper – organized groups; the satanic milieu with discursive communities and influential texts; the cultic milieu of which it is a part; and, finally, occulture itself, pointing towards and interacting with mainstream society and conventional "culture." Pathways exist within and between all of these levels, and socialization into Satanism, or indeed other decentralized "religiosities," can take many directions.[33]

As a thought experiment, we can follow an adolescent into the satanic milieu. A "traditional" model of "recruitment" would have us see the individual in relation to a small group of peers, a local "scene" or local events – for example a local Goth club, an occult lecture group, or a heavy metal band or rock bar. Through a combination of intellectual "fit," emotional support, and social networks, our young Satanist can gradually develop the resources, practices, and attitudes necessary to internalize a "satanic identity" and express it together with others. This can lead to a more serious affiliation with a specific group online or in real life, making the maturing Satanist more assured of his or her choices as well as containing future choices and restricting the Satanic social network within which he or she moves.[34]

This is fine as far as it goes, but looking merely at the individual's path into Satanism while neglecting the opposite direction, how the satanic milieu reaches out to the individual, seems to miss something essential. An important element noticed by recent studies in new religions is that the individual is often "primed" by wider occultural influences borne by popular culture: music, literature, movies, television shows, and so on.[35] The consumption of material deemed relevant in the satanic milieu makes the topics and styles familiar, and serves to "prime" the individual seeker, and can make later choices seem natural: they are "born" Satanists, or in the rhetoric of modern Paganism are "coming home."

There is, of course, nothing automatic in this process. But just as *Charmed* or *Buffy the Vampire Slayer* can stimulate an interest in witchcraft, so Marilyn Manson, *Rosemary's Baby*, or H. P. Lovecraft can lead our adolescent to a more serious involvement with Satanism, as can the general secular values and libertarian attitudes of much middle-class life. The active words here are "can lead" and "stimulate," not "coerce" or "brainwash."

Aside from "traditional" socialization and priming, we see two additional vectors of analysis. The first is from occulture and the wider cultic milieu to specific groups and local scenes. Here the interesting element is the distribution and availability of material for use in collective consumption.[36] This relates on the one hand to more esoteric and occult elements, and on the other to popular culture using religious or "satanic" elements. The distribution and availability of, say, key esoteric texts and philosophical material in a wider milieu obviously has a bearing on their influence on specific rationalist and esoteric groups. The popularity of various mass-mediated and -marketed products makes identity construction based on them easier, as the items are visible and available for appropriation.

It also makes their use more difficult for Satanists, because they are *widely* used and thus problematic in a setting where "herd conformity" is a sin. A delicate balance has to be struck between something unique and provocative and something understandable and communicable – a factor in discussions of "authenticity" in subcultural choice in relation to the marketplace.[37] This leads us to the next vector, which goes from individual, scene, and group to milieu and occulture.

Individual creativity in producing material, interpretations, and strategies of consumption plays an important role in forming specific scenes and groups. These again influence each other and the larger milieu, with regard to identity and difference, harmony, and conflict: while individual creativity is necessary to create bonds and identity, it is also centrifugal and disruptive. Whether expressed as solitary engagement or as spokespersons through central movement texts, creativity also creates conflicts. The easier accessibility and availability of different ideas via the Internet makes these ideas clash more often.[38] Sometimes they do so on an individual basis, but on the larger scale, the satanic interpretation of cultural materials (or the decision whether they are "satanic as such" or "satanic for me") is usually mediated by groups and scenes. For example, discussions on message boards of whether heavy metal music is satanic, or if specific television shows qualify as such or not, is a testing ground for making individual choices, but they are also a battleground for learning what Satanism is supposed to be.[39] All in all, it is the creative use of cultural materials by individuals, elaborated and given prominence by their reception in groups and scenes that produces the specific satanic materials that give the satanic milieu its coherence and content.

CONCLUSION

As discussed in the introduction to this chapter, the phenomenon of Satanism changes character depending on the questions posed and the definitions offered. Aside from the somewhat uniform Christian under-standing and the popular receptions of that framework, Satanism today has been appropriated and extended into an evocative modern symbol of resistance and self-understanding. Although a minority in contem-porary decentralized religious life, the milieu of individuals and groups exploring satanic discourses and practices has a presence in mainstream culture far greater than their numerical strength would seem to war-rant – which again links back to the Christian heritage of the West, and the appeal of the sinister.

Notes

1   See M. Farren, "The Devil's Advocate," *Citybeat* 158 (2006), and the CBS report on the Church of Satan's fortieth-anniversary High Mass at www.youtube.com/watch?v=fcE9JZZgmc8&mode=related&search= (all www references in this chapter were accessed in September 2011).

2   See for example www.satansrapture.com/maitreya.htm.

3   A point powerfully asserted by Christopher Partridge in *The Re-enchantment of the West*, 2 vols. (London, 2004–5).

4   On processes of dis- and re-embedding, see Anthony Giddens, *The Consequences of Modernity* (Cambridge, 1990); Olav Hammer, "Same Message from Everywhere: The Sources of Modern Revelation," in Mikael Rothstein (ed.), *New Age Religion and Globalization* (Aarhus, 2001), pp. 42–57. The disembedding of Satan is discussed in Jesper Aa. Petersen, "Introduction: Embracing Satan," in Petersen (ed.), *Contemporary Religious Satanism: A Critical Reader* (Farnham, UK, and Burlington, VT, 2009), pp. 1–24, at pp. 10–14.

5   For a few critical treatments of Satanic panic and Satanic ritual abuse scares, see Bill Ellis, *Raising the Devil: Satanism, New Religions, and the Media* (Louisville, 2000); James R. Lewis and Jesper Aa. Petersen (eds.), *The Encyclopedic Sourcebook of Satanism* (Amherst, NY, 2008); and James T. Richardson, Joel Best, and David G. Bromley (eds.), *The Satanism Scare* (New York, 1991).

6   See James R. Lewis, "Infernal Legitimacy," in Petersen (ed.) *Contemporary Religious Satanism*, pp. 41–58, at p. 45. Good studies on Satanism and popular culture are Gavin Baddeley, *Lucifer Rising: Sin, Devil Worship and Rock 'n' Roll* (London, 2000); Christopher Partridge and Eric Christianson (eds.), *The Lure of the Dark Side: Satan and Western Demonology in Popular Culture* (London and Oakville, 2009); and Partridge, *Re-enchantment*, vol. II, pp. 207–55.

7   For example, Robert Muchembled, *A History of the Devil* (Cambridge, 2003).

8   See Peter A. Schock, *Romantic Satanism: Myth and the Historical Moment in Blake, Shelley, and Byron* (Houndmills, UK, and New York, 2003).

9   Petersen, "Introduction," pp. 12–13.

10 See Muchembled, *History of the Devil*, pp. 187–227; Jeffrey Burton Russell, *Mephistopheles: The Devil in the Modern World* (Ithaca, NY, and London, 1986), pp. 214–51.

11 On Fraternitas Saturni, see for example Hans Thomas Hakl, "Fraternitas Saturni," in Wouter J. Hanegraaff *et al.* (eds.), *Dictionary of Gnosis and Western Esotericism* (Leiden, 2006), pp. 379–82; on Herbert Sloane, see the popular account in Susan Roberts, *Witches, U.S.A* (New York, 1971), pp. 200–16.

12 See Blanche Barton, *The Church of Satan* (New York, 1990) and Blanche Barton, *The Secret Life of a Satanist* (Los Angeles, 1992) for more information. Notice that both texts are church material. On the occult explosion, see for example Gary Lachman, *Turn Off Your Mind: The Mystic Sixties and the Dark Side of the Age of Aquarius* (New York, 2001).

13 On the history of modern Satanism, see Baddeley, *Lucifer Rising*; Jesper Aa. Petersen, "Modern Satanism" in James R. Lewis and Jesper Aa. Petersen (eds.), *Controversial New Religions* (Oxford and New York, 2005), pp. 423–59; Jesper Aa. Petersen, "Satanists and Nuts: Schisms in Modern Satanism," in Sarah Lewis and James R. Lewis (eds.), *Sacred Schisms: How Religions Divide* (Cambridge and New York, 2009), pp. 218–47.

14 On the cultic milieu, see Colin Campbell, "The Cult, the Cultic Milieu and Secularization," in *A Sociological Yearbook of Religion in Britain* 5 (London, 1972), pp. 119–36; on occulture, see Partridge, *Re-enchantment*, vol. 1; on self-religion, see Paul Heelas, *The New Age Movement* (Oxford, 1996).

15 On world-affirming religions, see Roy Wallis, *The Elementary Forms of the New Religious Life* (London, 1984); on hyper-consumerist religion, see Asbjørn Dyrendal, "Devilish Consumption: Popular Culture in Satanic Socialization," *Numen* 55:1 (2008), pp. 68–98, and Adam Possamai, *Religion and Popular Culture: A Hyper-Real Testament* (Brussels, 2005); on Satanism as self-religion, see Asbjørn Dyrendal, "Darkness Within: Satanism as a Self-Religion," pp. 59–74, and Petersen, "Introduction," pp. 3, 8, both in Petersen (ed.), *Contemporary Religious Satanism*.

16 See Dyrendal, "Devilish Consumption."

17 Petersen, "Introduction," pp. 10–14.

18 Ibid., pp. 7–8.

19 Dyrendal, "Devilish Consumption," p. 74; Petersen, "Introduction," pp. 6–7.

20 To get some idea of the broader spectrum here, one should review a collection of primary sources. For books we suggest all of Anton LaVey's books, and Blanche Barton's *The Church of Satan* (New York, 1990), for official church history. High Priest Peter Gilmore's *The Satanic Scriptures* (Baltimore, MD, 2007) shows a contemporary turn within the Church of Satan, as does M. G. Paradise, *Bearing the Devil's Mark* (n.p., 2007). Of the main and good venues for rationalist Satanism online associated with the Church of Satan, one may start out with Lestat Ventrue's *Letters to the Devil* (www.satannet.com/forum/ubbthreads.

php) and Matt G. Paradise's *Purging Talon*, including The Sinister Screen and the Diabologue (purgingtalon.com/main/). Vexen Crabtree's *Description, Philosophies and Justification of Satanism* (www.dpjs. co.uk/index.html) is one of the more articulate online presentations. There are many unaffiliated online sources, among which Modern Church of Satan (www.modernchurchofsatan.com/index.html) is one of the rationalist ones.

21 The central example here is, as we return to briefly, the Temple of Set. Central public sources include former High Priest Don Webb's *Uncle Setnakt's Essential Guide to the Left-Hand Path* (Smithville, TX, 1999), and *Mysteries of the Temple of Set* (Smithville, TX, 2004). Founder and former High Priest Michael Aquino's ebooks on the Church of Satan, *The Church of Satan*, 6th edn. (San Francisco, 2009), available at www.xeper. org/maquino/nm/COS.pdf, and the *The Temple of Set*, 11th edn. (San Francisco, 2010), available at www.xeper.org/maquino/nm/TOSd11.pdf, are highly recommended. The Temple of Set is far from the only esoteric example. A selection of others are *Satanic Reds* (www.satanicreds.org/ satanicreds/), Diane Vera's *Theistic Satanism* (theisticsatanism.com/), *Temple of the Black Light* (www.templeoftheblacklight.net/main.html), Venus Satanas' *Spiritual Satanist* site (www.spiritualsatanist.com), and NocTifer's *Satanservice* (www.satanservice.org).

22 Sources here have an even more unstable, temporary presence than for online "groups" in the other categories. An example of online source was at the time of writing the MySpace site Satanspace (www.satans-pace.com).

23 Joachim Schmidt, *Satanismus. Mythos und Wirklichkeit* (Marburg, 2003 [1992]), pp. 11–12.

24 Bill Ellis, "Legend-Trips and Satanism: Adolescents' Ostensive Traditions as 'Cult' Activity," in Richardson *et al.* (eds.), *Satanism Scare*, pp. 279–95.

25 See for example Kathleen S. Lowney, "Teenage Satanism as Oppositional Youth Subculture," *Journal of Contemporary Ethnography* 23:4 (1995), pp. 453–84; Gry Mørk, "'With my Art I am the Fist in the Face of god': On Old-School Black Metal," in Petersen (ed.), *Contemporary Religious Satanism*, pp. 171–99; and Jesper Aa. Petersen, "'Smite Him Hip and Thigh': Satanism, Violence and Transgression," in James R. Lewis (ed.), *Violence in New Religious Movements* (Oxford, 2011), pp. 351–76.

26 The degrees are: 1. Active Member; 2. Witch/Warlock; 3. Priestess/ Priest; 4. Magistra/Magister; 5. Maga/Magus. The Priesthood consists of levels three through five.

27 Petersen, "Satanists and Nuts," pp. 234–39.

28 For example, Dyrendal, "Darkness Within," pp. 62–70.

29 The degrees are: 1. Setian; 2. Adept; 3. Priest/Priestess; 4. Magister/ Magistra Templi; 5. Magus/Maga; 6. Ipsissimus/Ipsissima.

30 Cited from James R. Lewis, "Fit for the Devil: Toward an Understanding of 'Conversion' to Satanism," *International Journal for the Study of New Religions* 1:1 (2010), p. 120; the original, shorter version is in James R. Lewis, "Who Serves Satan? A Demographic and Ideological Profile,"

Marburg Journal of Religious Studies 6:2 (2001), http://archiv.ub.uni-marburg.de/mjr/lewis2.html, p. 5. The small-scale statistical study of 2000–1, SS1 ("Satan Survey One"), was elaborated and further tested in 2009 (SS2) and partially published in "Fit for the Devil."

31 Survey data are few and cannot formally be generalized. They do fit well with the picture presented by observational data and other investigations, e.g., Dagmar Fügmann, *Zeitgenössischer Satanismus in Deutschland: Weltbilder und Wertvorstellungen im Satanismus* (Marburg, 2009).

32 Lewis, "Who Serves Satan?" pp. 2, 6.

33 See Partridge, *Re-enchantment*, vol. 1; cf. Colin Campbell and Shirley McIver, "Cultural Sources for Support for Contemporary Occultism," *Social Compass* 34:1 (1987), pp. 41–60. The circles of analysis are partly inspired by Helen A. Berger, *A Community of Witches: Contemporary Neo-Paganism and Witchcraft in the United States* (Columbia, SC, 1999).

34 Lewis, "Fit for the Devil," pp. 120–21 and 125–26. For such approaches to recruitment, conversion, and socialization, see, e.g., Peter L. Berger, *The Sacred Canopy: Elements of a Sociological Theory of Religion* (New York, 1990 [first published 1967]), James Richardson (ed.), *Conversion Careers: In and Out of New Religions* (Beverly Hills and London, 1978), and Dick Anthony and Thomas Robbins, "Conversion and 'Brainwashing' in New Religious Movements," in James R. Lewis (ed.), *The Oxford Handbook of New Religious Movements* (Oxford and New York, 2004), pp. 243–98.

35 Lewis, "Fit for the Devil," pp. 4–9. Our concept of "priming" is analogous to the "cultural orientation" proposed in Douglas Ezzy and Helen A. Berger, "Becoming a Witch: Changing Paths of Conversion in Contemporary Witchcraft," in Helen E. Johnston and Peg Aloi (eds.), *The New Generation Witches: Teenage Witchcraft in Contemporary Culture* (Aldershot, UK, and Burlington, VT, 2007), pp. 41–56, and Helen A. Berger and Douglas Ezzy, *Teenage Witches: Magical Youth and the Search for the Self* (New Brunswick, NJ, and London, 2007); see also Sian Reid, "'A Religion without Converts' Revisited: Individuals, Identity and Community in Contemporary Paganism," in Murphy Pizza and James R. Lewis (eds.), *Handbook of Contemporary Paganism* (Leiden and Boston, 2009), pp. 171–94; Steven Sutcliffe, "The Dynamics of Alternative Spirituality: Seekers, Networks, and 'New Age'," in Lewis (ed.), *Oxford Handbook*, pp. 466–90.

36 See, e.g., Peg Aloi, "Rooted in the Occult Revival: Neo-Paganism's Evolving Relationship with Popular Media," in Pizza and Lewis (eds.), *Contemporary Paganism*, pp. 539–74.

37 See Dyrendal, "Devilish Consumption"; on authenticity, Keith Kahn-Harris, *Extreme Metal: Music and Culture on the Edge* (Oxford, 2007) is particularly useful.

38 See Jesper Aa. Petersen, "From Book to Bit: Enacting Satanism Online," in Egil Asprem and Kennet Granholm (eds.), *Contemporary Esotericism* (London, 2012).

39 See Asbjørn Dyrendal, "Satanism and Popular Music," in Partridge and Christianson (eds.), *Lure of the Dark Side*; Dyrendal, "Devilish Consumption," pp. 85–89.

Further reading

Baddeley, Gavin, *Lucifer Rising: Sin, Devil Worship and Rock 'n' Roll* (London, 2000).

Ellis, Bill, *Raising the Devil: Satanism, New Religions, and the Media* (Louisville, 2000).

Lewis, James R. and Jesper Aa. Petersen (eds.), *The Encyclopedic Sourcebook of Satanism* (Amherst, NY, 2008).

Petersen, Jesper Aa. (ed.), *Contemporary Religious Satanism: A Critical Reader* (Farnham, UK, and Burlington, VT, 2009).

Petersen, Jesper Aa. and Per Faxneld (eds.), *The Devil's Party: Satanism in Modernity* (Oxford, 2012).

Richardson, James T., Joel Best, and David G. Bromley (eds.), *The Satanism Scare* (New York, 1991).

14 Theosophy

JAMES A. SANTUCCI

INTRODUCTION

From a modern and popular perspective, theosophy refers to the teachings espoused by the Theosophical Society, an organization founded on November 17, 1875 in New York City by sixteen individuals primarily from spiritualist, cabalistic, and Western esoteric backgrounds and interests. Chief among those founders was the Russian *émigrée* Helena Petrovna Blavatsky (1831–1891), who synthesized and interpreted ancient and modern teachings that in her view adhered neither to dogmatic religion nor materialistic science. Modern theosophy mainly reflects Blavatsky's vision and exposition of what is identified as *theosophy*. All subsequent texts, with some exceptions, within the Theosophical movement are summaries of, reactions to, expositions of, or enlargements upon her own extensive writings. Just as Blavatsky's teachings developed from the early 1870s to her death in 1891, so too did the Theosophical Society undergo ruptures based in large part on the degree of adherence to the Blavatskyan body of teachings. At present, three principal organizations that propound theosophical teachings are the Theosophical Society (Adyar), the Theosophical Society (Pasadena), and the United Lodge of Theosophists.

The purpose of this chapter is fivefold: (a) to present the principal characters responsible for the Society's founding and the events leading up to its inception, (b) to define and describe theosophy, (c) to outline its main teachings, (d) to give a brief historical overview principally of the Theosophical Society (Adyar) together with brief mention of the Theosophical Society (Pasadena) and the United Lodge of Theosophists, and (e) to survey the impact of theosophy and the Theosophical Society on the contemporary religious landscape.

ANTECEDENTS

The foundations of the Theosophical Society take its cue from the life of H. P. Blavatsky in her pre-New York years (before 1873) and the narrative of Henry Steel Olcott (1832–1907) of the Society's origin. Blavatsky, *née* Helena von Hahn, was born in Ekaterinoslav (Dnepropetrovsk), Ukraine on August 12, 1831. From age 18, she led a rather unconventional life undergoing years of wandering, ostensibly in search of the Hidden Truth that lay behind the cosmos. As a seeker, Blavatsky was mainly an autodidact, but she also claimed to have received training from spiritually evolved living teachers or "Masters" in esoteric Truth. This knowledge allowed her in her middle years to play a crucial role in the founding of a movement dedicated to the pursuit of this Secret Wisdom, the Theosophical Society. Her purpose in coming to the United States from France, so she stated, was to expose the truth about modern spiritualism[1] and to reveal esoteric wisdom or, in the language of the time, "ancient Spiritualism" or "Occultism."[2]

Although aspects of this topic as discussed by Blavatsky attracted several interested individuals to her and her colleague Olcott's New York apartment and eventually led to the establishment of the Theosophical Society, the direct inspiration behind the Society's establishment was a lecture by an invited guest, George Henry Felt (1831–1906), which motivated Olcott to suggest the formation of a society to investigate subjects similar to Felt's topic, the Cabala of the Egyptians, the Greek Canon of Proportion, and the ability to evoke "elementals" or "creatures evolved in the four kingdoms of earth, air, fire, and water" (identified by the cabalists as gnomes, sylphs, salamanders, and undines). Thus it was *"that a society [was] formed for the study and elucidation of Occultism, the Cabala & c."*[3]

From September 8 to November 17, 1875 a constitution and by-laws were drafted, the new society was named "Theosophical"[4] and the inaugural address given by Olcott on November 17 at Mott Memorial Hall. The Society has since gone through periods of turbulence and controversy, but the language of its current objects (introduced in 1896) has retained the confidence first exhibited by Olcott in his inaugural address:

1. To form a nucleus of the universal brotherhood of humanity, without distinction of race, creed, sex, caste, or color.
2. To encourage the study of comparative religion, philosophy, and science.
3. To investigate unexplained laws of nature and the powers latent in man.

THEOSOPHY

The question of just what the term "theosophy" meant to the founders and formers of the Theosophical Society is not as obvious as one might think. Did the term accurately define the purpose of the society? Indeed, before "theosophical" was chosen, Olcott reported other proposed modifiers introduced in the discussion of a title: "Egyptological, the Hermetic, and the Rosicrucian."[5] "Theosophical" was selected because it "covered the ground of Felt's methods of occult scientific research."[6] Indeed, the dictionary that was used, presumably the 1875 *Webster's Dictionary*,[7] contained the following definition:

> Supposed intercourse with God and superior spirits, and consequent attainment of superhuman knowledge by physical processes, as by the theurgic operations of some ancient Platonists, or by the chemical processes of the German fire philosophers; also, a direct, as distinguished from a revealed, knowledge of God, supposed to be attained by extraordinary illumination; especially, a direct insight into the processes of the divine mind, and the interior relations of the divine nature.[8]

The first part of the definition mentions the theurgy of the Neoplatonists, such as Iamblichus,[9] and the fire-philosophers as described by such contemporaries as Hargrave Jennings (?1817–1890).[10] The second part reflects a "direct seeing," what some might identify as a mystical illumination or gnosis.

The practice of "theurgy" agreed more with Olcott's main interest at the time as evidenced by his highly complimentary remarks regarding Felt's experiments in manifesting "Elementary Spirits" in his "Inaugural Address."[11] Indeed, the Preamble of the Society asserts that the appellation "Theosophical Society," according to the founders, sought "to obtain knowledge of the nature and attributes of the Supreme Power *and of the higher spirits*, by the aid of physical processes."[12]

It would appear from these remarks that Olcott *et al.* had placed more emphasis on experimentation to reveal "proof of the existence of an 'Unseen Universe,' the nature of its inhabitants, *if such there be*, and the laws which govern them, and their relations with mankind."[13]

When she first turned to this topic, Blavatsky was more concerned with the wisdom or transformative vision that it brings rather than the more scientific or theurgic demonstration that appeared to excite Olcott. It is in her article "What is Theosophy?"[14] that she states that the *Webster's* definition was "poor and flippant."[15] Rather, she quotes

Robert A. Vaughan's *Hours with the Mystics*: "A Theosophist is one who gives you a theory of God or the works of God, which has not revelation, but an inspiration of his own for its basis."[16] This is then followed by her full description of theosophy:

> The interior world has not been hidden from all by impenetrable darkness. By that higher intuition acquired by Theosophia – or God-knowledge, which carries the mind from the world of form into that of formless spirit, man has been sometimes enabled in every age and every country to perceive things in the interior or invisible world.

All earlier theosophists that she subsequently mentions – among whom are the Hindu ascetics (i.e., the *yogins* who practice meditation or *samādhi*), the Neoplatonists, and the Rosicrucians or Fire-philosophers – were involved with the "search after man's diviner 'self',"[17] which conformed to Blavatsky's description of theurgy, as opposed to Olcott's more limited understanding. In accordance with the description of Iamblichus (c. 250–330 CE), as mentioned in her article, theurgy was defined as "the art of applying the divine powers of man to the subordination of the blind forces of nature."[18] Furthermore, in the subsequent EST (Eastern School of Theosophy) Instruction No. II, theurgy is characterized as that which "unites us most strongly to divine nature."[19]

To conclude this section, most Theosophists would view "Theosophy"[20] as "a system that claims to embrace the essential truth underlying all systems of religion, philosophy, and science."[21] Theosophists also recognize in varying degrees the term as a "gnosis" or in Hartmann's words "self-knowledge of the awakened spirit in man; *i.e.*, the knowledge by which the god in man knows that he is."[22]

THE TEACHINGS

Theosophy, according to Blavatsky and her successors, refers to a nexus of teachings associated with the Supreme, the macrocosmos (the universe or Nature), and microcosmos (humanity). The Supreme is discussed in a number of sources, with the first clearly articulated Theosophical statement offered in 1879 in Blavatsky's "What is Theosophy?" Therein she concludes what she explains in more detail in *Isis Unveiled*:[23] "a single Supreme Essence, Unknown and Unknowable."[24] This statement is expanded in the Proem to *The Secret Doctrine* as an "omnipresent, Eternal, Boundless, and Immutable PRINCIPLE on which all speculation is impossible, since it transcends the power of human conception and could only be dwarfed by any human expression or similitude."[25]

The relation between the Supreme and nature may be expressed in the following manner: "God is nature, visible and invisible, and nature or Cosmos in its infinity is God!"[26] As explained by Blavatsky, from the Eternal and Immutable Principle, which is also the "causeless Cause" and "rootless root," emits the "First Cause," the unmanifested First Logos, or the potential to the creation to come. From the First Logos derives a duality of Spirit (consciousness) and Matter followed by the Cosmic Ideation: the Mahat or Intelligence of the Universal World Soul and the individual mind (*manas*) of humans.[27] Thus the Divine Mind is reflected in the Universe: "The *Logos* is the mirror reflecting DIVINE MIND, and the Universe is the mirror of the Logos though the latter is the *esse* of that Universe."[28]

The universe that evolves and reflects the Logos is dualistic – reflecting Spirit and Matter – and cyclic, in its manifestation and dissolution on both macro- and microcosmic planes. Furthermore, the structure of both planes is septenary in nature: on the macrocosmic level, for instance, the seven planes[29] and seven Globes;[30] on the more microcosmic or human level the seven sub-races and root races, and the septenary composition of humans. In other words the Theosophical teaching promotes the correspondence between the microcosm of the human being and macrocosm of the universe.[31]

The universe is not static, however. It is in motion, reflecting that symbol of "Be-ness" or the Eternal Cause as "absolute Abstract Motion" that represents "unconditioned Consciousness."[32] For the individual, the cyclic motion is represented by reincarnation, a teaching that entered a later version of Theosophical teaching during the 1880s. Reincarnation actually took on the Greek teaching of "metempsychosis," which was a type of progressive embodiment in the hierarchy of nature: "A stone becomes a plant, a plant an animal, an animal a man, a man a spirit, and a spirit a god."[33]

THE HISTORY OF THE THEOSOPHICAL SOCIETY

Although the Theosophical Society commenced with great enthusiasm, it soon became moribund during the New York years (1875–78).[34] This was partly due to the failure to prove the existence of the "Unseen Universe," its laws and inhabitants initially promised by G. H. Felt. The one positive development was the publication in 1877 of Blavatsky's first major synthesis of the Ancient Wisdom, *Isis Unveiled*. Moreover, the Society itself changed from an open to a hierarchical secret society in early 1876 because of disruptions from outside parties.[35] This was short-lived, however, lasting only until the early to mid 1880s.

In the final year of the founders' New York residency the Society joined with the Ārya Samāj of Swami Dayānand Sarasvati (1824–1883).[36] Convinced that the two societies agreed in their interpretation of the Ancient Wisdom, the Council of the Theosophical Society agreed to this merger on May 22, 1878. Named the "Theosophical Society of the Arya Samaj," the merged body lasted only until July 1882 after it became obvious that the goals of the Ārya Samāj and its leader were incompatible with those of the Theosophical Society.[37]

On December 18, 1878 Blavatsky and Olcott departed New York for India, with a stopover of seventeen days in Britain before arriving in Bombay Harbor on February 16, 1879. The decision to travel to India converted the Society from a local institution to one that was genuinely universal. Foreign branches were organized, beginning with the "British Theosophical Society of the Arya Samaj of Aryawart,"[38] (June 1878).[39] Following the British Theosophical Society came the establishment of the Bombay branch in 1879, the new headquarters of the society and its founders, with an increasing number of charters being granted to local branches over the ensuing years: from 10 in 1880 to 179 in 1888 to 607 charters in 1900[40] located in North and Central America, Asia, Europe, Australia, Africa, and various islands chains (Hawai'i, Canary Islands, Borneo, and West Indies).[41]

Success, however, was not without its setbacks. In 1882, the newly established Society for Psychical Research (SPR) decided to examine the claims of the Theosophical Society in 1884. Specific to the investigation was the latter's claim to the existence of Masters of Wisdom or Mahatmas, from whom the Society claimed to have received communications through letters addressed primarily to one of its members, A. P. Sinnett (1840–1921), over a period of approximately five years (1880–85). Because the correspondent Mahatmas were considered the sources of Blavatsky's interpretation of the Ancient Wisdom, Sinnett's summary of their letters in *Esoteric Buddhism* in 1883 greatly promoted both Theosophical teachings and the source of those teachings. The SPR took on the claims of the existence of these Mahatmas and the authenticity of their letters and their means of delivery to the Theosophists, the latter achieved by means of "precipitation" of the writing on blank paper and their transportation "through solid matter."[42] The first preliminary report released in December 1884 arrived at a tentative conclusion; however, the second (1885) report prepared by Richard Hodgson (1855–1905) was one that inflicted considerable damage upon Blavatsky and the Society. The reason for the second report originated with an exposé by the former housekeeper of Blavatsky and Assistant Corresponding Secretary, Emma Coulomb, of a number of letters allegedly written by Blavatsky affirming her involvement in producing fraudulent phenomena surrounding the Mahatma letters. Hodgson's conclusions were devastating to the Society: the Mahatmas did not exist, and Blavatsky herself wrote the letters in the Masters' names. Furthermore, he raised the suspicion that she was a Russian spy and the Society in reality a political organization.[43] The Society's and Blavatsky's reputations never fully recovered from this assessment.

After Blavatsky's death in 1891, a major challenge confronted the Theosophical Society with the Vice-President of the Society, William Q. Judge, being charged with forging documents in the name of the Mahatmas. This led Annie Besant (1847–1933), the Outer Head of the Eastern School of Theosophy (the new name for the Esoteric Section of the Theosophical Society, founded in 1888), to call for Judge's resignation of the vice-presidency at the Society's December 1894 convention in Adyar. Rather than resigning, Judge and the American Section voted to withdraw from the Adyar Society at the American Section's convention in April 1895. The newly constituted organization, the Theosophical Society in America, appointed Judge President for life. Following Judge's death in 1896, the Theosophical Society in America soon came under the Presidency of Ernest T. Hargrove (d.1939) for a brief time before Katherine Tingley (1847–1929), the Outer Head of the Eastern School of Theosophy, became the sole leader after Hargrove resigned the Presidency in 1897.[44] The Theosophical Society in America continues to this day, having moved its headquarters to Point Loma (San Diego, California) in 1897, Covina (California) in 1942, and finally to Altadena (California) in 1951. Now known as the Theosophical Society with International Headquarters in Pasadena, its current Leader is Randell C. Grubb. The work of the Society is to conduct correspondence courses, study groups, and publication work through its Theosophical University Press both in printed and online versions,[45] and to maintain the Theosophical Library Center in Altadena. Eight National Sections remain active (America, Australia, Germany, Netherlands, Nigeria, South Africa, Sweden, and the United Kingdom).

In addition to the separation of the Theosophical Society in America from the Theosophical Society (Adyar), a third major group was inaugurated in 1909: the United Lodge of Theosophists in Los Angeles. Founded by Robert Crosbie (1849–1919), a staunch follower of William

Q. Judge, established the ULT expressly to study the Source Theosophy of Blavatsky and Judge. The organization defines itself as a group of students dedicated to the investigation and understanding of the writings of Blavatsky and Judge.

The largest Theosophical society, however, remains the Society with headquarters established in Adyar, India in 1882. The work of the Society during Olcott's tenure as president (1875–1907) was expanded to include social activism, such as initiating the Buddhist revival in Sri Lanka and India, upgrading the position of the outcastes in India by establishing "Pariah schools," and establishing an Oriental Library to preserve Indian Sanskrit and other manuscripts.[46]

The former socialist and freethinker Annie Besant quickly became a leading propagandist and spokesperson after joining the Society on May 10, 1889. As noted above, she became Outer Head of the Esoteric Section after Blavatsky's death in 1891 and the Society's second President following Olcott's death in 1907. Besant was a major propagandist of the Theosophical teachings of Blavatsky in the earlier part of her career as well as a social activist after her arrival in India in 1893, attempting to uplift Hindus and to advance their education by helping establish the Central Hindu College in Benares (now Vārānasī) in 1898 and the Central Hindu Girls' School in 1904. More controversially, she engaged in the struggle for Indian independence from British rule, establishing the Home Rule League in 1916, and working with other nationalist leaders such as Lokamanya Bal Gangadhar Tilak (1856–1920) and becoming active in the Indian National Congress as well as its President in 1917.

Of direct concern to the Society, however, was the new direction undertaken by Charles Webster Leadbeater (1854–1934), with the help and cooperation of Mrs. Besant, from the mid 1890s on. Both conducted occult or psychic research in order to discover direct insight into the astral plane, past lives, and other supraphysical phenomena. Since this research seemed to provide direct access to such phenomena, the results of Besant's and Leadbeater's investigations appeared convincing to many members of the Adyar Society. Such was the beginning of what was originally called neo-Theosophy, a term first used by Besant in 1912.[47]

Those who opposed what was regarded as Besant's and Leadbeater's usurpation of Blavatsky's teaching authority also included two other deviations from the original teachings: the discovery in 1909 of the coming World Teacher – the Maitreya or the Christ – eventually embodied in the physical vehicle of Jiddu Krishnamurti (1895–1986) – and the inclusion of a pro-clerical component through the Liberal Catholic Church as part of the Theosophical enterprise beginning in 1917. Both antagonized the Blavatskyite Theosophists, but there is no doubt that the popularity of the Adyar Society benefited from the World Teacher project. During the 1920s, the ritual of the Liberal Catholic Church was combined with the claims that focused on the World Teacher. The popularity of both continued until 1929, when Krishnamurti publicly rejected the role he was supposed to have played in the Theosophical context by dissolving the allied organization that furthered the goals of the World Teacher, the Order of the Star.

Following this event, the Society's membership declined,[48] but it continued to remain an activist organization, only more focused on its own needs. The successor to Mrs. Besant, George Arundale (1878–1945, President from 1933–45), contributed to defining the role of the Theosophical Society, whose purpose was the "spread of Friendship and Freedom"; furthermore, and rather surprisingly, although Theosophy and the Theosophical Society were considered "twins," there was no requirement that the membership be obliged to study Theosophy. Finally, Arundale summarized the contributions of his predecessors to the understanding of Theosophy in the following manner: Blavatsky viewed Theosophy as Wisdom, Besant advanced it as Will and Activity, Leadbeater revealed it as Science, Krishnamurti maintained that it was a science of self-contained Individuality, and Arundale's wife, Rukmini (1904–1986), founder of the International Academy of the Arts (later known as Kālakshetra), advanced it as Beauty.[49]

His successor, C. Jinarājadāsa (1875–1953, President from 1946–53), took more of an interest in the third object of the Society by establishing the School of the Wisdom in the grounds of the international headquarters in Adyar in 1949. Following Jinarājadāsa came N. Sri Ram (1889–1973, President from 1953–73), whose presidency is noted for the construction of the Adyar Library and Research Centre, a new building for the Vasanta Press, and the publication of Theosophical books in regional languages.[50]

The relatively short presidency of John S. Coats (1906–1979, President from 1973 to 1979) was marked by efforts to reach out to other similar organizations to further the cause of brotherhood, the first of three objects of the Society.[51]

The current President from 1980, Radha S. Burnier (b.1923), the daughter of N. Sri Ram, has continued the work to reinvigorate the activities of the Society, such as revitalizing the Olcott Memorial School, conducting numerous welfare activities, and serving as President of the Theosophical Order of Service, an organization founded in 1908 by

Mr. Besant for the purpose of engaging in humanitarian endeavors "in a theosophical spirit."[52]

The Theosophical Society is currently represented by national sections in fifty-two countries with the largest national section being India (over 11,000 members) and the oldest section located in the USA. The most recently organized sections were established in 2007 in the Ukraine and Croatia. The current membership is estimated to be about 28,607 as of 2008.

THE IMPACT OF THEOSOPHY AND THE THEOSOPHICAL SOCIETY

The Theosophical Society and its adherents have made a profound impact on the contemporary religious landscape. As observed above, the Society influenced many prominent individuals especially in the humanities and the arts, contributed to the foundation of many esoteric-ally based new religious movements, contributed to an interest of South Asian religious ideas and Sanskrit terminology to express its ideas, popularized the notion of Masters or Mahatmas, incorporated science and the work of scientists in the exposition of the Ancient Wisdom, and became the first organization in modern times to become a truly international organization (see above) emphasizing the universality of the Ancient Wisdom as encompassed in scriptures, philosophical texts, and ancient science found around the world.

Many prominent individuals were attracted to Theosophical ideas or members of the Theosophical Society for at least part of their lives. Examples include Thomas A. Edison (1847–1931), William Butler Yeats (1865–1935), George W. Russell (1867–1935), Talbot Mundy (1879–1940), Lyman Frank Baum (1851–1919), Algernon Blackwood (1869–1951), the translator of Buddhist Pali texts F. L. Woodward (1871–1952), the Buddhist popularizer Christmas Humphreys (1901–1983), the Buddhologist Edward Conze (1904–1979), the philologist, Sanskritist, and one-time Director of the Adyar Library (TS) F. Otto Schrader (1876–1961), the artists Wassily Kandinsky (1866–1944), Piet Mondrian (1872–1944), and Paul Klee (1879–1940), Maria Montessori (1870–1952), and Walter Y. Evans-Wentz (1878–1965), the translator of the *Tibetan Book of the Dead*.

Many founders of modern esoteric movements were originally connected with the Theosophical Society or with Theosophical ideas, including Theodor Reuss (1855–1923: the founder of the Order of the Templars of the Orient, or OTO), Gustav Meyrink (1868–1932: novelist and a founder of the Blue Star Theosophical Lodge in Prague), Dion Fortune (Violet Mary Firth, 1890–1946: a Western esoteric writer who formed the Christian Mystic Lodge of the TS), Alice Bailey (1880–1949: founder of the Arcane School), Guy and Edna Ballard (1878–1939 and 1886–1971: founders of the "I AM" Religious Activity), Mark L. Prophet (1918–1973: founder of the Summit Lighthouse) and Elizabeth Clare Prophet (1939–2009: founder of the Church Universal and Triumphant), Nicholas and Helena Roerich (1874–1947 and 1879–1955: founders of the Agni Yoga Society), Max Heindel (Louis van Grasshoff: 1865–1919: founder of the Rosicrucian Fellowship), and Rudolf Steiner (1861–1925: founder of the Anthroposophical Society). More recent new religious movements that have been influenced by Theosophical teachings are the Aetherius Foundation, founded by George King (1919–1997) in 1955, and Share International (formerly the Tara Center [Los Angeles] and Tara Press [London]), founded by Benjamin Creme (b.1922) around the late 1970s or early 1980s. In Italy, Damanhur, a spiritual community situated in the Valchiusella Valley, was founded by Oberto Airaudi (b.1950), who came under some Theosophical influence.

The connection of the Theosophical Society primarily to the Eastern (i.e., mainly South Asian) religions of Hinduism and Buddhism is evident from the Society's inception, although this influence only becomes prominent after the founders went to India in 1879. In the section above on "Theosophy," I suggested that the incipient society based its teachings on Western esotericism, identified as the Ancient Wisdom, purportedly known in every ancient civilized country. The South Asian connection to Theosophy was introduced by Sinnett in the early 1880s with the publication of his *Esoteric Buddhism*, based upon the letters said to have been sent to Sinnett by Blavatsky's Masters Koot Hoomi Lal Singh and Morya, or whoever represented these Masters. Blavatsky contributed to this South Asian (i.e., Hindu and Buddhist) emphasis in *The Secret Doctrine* (1888) and her subsequent writings. Other contributing factors include the establishment of the Adyar Library in 1886, which attracted Hindu pundits who helped collect and translate many Sanskrit manuscripts. The use of Sanskrit terminology to portray Theosophical ideas together with the incorporation of Vedantic and selected Buddhist teachings contributed to an Eastern flavor, although one can argue that Sanskrit terminology provided a veneer for the primarily Western esoteric content. Many Sanskrit words entered the English lexicon through Funk and Wagnall's Dictionary,[53] including *karma*, *karmic*, *brahm* (*brahmā*, *brahma*), *brahmakalpa*, *brahman/brahmin* (one of the priests in the Vedic ritual; the first social class: *brāhmaṇa*), *ātman*, and *sannyāsa*. Because of the location of the headquarters of the Adyar Society, the promotion of Sanskrit philosophical texts, and the importance of Sanskrit in the presentation of Theosophical ideas, the transformation of the Society into an Eastern movement qualified it, to at least one scholar, as a neo-Hindu reform movement.[54] Furthermore, it is not surprising that Sanskrit terminology is ubiquitous in subsequent religious movements.

One of the most important contributions to new religions has been the concept of Masters, Mahatmas, or the Great White Brotherhood. Although Blavatsky did not invent or introduce the idea of highly advanced and spiritualized wise men, it was she who excited the public about them. Letters from the Masters to Sinnett and subsequent letters to other Theosophists,[55] and Leadbeater's[56] expositions on the hierarchies of Masters and Brotherhoods (the Great White Brotherhood or Great White Lodge) struck a chord with more recent organizations, such as the "I AM" Religious Activity,[57] the Church Universal Triumphant, the Arcane School, the Movement of Spiritual Inner Awareness (John-Roger), Share International, the Agni Yoga Society, Eckankar (Paul Twitchell), and AMORC (Ancient Mystical Order Rosae Crucis: H. Spencer Lewis [1883–1939]). Individuals such as Baird T. Spalding (1872–1953) discuss the Great White Brotherhood in the pursuit of world peace, suggesting that the Brotherhood exerted an influence on the League of Nations.[58]

Another noteworthy contribution of Blavatsky and the Theosophical Society was the frequent reference to science as an instrument of legitimizing the Ancient Wisdom, as evidenced in the second object of the Society. Wherever scientific knowledge could be interpreted to support the Ancient Wisdom, Blavatsky and her disciples encouraged its conclusions, for ultimately, she felt, philosophy, myth, religion, and science all contribute to the Truth, reflecting the motto of the Theosophical Society: "There is nothing higher than Truth." Although critical of the ideology of scientism, the materialistic, positivistic approach to science, Blavatsky insisted that certain spiritual truths could be corroborated by scientific study.[59] Therefore, the names of numerous scientists appear in Blavatsky's writings: the chemist Sir William Crookes, the astronomer Simon Newcomb (*Popular Astronomy*), the geologist Alexander Winchell, the chemist Jean-Baptiste Dumas, Isaac Newton, A. Butlerof, Tycho Brahe, and the astronomer Sir W. Herschel. A typical example of Blavatsky's union of esoteric and scientific assessment appears in *The Secret Doctrine* (1, 588f.): "Scientific and Esoteric Evidence for, and Objections to, the Modern Nebular Theory." In this respect, Theosophy paved the way for the almost universal insistence of contemporary religions that they are in harmony with the findings of science.

Notes

1 This appears in a letter to Professor H. P. Corson (1828–1911) dated February 16, 1875, appearing in John Algeo (ed.), *The Letters of H. P. Blavatsky*, vol. I, *1861–1879* (Wheaton, IL, and Chennai, India, 2003), p. 86. A similar entry appears in her *Scrapbook*, reproduced in Helena Petrovna Blavatsky, *H. P. Blavatsky Collected Writings*, vol. I, *1874–1878*, 3rd edn. (Wheaton, IL, 1988), p. 73.
2 H. P. Blavatsky, "A Crisis for Spiritualism," in *Blavatsky Collected Writings*, vol. I, p. 199 (originally published in *Spiritual Scientist* [Boston], 4 [March 23, 1876], pp. 32–34).
3 Quoted from the *Minute Book of the Theosophical Society*, located in the Archives of the Theosophical Society (Pasadena, California). Reproduced in *H. P. Blavatsky Collected Writings*, vol. I, p. 125, and Henry Steel Olcott, *Old Diary Leaves: The History of The Theosophical Society*, vol. I (Adyar, Madras, 1974 [based on 2nd edn., 1941]), p. 121.
4 Most likely suggested by Charles Sotheran (1847–1902).
5 Olcott, *Old Diary Leaves*, vol. I, p. 135.
6 Ibid.
7 Noah Webster, *An American Dictionary of the English Language*, revised by Chauncey A. Goodrich and Noah Porter (Springfield, MA, 1875), p. 1373. See note 142.
8 The 1913 *Webster's Revised Unabridged Dictionary* retains a similar definition in the online edition at http://machaut.uchicago.edu/?resource=Webster%27s&word=theosophy&use1913=on&use1828=on (accessed November 28, 2011).
9 See Gregory Shaw, *Theurgy and the Soul: The Neoplatonism of Iamblichus* (University Park, PA, 1995).
10 Joscelyn Godwin, *The Theosophical Enlightenment* (Albany, NY, 1994), pp. 261–75; Hargrave Jennings, *The Rosicrucians* (Montana, n.d.; originally published in 1870), pp. 77–88. See also Albert Gallatin Mackey, *An Encyclopædia of Freemasonry*, new and revised edn. by William J. Hugan and Edward L. Hawkins (New York and London, 1913; originally published in 1873), Vol. I, p. 266.
11 Henry S. Olcott, "Inaugural Address of the President." Pamphlet printed by The Theosophical Society (November 17, 1875), p. 21. [Archives of The Theosophical Society (Pasadena).] "Elementary Spirits," or "elementals" are "forces of nature" dwelling in air, water, earth, and fire, and associated with gnomes sylphs, salamanders, and undines. For an explanation, see H. P. Blavatsky, *Isis Unveiled*, vol. I (Los Angeles, 1982; photographic facsimile of the 1877 edn.), pp. xxix–xxx, and Franz Hartmann, *The Life and the Doctrines of Philippus Theophrastus, Bombast of Hohenheim, known by the name of Paracelsus* (New York, 1910), pp. 5–6, 44, 110, 146 (note), 150–60.

12 "Preamble and By-Laws of the Theosophical Society. Organized in the City of New-York. October 30, 1875," p. 5. The Preamble was delivered on November 17, 1875.

13 Ibid.

14 Helena P. Blavatsky, "What is Theosophy?" in *H. P. Blavatsky Collected Writings*, vol. II, *1879–1880* (Wheaton, IL, n.d.), pp. 87–97 (originally published in *The Theosophist* 1:1 [October 1879], pp. 2–5).

15 Ibid., p. 87.

16 Ibid. Robert Alfred Vaughan, *Hours with the Mystics: A Contribution to the History of Religious Opinion* (New York, 1893), p. 40.

17 Blavatsky, "What is Theosophy?" p. 92.

18 Ibid., p. 90.

19 Helena P. Blavatsky, "Instruction No. II," in *H. P. Blavatsky Collected Writings*, vol. XII, *1889–1890*, p. 560, www.katinkahesselink.net/blavatsky/articles/v12/y1890_054.htm (accessed November 2011).

20 "Theosophy," with a capital "T," represents the modern Theosophy of the Theosophical societies, while theosophy (with a lower-case "t") represents other and usually earlier forms of theosophy.

21 *Standard Dictionary of the English Language* (New York and London, 1898), p. 1871. This reference work, Funk and Wagnall's Dictionary (with copyrights in 1890, 1893, and 1894), had on its editorial board William Q. Judge, the General Secretary of the American Section of the Theosophical Society, and C. H. A. Bjerregaard, a Theosophist, both responsible for defining Theosophical terms.

22 Hartmann, *The Life and the Doctrines of Philippus Theophrastus*, p. 54.

23 Blavatsky, *Isis Unveiled*, vol. I, pp. 16, 36, 92–93.

24 Blavatsky, "What is Theosophy?" p. 90.

25 Helena Petrovna Blavatsky, *The Secret Doctrine*, vol. I (London, 1888; reprinted 1974), p. 14.

26 Helena Petrovna Blavatsky, "Notes and Footnotes to 'Three Unpublished Essays'," in *H. P. Blavatsky Collected Writings*, vol. VI (Los Angeles, 1954), p. 180.

27 Blavatsky, *The Secret Doctrine*, vol. I, pp. 14–17.

28 Blavatsky, *The Secret Doctrine*, vol. II, p. 25.

29 A diagram appears in Helena Petrovna Blavatsky, "Instruction No. IV: The Eastern School of Theosophy," in *Blavatsky Collected Writings*, vol. XII, p. 658. For an explanation, see Geoffrey A. Barborka, *The Divine Plan* (Adyar, Madras, 1980), pp. 164–68.

30 Barborka, *The Divine Plan*, pp. 206–17.

31 Blavatsky, *The Secret Doctrine*, vol. I, p. 274.

32 Ibid., p. 14.

33 Blavatsky, *Isis Unveiled*, vol. I, p. xxxvii.

34 Olcott, *Old Diary Leaves*, vol. I, p. 394.

35 This is mentioned in the *Scrapbook*, as recorded in *Blavatsky Collected Writings*, vol. I, pp. 193–94, and in a circular dated May 3, 1878, published in ibid., pp. 375–78.

36 The full account is given in Olcott, *Old Diary Leaves*, vol. i, pp. 395–98. See also *A Short History of the Theosophical Society*, compiled by Josephine Ransom (Adyar, Madras, 1938), pp. 103–4.

37 The reasons are given in Olcott, *Old Diary Leaves*, vol. i, pp. 405–6.

38 Michael Gomes, *The Dawning of the Theosophical Movement* (Wheaton, IL, 1987), pp. 169–71.

39 Corfu, one of the Ionian Islands, is also mentioned by Olcott in his "Theosophy and Theosophists," *Overland Monthly* (May 1901), p. 993.

40 Ibid., p. 995.

41 Ibid.

42 A discussion of "precipitation" is given in Geoffrey A. Barborka, *The Mahatmas and their Letters* (Adyar, Madras, 1973), pp. 109–22.

43 Richard Hodgson, "Account of Personal Investigations in India, and Discussion of the Authorship of the 'Koot Hoomi' Letters," in "Report of the Committee appointed to Investigate Phenomena Connected with the Theosophical Society", *Society for Psychical Research: Proceedings* 3 (1885), pp. 201–7 and 313–17. See also James A. Santucci, "Theosophical Society," in Wouter J. Hanegraaff (ed.), *Dictionary of Gnosis and Western Esotericism* (Leiden, 2005), pp. 1118–19.

44 Hargrove founded his own Theosophical Society, known also as the Theosophical Society in America, in 1898 after failing to regain control of Tingley's society. It is no longer active.

45 See www.theosociety.org/pasadena/tup-onl.htm (accessed November 2011).

46 Santucci, "Theosophical Society," pp. 1116–20.

47 Michael Gomes, "Nehru's Theosophical Tutor," *Theosophical History* 7:3 (July 1998), p. 108n. 31. The current label for this version of Theosophy is Second Generation Theosophy.

48 This is also mentioned in René Dybdal Pedersen, "Theosophy in Denmark: A Second Golden Age?" *Theosophical History* 13:2 (April 2007), p. 25.

49 George S. Arundale, "What is My Policy?" in *The International Theosophical Year Book: 1937* (Adyar, Madras, 1937), p. 22.

50 www.ts-adyar.org/content/n-sri-ram-1889-1973#President_of_the_Theosophical_Society (accessed November 2011).

51 www.ts-adyar.org/content/john-b-s-coats-1906-1979 (accessed November 2011).

52 http://international.theoservice.org (accessed November 2011).

53 See note 21, above.

54 Axel Michaels, *Hinduism: Past and Present*, trans. Barbara Harshaw (Princeton and Oxford, 2004), p. 45.

55 *The Mahatma Letters to A. P. Sinnett from the Mahatmas M. & K. H.*, transcribed, compiled, and with an introduction by A. T. Barker, 2nd edn. (London, 1926).

56 *The Masters and the Path* (Adyar, Madras, 1925); *The Masters of Wisdom*, Adyar Pamphlet 86 (Adyar, Madras, n.d.).

57   The Ballards introduced the Ascended Masters, Masters who died and ascended to higher realms, whereas the Masters of Theosophy are living beings.
58   Baird T. Spalding, *Life and Teachings of the Masters of the Far East*, 5 vols. (Santa Monica, 1924).
59   Blavatsky, *The Secret Doctrine*, vol. 1, p. 579: "Modern Science is Ancient Thought Distorted, and no more."

Further reading

Campbell, Bruce, *Ancient Wisdom Revived: A History of the Theosophical Movement* (Berkeley, 1980).

Godwin, Joscelyn, *The Theosophical Enlightenment* (Albany, NY, 1994).

Gomes, Michael, *The Dawning of the Theosophical Movement* (Wheaton, IL, 1987).

Hammer, Olav and Mikael Rothstein (eds.), *Handbook of the Theosophical Current* (Leiden, forthcoming).

15 The New Age

GEORGE D. CHRYSSIDES

The term "New Age" is generally associated with a variety of new and alternative forms of spirituality that gained popularity in the West from the early 1970s. Its proponents have frequently referred to it as a "paradigm shift," signifying alternative and new ways of understanding the human mind, one's spiritual life, emergent culture, and the nature of the world. The New Age Movement (NAM) is somewhat amorphous, encompassing a variety of seemingly diverse, yet interconnected interests, spanning spiritual healing, yoga and meditation, crystals, psychic phenomena, astrology, earth mysteries such as UFOs and crop circles, human potential, and Eastern religions, among others. It is not a unified movement with an agreed set of objectives, and it is to be differentiated from new religious movements (NRMs), which normally have a clear organizational structure and whose followers give them exclusive allegiance. Since the New Age sometimes relies on ideas that pre-date the 1970s, some mention will be made of these in the ensuing account.

The NAM's nebulous nature has caused different scholars to draw different boundaries around it. Wouter J. Hanegraaff distinguishes between a restricted sense and a general sense of the term "New Age."[1] The restricted sense is the form of esotericism based on the 1950s interest in ufology, which anticipated a coming apocalypse, followed by a period of world peace. While early New Age proponents, such as George Trevelyan and David Spangler, emphasized a new age as central to their teachings, Hanegraaff's general sense of the concept spans a wide range of esoteric activities, including channeling, healing, spiritual growth, holistic science, and neopaganism.

Paul Heelas[2] adopts a somewhat liberal stance, allowing the term to encompass NRMs like the International Society for Krishna Consciousness and the Rajneesh/Osho organization, as well as the human potential movement (HPM), including organizations like The Forum (formerly Erhard Seminars Training) and techniques such as neuro-linguistic programming (NLP). Marilyn Ferguson defines it in terms of transformation and "psychotechnologies,"[3] spanning techniques for developing human potential, dream work, channeling, alternative health, meditation, and Eastern spirituality, but not specific NRMs. Steven Sutcliffe has argued that the term "New Age" is not a meaningful category, since it is impossible to specify what counts as a "New Age" activity and what does not.[4] In Rodney Stark and William S. Bainbridge's typology the New Age Movement is more akin to a "cult movement," consisting of "client cults" – spiritual services that are offered to clients on a commercial basis.[5] Dominic Corrywright employs the concept of SPIN (Segmented Polycentric Integrated Network), as a means of understanding the New Age.[6]

The term "New Age" signifies a passing beyond traditional Christianity. It is the Age of Aquarius, which is held to supersede the previous age of Pisces. Pisces, meaning "fish," is the symbol of Christianity, and thus the zodiacal sign of Aquarius signifies the presumed post-Christian nature of the New Age. Astrologically, each age has a zodiacal constellation that is believed to dominate our planet. This dominance lasts for a period of roughly 2,000 years, and the earth is currently in transition between zodiacal ages. The exact timing of this transition is somewhat indeterminate; hence there is disagreement about the exact point of transition. Some believe that the transition has occurred, some expect it soon, and some hold that the earth is currently "on the cusp."

PRECURSORS OF THE "NEW AGE"

Despite the adjective "new" in New Age, many New Age ideas are not new, but have their precursors. Even the term is not novel. William Blake (1757–1827) used it to designate a new expression of Christianity influenced by gnosticism, and the expression was also used by Alice Bailey (1880–1949), whose Arcane School offered "training in new age discipleship."

Emanuel Swedenborg (1688–1772), a mathematician and engineer who in his mid fifties began to receive a series of supernatural visions, is sometimes regarded as the "father of the New Age." He was particularly influential on Ralph Waldo Emerson (1803–1882), who advocated a kind of nature mysticism, in which the soul is one with God, and both are one with nature.[7] His notion of the self–God relationship was in part influenced by the Upanishads; he was one of the first Westerners to possess a copy and to study it. The Chandogya Upanishad contains the famous assertion *tat tvam asi* ("You are that"), frequently construed as asserting an identity between the *atman* (the soul) and *brahman* (the eternal). Emerson's legacy to the New Age lies in his anti-establishment, anti-Enlightenment ideas, his idealism, his emphasis on direct spiritual experience and the intellect's limits in discovering the divine, his rejection of organized religion, and his drawing on spirituality outside the Christian tradition.

More directly, the movement can be traced to Anton Franz (Friedrich) Mesmer (1734–1815), who held that a magnetic field or fluid surrounded one's physical body, transmitting "universal forces." Mesmer is particularly associated with the trance states into which he induced patients, some of whom purportedly manifested clairvoyant powers. He had an important bearing on the development of New Thought, which taught methods of healing through the powers of the mind. Warren Felt Evans (1817–1889), one of New Thought's leading proponents, wrote several books on "mind cure," and is particularly remembered for recommending the use of "affirmations" – positive statements about one's personal progress, which the follower was urged to recite at regular intervals – as a means of furthering health and prosperity.

Despite its subsequent decline, the role of the Theosophical Society can hardly be underestimated. Founded in New York in 1875, with the aims of investigating unexplained natural phenomena, and the study of "comparative religion" and philosophy, it drew largely on the writings of Helena P. Blavatsky (1831–1891), who claimed to have traveled the world between 1848 and 1858, eventually reaching Tibet, and meeting Canadian Red Indians, Egyptian cabbalists, and voodoo magicians in the course of her journeys. In Tibet, she purportedly studied under Secret Masters, who continued to contact and influence her. (Such claims, of course, are unsubstantiated, although her later journey to India and Sri Lanka is much better attested.)

Annie Besant (1847–1933) and Charles W. Leadbeater (1854–1934) were important second-generation Theosophists on whose legacy the New Age draws. Both had a mainstream Christian background, which they mingled with esotericism and Eastern religion. On a visit to India in 1908, Leadbeater "discovered" the boy Jiddu Krishnamurti (1895–1986), whom he and Besant proclaimed as Maitreya, the expected Buddha of the next eon, and they set up the Order of the Star in the East as his organization. In 1929, however, Krishnamurti renounced this imposed identity, establishing himself as an independent teacher, whose popularity continues within New Age circles.

Alice Bailey also claimed contact with a number of Ascended Masters, particularly one by the name of Djwahl Khul, who allegedly "channeled" her earliest writing, *Initiation: Human and Solar* (1922).[8] Her best known work is *The Reappearance of the Christ* (1948) which, far from propagating mainstream Christianity, portrayed Jesus as a medium whose body was inhabited by the Christ. Christ, she contended, would reappear towards the end of the twentieth century, heralding a "new age."[9]

A further important exponent of esoteric Christianity was Edgar Cayce (1877–1945), whose writings continue to be read in New Age circles. He was reared a conservative Christian, but began to have out-of-the-body experiences, affording esoteric knowledge about the natural and spiritual worlds. Cayce gave "readings" to inquirers – pronouncements given in a trance state and noted by a stenographer – on subjects which ranged from personal health to the nature of the universe. When asked about his sources of knowledge, Cayce declared that they derived from telepathic knowledge of the inquirer's subconscious, and from the Akashic Records – a kind of metaphysical database containing the totality of the universe's knowledge. Cayce's view of Jesus was bound up with occultism and belief in reincarnation. He believed that Jesus was an Essene, who traveled to the East, studying Eastern spirituality and astrology.

In addition to healing and psychic powers, two further New Age preoccupations can be traced back to Cayce: the use of crystals and its interest in lost civilizations. Cayce believed that the inhabitants of Atlantis utilized enormous crystals as a source of energy, but these became over-charged, causing a gigantic explosion which destroyed their civilization, causing it to sink beneath the ocean. Cayce's psychic readings frequently referred to crystals, which he believed were related to human vibrations and past lives, and he recommended the use of gemstones to his clients.

G. I. Gurdjieff (c.1874–1949) is also significant: his "Fourth Way" is a spiritual path that is distinct from those of the body, the emotions, and the mind. These three ways, he contended, are represented by the fakir (who seeks to control the body), the monk (who seeks emotional non-attachment), and the yogi (who practices mental training), and all are connected with organized religious institutions. Gurdjieff's Fourth Way was not bounded by religious organizations: the seeker conducts his or her own search, achieving inner development and higher states of consciousness. Gurdjieff is also credited with the invention of the enneagram, which continues to arouse interest: this is a nine-pointed diagram, whose meaning is undisclosed, but may be connected with the Kabbalah.

Many of the interests of Swedenborg, Emerson, the Theosophists, New Thought, and Gurdjieff are reflected in New Age thinking. The New Age offers spirituality outside mainstream religion, with an interest in Ascended Masters, healing, the powers of the mind, esotericism, and paranormal phenomena. These earlier forms of alternative spirituality tended to be self-contained, being membership organizations with their own distinctive teachings and practices. In contrast, the New Age popularized the occult, bringing it to the high street with its shops and book stores. A further point of contrast was the New Age's move away from the idea of eschatological savior figures, such as the returning Ascended Masters, Bailey's notion of the reappearance of the Christ, or the expectation of the Maitreya, the Buddha of the next eon.

BACKGROUND AND EARLY DEVELOPMENTS

The backdrop against which the New Age Movement emerged was a concern for peace, an interest in environmental protection, and a belief in a plurality of truths rather than a single objective one. Thomas Kuhn's *The Structure of Scientific Revolutions*,[10] which focused on "paradigm shifts," was roughly contemporaneous with Peter Winch's famous essay "Understanding a Primitive Society," which argued that the Azande belief in witchcraft and magic was as internally coherent as a Western scientific worldview, and suggested not only a culture-relative view of truth, but an added respect for the ideas of alternative, and indeed primal, cultures.[11] Some popular works on alternative science served to undermine confidence in conventional science, most notably Lyall Watson's *Supernature* (1973), which explored paranormal phenomena,[12] and Uri Geller, whose famous psychokinetic spoon-bending, demonstrated worldwide on television, supposedly demonstrated psychic powers given to him by extraterrestrials. Other themes of the 1960s and early 1970s were world peace and environmental protection. The Campaign for Nuclear Disarmament (CND) had been founded in 1957, and gained momentum with the 1962 Cuba Crisis and the US involvement in the Vietnam War. Friends of the Earth was established in 1969, and Greenpeace in 1971. The Club of Rome's 1972 *Limits to Growth* report suggested that it was now too late for humankind to mend its ways environmentally, and that population growth would soon outstrip the earth's available natural resources.[13] E. F. Schumacher's *Small is Beautiful*,[14] first published in 1973, argued the case against large multinational corporations, advocating smaller-scale businesses with concern for people above profits, in order to save the environment and acknowledge the worth of the individual. One chapter was entitled "Buddhist Economics," linking his ideas with Eastern religion.

The Findhorn Community, set up by Peter and Eileen Caddy in early 1962, was initially a project in small-scale vegetable farming, and was one of the earliest New Age centers. The Esalen Institute at Big Sur in California commenced in the same year, and offered a range of New Age practices, including visualization, Gestalt therapy, and study of the enneagram. By the mid 1970s a number of centers, bookstores, and gift shops had been set up, often describing themselves as "New Age," and offering literature on peace, ecology, alternative spirituality, and paranormal phenomena. The term was taken up by the popular media, and came to describe the network of groups interested in the phenomena associated with the movement. One book which was particularly significant in the development of New Age ideas was Shirley MacLaine's *Out on a Limb* (1983),[15] an autobiographical work in which she revealed her belief in reincarnation, mediumship and channeling, and UFOs. The book became the subject of a television series in 1987, giving the ideas wide circulation.

TURNING EAST

One of the manifestations of the New Age's turning away from Christianity was its tendency to turn eastward for spiritual inspiration. Of particular interest were Hinduism, Buddhism and philosophical Taoism, although these religious systems tended to be propagated in a Westernized and often romanticized form. Herman Hesse's *Siddhartha*,[16] originally written in 1922, underwent a revival after the author's death forty years later.

Zen – previously part of the US "hippie" counterculture – continued to be propagated, largely through the writings of D. T. Suzuki, a Japanese Zen practitioner, who came to the USA in the 1890s and wrote prolifically, in English, with the aim of devising and propagating a form of Zen to which Westerners could relate. Later authors took up the theme that *satori* (enlightenment) could be experienced in any human activity, not just sitting meditating, and produced titles such as *Zen in the Art of Archery* (1953),[17] and *Zen in the Art of Flower Arrangement* (1958),[18] both reprinted in the 1970s. Sometime later Robert M. Pirsig's *Zen and the Art of Motorcycle Maintenance* (1974)[19] became a New Age cult book, linking Zen to ideas in the history of Western philosophy. Numerous titles followed, linking Zen to a plethora of professions and interests, spanning social work, management, and education, among others. The fascination for Zen was followed by a surge of interest in Tibetan Buddhism, aided by the somewhat suspect novels of T. Lobsang Rampa, whose *The Third Eye* attained popularity.[20] (Rampa claimed to be a Tibetan lama, but in reality was a plumber's son from Devon.) More reputable spiritual classics such as *The Tibetan Book of the Dead* and *The Tibetan Book of the Great Liberation*[21] were studied, and several spiritual teachers from Tibet took up residence in the USA and Britain.

A comparable interest in Taoism can also be noted. The popularity of Chinese classics like the *Tao Te Ching* and the *I Ching* generated an after-market in literature and paraphernalia. The latter text, being a method of divination, was backed up by sales of commodities such as I Ching cards, boards, and coins, and several book titles, such as *The Tao of Love and Sex* (1977), *The Tao of Health and Longevity* (1978), *The Tao of Leadership* (1984), and many more. Fritjof Capra's *The Tao of Physics* (1975) is especially memorable for its linkage of Taoist thought with nuclear physics and Eastern philosophical notions of impermanence and insubstantiality.[22] The fascination for Chinese culture also brought with it an interest in the martial arts, such as kung fu and t'ai chi, and President Nixon's visit to China in 1972 heralded the introduction of *feng shui*, a form of geomancy which has become adapted for interior decoration.

Hindu gurus also provided wisdom for the New Age. Yogananda (1893–1952), one of the first Hindu swamis to visit the West, published his *Autobiography of a Yogi* in 1946, a work which remains a spiritual classic.[23] Better known was the Maharishi Mahesh Yogi, renowned for his Transcendental Meditation, Swami Prabhupada came to public attention in the late 1960s as the founder of the International Society for Krishna Consciousness (ISKCON); and Satya Sai Baba was famed for his apparent ability to perform miraculous healings and materializations of objects. A number of Western teachers studied in the Eastern tradition, such as Ram Dass (born Richard Alpert) and Andrew Cohen, who have developed somewhat syncretistic teachings combining aspects of Hindu teaching with Buddhism and Sufism. Ram Dass' *Be Here Now* (1971) and *Grist for the Mill* (1977) proved to be a source of inspiration to many seekers.[24] The Brahma Kumaris, a female-led Hindu organization in the Saivite tradition, is sometimes reckoned to have "gone New Age," having supplemented its traditional practice of raja yoga with self-development seminars, including topics such as positive thinking, stress management, and time management.

Hinduism and Buddhism do not merely offer a spiritual path for New Agers, who have drawn on these traditions as a means of understanding the human body. The concept of chakras offers such a method. Early Western interest in the chakras was aroused by Charles W. Leadbeater's book *The Chakras*,[25] and Rudolf Steiner also employed the system. It is an occult system of anatomy, postulating energy centers in the body – vortices corresponding to one's subtle or etheric body and which are associated with different bodily or mental functions. There are usually held to be seven of these (located at the spinal base, the genitals, the solar plexus, the heart, the throat, the forehead, and the crown), although some systems posit only five or six. This system can be used medically: these energy centers can allegedly be over-active or under-active, giving rise to various ailments. The chakras are also believed to have their associated colors, sounds, and vibrations: various New Age skills can be used to apprehend them, including clairvoyance, color therapy, pendulum dowsing, and crystal therapy. The practice of kundalini yoga aims to raise one's *kundalini*, a snake-like coil in one's spinal-base chakra, so that it resides in the crown chakra, resulting in enlightenment.

Hindu and Buddhist belief in karma and reincarnation (or rebirth) also became related to health and healing. A number of New Age therapists inferred that ailments might be related not merely to physical causes within their clients' present lives, but to events in past lives, the effects of which were now manifesting themselves. Accordingly, services such as karmic counseling and past-life regression are offered within New Age networks. Karmic counseling can supposedly reveal the reasons for the counselee's lot in life, yielding empowerment for living, knowledge of the goals that he or she should seek in the present life, and an ability to face death with hope and confidence.

HEALING

The previous section introduced the subject of alternative therapies. Healing is a major theme in New Age thought and practice: in addition to Ayurvedic and Tibetan medicine, a number of therapies proved popular in New Age circles, although many are not particularly new. One such example is aromatherapy: the practice of mixing dried plants with oils may go back as far as the first century. Homoeopathy, invented in the late eighteenth century by the German physician Samuel Hahnemann (1755–1843), works on the principle of *similia similibus curentur* ("like is cured by like"), and utilizes plant, animal, and mineral substances in high dilution. Bach flower remedies, devised by Dr. Edward Bach (1886–1936) in the 1930s, draw on the homoeopathic practice of high dilution, often leaving the preparation devoid of any curative substance; hence the principle of "water memory" is invoked to explain the preparation's alleged curative effects. Unlike homoeopathy, however, Bach's therapies do not presuppose a "law of similars."

Healing is not merely about physical and mental health, but about life in general. *You Can Heal Your Life* (1984) by Louise Hay remains a best-selling New Age classic. At one time a New Thought practitioner, Hay was diagnosed in the late 1970s as having cervical cancer, which she claimed to have successfully treated through mind cure. Hay's writing emphasizes motivation, personal responsibility, and positive thinking, and in common with Religious Science, (established in 1949 by Ernest Holmes [1887–1960] as one of the several religious movements propagating mind over matter) makes much use of affirmations. Her key message is that thought can be changed, and that the substitution of positive for negative thoughts can bring about health, success, good personal relationships, and economic prosperity. Positive thinking suggests a regard for the self which differs from the traditional Christian view that humankind has separated itself from God through sin. New Age thinking emphasizes self-worth and human potential. Hay writes, "I am one with the very Power that created me, and this Power has given me the power to create my own circumstances."[26] Such statements distance New Agers from the traditional Christian perception of God as "Other," affirming a God who lies within the self.

Equally – if not more – prominent in the field of New Age health is Deepak Chopra. In 1973 Chopra qualified as a physician in the USA but, after taking up Transcendental Meditation in 1981, he came to meet the Maharishi Mahesh Yogi in 1985, and took up the study of Ayurvedic medicine. Chopra's writings recommend the elimination of negative emotions and the intuitive understanding of signals from one's body, which can improve health and increase one's lifespan. Among Chopra's many books, *Quantum Healing: Exploring the Frontiers of Mind–Body Medicine* (1984) and his later *The Seven Spiritual Laws of Success* (1994) are the best known.[27]

SUPERNATURAL HELP

Although New Age thought emphasizes self-help and responsibility, this does not rule out the availability of supernatural assistance. Recourse to powers outside oneself can be accomplished in a variety of ways. One such path is that of magic. Melton distinguishes three traditions, two of which substantially impinge on New Age. (The third is Satanism, although the satanic path is regarded as too "dark" by most New Agers.)

The first path is that of Aleister Crowley and the Hermetic Order of the Golden Dawn with which he was for some years associated. Crowley's *Magick in Theory and Practice* (1929) was detailed and influential.[28] His magical ideas owed much to Eliphas Levi (1810–1876), whose writings were translated into English as *Transcendental Magic: Its Doctrine and Ritual* and published in 1896.[29] Sometimes known as Enochian magic, it is a system of ceremonial magic, used for the summoning and commissioning of spirits, originating from the sixteenth-century occultists John Dee and Edward Kelley. The system was discovered by S. L. MacGregor Mathers, but much of its detail had been lost. Crowley expended considerable effort in endeavoring to reconstruct it, and it forms the basis of his own system. Dee and Kelley maintained that its contents were transmitted by angels, who revealed to them the secrets contained in the apocryphal *Book of Enoch*.

Melton's second magical tradition is found in Wicca, or witchcraft – a branch of a broader set of so-called pagan movements that attempt to recreate and adapt pre-Christian religious traditions for modern practitioners. Wicca is a tradition in its own right, which many have chosen as their own exclusive religion. Wiccans therefore deny that they are following "New Age religion," since they regard themselves as reviving ancient pre-Christian religious practices, and do not combine them with other New Age practices such as the use of crystals, channels, and Tarot. Nonetheless, New Agers may decide to appropriate elements of Wicca, of which the use of spells seems to have a particular appeal. Such books of spells are typically the idiosyncratic creations of their authors, recommending incantations to address themes like finding love, personal success, financial prosperity, breaking bad habits, and general protection against evil.

CHANNELING

A further source of external help lies in supernatural beings. Sometimes this is expressed in a belief in angels, who minister to humans, and some New Agers, in common with some Christians, profess a belief in a designated guardian angel who watches over them. Other ideas of supernatural help derive from belief in Ascended Masters, who provide humankind with spiritual teachings. The present-day New Age interest in "channeling" (a form of mediumship) draws on the Theosophical tradition, rather than from the practices of the Spiritualist churches. Spiritualism is organized religion, in contrast with the more eclectic explorations of the New Age, and the spirits with whom the medium

purportedly makes contact tend to be attendees' family and acquaint-
ances. New Age channelers – the preferred name for mediums – do not
normally convey messages from those who have recently died, but
either clairvoyantly communicate with spirit guides or angels, or else
employ trance mediumship to provide their audiences with the teachings of a Master to whom they specifically relate. Well-known examples
of the latter are J. Z. Knight, who mediates the spiritual master Ramtha,
and Jane Roberts, who served as the channel for Seth.

Other related forms of channeling make use of channeled writings,
which assume the role of sacred texts for their supporters. Well-known
examples include *The Urantia Book*, purportedly of composite celestial authorship between 1934 and 1935, although the human channel is
unknown.[30] The book was published in 1955, and recounts a history of
the universe that extends back 987 million years, providing an account
of the conflict between good and evil, including Jesus' role in enabling
humanity to evolve towards perfection. Helen Schucman's *A Course in
Miracles*, first published in 1975, swiftly became a popular book, both
for private study and for group seminars.[31] It was purportedly channeled
from Jesus, extolling the virtues of peace, love, joy, and oneness, and it
is accompanied by spiritual exercises to develop these.

JESUS IN THE NEW AGE

It will be noticed from the above that the New Age does not dispense with the figure of Jesus. What it typically rejects is the Jesus of
the Church. In his *The Third Jesus* (2009) Deepak Chopra rejects the
Jesus of history (the first Jesus), which he believes cannot be rediscovered.[32] Equally, he rejects the Church's Jesus (the second Jesus), who has
been theologized, given a metaphysical role in the ancient creeds, and
become the source of the sacraments. The third Jesus, by contrast, is
the consciousness of Jesus, which is the source of all creation, and on
which everyone can draw, and is particularly encapsulated in his sayings, which can trigger personal transformation.

Since the Bible does not provide a biography of Jesus, there are
years that are unaccounted for. These years span the period of Jesus'
adolescence and early adulthood before his teaching ministry, although
some have speculated that there remain lost years after the resurrection. This tradition goes back at least as far as Nicolas Notovich, who
wrote *The Unknown Life of Jesus Christ* in 1894.[33] Notovich claimed
to have arrived at Kashmir, where he found Issa's biography, revealing
that Jesus left Jerusalem in his youth and traveled to the East, where he

learned from various Brahmins and Buddhist teachers. Elizabeth Clare Prophet revived his account in her *The Lost Years of Jesus: Documentary Evidence of Jesus' 17-year Journey to the East* (1984),[34] and Notovich's work paved the way for further theories that Jesus lived in India. Levi Dowling in his *The Aquarian Gospel of Jesus Christ*, originally written in 1920, but rediscovered in the 1960s, tells of how Jesus visited India and Tibet, as well as Persia, Assyria, Greece, and Egypt.[35] Holger Kersten in his *Jesus Lived in India* (1986) claimed that Jesus had studied under Buddhist teachers.[36]

Allegations of a relationship between Jesus and Mary Magdalene provide a further theme for an alternative Jesus. The best-known work which explores the theme is *The Holy Blood and the Holy Grail* (1982), in which the authors Michael Baigent, Richard Leigh, and Henry Lincoln speculate that Jesus married Mary Magdalene and fathered two children who emigrated to southern France.[37] The famous Holy Grail is the bloodline of the Merovingian dynasty, the rightful claimants to the throne of France, a claim which the Priory of Sion champions. The theme, of course, is well known to readers of Dan Brown's *The Da Vinci Code* (2003),[38] and the plagiarism allegations that followed its publication fueled public interest, prompting an aftermath of books supporting the hypothesis that Jesus and Mary were lovers, for example Lynn Picknett's *Mary Magdalene: Christianity's Hidden Goddess* (2003).[39]

Mary Magdalene is bound up with the Holy Grail – a further source of New Age speculation and activity. Some New Age thought equates the grail with a cup that was held by Mary Magdalene beneath Christ's cross, and which captured some of his blood. According to one theory, Mary brought this to southern France. A rival tradition is that Joseph of Arimathea brought the grail to Glastonbury, thus associating the grail with the town's Arthurian legends. Yet another theory is that reference to the grail is itself a reference to Mary Magdalene, thus explaining why Arthur and his knights failed to discover it.

It would be inaccurate to portray mainstream Christianity and the New Age in stark contrast, however. A number of Christian organizations have grown up whose members remain open to some of the aspects of the New Age Movement. Examples are the Omega Order, the Bridge Trust, Christians Awakening to New Awareness (CANA), New Age Catholics, and numerous Creation Spirituality Groups. St James's Church in Piccadilly, London, under the leadership of the Revd. David Reeves, organized a weekly program in which exponents of New Age ideas engaged in dialogue with mainstream Christians. Daren Kemp refers to such organizations collectively as "Christaquarians."[40] The

Roman Catholic website New Age Catholics comments positively on New Age hopes and aspirations, and remarks favorably on some aspects of the movement, such as some of its music, and phenomena like near death experiences and belief in angels. However, it views the New Age's more occultist aspects, such as astrology, clairvoyance, and channeling, more critically.

THE DEMISE OF THE NEW AGE?

It has been claimed that the New Age Movement is now over. In 1987 José Argüelles, now a well-known proponent of the Mayan prophecy, noted and announced an unusual planetary alignment, which became known as the "harmonic convergence." This was expected to be a significant event, likely to cause a change in the earth's energy, resulting in a new era of peace. However, no significant subsequent change in the world became apparent.

David Spangler himself came to express doubts about a coming new age. In 1991 he wrote:

> I have personal doubts that there really is something called the "New Age movement." The New Age idea, yes, but a movement, no – at least not in any ideological, organised sense.[41]

Gordon Melton has suggested that a "new age" as a focus of interest has given way to the theme of "ascension," and cites the Solara as a group who seek to gain entrance through a "doorway" into a progressive series of gates – eleven in all – affording changes in one's individual consciousness.[42] Some groups have integrated the idea of individual transformation with the arrival of UFOs – for example the Raëlian organization. Although initially an individual quest, some writers have viewed individual ascension as a prelude to the establishment of a critical mass of individuals, who by their collective enhanced consciousness will transform the rest of the population. This idea can be found, for example, in James Redfield's highly popular novels *The Celestine Prophecy* (1994) and its sequel *The Tenth Insight* (1996).[43]

One further hope for individual transformation is found in the Mayan prophecy, which has recently attracted interest. The prophecy purportedly relies on the Native American Mayan calendar, which, its proponents explain, relies on an interaction of two cycles of 260 and 365 days respectively: the *Tzolk'in* and the *Haab* (the "short count" and the "long count"). When the short and long counts end simultaneously, a *b'ak'tun* is complete: this happens every 394 solar years, and the present *b'ak'tun* is due to end on December 21, 2012. However, this date does not signal the world's destruction: it is a period of opportunity to gain enlightenment, to reappraise one's materialistic values, to gain enhanced spiritual awareness and creativity.

A further undoubted development in New Age thought has been the spread of its ideas through globalization. World events, such as the collapse of communism in the early 1990s, have enabled New Age ideas to spread into Eastern Europe. Louise Hay and Deepak Chopra, among other New Age authors, are available in many different languages, and are on sale in places like airport bookshops. This globalization of New Age ideas has been accompanied by a mainstream acceptance of several of its components. Alternative health has gained a more sympathetic audience: many medical centers currently make techniques like acupuncture available to patients; it is now possible to obtain degrees in aromatherapy at some universities; meditation is increasingly recognized as being beneficial to health; and several multinational corporations employ human potential consultants. However, one should be cautious about claims that "the New Age has gone mainstream": many of its ideas have failed to gain acceptance in conventional society. Claims that Jesus visited India, or that the Bible recounts visits of extraterrestrials, find little credence among biblical scholars, historians, or archaeologists, and medical researchers remain skeptical about treatments such as Bach flower remedies.

CONCLUSION

While scholars remain divided on whether the New Age should be regarded as at an end, or whether it was ever appropriate to talk about a New Age movement in the first place, most of the phenomena associated with the concept continue. Festivals of Mind-Body-Spirit continue to be held regularly in major cities, psychic fairs continue to be advertised, books on Tarot, clairvoyance, the paranormal, meditation, and self-transformation continue to abound in bookstores, and New Age locations such as Mount Shasta, Findhorn, and Glastonbury still attract seekers. What the New Age has undoubtedly done is to bring the paranormal and the occult into the public arena. To let Melton sum up:

> The New Age in effect transformed the whole occult world. It also gave occultism an entirely new and positive image in society and did away with popular notions tying it to Satanism and black magic.[44]

Notes

1 Wouter J. Hanegraaff, "The New Age Movement and Western Esotericism," in Daren Kemp and James R. Lewis (eds.), *Handbook of the New Age* (Leiden, 2007), pp. 25–75.
2 Paul Heelas, *The New Age Movement* (Oxford, 1996).
3 Marilyn Ferguson, *The Aquarian Conspiracy: Personal and Social Transformation in Our Time* (New York, 1987; first published 1980).
4 Steven J. Sutcliffe, *Children of the New Age: A History of Spiritual Practices* (London, 2003).
5 Rodney Stark and William Sims Bainbridge, *The Future of Religion: Secularization, Revival, and Cult Formation* (Berkeley, 1985), pp. 24–30.
6 Dominic Corrywright, "Network Spirituality: The Schumacher-Resurgence-Kumar Nexus," *Journal of Contemporary Religion* 19:3 (2004), pp. 311–27.
7 Ralph Waldo Emerson, "Nature," in Joseph Forster (ed.), *Four Great Teachers: John Ruskin, Thomas Carlyle, Ralph Waldo Emerson, and Robert Browning* (London, 1890).
8 Alice Bailey, *Initiation: Human and Solar* (New York, 1922).
9 Alice Bailey, *The Reappearance of the Christ* (New York, 1948).
10 Thomas Kuhn, *The Structure of Scientific Revolutions* (Chicago, 1962).
11 Peter Winch, "Understanding a Primitive Society," *American Philosophical Quarterly* 1:4 (1964), pp. 307–24.
12 Lyall Watson, *Supernature* (London, 1973).
13 Donella H. Meadows, Dennis L. Meadowes, Jørgen Randers, and William W. Behrens III, *Limits to Growth* (London, 1972).
14 E. F. Schumacher, *Small is Beautiful* (London, 1973).
15 Shirley MacLaine, *Out on a Limb* (London, 1983).
16 Herman Hesse, *Siddhartha* (London, 2008).
17 Eugen Herrigel, *Zen in the Art of Archery* (London, 1975).
18 Gustie L. Herrigel, *Zen in the Art of Flower Arrangement* (London, 1979; first published 1958).
19 Robert M. Pirsig, *Zen and the Art of Motorcycle Maintenance* (London, 1976).
20 T. Lobsang Rampa, *The Third Eye: The Autobiography of a Tibetan Lama* (London, 1956).
21 Francesca Fremantle and Chögyam Trungpa (trans.), *The Tibetan Book of the Dead* (Boulder, CO, and London, 1975); W. Y. Evans-Wentz (ed.), *The Tibetan Book of the Great Liberation* (London and Oxford, 1954).
22 Fritjof Capra, *The Tao of Physics* (London, 1975).
23 Paramahansa Yogananda, *Autobiography of a Yogi* (New York, 1946).
24 Ram Dass, *Be Here Now* (San Cristobal, NM, 1973; first published 1971); Ram Dass, *Grist for the Mill* (London, 1978).
25 Charles W. Leadbeater, *The Chakras* (Adyar, Madras, 1927).
26 Louise Hay, *You Can Heal Your Life* (London, 1984), p. xiv.

27 Deepak Chopra, *Quantum Healing: Exploring the Frontiers of Mind–Body Medicine* (London, 1989); Deepak Chopra, *The Seven Spiritual Laws of Success* (London, 1996).
28 Aleister Crowley, *Magick in Theory and Practice* (New York, 1929).
29 Eliphas Levi, *Transcendental Magic: Its Doctrine and Ritual* (London, 1896 repr. 1995).
30 Urantia Foundation, *The Urantia Book* (Chicago, 1955).
31 Helen Schucman, *A Course in Miracles* (Tiburon, CA, 1975).
32 Deepak Chopra, *The Third Jesus: How to Find Truth and Love in Today's World* (London, 2009).
33 This and many other contemporary Jesus legends are surveyed in Olav Hammer, "Modern Jesus Legends," in Hammer (ed.), *Alternative Christs* (Cambridge, 2009), pp. 275–92.
34 Elizabeth Clare Prophet, *The Lost Years of Jesus: Documentary Evidence of Jesus' 17-year Journey to the East* (Corwin Springs, MT, 1984).
35 Levi H. Dowling, *The Aquarian Gospel of Jesus the Christ: The Philosophic and Practical Basis of the Religion of the Aquarian Age of the World, Transcribed from the Akashic Records by Levi* (Romford, UK, 1985).
36 Holger Kersten, *Jesus Lived in India* (Shaftesbury, 1986).
37 Michael Baigent, Richard Leigh, and Henry Lincoln, *The Holy Blood and the Holy Grail* (London, 1982).
38 Dan Brown, *The Da Vinci Code* (London, 2004).
39 Lynn Picknett, *Mary Magdalene: Christianity's Hidden Goddess* (London, 2003).
40 Daren Kemp, *The Christaquarians? A Sociology of Christians in the New Age* (Sidcup, UK, 2003).
41 D. Spangler and W. Thompson, *Reimagination of the World: A Critique of the New Age, Science, and Popular Culture* (Santa Fé, NM, 1991), p. 64.
42 Gordon Melton, "Beyond Millennialism: The New Age Transformed," in Kemp and Lewis (eds.), *Handbook*, pp. 77–97.
43 James Redfield, *The Celestine Prophecy* (1994) and *The Tenth Insight* (1996).
44 Melton, "Beyond Millennialism," p. 89.

Further reading

Hammer, Olav, *Claiming Knowledge: Strategies of Epistemology from Theosophy to the New Age* (Leiden, 2001).
Hanegraaff, Wouter J., *New Age Religion and Western Culture: Esotericism in the Mirror of Secular Thought* (Leiden, 1996).
Heelas, Paul, *The New Age Movement* (Oxford, 1996).
Kemp, Daren and James R. Lewis (eds.), *Handbook of the New Age* (Leiden, 2007).

16 "Jihadism" as a new religious movement

REUVEN FIRESTONE

INTRODUCTION

"Jihadism" is a term that has been constructed in Western languages to describe militant Islamic movements that are perceived as existentially threatening to the West. Western media have tended to refer to Jihadism as a military movement rooted in political Islam. Some Muslims have claimed that there is nothing authentically Islamic in these movements. Others have claimed that they represent true Islam. The question that will be addressed in this chapter is the extent to which radically violent Islamist movements might be identified as a kind of new sect formation within Islam or perhaps the emergence of a trend that may result in new religious movements. Criteria for examination will include belief structures, rituals, material culture, scriptural interpretation, and iconography in relation to traditional Islam and other religious and political traditions. Whereas NRM studies are usually confined to religious and sociological innovations in the West, the approach adopted here is somewhat different. In the context of the present volume the intention is to challenge this geographical demarcation and suggest a broader understanding of religious innovation.

JIHADISM AND CONTEMPORARY
ISLAMIC MOVEMENTS

"Jihadism,"[1] like the word *jihad* out of which it is constructed, is a difficult term to define precisely. The meaning of Jihadism is a virtual moving target because it remains a recent neologism and no single, generally accepted meaning has been developed for it. It would require too much space to parse out the full range of meanings and nuances associated with Jihadism and its root in *jihad* even in recent history, but it is important to articulate a working definition for the purposes of this discussion.[2] Jihadism applies here, therefore, to something akin to a transnational movement of militant Sunni Muslim activists, often called *jihadis*,[3] who feel that they must be engaged in a prolonged and perhaps even endless war with the forces of evil defined vaguely as the West, or the "Judeo-Christian" or "Crusader-Zionist" enemy.[4] It arises out of a Muslim religious and cultural context in response to the combination of contemporary Western economic, political, and cultural developments that have tended to be lumped together and defined over the last decade by the term globalism. Because of its genesis in response to conditions defined as globalism and because of its transnational reach, it is sometimes referred to as "global jihad."[5]

Jihadism has some commonalities with the modern, post-colonial trend in Islam called "Islamism," not the least of which is the difficulty of pinpointing the changing meanings associated with both terms.[6] Jihadism was strongly influenced by Islamism and its intellectual founders such as Sayyid Qutb in Egypt and Sayyid Abul-A'la Maududi in India.[7] Like Islamists, Jihadists consider Islam to be more than a creed or conviction that informs individual and group ritual and personal behaviors within a religious community and in relation to members of other religious communities, as religion has largely come to be understood during the last century in the West. That is, like Islamists, adherents of Jihadism believe that Islam has the right and responsibility not only to regulate the behaviors of Muslims, but also to regulate the behaviors of the state and of those residing within the state who are not Muslim. Like Islamism, therefore, Jihadism has a political orientation and can be considered to be situated within a general category referred to by journalists and some scholars and theoreticians as "political Islam." But unlike Islamism, which tends to function within the framework of the nation-state and strives to establish an Islamic state through political action, or a state informed by what are considered Islamic values and ethics, Jihadism does not confine itself to working for political change within the nation-state. It is transnational or global in nature and expresses little interest in articulating national-oriented political goals.

Like Jihadism, Islamism also incorporates many developments or vectors of thought and practice from Islamic tradition and history, and also like Jihadism, it has absorbed notions and patterns that originate outside of traditional Islamic categories (such as modern notions of nationalism and the nation-state for Islamism). A major and defining difference between the two is that Islamism focuses on political goals that can be realized within the framework of the nation-state, while Jihadism is less clear about specific, concrete political goals (if it has any). Islamism incorporates many well-known groups, such as Hamas in Palestine, Hizbullah in Lebanon, Jamaat-i-Islami in Pakistan, and the Taliban in Afghanistan. While every Islamist movement shares a vision of a broader world under Islamic rule, they concentrate on their own national territory and function largely as political movements. The conflict between Fatah and Hamas in the Palestinian arena, for example, is a political conflict between secular nationalism (Fatah) and Islamist nationalism (Hamas) within the territorial framework of Palestine.[8]

Olivier Roy notes that, unlike Islamists, the attackers of 9/11 and the killers of Sadat were unconcerned "about the day after" because they never cared to build a true political movement.[9] Jihadism has been defined as an "ethical" rather than political movement because, as Faisal Devji points out, politics are meant to be instrumental while ethics are not.[10] But Pedahzur notes correctly how Jihadi actions against the US embassies in Africa, the USS *Cole*, and the 9/11 attacks were carefully designed to affect the political and military policy of the USA in the Middle East.[11] The distinction is more accurately between the horizons of the two trends' aspirations. Islamism functions within the context of the modern nation-state and aspires to establishing an Islamic political system within it, while Jihadism is a post-modern trend with less specific political goals applied to a much larger world political arena, and with much less ability relative to world powers to actually accomplish them.[12] While it is clear that Jihadism has a vague but grand political agenda, the "politics" of the trend does not invalidate its religious nature or distinguish it particularly from some Christian religious movements that aspire to a world order in which Christianity will become the dominant driver of all human communities and polities.

Jihadism is situated within a larger fundamentalist trend in modern Islam because, like "Salafi" and "Wahhabi" trends, Jihadists claim to return to the fundamentals of Islamic faith and practice that they believe have been neglected as world Muslims acculturate to what are deemed the negative influence and temptations of Western modernity.[13] And like these trends and their parallels in religious revivalism among Christians and Jews, Jihadism is notably anti-intellectual.

Jihadism also exists within a larger trend of belligerent "Islamic radicalism" because it tends to stress narrow aspects of militant traditional Islamic practice and creed while downplaying or ignoring certain foundational Islamic practices and requirements that might counter or contradict its overwhelming militancy. While Jihadis of course claim that they are authentic Muslims, other Muslims have accused them of grossly distorting Islam through their lopsided emphasis on radical militancy and some of their behaviors and Manichaean perspective, including the practice, called *takfīr* (see below), of considering opponents (whether non-Muslim or Muslim) to be infidels and therefore the enemy that must be destroyed along with the unjust power of the Crusader-Zionist West.

Jihadism thus intersects with a number of other trends in contemporary Islam. We have mentioned the overlap in meaning and association with "political Islam," "Islamism," Wahhabi and Salafi expressions, and fundamentalism. There is a clear intersection also with some aspects of Sufism, including the popular ideals of the *ghāzī* or holy warriors in the Muslim world who were members of Sufi or mystic fraternities.[14]

I categorize Jihadism as a trend or movement rather than an organized group or even association, because while there is a leadership, a hierarchy and a general ideology (or basic perspective and outlook), organization within the trend is extremely loose and dispersed. The most obvious reason for this is its status as a hunted rogue organization whose leadership is sought out for destruction by most Western and many Muslim nations. A second and less obvious reason for its loose and decentralized structure is its transnational role as a kind of franchise or service provider that links a disparate community of individuals lacking any particular psychological profile or cultic or ideological uniformity to bind them together. Pedahzur observes, for example, that the very definition of the name al-Qa'ida ("the base") defines its nature as an umbrella organization that involves, with various degrees of affinity, affiliated groups in more than forty-five countries.[15] Even after his death in May, 2011, Osama bin Laden continues to serve as a symbolic centralizing figure within the movement, but participants within it "are connected by contingency of effects rather than by some common substance."[16]

Jihadism is therefore not merely a negative response to globalism. It is also a *product* of globalism and has been enabled by it.[17] To be more precise, Jihadism is itself a global movement with a certain phenomenological commonality with such global movements as environmentalism or, ironically, the anti-globalization movement. Jihadism is in part a reaction to the Western content and culture of globalism and strives to replace globalism's Western content with a particular expression of what Jihadis define as true Islam.

Now that a general identification for Jihadism has been established, we must ask what groups are included within that trend. That is, if we are attempting to determine whether a religious community is or is not an NRM, we must be able to identify the community so that we can observe its behaviors, learn its creeds, and read its literature or hear its public statements. This presents a problem in the case of Jihadism because, aside from the obvious al-Qa'ida, many groups either have no names, their names change as they morph in response to attempts to destroy them, or if they are protected within the borders of a national territory, they may represent something that is more akin to the religious/national/territorial movement of Islamism than Jihadism. Most of the information available for Jihadi communities, therefore, comes from studies of al-Qa'ida because of its central position and its obvious influence, but it applies to the larger network of groups – the Jihadi trend.

NEW RELIGIOUS MOVEMENT?

Literature on Jihadism rarely reflects explicitly on the relation between this phenomenon and the broader issue of religious innovation as addressed in NRM studies. The question as to whether Jihadism represents nothing more than a normative trend within Islam or whether it fits some definition of the term "new religious movement," and of subcategories such as "sect" or "cult," therefore requires consideration of the terminology employed. Several of the most commonly used labels, however, turn out to be nearly as slippery and difficult to define as the terms we have been struggling with in the previous section. As is well known, their meanings have shifted through the years and decades and depend heavily on religious and political context. In fact, as J. Gordon Melton has shown, a dominant or establishment religion in the United States such as the United Methodist Church can be labeled by the government of a different country as a sect or even "a destructive cult."[18]

One basic distinction that can be made at the outset is between substantive and relational approaches to the terminological question (roughly matching the common dichotomy between emic and etic definitions). A substantive approach could review the various characteristics that the extant literature has identified as typically distinctive of emergent religious movements, and that set them apart from more established trends. We shall shortly return to this question. A relational approach could, on the other hand, focus on whether the religious communities in question are accepted within a local context and are considered normative and legitimate by general consensus as "established" or "establishment" religions.

The determination of whether a particular group is a sect or new religious movement, on the relational view, depends not on any particular creed or behavior, but rather on the relationship of the practices, expectations, and beliefs of the community in question with those of the establishment religions of its environment. In this schema, there is no particular theological position, ritual practice, or set of theologies or practices that can identify a religious movement as a "religion," a "sect," or "NRM." All three categories rest on a continuum that is dependent on the assumptions and expectations of the religious and political context, and the assumptions and expectations are defined by and large by establishment religions and then negotiated by all the dramatis personae in the larger environment. These "players" consist of establishment religious leaderships, including the leaders of non-dominant but "normative" religions (i.e., those accepted as such within the religious environment), shapers of public opinion and the media, and leaders and members of religious movements and communities that are identified (or identify themselves) as sects or new religions.[19] As documented in a substantial body of literature, these criteria tend to be negotiated differently in different contexts, and they also change over time as they are influenced by migration and immigration, cultural and technological developments, and other considerations.

As with Christianity and Judaism, Islam has always contained within it many discrete religious communities that emphasize particular aspects of creed, practice, ideology, and theology while disregarding or de-emphasizing certain aspects deemed important to others. Usually, such trends remain within the margins of what coreligionists would consider to be authentic, though different. In some cases, they move beyond those margins and are then deemed heresies and/or new religious movements. The question at hand is whether what we define here as Jihadism can be considered a trend, even if a sectarian trend within Islam, or whether it has moved or is moving beyond the margins of traditional Islamic authenticity. One concluding observation: the final arbiter of this negotiation is never the academic, outside observer, or even religious functionary or office within a religious hierarchy,[20] and it is never based on any clearly articulated set of criteria, principles or norms. In the final analysis, it is the religious community in its largest (and most vague) articulation, sometimes with the help of general public opinion that it generates, which eventually negotiates the status of communities within it. The process is elusive and organic.

If such relational (or etic) considerations thus result in the conclusion that Jihadi movements are perceived in very different ways by different interested parties, a substantive (or emic) approach might perhaps yield more unambiguous results. A perusal of some of the literature on movements that are generally characterized by scholars as NRMs shows that there are a number of commonly accepted criteria. Three such criteria are summarized below: personal commitment, social action, and the historical and mythological relationship with existing religious traditions.

NRMs typically distance themselves from existing religions or existing versions of their own religious tradition by claiming to be, in some way or another, "better": their lifestyle is purer, their enthusiasm for the religious message is greater, their ideals closer to that of the founder, their understanding of the sacred texts more authentic, and so forth.[21] The reaction may furthermore be directed at society at large, which is perceived as too secular.[22] As a result of this self-perception of their own version of the tradition as "better," members of such schismatic NRMs often see themselves as constituting an elite.[23] Concomitantly, NRMs often have members who have actively chosen to be involved in the movement and who engage themselves more in religious activities. Max Weber is perhaps the best-known exponent of the idea that sects, in particular, demand that one actively chooses membership, while church membership is nearly automatic.[24]

NRMs typically suggest that one of the prime consequences of holding strong religious ideals should be direct, social action. James Beckford argues that NRM members belong to either a loosely engaged and numerically stronger cohort of people (with a presumably lower willingness to commit themselves to this social vision), and a much smaller group who are determined to carry out the social agenda of the movement.[25]

Some NRMs will acknowledge that by distancing themselves from their forebears and competitors, they have crafted a novel religious alternative. Most NRMs, however, insist that their seeming innovation is in fact a return to the true and original face of the entire religious tradition. Mormonism, for example, projects an image of itself as a revival of the very first community of Christians. Theosophy claims to represent an age-old wisdom religion traceable to ancient sages, and constructs an elaborate mythology around this theme. Other NRMs suggest that there are more indirect links to venerable, existing religions. Scientology is in many ways a very novel religion, and does in fact suggest that it represents a major advance in human history, but legitimating references to similarities with Buddhism, for example, are nevertheless common in Scientology's texts.

The relationship between the new movement and the parent tradition is usually neither as distant as critics with a theologically normative agenda may suggest or as close as members of the movement itself can insist that it is. Mormonism is not just a reconstruction of an original Christian Church, nor is it a blatant innovation with no semblance to "true" Christianity. Clearly, Mormon doctrines and rituals reuse and reinterpret extant elements from previous Christian denominations, add a number of innovations created by its prophet Joseph Smith and other influential spokespersons, and do so in ways that give Mormonism a flavor of its own. Other religious movements will similarly select and recombine already existing elements: the new always bears a recognizable relation to the existing.

As we now leave the broad comparative sweep and proceed to survey in greater detail the Jihadi attitude to well-established Islamic religious norms, it should become clear how these are indeed redescribed in order to produce a form of Islam that fits several or all of the NRM characteristics mentioned above.

MAKING SENSE OF RELIGIOUS NORMS IN ISLAM

Below we examine a number of key phenomena (norms, use of symbols, expectations) among Jihadis that may represent innovation and a turn away from established tradition, and add a brief comparative note on similar phenomena in other NRMs. It must be kept in mind, of course, that there is a significant range of thought and practice (and even lack of practice) among Jihadi activists, so we are dealing here with general observations. I have identified the items listed below as reimagined, or reinterpreted norms whose articulation among Jihadis would appear to contradict or at least conflict with current majority views; such an overview will contribute to addressing the question to what extent Jihadi movements constitute a variety of NRMs.

In most if not all cases, however, there is some precedent for the Jihadi views and actions among certain Muslim thinkers and communities in the past. Those past thinkers have tended to be in the minority and the communities have tended to be unconventional. Some have been considered radical, excessive, or labeled as heresies. They have threatened or exceeded the boundaries established by Sunni Muslim scholars and the established schools of Islamic thought and practice. While every one of these changes may have a precedent in Islamic history and tradition, their particular manifestations and combinations which occur in this moment of history and world culture create a unique expression that may or may not lie within the boundaries of Islam as defined by the community as a whole. This, of course, is quite similar to what we tend to find when more traditional NRMs are considered.

AUTHORITY

All dissident forms of religion are confronted with the problem of authority. By what authority can a movement diverge from the established religion and its positions? Unlike classical Christianity, traditional Islamic law is quite flexible, allowing for disagreements and a range of practice in a non-hierarchical structure of religious authority. In the post-colonial world, however, the modernization of Muslim societies under dictatorships has brought authorities of traditional religion into the grip of authoritarian regimes. This kind of relationship between religious jurisprudence and politics was not normative in traditional, pre-modern Muslim societies.[26] The forced centralization of religious authority under modern dictatorships has polarized religious representatives and has alienated many individuals and communities. What is more, the influence of Western norms such as democracy has further upset the traditional system, allowing individuals to claim that they need not follow any of the public authorities who claim to represent Islam.

A common claim for authority among new trends or movements within religion is to declare that it has bypassed the corruption of contemporary religious leaders and scholars and returned to the "original" sources. We observe this quite clearly among Islamic "fundamentalist" movements such as Salafis and Wahhabis, who claim to practice according to the true and authentic practice of the Prophet Muhammad and the very first generations of believers.

A related approach is to retain a semantic community with tradition and the past, but incorporate new content and therefore, meaning. Farhad Khosrokhavar describes this approach in reference to the traditional laws of jihad: "A reinterpretation of Islamic laws that combines what are often traditional minority views with innovations in the conduct of human behavior gives a legal vision a political extension. The political annexes the juridical by justifying itself in the name of Islamic jurisprudence (*fiqh*)."[27]

Al-Qa'ida engages in both strategies. In an interview in December of 2001, shortly after the 9/11 attacks, Osama bin Laden said, "Those youth who conducted the operations did not accept any *fiqh* (traditional Islamic jurisprudence and its legal pronouncements) in the popular terms, but they accepted the *fiqh* that the prophet Muhammad brought."[28] This position is not uncommon among militant radicals, but it completely disregards traditional forms of authority in Islam. It should not be surprising, therefore, that traditional clerical groups and religious authorities are vehemently opposed to Jihadism. In fact, perpetrators of the 9/11 attacks famously went out to bars and had sex with women outside of marriage in the period just before the attacks, both of which are unambiguously forbidden by all expressions of Islam.[29]

Jihadis do not seek juridical rulings from contemporary religious authorities in order to gain popular or religious credibility in the Muslim world, but they are sensitive to the general acceptance of the classical *form* of juridical rulings among Muslims. Osama bin Laden thus structured his interviews and disseminated remarks according to traditional Muslim public discourse. He did not bother to follow the rhetorical rules of this discourse, necessarily, but utilizing these forms "enables [him] to legitimate himself in relation to different traditions of religious authority."[30] The way in which he cited traditional authorities actually dismantles the very structures of authority that he relied on by personally and independently disaggregating certain rulings from the juridical system out of which they are produced. His claim as an untrained (and therefore untainted) authority reflects the modern, Western trend toward individuation and the authority of personal autonomy to confront scripture and tradition. This, then, contributes to the fragmentation of traditional forms of religious authority through his personalizing the "democratization" of juridical judgments.

Bin Laden thus discredited the operative and contemporary sources of religious authority and in effect dismantled traditional forms of authority by structuring the articulation of his innovations on those very forms. This is hardly a new phenomenon, but it provides evidence of a move away from established religion.

Aside from the structures of authority, the *persona* of authority in Islamic tradition is carefully cultivated by the Jihadi leadership. Within Sunni Islam, for example, the most revered leaders of the *umma* (the Muslim world community) were the Prophet Muhammad and his companions, some of whom became the first four caliphs, known as the *rashīdūn*, the "righteous caliphs." They are portrayed in popular tradition as unpretentious, humble, and living simply and without the luxuries and amenities that typically come with power and wealth. Their only concern was furthering God's will by expanding the *umma*, and they were totally dedicated to "jihad in the path of God."[31] The greatest religious leaders in later periods were likewise abstemious and humble, living modestly or even ascetically. In contrast, the political and religious leaders of the contemporary Muslim world, and particularly Saudi Arabia, are depicted by bin Laden as treacherously abandoning God and the *umma*.[32] His and other Jihadis' austere living conditions, abandoning of comfort for the jihad, all evoke traditional authority.

JIHAD

In traditional Islamic thought and practice, military jihad is a collective obligation (*fard kifāya*).[33] As soon as it is fulfilled by part of the community it is not obligatory on others. This means that engaging in military jihad is required of the community as a whole during military campaigns, but not required of every individual except in case of defense, especially when the defending forces are in danger of being overwhelmed. The term for individual obligation is *fard 'ayn*, and it typically applied to the Five Pillars of Islam: witnessing the unity of God, prayer, fasting, required almsgiving, and pilgrimage.

Jihadis reject the classical doctrine that jihad is a collective obligation and consider it to an individual obligation at all times (*fard 'ayn*), at least at this period of history.[34] This raises the status of jihad to that of the Pillars of Islam,[35] a blatant contradiction to Islamic tradition. As bin Laden put it in an interview reported on September 18, immediately after the 9/11 attacks, "Al-Qaeda wants to keep jihad alive and active and make it a part of the daily life of the Muslims. It wants to give it the status of worship," which is one of the Five Pillars of Islam.[36] Bin Laden often referred to the defensive nature of jihad at this time and the resultant obligation upon every individual Muslim to engage in jihad at every opportunity.[37] This inclusion of jihad within one's individual required duties is to add a sixth pillar to the five required by orthodoxy.[38]

Including jihad among the Pillars of Islam is not, however, an innovation with today's Jihadists. The radical militant sect known as the *khawārij* or "Kharijites" had already considered militant jihad an individual obligation during the earliest Muslim generations.[39] And parallels between Jihadis and the twelfth-century Isma'ili Hashshāshiyīn have been noted famously by Bernard Lewis.[40] Khosrokhavar shows that many aspects of modern violent activists were already present in early sectarian forms of Islam.[41] He points out a significant distinction in worldview, however, between pre-modern and contemporary militants:

> Members of premodern sects were usually willing to die and to kill their enemies because of their millenarian convictions ... and their positive image of the role they were playing ... Modern martyrs, in contrast, act out of hatred for a world in which, as they see it, they

are being denied access to a life of "dignity," no matter whether they are Iranian, Palestinian or members of transnational networks such as al-Qaeda. Whereas the sectarian martyrs of the Islam of the premodern age were convinced that their actions would bring about the advent of a new world and the destruction of the old, the actions of modern Muslim martyrs are intended to destroy a world in which there is no place for them as citizens of a nation or of an Islamic community.[42]

This new attitudinal variation within the powerful emphasis on a personal jihad is indicative of the unique situation of today's Jihadi militants, who make up a dispersed, global community that eschews all the many natural Muslim communities to create a cohort of pure activists.

KHARIJISM

Terribly destructive civil wars in the seventh century called *fitnas* (meaning "trial" or "civil strife") tore the early Muslim community into viciously competing communities.[43] One of the opposition groups to emerge from this strife was an extremely militant group called the Kharijites ("seceders/rebels" or "those who go out"). They considered themselves to be pious purists who upheld the true meaning of the Qur'an without exception. They demanded absolute obedience to their understanding of the divine will and totally rejected other Muslims who did not share their views, even to the extent of labeling them apostates (*kāfirs*), an act that is called *takfīr* (see below).[44] As noted above, the Kharijites considered jihad to be an individual obligation and therefore one of the Pillars of Islam.

The Kharijites were violently opposed to the caliphal leadership after the first *fitna* and continued to actively threaten the caliphate and its local representatives for about a century. They insisted that community leaders were required to be absolutely upright Muslims in order to lead, and they engaged in violent attacks and assassinations in order to further their cause. But their violent militancy and accompanying doctrine was rejected by the overwhelming community of Muslims because it was simply too destabilizing. It was finally accepted by most legalists that even if the ruler is not absolutely just, he must nevertheless be obeyed for the sake of the unity of the community.[45] The Kharijite approach was rejected by the community as a whole and their presence faded from history as an organized movement. But Kharijite or neo-kharijite groups continued to exist in the Muslim world on and off throughout history. They were feared and even hated, yet at a certain level they were also admired because of their pious willingness to die in their insistence on doing what they believed was right for the community.

The image and meaning of "Kharijism" remains a contested issue currently in the Muslim world. For example, the mythic position of Kharijites has become a key issue within contemporary legitimizing (and delegitimizing) discourse in modern arguments in Egypt.[46] Ayman al-Zawahiri, the closest partner of bin Laden, likened his Jihadi followers positively with the Kharijites, and Umar Abd al-Rahman, the leader of the World Trade Center bombing of 1993, also expressed a positive view of the historical Kharijites because of their absolute commitment and activism.[47]

TAKFĪR

Historically, it was the Kharijites who first engaged in the act of *takfīr* – declaring Muslims to be apostates by virtue of their not adhering adequately to a particular vision of Islam. This trend reached its zenith only recently with a radical Egyptian group called Al-Takfir wal-Hijra ("Declaring Apostate and Immigration"), which pronounced *takfīr* on the entire Muslim world outside of its own small community.[48] One of the assassins of Anwar Sadat, Muhammad Abd Al-Salam Farraj (or Farrag), wrote a pamphlet called "The Hidden Imperative" (or "The Missing Obligation" – *al-farīda al-ghā'iba*), in which he made a blanket declaration of apostasy on the Muslim leaders of his day and declared war against all Muslims who failed to implement true Islam.[49]

Most Islamists oppose the policy of *takfīr*, preferring to advocate *da'wa* or active engagement to return Muslims to the true path. Bin Laden defended his use of *takfīr* when criticized by the Saudi interior minister for it in 2001.[50] It is the relatively small community of radical Jihadis that are proponents of *takfīr* and along with it the necessary personal obligation of jihad, including jihad against those Muslim rulers who are, according to their standards, apostatizing.[51]

HIJRA

The phenomenon of *hijra*, or emigration, is another key element of some purist Islamists and Jihadists. It is a highly symbolic emulation of the Prophet Muhammad (and before him, the Prophet Abraham) who left his idolatrous community in Mecca in order to live out Islam away from the pollution of polytheism. After the Muslim community became strong enough, he returned with his followers to Mecca and took it over by force in order to impose monotheism on all its inhabitants.

The traditional Islamic perspective on *hijra* is to apply it to a situation where a Muslim is living outside of the Abode of Islam (*dār al-Islam*) where proper Islamic religious practice cannot be engaged because of the pressures of dominant non-Islamic religious and political power structures. In the traditional scenario, the world outside of the Abode of Islam is the Abode of War (*dār al-ḥarb*). According to the fourteenth-century Hanbali jurist Ibn Taymiyya, a Muslim who finds her/himself in such a situation is obliged to return to the Abode of Islam where proper religious life can be practiced fully and without interference.[52]

In the new understanding of Jihadis and some radical Islamists, *hijra* applies to living *within* the Abode of Islam because the modern perversion of religious practice within it prevents Muslims from practicing Islam properly. In such a situation, true Muslims must leave and live in separate communities where they can practice properly. In the case of the group called Al-Takfīr wal-Hijra, this meant living in caves in upper Egypt until the time would be ripe to take over the corrupted country and impose proper Islam throughout.[53] Bin Laden and others who have departed what they consider the Westernized Muslim world for the caves of Tora Bora, the deserts of Somalia and Afghanistan, and the Frontier Provinces of Pakistan, claim to follow Ibn Taymiyya in their act of *hijra* until, like the Prophet Muhammad, they can return to apply true Islam within the Abode of Islam.[54]

CULT OF MARTYRDOM

Devji notes deep similarities between al-Qaʾida and traditional Sufi or mystical brotherhoods, though Jihadis along with most other fundamentalist trends condemn Sufism as a distortion of true Islam. There is, for example, the very emphasis on military jihad and martyrdom through jihad among proto-Sufis in the early period of conquest, later reinterpreted by Sufis as a kind of spiritual jihad as personal obligation. There is a history of martyrdom among Sufis, who tended to be antinomian and therefore found themselves often in conflict with ruling elites.[55] This trend toward martyrdom became romanticized and developed among some into a cult of martyrs to whom are attributed supernatural powers, including the ability to intercede with God for the salvation of their families. The notion of intervention by martyrs or others is condemned by traditional Islam and particularly by anti-Sufi groups (based on Q. 2:48, 123), but has been supported by bin Laden himself.[56]

A number of Qur'an verses urge followers of Muhammad to go out and fight because they had been refusing to do so. One of these includes the statement, "Do not consider those killed in the path of God to be dead. No, they are alive with their Lord who sustains them" (3:169).[57] That verse, along with a number of others,[58] has elicited a great deal of interpretation about the fate of those martyred while fighting in the path of God. In the later tradition literature, and particularly under the influence of the Muslim Caliphate's need to promote its own interests through jihad, death in combat became established as "the noblest way to depart this life."[59]

The tremendous honor associated with the martyr in Islam, and especially the battlefield martyr, is naturally extolled in the words and actions of Jihadis. Asiem El Difraoui has conducted extensive research on the media productions of Jihadi groups and has noted the complex interplay between tradition and innovation in their use of martyrdom motifs.[60] Through his work with martyrology videos, he notes that despite the importance of martyrdom and traditional praise for martyrs and their transcendent rewards in the afterlife, Jihadis have far exceeded tradition in their creation of what he calls a "cult of death" that finds no precedent in traditional Islam. The videos impose photographs of suicide martyrs floating in clouds or sitting in gardens depicting a heavenly paradise. They provide a visual "proof" of martyrs already enjoying their heavenly reward, which produces what he calls a "virtual mausoleum" (or, more accurately, cenotaph) to serve as a public monument to the valor and reward of the martyr. This visual imagery immediately challenges the Islamic taboo against portraying the human image, a prohibition that is of the utmost concern among Sunni fundamentalist communities such as Wahhabis and Salafis. In fact it is very reminiscent of Shi'a depictions and, in particular, the common Shi'ite practice of the veneration of martyrs which is regularly condemned by Sunnis, and especially fundamentalist Sunni groups.

The videos also depict funeral rites based on the writings of bin Laden's mentor, Abdullah Azzam. These celebrate martyrdom and depict smiling martyrs, and they include graphic images of the mutilated bodies of the martyrs as well. Some actually depict the sniffing of the body of the martyr for the smell of musk, which the tradition literature teaches comes from the wounds of those who engaged in jihad.[61] This cult of the dead, which includes the expectation of martyrs' intercession with the powers of heaven on behalf of the living, is an innovation, as is its visual expression.

Devji notes how the videotaping of the martyrs' last testaments have become a kind of reality television show, and observes that the spectacle of martyrdom as a selfless sacrifice actually transforms jihad from the traditional goal-oriented, policy-driven act to a public display of a practice of ethics.[62] This conforms with Khosrokhavar's distinction between the expectation of traditional Muslim martyrs and those of today:

> Whereas the sectarian martyrs of the Islam of the premodern age were convinced that their actions would bring about the advent of a new world and the destruction of the old, the actions of modern Muslim martyrs are intended to destroy a world in which there is no place for them as citizens of a nation or of an Islamic community.[63]

TAQIYYA

Taqiyya is an act among Muslims of dissimulation and concealment of religious ideology and practice when there is a distinct possibility that articulations of these will result in harm.[64] The practice of *taqiyya* was discussed from the earliest period, debated and frowned upon in many cases, but never forbidden. It became a well-known practice among the Shi'a, a minority often in opposition to the dominant Sunni governance. The Shi'ite practice of *taqiyya* has therefore been resented by many Sunnis who condemn Shi'ism in general and therefore any practices that might distinguish them from the practice of "proper" Islam.

We have noted above how some Shi'ite traits or those closely associated with Shi'ism (and therefore criticized), such as the veneration of martyrs, have been absorbed by Jihadis. Another such trait is *taqiyya*, practiced by Sunni Jihadis who pretend they are Shi'ite, not for protection but in order to pass into Shi'ite mosques to blow them up and kill Shi'ites, whom they consider infidels.[65]

TOTAL JIHAD AGAINST NON-JIHADI MONOTHEISM

The Qur'an differentiates between Christian and Jewish monotheists on the one hand, and polytheists on the other. The two famous "sword verses" of the Qur'an are interpreted by Islamic tradition to call for different approaches to fighting monotheists and polytheists. According to the mainstream interpretive tradition associated with Q. 9:5, "kill the polytheists wherever you find them," God requires the complete elimination of idolatry. But according to the normative interpretation of Q. 9:29, "fight ... those who have been given scripture until they pay tribute willingly, as subjects," the object is the hegemony of Islam but not the destruction of other forms of monotheism or their adherents.

In the famous "declaration of war" published in the London-based Al-Quds al-Arabi in August 1996, however, bin Laden reversed this tradition by stressing the importance of war against the "People of the Book." "Those youths know that their rewards in fighting you, the USA, is double than their rewards in fighting someone else not from the people of the book."[66] The absolute evil that is associated with the United States and Israel (the "Crusader–Zionist alliance") places them in the role of a virtual antichrist (Arabic *al-dajjāl*). Although to my knowledge the particular term is not used in the discourse of bin Laden and al-Qaeda, associating the USA and especially Israel with *al-dajjāl* is common on the Internet.

The jihad directed against monotheists is extended by Jihadis also to Muslims who oppose them. However, declaring Jihad against nominal Muslims is not a modern innovation. It was used by Muslim rulers to consolidate their power by declaring jihad against "apostates" rebelling against proper Islamic authority (*murtaddūn*), against dissenting groups denouncing legitimate Muslim leadership (*baghī*), highway robbers, and other violent types. And in some cases, Muslim jurists accepted the notion of jihad against deviant or unislamic leadership.[67] However, Muslim legal authorities gave no free rein either to rulers to pursue their enemies or to rebels fighting against unjust rulers. The moderate stance of the classical jurists has collapsed as the traditional institutions that sustained this discourse have crumbled in the modern world, allowing both the state and their opponents to engage in far more radical actions than allowed by the tradition.[68]

A COMPARATIVE NOTE

All of the sections above discuss links with previous expressions of the Islamic tradition and differences in emphasis and interpretation in relation to the tradition as a whole. Besides such Islamic parallels, similarities with "classical" NRMs can also be highlighted. A few examples can illustrate such broader commonalities.

Legitimating one's own position by stressing continuities with ideologies or practices of earlier sects is not uncommon among Western

NRMs. Among Christian groups, for instance, it is commonplace to identify with the early Jesus movements, and several Hindu- and Buddhist-inspired NRMs will in similar ways forge rhetorical links with movements of an earlier date. All of these will, of course, also construct new ways of being Christian, Hindu, or Buddhist.

Legitimizing one's mode of exercising authority by means of such putative links to the past is also a well-documented strategy. Mormonism, for instance, not only claims to have restored the creed of the original church, but also the structures that ruled this church. As is well known, Mormon leadership in the first decades of the church even adopted polygamy, in a distinct echo of Old Testament patriarchal norms.

What seems to characterize Jihadi movements more specifically, and set them apart from run-of-the-mill NRMs, is their very high level of conflict with surrounding society. However, when one compares these movements with the relatively few truly high-conflict NRMs documented in the literature, many similarities strike the observer. The following paragraphs consider some of these.

While millenarian convictions are common in various NRMs, and the emphasis on the individual's personal piety and personal obligations as well as the need for an inward, psychological warfare against sinful thoughts and impure living are also found in various NRMs, violent activism of the kind associated with Jihadi movements is uncommon in the NRMs described in the literature. Nevertheless, the gas attacks perpetrated by members of the Aum Shinrikyo movement show that extreme violence is not unknown. Perhaps uniquely Jihadi, however, is the elevation to the status of martyr of individuals killed in violent action.

Other high-conflict NRMs conclude that the world is corrupt and should be abandoned. There are a number of examples of movements with a high degree of tension with surrounding society whose members decide to withdraw from the world and build an alternative existence apart from others, whether in the jungles of Guyana (as the Peoples Temple did) or in a commune for the like-minded (as was the case for the Branch Davidians and numerous other "sectarian" groups). Quite a few NRMs polemicize against other versions of the religious traditions to which they belong. The felt need to denounce others as apostates and heretics is, for quite a few movements, part and parcel of their self-presentation as a "better" religious alternative, as discussed above. The higher the degree of conflict, the greater is the temptation to see all others as destined to eternal damnation.

To conclude: while the specifics of the various Jihadi movements are the result of a more or less radical reinterpretation of a shared Islamic heritage, the direction taken by this reinterpretation is to a considerable extent driven by the sheer fact of living in a state of intense tension with outsiders.

CONCLUSION

Through the course of this exercise we have briefly examined seven realia of Jihadism and considered how they are expressed among Jihadis and in relation to established tradition. In virtually every case, the Jihadi expression was not entirely unprecedented. That is, similar expressions occurred or still occur within known expressions of Islam, though often among peripheral groups or, at least, groups that are considered by established Sunni religious leaders to be peripheral. The particular nuances of expression within the particularity of today's contemporary world, and the particular combination that forms the full "package" that is Jihadism are of course unique. But that can be said of any religious trend or movement that is defined as functioning fully within the norms of religious establishments. All expressions have certain commonalities along with certain aspects that are unique, thus representing an expression that is, one way or another, different from all other expressions.

The task, then, is to consider the extent of the unique views and articulations of Jihadism. Do they fit the general criteria we have established for sectarianism within Islam or for new religious movements? Readers will of course judge for themselves, but to this observer, a case can be made for Jihadism as a common term for a set of sectarian new religious movements. Like all sectarian movements within Islam, Jihadism strives to redefine what it means to be a Muslim. It has attracted a certain number of Muslims to its ranks, but it has been far more effective in redefining Islam for non-Muslims. Its overwhelming and bloody actions have significantly influenced citizens of the West to characterize most (if not all) Muslims as Jihadis – radical, militantly religious, violent Muslims. Effective use of the media and outrageously cruel acts of destruction have had a profound impact on Western views of Muslims and Islam. As Devji puts it:

> Islam comes to exist universally in the places where its
> particularity is destroyed, the presence of its ruins on television
> screens bearing witness to the Muslim's universality as martyr
> and militant. What makes Islam universal, then, is the forging

of a generic Muslim, one who loses all cultural and historical particularity by his or her destruction in an act of martyrdom.[69]

While Jihadis wish to project an image of their own take on Islam as "authentic" or "real" Islam, theirs is a particular construction of what it means to be a "true Muslim."

Notes

1 The Arabic term is *jihādiyya* (or *jihādīya*) – جهادية. For a helpful website that provides current information, developments, and analysis of jihadi media and its critics, see the "jihadica" website www.jihadica.com/about/ (accessed November 2011).

2 For the meanings of jihad, see Reuven Firestone, *Jihad: The Origin of Holy War in Islam* (New York, 1999), pp. 16–18; David Cook, *Understanding Jihad* (Berkeley and Los Angeles, 2005), pp. 1–4.

3 It is significant that Jihadi is a new term. The traditional term for a Muslim fighter, including those who engage in military jihad (and the Muslim warriors who fought against the Soviets in Afghanistan), is *mujāhid* (plural: *mujāhidūn*).

4 This terminology is ubiquitous in the articulations of Osama bin Laden. See Bruce Lawrence (ed.), *Messages to the World: The Statements of Osama Bin Laden* (London, 2005).

5 Jarret M. Brachman, *Global Jihadism: Theory and Practice* (London, 2009), pp. 4, 10.

6 For the range of meanings associated with Islamism, see Martin Kramer, "Coming to Terms: Fundamentalists or Islamists?" *Middle East Quarterly* (Spring 2003), pp. 65–77, www.geocities.com/martinkramerorg/Terms.htm (accessed May 2010).

7 See Gilles Kepel, *Jihad: The Trail of Political Islam* (Cambridge, 2002); Olivier Roy, *Globalized Islam* (New York, 2004).

8 Loren Lybarger, *Identity and Religion in Palestine* (Princeton, 2007).

9 Roy, *Globalized Islam*, p. 250 n. 41.

10 Faisal Devji, *Landscapes of the Jihad* (London, 2005), esp. pp. 4, 165 n. 3.

11 Ami Pedahzur, *Suicide Terrorism* (Cambridge, 2005), pp. 99–103. That bin Laden was interested in influencing US policy is clear from any serious reading of his writings and interviews.

12 A current school of thought led by Olivier Roy sees the failure of Islamism to realize its goals as a powerful motivation for globalized Jihadism; Olivier Roy, *The Failure of Political Islam* (Cambridge, 1995). A response to Roy may be found in François Burgat, *Face to Face with Political Islam* (London, 2003). For a study of the tensions between the two trends as they have played out within Palestinian refugee camps, see Bernard Rougier, *Everyday Jihad: The Rise of Militant Islam among Palestinians in Lebanon* (New York, 2007).

13 On "Wahhabi" and "Salafi" Islamic trends, see Khaled Abou El Fadl, *The Great Theft* (New York, 2005).

14 Devji, *Landscapes*, pp. 34–35.
15 Pedahzur, *Suicide*, p. 97. According to bin Laden, the name was not carefully chosen but was simply acquired from an actual training base set up to fight the Soviets in Afghanistan (Lawrence, *Messages*, p. 120).
16 Devji, *Landscapes*, p. 19.
17 Roy, *Globalized Islam*, p. 25.
18 J. Gordon Melton, "An Introduction to New Religions," in James R. Lewis (ed.), *The Oxford Handbook of New Religious Movements* (Oxford, 2004), pp. 16–35, at p. 25.
19 I am strongly influenced by Melton in this description; ibid.
20 Even a highly organized religious hierarchy such as the Catholic Church has not been successful in determining what is "religion" and what is "heresy" even within the church. These are categories that are constantly interrogated and negotiated by all its members.
21 See, e.g., the classic formulation of this thesis by H. Richard Niebuhr, *The Social Sources of Denominationalism* (New York, 1929).
22 Roy Wallis, *The Elementary Forms of the New Religious Life* (London, 1984); James A. Beckford, *Cult Controversies: The Societal Response to the New Religious Movements* (London, 1985).
23 John Saliba, *Perspectives on New Religious Movements* (London, 1995), pp. 55–56.
24 Max Weber, *Essays in Sociology* (London, 1991 [1948]), pp. 302–22.
25 James A. Beckford, "Introduction," in Beckford (ed.), *New Religious Movements and Rapid Social Change* (Paris and London, 1986), pp. xiii–xv.
26 Farhad Khosrokhavar, *Suicide Bombers: Allah's New Martyrs*, trans. David Macey (London, 2005), p. 37. Khaled Abou El Fadl, *Rebellion and Violence in Islamic Law* (Cambridge, 2006), pp. 234–94.
27 Khosrokhavar, *Suicide*, p. 36; see also p. 5.
28 www.defense.gov/news/Dec2001/d20011213ubl.pdf (accessed April 2010); Devji, *Landscapes*, pp. 16–17.
29 Such anarchic and antinomian behaviors are also associated with charismatic messianic movements. See also the chapter by Catherine Wessinger in this volume.
30 W. Flagg Miller, cited by Lawrence, *Messages*, p. xvi. See also, Devji, *Landscapes*, p. 113.
31 This term is qur'anic in origin (Q. 2:218; 4:95; 5:35; 8:74; 9:19–20, 41, 80; 49:15; 61:10) but becomes an idiom for piety among many groups ranging from extreme militants to other-worldly Sufis, depending on how the term jihad is understood.
32 Lawrence, *Messages*, pp. 33–38, 45, 212–32, 247–48. He specifically names six Muslim countries that need liberation from their current (Muslim) rulers: Jordan, Morocco, Nigeria, Pakistan, Saudi Arabia, and Yemen (p. 183).
33 Firestone, *Jihad*, pp. 60–61; Majid Khadduri, *War and Peace in the Law of Islam* (Baltimore, 1955), pp. 59–61; James Turner Johnson, *The Holy War Idea in Western and Islamic Traditions* (University Park, PA, 1997), pp. 157–66.

34 Bin Laden repeats this often (Lawrence, *Messages*, pp. 24–30, 41, 46–48, 60–61, 98, etc.).

35 "The new *jihad* is an individual and personal decision. As we shall see, most radical militants are engaged in action as individuals, cutting links with their 'natural' community (family, ethnic group and nation) to fight beyond the sphere of any real collective identity" (Roy, *Globalized Islam*, pp. 41, 179, 254).

36 Devji, *Landscapes*, p. 34. Bin Laden here is repeating the words of his own teacher, Abdullah Azzam, who said: "Jihad is the most excellent form of worship, and by means of it the Muslim can reach the highest of ranks" (Roy, *Globalized Islam*, p. 296).

37 See especially, "Declaration of Jihad," in Lawrence, *Messages*, pp. 23–30.

38 Roy, *Globalized Islam*, p. 179.

39 Khadduri, *War and Peace*, pp. 60, 67–68; Michael Bonner, *Jihad in Islamic History* (Princeton, 2006), p. 126.

40 Bernard Lewis, "The Revolt of Islam," *New Yorker* (November 19, 2001) www.newyorker.com/archive/2001/11/19/011119fa_FACT2 (accessed April 30, 2010). Lewis, however, has decided that such militancy is a normative aspect of Islam, which can only be argued successfully when all other vectors of Islamic practice and interpretation are ignored.

41 Khosrokhavar, *Suicide Bombers*, p. 23–24.

42 Ibid., 24–25.

43 Marshall Hodgson, *The Venture of Islam*, vol. I, *The Classical Age* (Chicago, 1974), pp. 213–17.

44 Michael Bonnor, *Jihad in Islamic History* (Princeton, 2006), pp. 127–28; J. O. Hunwick, "Takfir," in *Encyclopedia of Islam*, 2nd edn. (Leiden, 2000), vol. X, p. 182.

45 Abou El Fadl, *Rebellion and Violence*, pp. 237–41.

46 Jeffrey T. Kenney, *Muslim Rebels: Kharijites and the Politics of Extremism in Egypt* (New York, 2006).

47 Devji, *Landscapes*, pp. 49–50.

48 Kepel, *Jihad*, pp. 83–85. The group's name should be understood as meaning something like "the community that is true to the absolute meaning of Islam and will depart from the larger, polluted Muslim community in order to live Islam properly."

49 Muhammed Abdul Salam Faraj, *The Absent Obligation* (Birmingham, UK, 2000), pp. 24, 42–55, ia301530.us.archive.org/1/items/salamfaraj_obligation/22.pdf (accessed April 2010); Walter Lacqueur, *Voices of Terror* (New York, 2004), pp. 401–3.

50 Lawrence, *Messages*, p. 121. In the very same interview, he stated that whoever befriends Jews and Christians or even helps others to do so "with one word ... falls into apostasy." The interviewer then asks him if that is really his position, after which he repeats "even one word" (p. 123).

51 Roy, *Globalized Islam*, pp. 244–45.

52 Andrew March, *Islam and Liberal Citizenship* (New York, 2009), pp. 176–77.

53 Kepel, *Jihad*, pp. 84–85.
54 Devji, *Landscapes*, pp. 46–47.
55 David Cook, *Martyrdom in Islam* (Cambridge, 2007), pp. 63–73.
56 Devji, *Landscapes*, p. 42.
57 See the larger context: Q. 164–71, and Firestone, *Jihad*, pp. 77–84.
58 See Q. 3:157–58; 4:74; 9:111; 47:6. See Reuven Firestone, "Martyrdom in Islam," in Rona Fields (ed.), *Martyrdom: The Psychology, Theology and Politics of Self-Sacrifice* (Westport, CT, 2004), pp. 136–45.
59 Eitan Kohlberg, "Shahid," in *Encyclopedia of Islam*, vol. ix, p. 206.
60 Based on telephone conversations with Asiem El Difraoui in April 2010, and two unpublished papers, "Al Qaida et le culte du martyre en images" (2010), and "Wrestling for the Grand Narrative against Al Qaida: An Analysis of Two Saudi Counterpropaganda Films" (2009).
61 "The Prophet said, 'A wound which a Muslim receives in Allah's cause will appear on the Day of Resurrection as it was at the time of infliction; blood will be flowing from the wound and its color will be that of the blood but will smell like musk.'" (Muhammad Muhsin Khan, *The Translation of the Meanings of Sahih al-Bukhari – Arabic–English* (Lahore, 1983), Ablutions (book 4), *hadith* no. 238 (vol. 1, p. 150). This *hadith* is found repeatedly in the canonical Sunni *hadith* collections.
62 Devji, *Landscapes*, pp. 95 and 102.
63 Khosrokhavar, *Suicide Bombers*, p. 25.
64 R. Strothman and Moktar Djebli, "Takiyya," in *Encyclopedia of Islam*, vol. x, pp. 135–36.
65 Devji observes that the more that Sunni fundamentalists take on traits associated with Shi'ism that were markers of separation from Sunni Islam, the more threatened they are by Shi'ism and therefore, the more they hate them (Devji, *Landscapes*, pp. 54–58).
66 www.pbs.org/newshour/terrorism/international/fatwa_1996.html (accessed May 2010). Devji mistakenly dates this to 2001. An abbreviated version is in Lawrence, *Messages*, pp. 24–30), but it does not include this section about the added reward for fighting the People of the Book.
67 Khadduri, *War and Peace*, pp. 74–80; Joel Kramer, "Apostates, Rebels, Brigands," *Israel Oriental Studies* 10 (1980), pp. 34–73.
68 Khaled Abou El Fadl, "Islam and the Theology of Power," www.islam-fortoday.com/elfadl01.htm (accessed May 2010).
69 Devji, *Landscapes*, p. 94.

Further reading

Brachman, Jarret M., *Global Jihadism: Theory and Practice* (London, 2009).
Cook, David, *Understanding Jihad* (Berkeley and Los Angeles, 2005).
Firestone, Reuven, *Jihad: The Origin of Holy War in Islam* (New York, 1999).
Kepel, Gilles, *Jihad: The Trail of Political Islam* (Cambridge, 2002).

17 New religious movements in changing Russia

MARAT SHTERIN

The proliferation of NRMs in post-Soviet Russia after several decades of state-imposed atheism and secularism represents a particularly compelling case for thinking about their social and cultural provenance and of the effects of their presence on society. This chapter puts the discussion about NRMs into historical and social context. It argues that Soviet modernization paradoxically created conditions for new forms of religiosity and also contributed to post-Soviet society witnessing one of the most salient examples of "cult controversies." It provides a general overview of the Russian new religious scene and suggests possible directions of research, implying that focusing on these unconventional religious groups provides intriguing opportunities for understanding Soviet and post-Soviet versions of modern society.

UNINTENDED EFFECTS OF SOVIET MODERNITY: TRANSFORMATION OF RELIGION

One fruitful approach to understanding the provenance of the post-Soviet new religious scene is to examine some unintended consequences of the communist modernizing project.[1] The Bolsheviks translated Marx's vision of the ultimately just, prosperous, and enlightened society into a breakthrough modernization that involved a great amount of violence, including towards religious believers and institutions.[2] Impatient with waiting for the "opium of the people" to become redundant through the advancement of purely secular, rational, and scientific ways of seeing the world, militant atheism engaged in mass closures of religious associations, educational establishments, and places of worship, compounded by pervasive state surveillance of religious activities and believers. There is little doubt that, despite periodic "thaws," these policies severely undermined the transmission of traditional religious cultures. However, the available evidence points to a much more complex and intriguing situation than the oft-described

zero-sum game between atheism and faith. Instead, Soviet modernization is better seen as having resulted in the *transformation* of religion,
leading to the emergence of new forms of religious belief, practice, and
affiliation, which became particularly apparent as the last Soviet generation came of age.

To begin with, under state-imposed secularism and atheism, religion could no longer be taken for granted as being embedded in family
or community life; it became an object to be discovered, chosen, and
possessed.[3] The concept of religion was thus unintentionally modern-
ized, as chosen faith lends itself to becoming a basis for reconstructing
individual and group identities and to programs of personal and societal transformation. This considerably expanded "utopian spaces" for
religious search. Instead of creating the prescribed secularist and atheist cultural space, the enforced disruption of cultural continuity contributed to the proliferation of something akin to a pervasive "cultic
milieu." It was made up of the discarded debris of religious traditions,
mixed and matched with folk and occult sources, complemented by
whatever was available beyond official formulaic truths.[4] Furthermore,
Soviet culture was itself replete with quasi-religious connotations, such
as extraordinary achievement through indubitable faith, uncomprom-
ising commitment, and selfless effort. While promoting rational and
secular thought, Soviet ideology also popularized science as producing
miraculous tools with which to conquer nature and society.[5] An early
manifestation was the quasi-millenarian anticipation that the advent of
communism would fulfill the Marxist-Leninist "scientific prophecy."
In the 1940s and 1950s, academician Lysenko renounced Mendel's genetics in favor of a nature-defying communist agricultural science. In the
1980s, "scientific laboratories" emerged to study the paranormal in the
light of Marxist theory.

Christel Lane has described official Soviet communism as a "political religion," with its own rites of passage and ritualized expressions of
ultimate loyalty to the cause.[6] I would like to suggest that the effects of
this official religion were as much ideological as emotional: whether it
was embraced, denounced, or partially accepted, it was a *shared experience* that reinforced the "us" feeling of people living in a closed society,
a world apart from the rest of the world.

More generally, on the popular level the boundaries between science,
the occult, and folk beliefs remained blurred throughout the Soviet decades,
culminating in the appointment of Dzhuna Davitashvili, a self-proclaimed
"magic healer," as a "Kremlin doctor" to the ailing party leader Leonid
Brezhnev and some of his associates in the late 1970s and early 1980s. The

veneer of official rationalism faded away remarkably quickly when censorship was relaxed in the late 1980s: dozens of millions of viewers were attracted to the main state television channel when Anatoly Kashpirovski, a faith healer, demonstrated his power to cure the incurable diseases of those both in the studio and on the other side of the screen.

The official promotion of Russian high culture also unintentionally provided access to its rich repertoire of religious thinking, symbolism, and imagery. Conversely, the Soviet utopia produced its counter-cultural mirror-image in the form of anti-utopian critiques, rooted in the gnostic and occult, and articulated in increasingly popular underground or semi-official works of literature and arts, such as Mikhail Bulgakov's *Master and Margarita*, Evgeny Zamiatin's *We*, and Daniil Andreev's *The Rose of the World*.[7] One noteworthy phenomenon was the proliferation through official and semi-official channels of the ideas drawn from Agni Yoga, an esoteric teaching created by Elena and Nicholas Roerich, an artistic family who resided in Punjab, India, from 1929, while maintaining close ties with the USSR. Agni Yoga, which had its roots in Blavatsky's Theosophy, found relatively unimpeded routes to the Soviet cultural scene and was a significant channel for transmitting images, symbols, and concepts derived from esoteric and occult traditions.[8]

New religiosity was also created by the ways in which faith was – or rather, was *not* – practiced in Soviet Russia. I would describe this, using Michael Epstein's phrase with a somewhat different meaning, as "minimal religion," a milieu of religious imagery and projects maintained through informal interpersonal communication, rather than institutionally practiced and lived faiths. The "minimal religion," however, involved exuberant creativity: it was a breeding ground for utopian visions of alternatives to the Soviet system and for projects of creating alternative selves. It was this new religious milieu that came into the open in the 1990s.[9]

Finally, in thinking about the appeal of new religiosity, it is useful to consider the general effects of Soviet modernization, with its state-managed "breakthrough" industrialization, urbanization, and collectivization, compounded by two world wars and political repression. Uprooted from local communities and their traditional cultures, masses of people were subjected to socialization as "constructors of communism." However, in an apparent parallel to its Western counterpart and rival, Soviet modernity both stimulated aspirations and failed to provide opportunities for realizing them, the predicament exacerbated by a totalitarian style of social control. Hilary Pilkington points to the increasing discontent among successive post-World War II Soviet youth cohorts, evidenced in the proliferation of informal youth sub-cultures.[10] Among them, religious "utopian spaces" also gained their place, in particular from the 1970s onwards. It is hardly surprising that disillusionment and the search for alternatives were more common among urban and more educated sections of the population, that is, among those most exposed to the Soviet educational system and aspiring to benefit from it.

Two further paradoxes of religion in the USSR defined the categories in which NRMs were to be conceived in the post-Soviet decades. One concerns the relationship between religion and ethnicity. While officially aiming to create the collective "us" of the Soviet people, in reality, Soviet policy reinforced and often created sharp ethnic boundaries: ethnic origin as "nationality" was stated in all personal identity documents and it strongly defined constructions of individual and group identities and networks. Religion often played a paradoxical role in identity politics: officially excluded as a marker of ethnicity, it was largely preserved in collective memory and individual imagination as *a* – or sometimes *the* – root of ethnicity. Hence the apparent paradox of ethnically Russian, Ukrainian, and so on communists seeing themselves as *also "pravoslavnye"* (Eastern Orthodox), whereas their Tatar or Uzbek comrades were *"musulmane"* (Muslims). Conversely, Allah remained the Tatar, Chechen, or Uzbek god, whereas Jesus was the Russian or Ukrainian one.[11] With the developing crisis within the overarching Soviet identity, in particular from the 1970s onwards, the trend of "rediscovering" ethno-religious roots increasingly came to the fore.

Finally, at different periods of Soviet history, some minority groups, such as Evangelical Christians, underground Russian Orthodox, Jehovah's Witnesses, and Northern Caucasian Islamic brotherhoods, continued to defy official atheism and, by implication, the official regime. In the first Soviet decade such communities were treated as victims of tsarist oppression and therefore allies of the triumphant proletariat; however, with the consolidation of the Soviet system and increasing intolerance of social and ideological differences, the regime came to represent them as the dangerous "other," employing the label "sectarians" borrowed from the tsarist ideological vocabulary – but with much direr political implications.

THE NEW RELIGIOUS SCENE: THE QUEST FOR CERTAINTY, EMPOWERMENT, AND COMMUNITY

The dramatic changes in the country immediately before and after the collapse of the USSR in December 1991 can be broadly conceived of as an attempt to embrace the Western version of modernity, with its market economy, democratic system of government, and the recognition of individual freedoms and rights. Remarkably, the first act of legal liberalization was the 1990 Law on the Freedom of Religions, passed by the last Soviet Supreme Council. Later reinforced by the 1993 Constitution, it gave residents of Russia the freedom to choose their faith, form religious associations as full legal entities, profess commitment to them, and carry out religious activities without interference by government agencies.[12]

Existing scholarship indicates that NRMs can become attractive within a variety of socio-cultural settings, but particularly under conditions of social disruption and unsettling cultural change.[13] Indeed, post-Soviet changes brought about a mixture of frustrations and aspirations: the collapse of the USSR and the creation of independent nation-states; new economic opportunities and the loss of habitual safety nets; the freedom for new cultural pursuits; and the loss of shared meanings, symbols, and values. With the social structure and culture in flux, NRMs seemed more mobile and dynamic than mainstream religious institutions. They made a range of appealing offers, such as clearly defined and meaningful lifestyles, social networks, and friendships; ways of coping with everyday hardships; the basics and logistics of entrepreneurship; tackling health issues, and so forth. Moreover, while the newly open cultural market was overflowing with a bewildering variety of ideas and concepts, individual NRMs could offer cognitive and emotional certainties, something that Bryan Wilson succinctly described as a "surer, shorter, swifter, clearer way to salvation."[14] In some respects, new religions offered spiritual and practical solutions for many people who found themselves at a crossroads.

In the early 1990s, *transnational* NRMs were particularly effective in identifying gaps in the global religious market and relocating their resources.[15] Having had several decades of experience in the West, their mobility was much helped by accelerating globalizing trends, which facilitated missionaries' travel and the flow of financial, logistical, and informational resources.[16] In addition, it was Russia's previous relative *exclusion* from the global discourses on NRMs as "destructive cults" that perhaps partly accounts for their initial ability to insert themselves relatively smoothly into the post-Soviet environment.[17]

The International Society for Krishna Consciousness (ISKCON) seems a particularly interesting example of the ways in which a transnational NRM inserted itself in a local environment. In the early 1990s, after more than a decade in the Soviet religious underground, the movement was the first public organization to engage in a nationwide advertising campaign, its key text *Bhagavad-Gita as It Is* becoming a ubiquitous presence on major state television channels, underground stations, and national newspapers. Growing interest in oriental cultures, medicine, spiritual techniques, and vegetarianism created additional affinity with the movement. Also, in the mid 1990s, "Food for Life," the only charitable program in war-torn Chechnya, gave devotees a degree of respectability.

In its pursuit of "saving" the former abode of the "Communist Evil," the Unification Church (UC) made considerable investments in workshops and exchange programs held in the Crimea, the Baltic Coast, Hungary, and the USA. Thousands of Russian students, academics, and journalists were invited. The movement's anti-communist stance, unifying message, and program of moral and religious education, combined with opportunities to travel, appealed to some, mainly younger, Russians.

The Church of Scientology promised practical success, unlimited personal empowerment, and the attainment of personal freedom. These seemed in tune with the new spirit of unbounded economic possibilities and aspirations for personal growth among younger and more entrepreneurial Russians. Established in 1991, the Scientologists' Moscow Project Management set up Dianetics Centers in major Russian cities, soon complemented by regional public administration. Among those attracted were some high-profile entrepreneurs and officials who saw Scientology as a new science of prosperity and success.[18]

Despite the apparent demand, transnational NRMs have enjoyed only limited success in Russia. The UC's membership never exceeded 800–1,000 committed members, even at the peak of its success in the mid 1990s. Only a limited number of Scientology Centers have survived the effects of competition with other products within the same market niche combined with the restrictive policies of local officials. Despite the high expectations of the 1990s, ISKCON's fortunes declined steadily in the first decade of this century, not least due to the increasingly hostile social and political environment. However, despite their limited success in numerical terms, transnational NRMs, such as the UC, Scientology, Baha'i, Sahaja Yoga, the Osho movement, Transcendental Meditation, neo-Kabbalah, and a plethora of others introduced new concepts, ideas, and practices that have become part and parcel of the post-Soviet cultural milieu, often influencing even those opposed to their proliferation in the country.[19]

RUSSIAN HOMEGROWN NRMS

As with the general appeal of NRMs, uncertain times, such as those that immediately preceded and followed the collapse of the USSR, can be propitious for the emergence of charismatic leaders from within local societies.[20] Among other things, their appeal is often much enhanced by their being attuned to local concerns and able to address them through shared cultural templates and images. Some contemporary observers point to the surging numbers of aspiring gurus, prophets, and messiahs in the early 1990s; indeed, in 1995, dozens of them descended on an idyllic area near Yahroma (in the Moscow region) to debate the relative merits of their salvationist projects.[21]

It is noticeable that, in contrast to many of their optimistic Western competitors who emphasized the possibilities created by the collapse of the Soviet system, Russian indigenous NRMs in the early 1990s tended more towards apocalyptic millenarian expectations. However, rather than being indicative of their nostalgia for the Soviet past, such expectations are better explained as an articulation of the anxieties of those whose biographies intersected with the collapse of their habitual social world and the aspirations that had formed within it. In particular, the recognizable motif of Russia's special place in the salvation of humanity can be best interpreted as an extrapolation of their members' collective experience interpreted through the messianic templates within both Russian and Soviet culture.

The Great White Brotherhood (USMALOS) was the first homegrown NRM to make its presence known in a very dramatic way.[22] In the late 1980s, its original leaders, the "Divine Duo" of Maria Devi Christos and Uoann Swami, started a "Center for Non Traditional Medicine" based on oriental meditation techniques and ideas drawn from, among other sources, Theosophy and Agni Yoga. In the early 1990s, however, they began to prophesize the imminent destruction of the "satanic" world on November 23 in Kiev, the Ukrainian capital, featuring the "death" of the "Living God," Maria Devi Christos. Almost every public place in Russia and Ukraine was covered with leaflets carrying her stern image and apocalyptic message. The choice of Kiev, the city where in 988 Grand Prince Vladimir ordered the first mass baptism of the Eastern Slavs, was highly symbolic, pointing to their presumed salvationist mission. However, the failed attempt to stage the event led to the detention, trial, and imprisonment of the leaders and eventually to dramatic changes within the movement.

In contrast, the Mother of God Centre (MGC) can be best seen as an attempt to revitalize Eastern Orthodox tradition, by emphasizing

the importance of spiritual practice over and above ecclesiastical structures and even canonical scriptures. It was founded by the Revd. Ioann
Bereslavski (b.1946), who is believed to have had continuous revelations
from the Virgin Mary since 1984, providing spiritual guidance throughout the vicissitudes of Russia's recent history. According to these revelations, the collaboration of the official church with the Communist
evil meant the end of its spiritual authority. True Christianity survived
outside official structures through personal martyrdom, such as that of
the monks of the Solovki Islands, and through spirituality preserved in
Russian literature and philosophy. Spiritual salvation and happiness are
thus freed from institutional supervision, becoming a matter for each
individual believer. Since the late 1980s, the movement has changed
dramatically: its early messianic millenarianism has been steadily
mitigated by more global and ecumenical engagements, to the point of
including the Holy Grail in its repertoire of authentic spiritual sources.

The Church of the Last Testament represents another type of new
religious environment. Its leader, Vissarion (original name Sergei Torop,
b.1955), offers his followers the Final Truth that was previously partially
revealed in all of the major religions. In the early 1990s, his message was
strongly apocalyptic and messianic, conveying a "warning from Mother
Earth" of the impending Apocalypse due to irreversible climate change
and widespread immorality. Salvation was possible through human
effort, but only in a designated place in Russian Southern Siberia,
revealed to Vissarion by his Heavenly Father. Over almost two decades,
a 4,000-strong community of his followers has been engaged in realizing
his prophecy by building an "ecologically pure" Sun City in Southern
Siberia, connected to small home-based communities throughout
Russia and abroad.

The post-Soviet new religious scene has displayed remarkable
dynamism, driven by both internal changes in the movements and the
emergence of new groups articulating ever-evolving social and cultural
environments. Thus, in the late 1990s, the desire to live more closely
with nature within small-scale companionate communities rather than
within "oppressive and alienating market forces," found its expression in
the Anastasia movement (also known as the Ringing Cedars of Russia).
The movement was triggered by a series of books by the writer Vladimir
Megre about Anastasia, a hermit living in harmony with nature in her
millennia-old familial estate in the Siberian taiga. It teaches esoteric
knowledge, believed to be preserved in the mighty Siberian cedar, about
pure living and authentic kinship. Thousands of people have established
"familial estates" practicing "ecological farming" and looking for ideal
family relationships. In a recognizably messianic fashion, they believe

that Russia is uniquely positioned to transform itself, as Anastasia is the only surviving descendant of the autochthonous Russo-Vedic (sic) race. In a sense, new homegrown religious groups and their charismatic leaders make competing claims on exclusive representation of Russia's mission to save humanity while drawing on an array of religious sources and traditions.[23]

In recent years, the Russian new religious scene has expanded into the virtual space and now constitutes a distinctive part of the Russian Internet, or Runet, with a variety of forums representing diverse strands of modern religion and spirituality – from the New Age to neo-Goths and from neopagans to neo-Sufis. It can be argued that the Runet provides a space for free communication and exchange of ideas in a situation of increasing government control over the mass media and attempts at intellectual censorship by the dominant church.

"CULT CONTROVERSIES" IN RUSSIA: SOCIETY DECLARING ITSELF

As in other societies, the beliefs, practices, and lifestyles offered by NRMs in Russia can appear extreme, not least because some of them require a high degree of personal commitment, persistence, and consistency that may be at odds with what is generally expected of their participants' varied and complex roles as family members, work colleagues, and citizens. However, societies do not remain static in what they regard as, and how they deal with, social norms and deviance. James Beckford comments that the "extreme situation" of NRMs

> throws into sharp relief many assumptions hidden behind legal, cultural, and social structures. The operation of many NRMs has, as it were, forced society to show its hand and to declare itself.[24]

This comment has particularly intriguing implications for the analysis of disrupted societies where issues of social bonds can often come to the fore, be these issues of ethnicity, nationhood, statehood, or immediate socio-biological familial ties. Indeed, in the 1990s, two simultaneously accelerating trends can be detected in Russian society: either towards rediscoveries of "organic" ethno-religious ties or towards an increasing appreciation of personal religious choice. While many Russians have experienced the increasing diversity of religious offers as beneficial, it has also caused bewilderment and concerns that religious differences might cause conflicts and tensions.[25] As the least-known and worst-understood section of religious diversity, NRMs can be particularly vulnerable to becoming battlegrounds between competing notions of shared collective bonds and authority structures, for different concepts about the balance between individual and collective rights and about legitimate mechanisms of social control.[26] One useful approach to analyzing the related public debates is to look at the process of *frame alignment* among those opposed to NRMs, that is, how these different groups have come to shared ways of framing their conception of these groups as constituting threatening social phenomena that have to be dealt with at a societal level.

In the 1990s, the anti-cult movement (ACM) in Russia, which included the concerned relatives of some NRM members, representatives of the dominant church, mental health professionals, and politicians, had to press its case amidst public discourses on religious freedom and in opposition to groups prepared to defend it. On the other hand, public debates on NRMs were taking place at a time when the recently liberated mass media were increasingly focusing on "cults" or "sects" as a "newsworthy" topic. Indeed, as early as 1993, the Great White Brotherhood's preparations for the "final event" and the simultaneously unfolding drama of the Waco siege of the Branch Davidians provided ample opportunities for introducing the notion and images of the "destructive cult" to Russian audiences. The series of tragic events involving NRMs in the 1990s added further material for this continuing narrative.

The Moscow Patriarchate (MP), the leadership of the Russian Orthodox Church, provided a particularly potent power base for opposition to NRMs. As the most historically rooted institution, the church commanded considerable popularity, which boosted its claim to be the guardian of national identity vis-à-vis the corrosive effects of unfair religious competition. While initially welcoming religious freedom, it was increasingly opposed to the notion of "a free religious market," instead promoting the concept of Russia as its "canonical territory." Within that frame, NRMs had to be opposed on absolute grounds, as, according to the MP, they,

> destroy the traditional foundations of life that have been formed under the influence of the Orthodox Church, and the moral and spiritual ideal that we all share, and threaten the integrity of our national consciousness and cultural identity.[27]

However, some individuals within the MP and a number of church activists sought more than just cultural opposition. In their view, the church had been considerably weakened by Soviet atheist policies and had to be legally protected by the new Russian state. In this context, the first professional anti-cult centre was founded in 1993 within the structures of the Moscow Patriarchate by Alexander Dvorkin, a repatriate and US citizen, who had established close connections with Western anti-cult circles (mainly in the USA, Germany, and Denmark). Thus, somewhat ironically, the information, images, and solutions proffered on behalf of the Church had their origins in Western anti-cult circles. It was assumed that Russia now faced the same "cult epidemic" as had already been raging in the West for decades.[28] However, Dvorkin reframed the Western ACM rhetoric of destructive cults, brainwashing, and mind control, to align it with Russian public discourses of the 1990s. The "destructive cults" thus became "totalitarian sects," capturing an element of the public discourse about the recently rejected historical period *and* the lingering fear of sectarianism. In addition, in an uncanny attempt to push another sensitive button, Dvorkin portrayed NRMs as "criminal organizations" and "mafiosi structures" aimed at "seizing state power" and destroying democratic institutions.[29]

It is important to note that despite the existence within church circles of other approaches that either sought more research-based answers or attempted to find responses grounded in the Russian Orthodox theological tradition, the criminalizing anti-cult rhetoric proved to be particularly useful for the MP's lobbying for state protection. Claims to cultural superiority would not constitute sufficient grounds for legislative change to the extent to which the alleged criminality of "totalitarian sects" could. Similarly, this approach proved its suitability for forming "frame alliances" with the powerful social, cultural, and political actors in post-Soviet Russia, as they had shared interests in delegitimizing NRMs.

In the 1990s, the high symbolic capital of the church ensured that the new Russian political elite that was largely ungrounded in post-communist society took its interests seriously. Furthermore, church leaders themselves were becoming part of the social elite, as personal connections developed between politicians, government officials, and influential clergy.[30] Protectionist anti-cult rhetoric became a ritualized declaration of loyalty to the national church: it was routinely included in pre-election political manifestos and various agreements on co-operation between the Moscow Patriarchate and government agencies. Furthermore, some government agencies have used their authority to delegitimize NRMs by issuing semi-official reports, almost entirely informed by anti-cult sources, and containing highly unsound concepts of and unreliable information on NRMs. In addition, the increasing importance of religion in ethnic identity politics contributed to NRMs being a particularly sensitive issue for ethno-religious entrepreneurs: if there was one issue on which they agreed, it was about the "threat from totalitarian sects" to the integrity of their constituent ethnic groups.

Finally, the anti-cult alliance was given an aura of academic credibility by some mental health professionals. Though still not as influential in defining social deviance as their Western counterparts, they shared their view that searching for personal satisfaction outside the parameters of family life, professional career, civil responsibilities, and engaging in a certain range of other pursuits legitimized by dominant cultural values indicated an inability to make normal, "rational" choices. It pointed to some kind of underlying pathology.[31] However, in framing the "sect issue," Russian psychiatrists tended to align themselves with the MP-dominated Russian anti-cult movement. For instance, they referred to the "symphony" between the country's "traditional religions" and the state. They thus, by implication, made adherence to "traditional religions" a social norm, and membership of NRMs an expression of social and psychological pathology. In one influential representation, NRMs constituted a "secto-mafia" and their members were "secto-maniacs."[32]

The recognizably local phrasing notwithstanding, the framing of Russian "cult controversies" was significantly influenced by the Western ACM, involving the transmission of concepts, such as "brainwashing" and "mind control," and the direct involvement of its activists and government officials (e.g., French officials and the German Embassy). This provides an interesting example of the effects of a transnational lobbying movement on local policies involving religious minority groups.[33]

Major legislative changes resulted from the activities of the anti-cult alliance. Between 1993 and 1997, about a third of Russia's regions adopted local laws restricting missionary activities in general and specifically targeting NRMs.[34] In 1997, the Duma (Lower House of Parliament) introduced a new national Law on Freedom of Conscience and Religious Associations. Ideologically, it highlighted the significance of Russia's historic religions and imposed a number of restrictions on newer faiths, thus legitimizing the notion of their potentially anti-social nature.[35] This notion subsequently proved to be broad and unspecific enough to be applied to a wide variety of groups, including the Jehovah's Witnesses and new Pentecostal groups.

Analysis of "cult controversies" reveals early signs of rapid change in the country's prevailing political and philosophical climate in the 1990s and early 2000s. For example, the themes of external threat and the securitization of social issues were prominent in some political analyses of NRMs before these issues came to dominate the general public discourse on religion in the 2000s, as seen in the following assertion by experts from the Presidential Academy of Civil Service:

> The inculcation of alien religious orientations in the minds of even a small section of society becomes a problem of national security … The programs of evangelization of Russia must be subject to thorough investigation, not only by academic centers, but also by state authorities.[36]

However, post-communist political and legal changes enabled NRMs to defend their right to free exercise of religion through the courts, either as plaintiffs or defendants. The treatment of these groups within the Russian legal system constitutes a promising area of research. It reveals the contradictory ways in which the legal system operates, and the limitations of, and opportunities for, NRMs to use it to legitimize their right to free profession of their faiths. For example, analysis of some of the cases from the 1990s already indicates a trend towards limited judicial autonomy and a bias towards NRMs and, more broadly, newer minority groups.[37] This trend was later confirmed by cases involving a broader range of minority groups, such as Jehovah's Witnesses, the Salvation Army, and Pentecostal congregations.[38] In contrast, the lack of legal protection permits extra-judicial actions against NRMs, such as raids by security services and police, discrimination in registration, and a failure to protect against mob violence. The potential for judicial and extra-judicial discrimination was further facilitated by the introduction of the Law on Combating Extremism (2002; amended in 2007), which employs extremely broad and unspecific definitions, thus increasing the likelihood of arbitrariness in its application.

At the same time, some minority religions, such as the Unification Church, Scientology, neo-Pentecostals, and Jehovah's Witnesses, have, in some cases, used Russia's legal system more effectively, succeeding either in primary trials or on appeal. Also, these groups have partly succeeded through alternative channels provided by changes in the post-Soviet legal framework, such as the Russian Constitutional Court and the European Court of Human Rights.

CONCLUDING REMARKS

Russian NRMs have never attracted a large membership. According to my estimates, even counted together, they never had more than 30,000–40,000 committed members at any given point of time in the last two decades. However, their social significance goes well beyond their numerical presence and should merit more academic attention than it currently attracts. After nearly two decades of legitimate existence they provide a wealth of material for further insights into and knowledge of the ways in which individuals and groups can create social spaces in which to adapt to social and cultural trends in Russian and global modernity. Their relationships with wider Russian society reveal the emerging concepts of social norms and legitimate behavior, as well as the mechanisms of social control that society develops and employs in response to perceived challenges and threats.

Notes

1   Space does not permit a discussion of pre-Soviet non-mainstream religious trends, such as Russian sectarianism and the occult. For useful discussions, see Bernice G. Rosenthal (ed.), *The Occult in Russian and Soviet Culture* (Ithaca NY, and London, 1997), and William Ryan, *The Bathhouse at Midnight: A Historical Survey of Magic and Divination in Russia* (Stroud, UK, 1999).

2   Sabrina P. Ramet (ed.), *Religious Policy in the Soviet Union* (Cambridge, 1993).

3   Mathijs Pelkmans (ed.), *Conversion after Socialism: Disruptions, Modernisms and Technologies of Faith in the Former Soviet Union* (New York and Oxford, 2009), p. 9.

4   Maija Turunen, *Faith in the Heart of Russia: The Religiosity of Post-Soviet University Students* (Helsinki, 2005); Eliot Borenstein, "'Suspending Disbelief': 'Cults' and Postmodernism in Post-Soviet Russia," in Adele Barker (ed.), *Consuming Russia: Popular Culture, Sex and Society since Gorbachev* (Durham, NC, 1999), pp. 437–62.

5   Demyan Belyaev, "'Heterodox' Religiosity in Russia after the Fall of Communism: Does It Challenge 'Traditional' Religion?" *Religion, State and Society* 38:2 (2010), pp. 131–51.

6   Christel Lane, *The Rites and Rulers: Ritual in Industrial Society* (Cambridge, 1981).

7   On Soviet literary works as expressions of religious search, see Elena Volkova, "Religia i Khudozhestvennaja Kul'tura," in Alexei Malashenko and Sergei Filatov (eds.), *Dvadtsat' Let Religioznoi Svobody* (Moscow, 2009), pp. 190–239.

8   Roman Lunkin and Sergei Filatov, "The Rerikh Movement: A Homegrown Russian 'New Religious Movement'," *Religion, State and Society* 28:1 (2000), pp. 135–48; Anita Stasulane, "Theosophy of the Roerichs: Agni Yoga or Living Ethics," in Olav Hammer and Mikael Rothstein (eds.), *Handbook of the Theosophical Current* (Leiden, forthcoming).

9   Michael Epstein, "Post-Atheism: From Apophatic Theology to 'Minimal Religion'," in Michael Epstein, Alexander Genis, and Slobodanka Vladiv-Glover (eds.), *Russian Post-Modernism: New Perspectives on Post-Soviet Culture* (London, 1999), pp. 345–94.

10   Hilary Pilkington, *Russia's Youth and Its Culture: A Nation's Constructors and Constructed* (London and New York, 1994).

11   Pelkmans, *Conversion after Socialism*, p. 6.

12   Cole Durham and Lauren Homer, "Russia's 1997 Law on Freedom of Conscience and Religious Associations: Analytical Appraisal," *Emory Law Review* 12 (1998), pp. 101–246.

13   Eileen Barker, "New Religious Movements: Their Incidence and Significance," in Bryan Wilson and Jamie Cresswell (eds.), *New Religious Movements: Challenge and Response* (London, 1999), pp. 15–32.

14   Bryan Wilson, "The New Religions: Preliminary Considerations," in Eileen Barker (ed.), *New Religious Movements: A Perspective for Understanding Society* (New York, 1982), pp. 16–31, at p. 17.

15   James Beckford, "Religious Interaction in a Global Context," in Armin Geertz and Margit Warburg (eds.), *New Religions and Globalization* (Aarhus, 2008), pp. 23–42.

16   Missionaries of some NRMs, such as the Unification Church, Scientology, Sahaja Yoga, and others had been unofficially present in the Soviet Union before its collapse. Similarly, some of their publications, such as L. Ron Hubbard's book *Dianetics*, had been circulated by the *samizdat* (i.e., the network of dissident activity) from the 1970s.

17   In the early 1990s, Reverend Moon of the Unification Church had the sympathetic ear of President Gorbachev in the Kremlin. In 1992, Deputy Prime Minister Oleg Lobov discussed prospects of setting up a joint Russian–Japanese University with Shoko Asahara, the troubled guru of Aum Shinrikyo, coupled with $80,000 worth of humanitarian aid donated by this group to the Moscow Patriarchate.

18   Roman Lunkin, "Novye Religioznye Dvizhenia v Rossii," in Malashenko and Filatov (eds.), *Dvadtsat' Let*, p. 362.

19   Ibid.

20   Roy Wallis, "Charisma and Explanation," in James Beckford, Eileen Barker, and Karel Dobbelaere (eds.), *Secularization, Rationalism, and Sectarianism* (Oxford, 1993), pp. 167–79.

21   Igor Kanterov, *Novye Religioznye Dvizhenia v Rossii* (Moscow, 2007), pp. 105–19.

22   Although the Great White Brotherhood leadership was Ukrainian, it also saw the mainly Slavic republics of Russia and Belarus as its proselytizing area.

23   An interesting example of this is Pavel Globa, a prominent astrologer, whose horoscopes were announced on major state television channels in the 1990s and who has attracted a considerable following. He claims that his unique predictive power emanates from his Zoroastrian roots that, according to him, are autochthonous and not Persian. As a result, Russia is uniquely protected from global crises and catastrophes (I am thankful to Anna Tessmann for providing some of this information).

24 James Beckford, *Cult Controversies: Societal Responses to New Religious Movements* (London and New York, 1985), p. 11.

25 Vyacheslav Karpov and Elena Lisovskaya, "Religioznaja Neterpomost' v Sovremennoi Rossii," in Kimmo Kaariainen and Dmitri Furman (eds.), *Starye Tserkvi, Novye Verujushchie: Religia v Sovremennoi Rossii* (Moscow, 2007), pp. 400–15.

26 For a general discussion, see James Beckford, *Social Theory and Religion* (Cambridge, 2003), pp. 179–86; with respect to post-Soviet Russia, see Eileen Barker, "Democracy and Religious Pluralism in Post-Soviet Society," in David Hoekema and Alexei Bodrov (eds.), *The Rebirth of Religion and the Birth of Democracy in Russia* (Grand Rapids, MI, 2003), pp. 45–63.

27 Alexander Dvorkin, *Sekty Protiv Tserkvi* (Moscow, 2000) pp. 507–9.

28 Marat Shterin and James T. Richardson, "The Yakunin v. Dvorkin Trial and the Emerging Religious Pluralism in Russia," *Religion in Eastern Europe* 22 (2002), pp. 1–38; see also James T. Richardson, "Major controversies involving new religious movements" in this volume.

29 Dvorkin, *Sekty*, pp. 17–35.

30 Nikolai Mitrokhin, *Russkaya Pravoslavnaja Tserkov'* (Moscow, 2004), pp. 235–74.

31 Lawrence Lilliston and Gary Shepherd, "New Religious Movements and Mental Health," in Wilson and Cresswell (eds.), *New Religious Movements*, pp. 123–39.

32 Fyodor Kondratiev, "Narkomania i Sectomania – Yavlenia Odnotipnye," *Rossiyski Psychiatricheski Zhurnal* 1:13 (1996), pp. 47–8.

33 Marat Shterin and James Richardson, "Effects of the Western Anti-Cult Movement on Development of Laws Concerning Religion in Post-Communist Russia," *Journal of Church and State* 42 (2000), pp. 247–72.

34 Marat Shterin and James Richardson, "Local Laws on Religion in Russia: Precursors of Russia's National Law," *Journal of Church and State* 40 (1998), pp. 319–42.

35 Marat Shterin, "Legislating on Religion in the Face of Uncertainty," in James Gallighan and Marina Kurkchiyan (eds.), *Law and Informal Practices: Post-Communist Society* (Oxford, 2002), pp. 113–33.

36 www.state-religion.ru/cgi/ru (the site is now defunct; accessed 15 October 2002).

37 James Richardson, Galina Krylova, and Marat Shterin, "Legal Regulation of Religion in Russia," in James Richardson (ed.), *Regulating Religion: Case Studies from around the Globe* (New York, 2004), pp. 247–59.

38 James Richardson and Marat Shterin, "Constitutional Courts in Post-Communist Russia and Hungary: How Do They Treat Religion?" *Journal of Religion, State and Society* 36:3 (2008), pp. 251–67.

Further reading

Barker, Eileen, "The Opium Wars of the New Millennium: Religion in Eastern Europe and the Former Soviet Union," in Mark Silk (ed.) *Religion on the International News Agenda* (Hartford, CT, 2000), pp. 39–59.

Borowik, Irena and Grzegorz Babinski (eds.), *New Religious Phenomena in Central and Eastern Europe* (Krakow, 1997).

McKay, George and Christopher Williams (eds.), *Subcultures and New Religious Movements in Russia and East-Central Europe* (London, 2009).

Witte, John, Jr. and Michael Bourdeaux (eds.), *Proselytism and Orthodoxy in Russia: The New War for Souls* (Maryknoll, NY, 1999).

18 New religious movements in sub-Saharan Africa

PETER B. CLARKE

INTRODUCTION

There is no single interpretation of the purpose and objectives of African new religious movements (NRMs), some of which have been have interpreted as resistance movements, others as revivalist movements, others as embryonic forms of feminism, and yet others as essentially healing movements. Despite the diversity of these movements Turner attempted to provide a typology of African NRMs.[1] This chapter suggests that one way of understanding many of the NRMs discussed below is to see them as defenders of cultural capital.

While established or standard religion is usually seen as conservative in its response to the world and in its attitude to change, so called "new" religion is thought of as radical in these respects. However, in certain contexts, as in modern Africa during the colonial era, it was the new religions that attempted, albeit not indiscriminately, to preserve cultural capital, a term that includes religious culture, while the so-called historical or mission churches, and mainstream Islam, attempted to transform the local religious landscape. The adoption of the role of defenders of cultural capital accounts in great measure, as Stark's theory of religious success and failure would expect it to do, for the success of many African NRMs, including African Independent Churches (AICs), new Islamic movements such as the Murid brotherhood of Senegal, and neo-traditional movements, such as the Mungiki movement in present-day Kenya.[2]

Africa has produced its own NRMs and has also experienced the arrival in relatively recent times of NRMs from the rest of the world, some of which have African roots, an example being Candomblé, an African-Brazilian religion, which developed in its present form in Brazil during the era of slavery (c. 1550–1888) and from there has returned, transformed, to Africa. The scope of this chapter, thus, is wider than is usually the case when discussing religious innovation in Africa, where the tendency is to concentrate almost exclusively on the rise and impact of Christian forms of new religion in Africa.[3] The historical framework within which NRMs are discussed here stretches from approximately the 1890s to the present day, covering the colonial and the post-colonial era to the present. It is contended here that NRMs in Africa are not simply responses to the colonial, post-colonial, and Western missionary impact, and to modernization, but rather rational responses to changes some of which were external and some of which came from within.

As Robin Horton pointed out, many of the changes that were occurring in Africa during the colonial era when foreign missionary activity was at its height were actually "in the air anyway," so to speak, and would probably have happened independently of the presence of these external influences.[4] These changes include the greater centrality and significance being given to the Supreme Being, for not only was monotheism always present but was becoming, Horton argues, a more integral part of African religious life prior to colonization and Christian, and Islamic, missionary activity. Furthermore economic historians such as A. G. Hopkins have argued that parts of Africa were modernizing prior to colonialism and may well have done so more efficiently and effectively but for the colonial presence.

Religious change and innovation in modern Africa, then, are best understood if seen as interactive processes that have sought and continue to seek to discover and then construct the most viable and culturally and spiritually meaningful form of religion in new and rapidly changing cultural, social, political, and economic circumstances. They cannot be properly understood if seen simply as responses to colonialism, neo-colonialism, Christian and Islamic missionary activity, and the failures of post-independence governments. To see religious innovation in modern Africa in the form of NRMs solely through the lens of external impact–local response theory is to over-simplify the dynamics of such innovation. We must look for explanations of religious innovation within African society itself while at the same time seeing such innovation as an integral part of the process of rationalizing and streamlining the outcome of the encounter between several forces, some of which came from within and others from without, the most important of the latter being colonialism, modernization, missionary activity both Christian and Islamic, and more recently Hindu and Buddhist, and globalization.

AICS (c. 1890 TO THE PRESENT)

The demand for independence in church affairs which was articulated principally by the AICs began to gain momentum in the late 1880s when many of the historical or mission churches began in practice to abandon their goal of establishing self-governing, self-supporting African churches. In the 1890s this became manifest with the removal from his post and his replacement by the Anglican Church of the Nigerian bishop of the Niger Delta, Samuel Ajayi Crowther (1857–1890). As the Nigerian historian Ajayi remarked the investigation and subsequent dismissal of Crowther by the Church Missionary Society (CMS) had the psychological effect of putting on trial the capacity of a whole race to govern itself, and finding it wanting.[5]

Prior to Crowther's dismissal in 1888 a new wing of the American Baptist Missionary Society emerged in the form of the African Baptist Church, which temporarily split off from the American Baptist Missionary Society over, among other things, the question of leadership. Also important in bringing about this split was the issue of African identity, which the Nigerian Christian elite in Lagos and elsewhere in western Africa felt was being destroyed by the Eurocentric outlook and approach of mission Christianity as a whole. Dissatisfaction emerged over the imposition of European names at baptism, the wearing of European dress, the use of European musical instruments and English in worship, and the veneration of white-only representations of Christ. These same criticisms were also made later by Black Americans including Ali Drew, who helped found the Nation of Islam and Rastafarians, among other diaspora Africans.

Also rejected was the imposition of what were subjectively interpreted by the missionaries as immutable moral laws but which in practice were "foreign social arrangements," and these included such practices as monogamy. Africa, it was argued, was polygamous for entirely worthy social, cultural, and economic reasons which in no way violated God's moral law. One of the Nigerian founder members of the African Baptist Church, Mojola Agbebi (baptized David Vincent), expressed many of these objections and the anxieties over cultural and personal identity and African self-esteem to which they gave rise when he spoke out against mission Christianity in Africa as "foreign" and as preoccupied with: "Hymn books, harmonium, dedications, pew constructions, surpliced choir, the white man's names, the white man's dress ... so many non-essentials, so many props and crutches affecting the religious manhood of the Christian Africans."[6]

The AIC movement in Africa owed much to inspirational and charismatic figures, such as the Liberian prophet William Wade Harris (c. 1860–1929). A former Methodist, and then a lay preacher in the Episcopal Church of Liberia, Harris revolutionized the religious life of parts of southern Ghana and right across the southern Ivory Coast between 1913 and 1915. According to one official report compiled in 1915 by a French colonial civil servant, Harris' effect on the region was hypnotic.[7] The Harris movement, whose leader dressed in the style of a traditional prophet, was about continuity and change. While he challenged the power and authority of the traditional priests, chiefs, and elders, Harris at the same time offered them an opportunity to wield that authority and power even more effectively by becoming Christians.

Millions responded and Harris' success can be partly accounted for by his application of Christianity to traditional problems, both existential and material. He stressed, for example, that Christian baptism was the new and most effective remedy for evil, moral and social, as traditionally understood, and preached what today would be referred to as the gospel of prosperity: confess your sins, turn to Jesus, and prosper. Harris' mission was also helped by his acceptance into the Christian church as full members even those who were polygamous, in contrast with the Christian mission churches that insisted on monogamy for full participation.

Today there are over twenty Harris Churches in the Ivory Coast, one of which has an estimated membership of 100,000. The Ghanaian Grace Thannie, known as Madam Harris, who accompanied the prophet on his mission in the southern Ivory Coast, established in Ghana the Church of William Wade Harris and His Twelve Apostles, better known simply as the Church of the Twelve Apostles, a Spiritist Church in which great emphasis was placed on healing through the Holy Spirit and blessed water.

Among other new healing movements to emerge around this time were the Aladura or praying churches such as the Precious Stone-Faith Tabernacle movement. Dreams and visions played a crucial role in this development, as did the influenza pandemic that struck the world at the end of World War I. The Nigerian Anglican pastor Joseph Shadare, from St. Saviours Church, Ijebu Ode, 45 miles north of Lagos, claimed that it was in a divinely inspired dream that he learnt that much of the world was being ravaged by influenza and that with a young teacher, Sophia Adefobe Odunlami, he was called by God to found a church to combat the epidemic. Odunlami, who herself had recovered from influenza, claimed to have received a personal revelation from the Holy Spirit in which she was instructed to meet Shadare and help him form a prayer association for this purpose. Shadare's son explained to this writer that his father regarded Sophia Odunlami as a very special sign from God, for women prophets like her were most unusual.[8]

What Shadare and Odunlami essentially proclaimed was healing exclusively through the means of prayer and blessed water, a message that became the core teaching of the Aladura movement. This was not a radically new idea, for recourse was traditionally had to incantations and rituals for the cure and prevention of sickness. The Aladura message did not, therefore, conflict with the traditional understanding of illness and disease but rather reaffirmed it from a different perspective. What it did was to reaffirm in opposition to Western medicine the traditional idea that the cause of sickness was spiritual and hence could only be treated effectively by recourse to spiritual remedies.

The Cherubim and Seraphim movement – a group of indigenous Aladura churches founded by Moses Orinmolade Tunolase, an itinerant preacher from Ikare in the eastern sector of Yorubaland, southwestern Nigeria, and Christianah Abiodun Emmanuel – also insisted that prayer, faith in God and Jesus, and consecrated water, oil and traditional soap, were the most effective means of healing. It also insisted that witchcraft was at the root of most sickness, disease, and disharmony. At the same time it affirmed the central teachings of Christianity and retained the Anglican Book of Common Prayer, Sunday as the day of worship, and several of the sacraments.

Among the liturgical differences between the Aladura and mission-church Christianity were the former's practice of hand clapping, stamping on the ground – a way of obtaining spiritual power, prosperity and peace – drumming, demonstrations of the efficacy of sacred words through such exclamations as "Hallelujah," "Hosannah," and "Iye" (life), and pilgrimages to traditional sacred places such as mountain tops. The Aladura churches used a number of rituals – some of them familiar to Muslims – to protect the sacredness of the house of prayer as the church was called, including the prohibition on the wearing of shoes, and on menstruating women entering the church. There was also a ban on the use of alcohol, the eating of pork, and the use of charms, and bathing was compulsory after sexual intercourse before entering the house of prayer.

Somewhat different in its teachings and liturgy from other West African NRMs is the Brotherhood of the Cross and Star, also known as the Christ Universal School of Practical Christianity. This movement began in Calabar, Nigeria, in the 1950s.[9] Founded by the trader and itinerant preacher Olumba Olumba Obu (b.1918) the movement's teachings consist of a strong belief in the presence of the "living dead" at all meetings and ceremonies, in the widespread influence of sorcery, and in the sanctity of the earth, all of which are traditional beliefs. On the other hand it rejects polygyny, secret societies, and divination, all of which are traditional institutions. Obu's Brotherhood places the emphasis on the creation of communities and/or brotherhoods that bond through love rather than on purification and cleansing and on the leader as a new manifestation of God. Adam, the first man, is described as the "first divine incarnation" followed by six others before God came into "mortal life" through Obu to judge the living and the dead.

The terms "Ethiopian" and "Zionist" churches are labels applied to the AICs of southern Africa. The word "Ethiopian" appears to have been used for the first time to designate a new church started in Lesotho by Mangena Makone, a former Wesleyan minister. One of the largest and most influential of the new churches called Zionist is amaNazaretha (Nazareth and/or Nazerite Baptist Church). This church was founded in Zululand, South Africa, in 1913, by Mdlimawafa Mloyisa Isaiah Shembe (1867–1935), described by Sundkler as an "unusually quiet, withdrawn and soft-spoken Zionist prophet."[10]

Shembe, a well-known member of the Methodist and later the African Native Baptist Church, which had seceded from the White Baptist Church, began to innovate by baptizing converts in the sea, by triune emersion, a practice derived from the liturgy of the Zion Church in Illinois. This practice was later adopted by many churches in South Africa, who regarded it as a means of healing, understood in a holistic sense. Among other practices introduced by Shembe were the removal of shoes in worship, the wearing of long hair – a sign of resistance – abstention from pork, night communion with the washing of feet, and the seventh-day Sabbath.

Baptism became the main ritual of the amaNazaretha church, and the sacred wooden drum, not used in mission churches, where it was regarded a separatist symbol, became its main ritual instrument. The import of the hymn was also radically changed from being primarily a statement in verse about certain religious facts to being a sacred rhythm expressed chiefly through the medium of sacred dance that paralleled Zulu dances. NRMs with similar teachings and practices to the amaNazaretha became numerous in South Africa itself and across southern and central Africa, including the Democratic Republic of the Congo. There the largest AIC in Africa, the Kimbanguist Church, was founded in 1921 by the prophet Simon Kimbangu (c. 1887–1951) and is known as the Église de Jésus-Christ sur la Terre par le Prophète Simon Kimbangu (henceforth EJCSK).

Like Harris, Shembe, and other African prophets of the period, Kimbangu preached against the use of traditional rituals to combat evil. Like the amaNazaretha and the Aladura churches of western Africa the EJCSK introduced the use of blessed water for healing, purification, and protection. The EJCSK was also to become, like other AICs, a major enterprise with schools, hospitals, brick-built factories, and various large companies. However, in contrast to many other African prophets of the time, Kimbangu emphasized the importance of monogamy.

The Belgian colonial government, fearing the growth of this kind of movement, had Kimbangu court-martialed without any defense on charges that included sedition and hostility to whites. He was found guilty, sentenced to 120 lashes, and then to death. The latter sentence was commuted to life in solitary confinement, in Lumumbashi, 2,000 kilometers from his home in the village of Nkamba in the western region of what is presently the Democratic Republic of the Congo.

Among East Africa's NRMs is the Lord's Resistance Army (LRA) and the Movement for the Restoration of the Ten Commandments of God.[11] The first of these two movements, the LRA, started in Acholi territory in northern Uganda in the 1980s when self-proclaimed prophets announced that they had been entrusted with a mission to overthrow the National Resistance Army (NRA), which at the time was under the command of Yoweri Museveni, later President of Uganda,[12] and who continues in that role at the time of writing. Among these prophets of resistance was Alice Auma from Gulu in Acholi, who claimed to be possessed by a previously unknown Christian spirit named Lakwena, meaning messenger or apostle in Acholi. In pre-colonial and pre-Christian times possession by *jok* (spirit) of humans, animals, and material objects could endow the one possessed with the power to heal or make the land fertile and turn an immoral, decadent society into a moral and upright one. Such possession could also result in "evil" in the form of moral, social, and natural catastrophes. Alice, who came to be called after the name of her possessing spirit Lakwena, declared that she had been endowed with the powers to heal society.

This kind of mission made a fit with the Christian notion of the spirit that had started to spread in the region from the early years of the twentieth century, and especially the idea that spirits were thought to heal and purify from witchcraft without harming the one who was responsible for bringing it about, and thus breaking the cycle of retaliatory bewitching. This came to be contrasted with the traditional spirits or *joki* (plural of *jok*), who were believed not only to heal and release from witchcraft but also to kill the one who had perpetrated the affliction.

It was this new, Christian understanding which, under Lakwena's guidance, Alice tried to popularize by working as a healer and diviner, but not for long. She soon resorted to the traditional interpretation and in August 1986 organized the "Holy Spirit Mobile Forces" (HSMF), a movement that was joined by many regular soldiers for the purpose of waging war on the government, witches, and "impure" soldiers. Initial successes against the NRA were attributed by Alice Lakwena to "Holy Spirit Tactics" – a method of warfare that combined modern techniques with magical practices – and led to further support from among the Acholi population at large for her armed resistance.

After Alice's flight to Kenya in 1987 the spirit Lakwena then took possession of her father, Severino Lukoya, who for a short time led the various remaining HSMF forces until a soldier in another of Acholi's rebel groups, Joseph Kony, took over. Kony is also from Gulu and claims to be a cousin of Alice. After taking control from Severino, Kony renamed the movement the Lord's Resistance Army (LRA), while retaining many of the rites and ritual techniques that Alice devised including the same rite of initiation for army recruits. Kony claims to have been possessed not by Lakwena but by the spirit Juma Oris, who replaced Lakwena as chairman and commander of his army. Another of his spirits is Silli Sillindi (St. Cecilia) from the Sudan who leads the Mary Company, which consists of the women soldiers of the movement, and acts as commander of operations. Kony has even established an international network of spirits that goes well beyond Africa to China, Korea, and the United States, and though their names are new the functions they perform are very often the same as those undertaken by Alice's spirits.

Under Kony the abduction of children for initiation into the army has become commonplace, as have drug use by soldiers and the practices of torture, rape, and pillaging. Thus, a movement that began with the aim of healing and unifying society and of reconstituting the moral order has turned into one of random kidnapping, violence, and killing.

The Movement for the Restoration of the Ten Commandments, a millenarian movement that appears to have started in Rwanda in the 1970s, was brought to Uganda by Credonia Mwerinde, one of the principal members of a newly formed cult of the Virgin Mary which came into existence in the late 1980s. Mwerinde and her peers approached Joseph Kibwetere, a wealthy Catholic teacher from Kabumba in southeastern Uganda, and asked him to become the movement's leader. Kibwetere's farm became the movement's headquarters until it moved to Kanunga in 1992, the year he was excommunicated by the Catholic Church.

The movement's teachings were set out in a document entitled "A Timely Message from Heaven: The End of the Present Times," which contains the revelations received by Kibwetere, Mwerinde, and other apostles. While the movement's principal goal was the creation of a world based on the Ten Commandments, much emphasis was placed on the renunciation of material possessions – which were to be handed over to the leadership – abstinence from sexual relations, and the importance of silence. Sign language was the main means of everyday communication between the members. All of this was rationalized by reference to visions which told of the imminent end of the world (1999 was the date given for this). When this prediction of the end failed to come to pass, strong differences surfaced between the members, some deciding to leave but not before their possessions were returned to them. Some investigators are convinced that these members were put to death before the fire on March 17, 2000 in which others also tragically died. Others reportedly committed suicide or were eliminated later. Kibwetere and Mwerinde both escaped death, along with an unspecified number of members, leaving the precise number of those who died unknown. Mayer estimated the number of dead to be about 780.[13]

AFRICA'S NEW CHARISMATIC AND EVANGELICAL MOVEMENTS

In the 1970s a new wave of charismatic Christianity that started from within the existing churches began to sweep across Africa. Essentially composed of young, educated high school and university students, this movement emphasizes baptism in the Holy Spirit, the ready availability for Christians of the gifts and fruits of the Spirit, and speaking in tongues (*glossolalia*). Among the attractions of this ecstatic, optimistic religion is the contrast it makes with the despair generated by politics, which, despite the pledges, seems to be incapable of radically tackling such serious concerns as corruption in public life, managing efficiently and effectively public resources, and guaranteeing safety and basic educational, social, and medical facilities.

Also significant are movements that have emerged from within the churches, but, while using the language, symbols, and concepts of these churches, they are not supported by the ecclesiastical authorities. Such movements include the Marian Faith Healing ministry which has been very active in Dar-es-Salam, Tanzania, and which criticizes the church for too readily accepting a "secular" understanding of the world and proposes that it embrace with greater conviction the belief that ultimately the social world is controlled, influenced, or changed by the active intervention of spiritual beings. This is reminiscent of what might be termed for want of a better word a "traditional" African worldview.[14]

Neo-Pentecostalism from abroad runs parallel to, and sometimes overlaps with, the charismatic renewal movement in Africa.[15] It involves missionaries from many parts of the world not associated historically with Christian missionary activity in Africa, including Korea and Brazil. The objective is to present Africa with the real, authentic conversion to Christianity, as opposed to that incomplete and harmful form brought by the historical mission churches. Moreover, in contrast to the more ecumenical and conciliatory spirit of the historical churches to other non-Christian religions, the evangelical and charismatic religions, paradoxically, denounce on the one hand all forms of belief and practice that diverge from their own and, on the other hand, reinforce the traditional worldview by insisting on the power and hold of the devil and evil spirits over those involved in so-called false religion and superstition.

The Brazilian Igreja Universal do Reino de Deus (Universal Church of the Kingdom of God) is but one of the new Pentecostal churches to enter Africa since the 1970s and is growing rapidly not only in lusophone or Portuguese-speaking Africa but also in anglophone and francophone Africa, including Nigeria and the Ivory Coast. Quick to adapt and employ local ministers and ready to use the local language, this church insists on the reality of the spiritual world and on its direct influence on success and failure. As is the case with many other new churches of its kind, the Universal Church gives priority in its practice to the rite of exorcism of evil spirits, which are said to block progress to the kingdom of God. This psychologically uncomfortable theology is balanced by a doctrine of prosperity, not unfamiliar to African traditional religion, which promises that turning to Jesus can lead from poverty and sickness to wealth and well-being.

NEO-TRADITIONAL RELIGIONS

Revitalization movements grounded in the indigenous religious tradition are not infrequent in Africa among people who are persuaded that Westernization and modernization have brought them little but suffering and cultural degradation. While some of these movements have a local or regional vision of revitalization of indigenous culture, others have a pan-African vision. In the 1930s a movement of Nigerian (Yoruba) Christians formed the neo-traditional church of the Ijo Orunmila to ensure that core elements of their religious culture were not destroyed. Again in Nigeria in the 1960s the neo-traditional National Church of Nigeria espoused Godianism, a belief system which focused on belief in a single god of Africa as understood in ancient Egyptian sources.

The Mungiki is another revitalization movement to have emerged in recent times, also in East Africa.[16] Mungiki was started by two schoolboys, Ndura Waruinge, grandson of a Mau Mau warrior, General Waruinge, with whose spirit he often communicates, and Maina Njenga, the recipient of a vision from the god Ngai, who called him to lead his people out of bondage to Western ideologies and ways of living. The movement began as the Tent of the Living God movement and has appealed in the main to impoverished youth and young men and women who, lacking the resources to enter secondary education, are clearly inspired by the Mau Mau struggle for their land, freedom, and indigenous culture.

Following the practice of the Mau Mau, whom they aspire to imitate not only in their thinking but also in their lifestyle, the Mungiki wear dreadlocks and undergo initiation by means of which they are purified or cleansed of the impure, contaminating influences of the West. In their prayers they ask the god Ngai, who dwells on Mount Kenya, for mercy. The Mungiki disciplinary code rejects Western values and prohibits the use of tobacco and alcohol and will often employ extremely harsh methods to enforce its code of conduct. In what it forbids the Mungiki movement resembles evangelical Christianity. Though hostile to the type of Christianity brought by the missionaries the Mungiki are not opposed to Christianity in principle, nor to Islam or other religions. The movement has undergone persecution from the authorities in recent times.

NEW ISLAMIC AND ISLAMIC-RELATED MOVEMENTS

Among Africa's new Islamic NRMs are various branches of al-Qa'ida and of the Ikhwan or Muslim Brotherhood, and the previously mentioned Murid *tariqa* (brotherhood) founded in Senegal in the late nineteenth century by the Wolof Muslim cleric Ahmadu Bamba (1850/1–1927).[17] Bamba combined Sufism or mysticism with an unrelenting commitment to hard and continuous agricultural work. The outcome is the Murid brotherhood, a thriving entrepreneurial movement with considerable assets and political influence in Senegal, the Gambia, elsewhere in francophone West Africa, and a trading diaspora that extends to Europe and the United States. One of its members, Abdoulaye Wade, rose to become President of Senegal.

Mahdism, the Islamic version of millenarianism that believes in the advent of the Mahdi or god-guided one who will ensure the triumph of authentic Islam, has been a strong feature of several other new African Muslim movements. Among these is the exclusive Bamidele movement founded in Ibadan, Nigeria in the 1930s by a former Christian, Abdul Salami Bamidele. It is also the main belief of the Mahdiyya movement which began in the early 1940s in Ijebu-Ode, southwestern Nigeria, under the leadership of the charismatic Al-Hajj Jumat Imam, who, perhaps uniquely, endeavored to develop a theology that would integrate Muslims, Christians, and traditionalists.[18] Pacifism is a distinguishing feature not only of the Murids but of these movements also.

Mahdism has, however, contributed to outbreaks of violence, the worst case being that of the Maitatsine movement which originated in northern Cameroon and spread to northern Nigeria.[19] The movement ended in catastrophe in the 1980s when an estimated 6,000 people lost their lives in riots in Kano City. This was a movement of the "lonely" poor, of the displaced and marginalized – the street vendors, water carriers, and so on – who had received no benefits whatsoever from the oil boom of the 1960s and 1970s and who were without any protection against dire poverty.

Women often play a leading role both as founders and as supporters of religious change in Africa, as we saw in the case of the Cherubim and Seraphim movement in Nigeria. While there are exceptions, women leaders of NRMs do not necessarily seek to radically change the position of women in society.[20] In African-Brazilian religion women are the priests, teachers, and spiritual leaders, and while they themselves exercise considerable power over both men and women these women do not encourage their female followers to seek equality with men where this would mean abandoning their traditional role as women by assuming the roles traditionally performed by men, such as that of performing animal sacrifice.[21] On the other hand Lewis maintains that new cults such as the Zar movement can best be interpreted as embryonic forms of feminism.[22]

The Zar movement is composed in the main of women who are of low social and economic status. It has links with the West African Islamic Bori cult, which appealed to women whose husbands converted to Islam. The Zar has its largest followings among women in Ethiopia, Somalia, Djibouti, Sudan, North Africa, and the Gulf States. Although followers are mostly Muslim, some Christians are also involved in Zar, whose basic assumption is that various categories of spirits – some Muslim, some former colonial administrators including General

Gordon, some European Christians, some spirits of the River Nile – can invade and possess individuals.

Those whom the spirits enter manifest this presence through an illness, which can only be cured by the spirits being placated. The usual response is to treat the "illness," and this can be done in a number of different ways including through the performance of elaborate rituals known in Somalia as "beating the zar." Sessions are presided over by female shamanic leaders known by different names such as *alaqa* in Christian Ethiopia and *shaikha* in Somalia. Exorcism is also used as a form of treatment. In this rite, either a Christian or Muslim cleric uses the power of their holy scriptures to expel the spirit in question. The one possessed will usually enter a trance during the performance of these therapeutic rites.

Lewis, as we have mentioned, interprets the possession of women in this way as an embryonic form of female protest against their inferior status in relation to men. It can also be a means of attaining higher status and authority as it provides the opportunity for those possessed to become cult leaders, a position that gives considerable influence over others. The content of the Zar movement is forever changing as it incorporates new spirits and addresses new concerns thrown up by rapid social change.

Unlike the Zar in every respect and resembling more the new evangelical and fundamentalist Christian movements are the Islamic reform and missionary-minded movements composed in the main of committed, fervent young educated Muslims – mainly high-school and university students – guided by Muslim scholars, often of considerable standing in society. Such movements began to emerge across Africa in the 1970s and were dedicated to the advancement of a more orthodox, more assertive Islam. One such was the Bid'a Yan Izala of northern Nigeria, whose members were inspired by, among others, the Muslim jurist and judge or *qadi* Al-Hajj Gumi, who espoused Wahhabism.

Outside influences, including the arrival from the West of more assertive styles of evangelical and charismatic Christianity that actively proselytized in Muslim areas, contributed to this development, as did support, both intellectual and financial, for a more radical Islam from North African and Middle Eastern countries. The writings of such Muslim reformers as the Egyptian teacher and scholar Al-Imam Hassan al-Banna (1906–1949), founder of the Ikhwan al-Muslimin or Muslim Brotherhood in Cairo, have also been influential. Al-Banna's advocacy of the creation of an Islamic state in Egypt and his active opposition to the proclamation of the state of Israel in 1948 have proved to be particularly attractive to young educated Muslims. The works of Sayyid Qutb (1906–1966), a leading member of the Ikhwan, were also widely read, especially his *Ma'alim fi al-tariq* ("Milestones"), as were the writings of the Muslim reformer Abul Ala Maududi (1903–1979), founder of the Jama'at-i-Islam, which addressed head-on the thorny and vexed question of the relationship between Islam and Western culture, by stressing that Islam was a complete and independent way of life.

Thus, various Muslim associations – the mirror-image of evangelical, neo-Pentecostal, and charismatic renewal movements – influenced by Muslim revivalism in the wider world, began to embark on *da'wa* or mission, ignoring, as did their Christian counterparts, the "traditional" boundaries between Christians and Muslims. This new, more assertive Islam was facilitated by the politics of integration and attempts at nation building which made the old colonial notions of Christian, Muslim, and pagan areas untenable. In the new context of the nation-state which was committed to equality for all religions throughout the federation, neither Islam nor Christianity felt obliged any longer to respect the old boundaries that had been put in place under colonial rule to avoid inter-religious strife.

Several Muslim missionary movements from outside Africa have become well established on the continent and among these is the Ahmadiyya movement founded in what is today Pakistan by Ghulam Ahmad and which is particularly strong in West Africa.[23] A modernizing movement, the Ahmadiyya, regarded as heretical by mainstream Islam for its apparent refusal to accept the Prophet Muhammad as the last of the Prophets, promotes a balanced school curriculum of Islamic and Western subjects, accepts Western dress, strictly forbidden by many other more conservative Muslim reformers, and conducts marriage ceremonies in a Western, Christian style. The objective of such adaptations as these is to persuade young, educated Muslims that they can be modern and advanced without becoming Christians.

NRMS OF ASIAN ORIGIN

A variety of NRMs of Asian origin have established themselves mainly in West, East, and South Africa, in recent times, among them neo-Hindu movements such as the Sathya Sai Baba, Brahmakumaris (BK), and the International Society for Krishna Consciousness (ISKCON), more widely known as Hare Krishna, movements. These movements add to the strength of Hinduism, which has long been part of the religious culture of both East and South Africa. The Baha'i religion of

Iranian origin can be found in many African countries, both north and south of the Sahara, and even in the Sahara itself in the overwhelmingly Muslim, self-proclaimed Sahara Democratic Republic which is located in the westernmost segment of the desert to the south of Morocco.

Although there is evidence of Buddhism, mainly in the form of Indian Buddhists but also some Chinese Buddhists, in South Africa from the early part of the twentieth century, a Buddhist *sangha* (community) did not emerge until the 1970s. In 1979 a Buddhist Retreat Centre and a Buddhist Institute were opened in Natal, and from that point on various Buddhist traditions – Zen, Theravāda, Mahāyāna, and Pure Land – started to open centers in all the main towns of South Africa.

Since the 1970s modern forms of mainly lay Buddhism of Japanese origin have been making an even greater impact than these older traditions on African culture and spirituality. These new movements include Sōka Gakkai, present in Nigeria and South Africa, among other places.

Ritually Shinto and philosophically Buddhist Japanese NRMs are also widely spread across Africa and include Tenrikyo (Religion of Heavenly Wisdom), which has been active in the Congo since the early 1960s, and more recently (1992) Sekai Kyusei Kyo (Church of World Messianity, SKK). This last-mentioned movement entered Africa via Brazil and began to disseminate its message of divine healing (*johrei*) in lusophone Africa – Angola and Mozambique – before moving into South Africa and the Democratic Republic of the Congo. The movement has plans to send African-Brazilian missionaries to open centers in Nigeria.

Often seen as differing greatly from one another, there are clear parallels, nonetheless, between Japanese and African NRMs at the level of belief and ritual. These religions also tend to serve similar purposes. For example, the previously mentioned Japanese movement SKK not only emphasizes the importance of dreams and visions as guides to action, and the fundamental importance of pacifying the ancestors, as do many AICs, but also offers both a spiritual explanation of sickness and faith healing as the sole remedy.

CONCLUSIONS

The NRMs of Africa have, then, often been instrumental in rationalizing and making tolerable the process of rapid change. The Harris Churches, like the AICs, Zionist and Ethiopian churches, the Kimbanguist church, and the Islamic NRMs – the Zar cult, the Murid brotherhood, and the Ahmadiyya – discussed here were not uncritical of traditional society nor did they completely reject modernization. Their response to change was grounded in a more realistic understanding of the negative consequences of a root-and-branch approach to African culture, and cosmology. The neo-traditional NRMs also discussed here have been and continue to be more thoroughgoing in their commitment to the preservation of the traditional religious and cultural heritage of Africa. Some of the new NRMs from Asia briefly described have a considerable amount in common with African religion and spirituality and offer more recent and interesting examples of the dynamics of what is referred to widely as the process of "glocalization."[24]

Notes

1   Harold W. Turner, "Africa," in R. Sutherland and Peter B. Clarke (eds.), *The Study of Religion: Traditional and New Religion* (London, 1991), pp. 187–94.
2   Rodney Stark, "Why Religious Movements Succeed or Fail: A Revised General Model," *Journal of Contemporary Religion* 11:2 (1996), pp. 133–46.
3   See Aylward Shorter and Joseph Njiru, *New Religious Movements in Africa* (Nairobi, 2001).
4   Robin Horton, "African Conversion," *Africa* 41:2 (1971), pp. 85–108.
5   Jacob Festus Ade Ajayi, *Christian Missions in Nigeria, 1841–91: The Making of a New Elite* (London, 1966).
6   Peter B. Clarke, *West Africa and Christianity* (London, 1986), p. 160.
7   Ibid., p. 181.
8   Ibid., p. 167.
9   Friday M. M'bon, "The Social Impact of Nigeria's New Religious Movements," in James A. Beckford (ed.), *New Religious Movements and Rapid Social Change* (London, 1986), pp. 177–97.
10 Bengt G. M. Sundkler, *Bantu Prophets in South Africa* (London, 1970), p. 164.
11 J. Gordon Melton and David Bromley, "Lessons from the Past, Perspectives for the Future," in David Bromley and J. Gordon Melton (eds.), *Cults, Religion and Violence* (Cambridge, 2002), pp. 229–45.
12 Heike Behrend, "Power to Heal, Power to Kill. Spirit Possession and War in Northern Uganda," in Heike Behrend and Ute Luig (eds.), *Spirit Possession: Modernity and Power in Africa* (Oxford, 1999), pp. 20–34.
13 Jean-François Mayer, "Field Notes: The Movement for the Restoration of the Ten Commandments of God," *Nova Religio* 5:1 (2001), pp. 203–10.
14 Christopher Sivalon and John Comoro, "Contending for the Faith: Spiritual Revival and the Fellowship Church in Tanzania," in Thomas Spear and Isaria N. Kimambo (eds.), *East African Expressions of Christianity* (Oxford and Athens, OH, 1998).

15 Paul Gifford, *Ghana's New Christianity: Pentecostalism in a Globalizing African Economy* (London, 2004).
16 Ben Knighton, "Mungiki," in Peter Clarke (ed.), *Encyclopedia of New Religious Movements* (London, 2006), pp. 376–77.
17 D. B. C. O'Brien, *The Mourides of Senegal* (Oxford, 1971).
18 Peter B. Clarke, *Mahdism in West Africa* (London, 1995).
19 Peter B. Clarke, "The Maitatsine Movement in Northern Nigeria in Historical and Current Perspective," in Rosalind Hackett (ed.), *New Religious Movements in Nigeria* (New York, 1987), pp. 93–117.
20 Elizabeth Puttick and Peter B. Clarke (eds.), *Women as Teachers and Disciples in Traditional and New Religions* (Lewiston, NY, 1993); Elisabeth Puttick, *Women in New Religions: In Search of Community, Spirituality and Spiritual Power* (London, 1997).
21 Peter B. Clarke, "Why Women are Priests and Teachers in Bahian Candomble," in Puttick and Clarke (eds.), *Women as Teachers and Disciples*, pp. 97–115.
22 I. M. Lewis, *Ecstatic Religion* (Harmondsworth, 1971).
23 Humphrey J. Fisher, *Ahmadiyyah: A Study in Contemporary Islam on the African West Coast* (London, 1963).
24 Roland Robertson, *Globalization: Social Theory and Global Culture* (London, 1992).

Further reading

Hackett, Rosalind (ed.), *New Religious Movements in Nigeria* (New York, 1987).
Olupona, Jacob K. and Sulayman S. Nyang (eds.), *Religious Plurality in Africa* (Berlin and New York, 1993).
Peel, John D. Y., *Aladura: A Religious Movement among the Yoruba* (Oxford, 1968).
Turner, Harold W., *History of an Independent Church: The Church of the Lord*, 2 vols. (Oxford, 1967).
Wilson, Bryan R., *Magic and the Millennium: A Sociological Study of Religious Movements of Protest among Tribal and Third World Peoples* (London, 1973).
Zahan, Dominique, *The Religion, Spirituality and Thought of Traditional Africa*, trans. Kate Ezra Martin and Lawrence M. Martin (Chicago, 1979).

Index

Abd al-Rahman, Umar, 275
Abd Al-Salam Farraj, Muhammad, 275
ACIM, see Course In Miracles, A
Acts, 84
Adam, 64
adaptive movements, 17
Adi Granth, see Granth Sahib
Adi Shakti, 73
adventism, 65
Aetherius Society, 72
African Baptist Church, 305
African Independent Churches, 76
Afro-Brazilian religion, 303
Agbebi, Mojola, 305
Agni Yoga Society, 241
Aguéli, Ivan, 204
Ahmad, Ghulam, 316
Ahmadiyya movement, 316
Airaudi, Oberto, 241
Aiwass, 115
Akashic records, 67
Aladura movement, 307
Alawiyya
    neo-Sufi movement, renamed
    Maryamiyya, 206
    Sufi order, 204
al-Banna, Hassan, 315
Alexandrian Witchcraft, 159
Alice Lakwena, 309
Alpert, Richard, see Ram Dass
Al-Qa'ida, 266, 267, 271, 273, 279, 313
Al-Takfir wal-Hijra, 275
al-Zawahiri, Ayman, 275
AmaNazaretha, 308
Amish, 141
Amitabha Society for Collective
    Practice, see Li Yuansong
Amitabha Village, see Li Yuansong

Amway, 25
Ancient Mystical Order Rosae Crucis, 242
Ananda Marga movement, 74
Anandamurti, 73
Anastasia movement, 293
ancient astronaut theory, 168
Anglican Book of Common Prayer, 307
Anglican Church of the Nigeria, 305
Anonymous (Internet activist group), 38–39
Anthony, Dick, 88
Anthroposophy, 115
Anthroposophical Society, 67
anti-cult movement, see NRMs,
    tension with surrounding society
Apocalypse (New Testament book),
    see Revelation (New Testament
    book)
Apocalypse (newsletter of Raelian
    movement), 173
Applewhite, Marshall Herff, 90
Aquarian Gospel of Jesus Christ, The
    258
Aquino, Michael, 222
Arabiyya order, 204
ARAMIS (Raëlian Association of
    Sexual Minorities), 177
Arcane School, 67
Argüelles, José, 259
Arnold, Kenneth, 168
Arundale, George, 239
Arundale, Rukmini, 239
Arya Samaj, 64
astrology, 161
Atlantis, 67
audience cult, 118
auditing (in Scientology), 18
Aum Shinrikyo, 3

government action against, 46–48
life cycle of, 1–2
membership decline in, 24
myths in, 17–18
organization of, 19
rituals in, 18
scholarship on, 2–3
tension with surrounding society, 2
typology of, 16
Nye, Malory, 110

Oberon Zell, *see* Zell, Tim
occulture, 218
Odunlami, Sophia Adefobe, 306
Okada Yoshikazu, 73
Olcott, Henry Steel, 232
Olumba Olumba Obu, 76
Operating Thetan (OT), 137
Order of the Golden Dawn, 99
Ordo Templi Orientis (OTO), 217
Orientalism, 202–3
Orthodox Church, 295
Osho movement, *see* Rajneesh
    movement
Otter Zell, *see* Zell, Tim
Our Lady of Endor Coven, 217
Our Mother's Loving Children, 88
Ouspensky, Pyotr, 72
Out on a Limb, 252

Pagan Alliance, 157
Paganism, 7
    altered states of consciousness in,
        162–63
    controversies involving, 164
    demographics of, 156–57
    history of the term, 134
    material culture of, 163–64
    rituals in, 98–100
    role of folklore in, 156
    social organization of, 157–58
    varieties of, 158–60
Paradise Lost, 217
Paramahansa, Yogananda, 69
Path, The 204
Patrick, Ted, 48
Paulsen, Norman, 68
Peace Mission, 77
Pentecost, 84–85
Pentecostalism, 298
People's Temple, 3
philosophia perennis, 200
Picknett, Lynn, 258

Pirsig, Robert M., 252
Plato, 127
Popkin, Richard, 200
possession, *see* spirit possession
Prabhupada, Swami Bhaktivedanta,
    25
Practical Magic, 33
Prasanthi Nilayam, 188
Precious Stone-Faith Tabernacle
    movement, 306
Principle, The, see Divine Principle
prophet, definition of, 82
Prophet, Elizabeth Clare, 241
Prophet, Mark, 241
Protestantism, 99
PROUT (Progressive Utilization
    Theory), 74
Pure Land Buddhism, 93

qigong, 29
Quantum Healing, 255
Qur'an, 85
Qutb, Sayyid, 316

Raël, 8
    biography of, 167
Raël's Angels, 170
Raëlian Association of Sexual
    Minorities, *see* ARAMIS
Raelian movement, 8
    appeal to science in, 170–72
    doctrines of, 169–73
    history of, 168–259
    rituals in, 175
    social organization of, 175–76
Rahmaniyya order, 204
Rajneesh movement, 2–25
Ram Dass, 253
Ramtha, 18
Rapture, 65
Rastafarians, 76
Reappearance of the Christ, The 250
Reclaiming, 153
Redfield, James, 118
reincarnation, 137
religious genres, 113
Religious Science, 255
Renunciation and Reformation, 134
restorationism, 65
Reuss, Theodor, 240
Revelation (New Testament book),
    90
Road to Total Freedom, The, 134

Other titles in the series (Continued from page iii)

THE CAMBRIDGE COMPANION TO ORTHODOX CHRISTIAN THEOLOGY
edited by Mary Cunningham and Elizabeth Theokritoff (2008)
9780521864848 hardback   9780521683388 paperback

THE CAMBRIDGE COMPANION TO PAUL TILLICH
edited by Russell Re Manning (2009)
9780521859899 hardback   9780521677356 paperback

THE CAMBRIDGE COMPANION TO JOHN HENRY NEWMAN
edited by Ian Ker and Terrence Merrigan (2009)
9780521871860 hardback   9780521692724 paperback

THE CAMBRIDGE COMPANION TO JOHN WESLEY
edited by Randy L. Maddox, Jason E. Vickers (2010)
9780521886536 hardback   9780521714037 paperback

THE CAMBRIDGE COMPANION TO CHRISTIAN PHILOSOPHICAL
THEOLOGY
edited by Charles Taliaferro, Chad Meister (2010)
9780521514330 hardback   9780521730372 paperback

THE CAMBRIDGE COMPANION TO MUHAMMAD
edited by Jonathan E. Brockopp (2010)
9780521886079 hardback   9780521713726 paperback

THE CAMBRIDGE COMPANION TO SCIENCE AND RELIGION
edited by Peter Harrison (2010)
9780521885386 hardback   9780521712514 paperback

THE CAMBRIDGE COMPANION TO GANDHI
edited by Judith Brown and Anthony Parel (2011)
9780521116701 hardback   9780521133456 paperback

THE CAMBRIDGE COMPANION TO THOMAS MORE
edited by George Logan (2011)
9780521888622 hardback   9780521716871 paperback

THE CAMBRIDGE COMPANION TO MIRACLES
edited by Graham H. Twelftree (2011)
9780521899864 hardback   9780521728515 paperback

THE CAMBRIDGE COMPANION TO FRANCIS OF ASSISI
edited by Michael J. P. Robson (2011)
9780521760430 hardback   9780521757829 paperback

THE CAMBRIDGE COMPANION TO CHRISTIAN ETHICS, SECOND EDITION
edited by Robin Gill (2011) 9781107000070 hardback   9780521164832
paperback

THE CAMBRIDGE COMPANION TO BLACK THEOLOGY
edited by Dwight Hopkins and Edward Antonio (2012)
9780521879866 hardback   9780521705691 paperback

THE CAMBRIDGE COMPANION TO NEW RELIGIOUS MOVEMENTS
edited by Olav Hammer and Mikael Rothstein
9780521196505 hardback   9780521145657 paperback